CALVIN'S WISDOM

CALVIN'S WISDOM

*An Anthology Arranged Alphabetically
by a Grateful Reader*

J. Graham Miller

THE BANNER OF TRUTH TRUST

THE BANNER OF TRUTH TRUST
3 Murrayfield Road, Edinburgh EH12 6EL
PO Box 621, Carlisle, Pennsylvania 17013, USA

*

© J. Graham Miller 1992
First Banner of Truth edition 1992
ISBN 0 85151 624 6

*

Typeset in 11/12pt Linotron Baskerville
at The Spartan Press Ltd,
Lymington, Hants
Printed in Great Britain by
The Bath Press, Avon

TO THE MEMORY OF MY FATHER
THE REVEREND THOMAS MILLER MA
MINISTER OF CHRIST
WITHIN THE PRESBYTERIAN CHURCH
OF NEW ZEALAND
1908 – 1948

AND TO THE MEMORY OF MY MOTHER
MRS MARION M. MILLER MA (NÉE STRANG)
WHO SHOWED THEIR SEVEN CHILDREN
THE WAY OF LIFE

Contents

PROLOGUE   XXV

Adoption   1
Afflictions   3
Allegory   4
Ambition   5
Angels   6
Anger   7
Antichrist   7
Apostles and apostolic succession   8
Ascension of Christ   9
Assurance of salvation   10
Astrology   12
Atonement   12
Authority in the church   13

Backsliding   15
Baptism   16
   Roman Catholic
   Infants of believers
Bible   18
   God's Word
   Testimony of the Spirit
   Word and Spirit
   Limits of rational proofs
   And unbelief

[vii]

Bible Study
Interpretation
Blood of Christ   30
Burial   32

Ceremonies   33
Character   33
Charismatic Gifts   34
Chastening   35
Children   36
Christ   38
    Person of Christ
    Work of Christ
    Cross
    Bearing the cross
    Christ's kingly rule
    Kingdom of Christ
Church   50
    In the Old Testament
    Marks
    And the Word
    Purity
    Unity
    Reproach
    Chastening
    Apostasy
    And the remnant
    Invincibility
    Growth
    Triumph
Conscience   61
Constancy   63
Controversy   63
Conversion   66
Conviction of Sin   68
Courage   69
Covenant of Grace   70

Contents

Death 72

Deception 75

Decrees of God 75

Defamation 76

Depravity of Man 76

Difficulties in the Scriptures 78

Discipleship 79

Discipline in the church 80

Doctrine 82

Sound doctrine
Drawn from Scripture
Centres on Christ
Bears good fruit
Power of sound doctrine
Ruinous effects of unsound doctrine

Doubt 86

Effectual Calling 88

Egotism and Envy 89

Election 90

Cause
In Christ
Extent
Misrepresentation
Purpose
Fruit

Error 96

Evil 98

Faith 98

Defined
And obedience
And the Word
And promises
And divine election
Certainty
Humility
Temporary

Weak
Justifying
Gift of God
Fragrance
And works
Power
Testing
And hope
And prayer
Victory of
Vision of
And knowledge
Hunger of
And worship

False Prophets   111
    Described
    Man's readiness to listen to
    God's purpose in

Family   113
Fasting   113
Fatherhood of God   114
Fear   114
    Of God
    Of man
    In the Christian
    In ministry

Flattery   117
Flesh   117
Forgiveness   118
Free Offer of the Gospel   119
Free Will   120

Gifts   121
Giving   122
God   122
    Person
    Name
    Glory

Contents

Attributes
Good Works   128
Gospel   131
Government   132
Grace   132
   Illustrations
   And faith
   And works
   And election
   And conversion
   Maligned
Gratitude   135
Guidance   135
Happiness   136
Healing   138
Heathen   138
Heaven   139
   Won for God's people
   And Old Testament saints
   Meditation on
   Link between heaven and earth
   Prayers on
Heavenly Session of Christ   141
Hell   142
   Described
   Anticipated
Heresy   143
   Causes
   Character
   Examples
   Warning
Holiness   144
   Origin
   Brought by God's Word
   Imparted by Christ
   Fruitful
   Warnings

[xi]

Holy Spirit   145
  Personality
  Spirit and Word
  Spirit and Christ
  Work of
  Gifts of
  Sin against

Hope   151
Humanity of Christ   152
Humility   153
Hypocrisy   156

Idolatry   157
  The Remedy

Ignorance   158
  Character
  Consequences
  Learned ignorance

Illumination   159
  A prayer of Calvin for

  Gift of God
  Through the Spirit
  Opens Scripture
  Fruits of
  Warnings
  Prayer for

Image of God   163
Immortality   164
Imputation   165
Incarnation   166
Ingratitude   167
Inspiration   167
Intellect   168

  In the Christian
  In the natural man
  Effects of the fall
  Limits of Christian inquiry

Contents

Intercession of Christ   173
Intermediate State   174

Jesting   174
Jews   174
Joy   175
Judgment   176
   Human
   Divine
   On Christ
   Last
Justice of God   179
   Definition
   Different from human
   Principles
Justification by Faith   181
   Definition
   Importance
   Justifying faith
   Works?
   Opposition to
   Affirmation

Kindness   183
Kingdom of God and of Heaven   183
Kingly Rule of Christ   184
Knowledge of God   186
   Definition
   Source
   Hindrances
   Fruits
   Limits
   Warnings

Last Days   188
Law of God   189
   Definition
   Purpose
   Permanence

And the prophets
And the covenant
And gospel
Abrogation
Christ and the law
Preaching
Law of conscience
Opposition to

Laziness   194
Liberty   194
Life   195

Gift of God
Blessings
Limits
And death

Light   196
Lord's Supper   197
Love to God   198
Love to Others   199

Man   201

As created
As fallen
Not the measure of all things

Marriage   204

Disorder in
Single life

Martyrdom   206
Mass   207
Mediator   207
Meekness   208
Millennium   208
Ministry   209

Call to
Qualifications
Authority
Fidelity
Bible-based

Contents

Prayer in
Harmony of ministers
Plague of ambition
Opposition in
Warnings
Priorities
Miracles   218
Mission of Christ   219
  God's purpose
  Christ's commission
  Church's goal
  Prayer for
Modesty   221
Monotheism   221
Mortification   222
Music   222

Natural Man   223
Natural Theology   223
Nature   224
Novelty   224
Numbers in Scripture   225
Numbers in the church   225

Oaths and Vows   225
Obedience   226
  Expected by God
  And faith
  Directed by God's Word
  Enabled by Spirit
  Prompted by love for God
  Proves adoption
  Practice of
  And maturity
  Accepted by God
  Fruits
Old Age   229
Old Testament   229

Revelation in
Salvation in
Christ in
Holy Spirit in
Church in
Heaven in
Quotations in New Testament

Opposition 232
Ordination 234
Original Sin 235

Patience 236
Peace 236
  With God
  Within
  With others
Perfection 238
  Present perfection
  No sinless perfection
Persecution 239
  Defined
  Satan's aim in
  God's purpose
  Certain outcome
  Victory song
Perseverance 241
  Definition
  Grounded in God
  Accomplished by Spirit
  Our part in
Philosophy 243
Praise 244
  Ordained by God
  Chief part of worship
  Aids for
  Warnings
Prayer 245
  Principal exercise of faith

Contents

Medium of receiving blessing
Invocation of God's name
And Spirit of Adoption
Christ's intercession
And the Word
Defective prayer
Method in
Scope of
General
A prayer of Calvin

Preaching   252

Focus
First preacher
Definition
Biblical content
Accompanied by God's majesty
Spirit with the Word
Focus on the preacher
Sceptre of Christ's government
Sound Method
Deviations
Free offer of the gospel
Opposition to
A prayer for

Predestination   260

Definition
And salvation
And faith
And assurance
And the church
Criticism
Calvin's testimony

Pride   262

Root
Evil character
Evil fruit
Divine restraint
Cure
Judgment

Promises of God   267
God's design
God's glory paramount
God's covenant the guarantee
Christ the foundation
Role of the Spirit
To Abraham
And prayer
And our need
And doubt
And delay
And God's liberality

Prophecy   273
Prosperity   274
A Prayer of Calvin

Protection   274
Providence   275
Not chance
Objections
Explanations
Benefits

Punishment   278
Of God's people

Race   279
Reason   279
Reconciliation   281
Redemption   282
Reformers and Reformation   283
Doctrine
Worship
God's work
Opposition
Peace and unity
State of church before
Calvin's modesty

Regeneration   286
Necessity

Contents

Origin
In Old Testament
And adoption
And covenant children
And justification
Fruits
Religion   288
  Foundation
  Perversion
  Ridiculed
Remnant   290
Repentance   290
  Definition
  Need
  Roots
  A work of God
  And faith
  Evidences
  Lifelong
  False
  Preaching
  Prayer for
Reprobation   295
  Definition
  God sovereign
  Man responsible
  Explanations
  Objections
  Practical duty
Reputation   299
Responsibility   300
Resurrection   300
  Importance
  Of Christ
  Preaching on
  Of the Christian
  Of the soul
  Of the church
  Of the body

[xix]

And burial
Old Testament figures
Unbelief
Revelation   304
    Definition
    Necessity
    In creation
    Special revelation
    Progressive
    Accommodation in
    Submission to
    Deviations
Revenge   309
Reverence   309
Revival   310
Rewards   311
Righteousness   311
    God's
    Christ's
    Ours
Roman Catholicism   313
    Context
    Theology
    Scripture
    Church
    And Christ
    Worship
    Ceremonies
    Antichrist
    Papacy

Sabbath   318
Sacraments   319
    Purpose
    Scope
    And Word
    Christ-centred
    Necessity of faith
    Abuse of

Contents

Salvation   321
> *Definition*
> *Source*
> *Substance*
> *Scope*
> *Word*
> *Preparation*

Sanctification   324
> *Definition*
> *And election*
> *And justification*
> *Mortification*
> *Through Christ, by Spirit*
> *A gradual work*
> *Aids to*
> *Not sinless perfection*
> *Evidence of*
> *Opposition to*

Satan   327
> *Origin*
> *Character*
> *Assails Adam and Eve*
> *Strategies*
> *Christ's victory*
> *Our victory*
> *His 'miracles'*
> *His dupes*
> *God's control over*

Schism   334
Sciences   335
Second Advent   336
> *Purpose*
> *'Last days'*
> *Times and seasons*
> *'Soon'*
> *Moral power*

Sects   338
Security of Believers   338

Self Denial   339
Self Examination   339
Self Love   339
Self Praise   340
Separation   341
Service of God   341
   Importance
   Qualifications
   Disposition
   Warnings
   Prayer
Silence   344
Simplicity   344
Sin   344
   And a sovereign God
   Definitions
   Adam's and ours
   Old self crucified
   Indwelling sin
   Past sin remembered
   Wrath of God against
   Hardening
   Consequences
   Not due to ignorance
   Miscellaneous thoughts
Sorrow   348
Soul   349
Sovereignty of God   349
   Over the world
   Over the wicked and Satan
   Over God's people
Speech   352
State   352
Study   353
Success   353
Suffering   354
Superstition   355

Contents

Teacher   356

Temptation   356
Trial from God
Assault of Satan
Satan's snares
Susceptibility to
Use
Our armour
Victory

Testimony   359
Calvin's
Beza's on Calvin

Thanksgiving   360
Theology and theologians   361
Tradition   362
Trinity   362
Truth   363

Unbelief   365
Roots
Character
Gravity of
Fruits
Cost
Impotence

Union with Christ   367
Described
Explained
Enjoyed
Attested

Unity   369
A reality
Basis of
Headship of Christ
Subject to Scripture
And truth
Not with papacy
Violation of
Prayer for

Universalistic language 373

Victory 373
Virgin Mary 374
Vocation 374

War 375
Wealth 376
Will 376
Wisdom 377
  True
  Comes from God
  By divine illumination
  Through the Word
  Through the Cross
  Blindness of human conceit
  Teachable spirit
Works of the believer 380
World 381
  As created
  Vitiated by sin
  Platform for salvation
  Present evil world
Worldliness 384
Worship 385
  Principles
  Governed by Scripture
  Old Testament worship
  Corruption of
  Gravity of departure from

EPILOGUE 392

Prologue

In the 1920s my father, the Rev. Thomas Miller, M.A., was minister of St Paul's Presbyterian Church, Feilding, New Zealand. He was a lifelong student and had accumulated a fine library. He dealt with W. F. Henderson, bookseller of second-hand books in Edinburgh. As a small boy I used to rummage about in father's waste-paper basket for the British half-crown stamps off his parcels.

One day father had a phone call to say that a batch of heavy book parcels was awaiting him at the Post Office. He hurried off in his old Oakland car, crossed the railway line just ahead of the New Plymouth-Wellington express, and incurred a fine for breach of the law. It was worth the fine to pick up the full set of Calvin's works in the old black-and-gold Calvin Translation Society edition; some fifty-five volumes.

John Calvin was then in limbo and his works with him. I never heard how much father paid W. F. Henderson for this priceless set. Calvin's Institutes were unprocurable when I began theological training in Knox College, Dunedin, in 1939. Little attention was paid to Calvin and his writings.

Ten years earlier a cloud like a man's hand appeared in Scotland. The faculty of the Free Kirk theological hall began a new journal, *The Evangelical Quarterly*. Father subscribed from the first number. I have these copies down to the 1950s. Here Calvin came to life, and with him the Institutes, the Commentaries and the Tracts.

As a teenager I was aware that mother used Calvin for her own purpose. She was the treasurer for the manse family budget. She cashed the monthly salary cheque for about £26 and kept the cash in a small canvas bag. Every night she secreted this behind Calvin's commentaries in father's study. If thieves broke in, she reckoned that those black volumes, row on row, would be the last place they would go to for the family treasure. Calvin was protected, above and below, by rows of the Puritans in faded brown covers, and the Works of Augustine in the Marcus Dods edition.

In April 1941 my wife and I sailed for the New Hebrides as missionaries. We spent some weeks in Sydney buying household stuff. I browsed about in second-hand book shops in the city and came across a Latin edition of the Institutes. I took it, hoping it would assist both my Latin and my doctrine. Island conditions furnished scant opportunities for serious reading as we sought to master the language and culture of the people of the central New Hebrides.

On 17 March 1942 a present arrived from father – the Institutes, in John Allen's edition, published in 1936 by the Presbyterian Board of Christian Education, Philadelphia, in two well-bound volumes. I was grateful for this unexpected answer to a long-felt need, and inscribed I Corinthians 4:15 in Greek on the title page:

> Though you have ten thousand instructors in Christ,
> yet have you not many fathers . . .

Amidst the demands of that many-sided missionary task we made time to read, mark, learn and inwardly digest Calvin's Institutes. I had devised a simple system for the recording of my readings: a file-index of cards for themes treated, quotation books, large and durable, into which I transferred striking extracts, and cross-references to my Bible of apt textual comment which could be concisely noted in the margin. That system has gone with me through my life and paid handsome dividends. War in the South Pacific assisted our isolation and our study of Calvin's Institutes. Bookworms have got at the quotation books. They are with me in retirement, a treasury of Calvin's best thoughts.

At the end of 1943 we reached New Zealand on an American auxiliary cruiser for a furlough of three months. As I looked at father's library, I felt prompted to ask if he would inscribe my name, by anticipation, in Calvin's Commentaries and Tracts, and in his set of Augustine's Works. He did so at once, writing the inscription:

> To my dear son Graham this set of Calvin's works
> was presented by his father
> December 1943.

In 1940 Duckworth's Theology Series published a volume on Calvinism by the Rev. Dr A. Dakin, President of Bristol Baptist College, England. In his introduction he spoke of 'the revival of interest in Calvinism' and wished that his study might send others to 'the Reformer's monumental work' – The Institutes. I bought my copy of Dakin's book when passing through Sydney in April 1941. By June I had noted on the title page, 'spiritless compared with Calvin himself'. This taught me a valuable lesson. To know Calvin, we must first read Calvin, not his biographers.

During many years in the ministry in New Zealand and Australia I found my final court of appeal on difficult textual questions in Calvin's Commentaries. His material was preachworthy, practical, profound.

Then came retirement in my sixty-seventh year. By 1986 I had completed the disciplined reading of all fifty-five volumes inherited from father, easily the most rewarding and enduring reading experience of my life. I followed my system of recording the fruits of this reading.

The quotations extracted from Calvin's Institutes and Calvin's Commentaries have been arranged in themes which should appeal to the serious reader as an introduction to the actual words of Calvin. The source reference is given in each case. In the case of The Institutes, the edition employed is Allen's translation; in the case of the Commentaries and Tracts, the references are to the Calvin Translation Society's edition of the mid-19th century, with the exception of Romans and Thessalonians, which are from the 1960 Oliver & Boyd edition of that volume, translated by R. Mackenzie. The Banner of Truth Trust edition of Calvin's Letters (1980) is the source for the quotations from the letters.

The aim is to let Calvin speak for himself, and for the reader to find for himself what I have found, 'good measure, pressed down, shaken together and running over'. It is expected that

the serious reader will gain most benefit by taking one theme or
sub-theme a day, giving time for assimilation and reflection. In
this way the Anthology may prove an ideal primer in Reformed
doctrine and practice, worship and churchmanship, personal
and social life. And it will serve the reader for the best part of a
year if read in this way.

Explanatory note: In the text, round brackets are used when the
material belongs to the original; square brackets are used when I have
added my own explanations. Translators varied in their use of
capitals; I have followed them whether they used a capital for the
pronouns of the Divine names or not. The following words vary:
Gospel, Word, Divine, Divinity and the pronouns for the Godhead.
The reader will find an occasional quotation of the same source in
more than one place in the Anthology where it seemed appropriate.
In many cases I have given the Scripture references to provide the
context for Calvin's remarks.

J. Graham Miller
14 Franklin Street
Wangaratta, Vic. 3677
Australia.

Because Adam was made in the image of God, his posterity were always reckoned, in a certain sense, to be the children of God . . . Still we must come to Christ, the only head, in order that the adoption should be sure . . . Christ is the root of our calling. *Four Last Bks of Moses I: 103, 104.*

The adoption of Jacob was founded on the sole good pleasure of God . . . lest men should attribute something to their own preparatory acts. *Gen. II:49.*

We can only begin an upright course of life when God, of his good pleasure, adopts us into his family. *Ps. I:280.*

The pardon which we daily receive flows from our adoption, and on it also are all our prayers founded. *Ps. II:456.*

It is . . . in consequence of God's having freely and sovereignly adopted us as his children that he continually pardons our sins. *Ps. IV:137.*

[Our adoption] depends upon his free choice, by which he condescends before we were born to take us into the number and rank of his followers. *Ps. V:259.*

An unfeigned love of God's law is an undoubted evidence of adoption, since this love is the work of the Holy Spirit. *Ps. V:35.*

Those who owe their birth to believers, are delivered from the common perdition by supernatural grace and special adoption. *Four Last Bks of Moses I:500.*

Circumcision was a sign of their adoption from their mother's womb . . . Thus, nowadays, infants are initiated into the service of God, whom they do not yet know, by baptism; because He marks them as His children, when He ingrafts them into the body of Christ. *Four Last Bks of Moses III:274.*

Although [Israel's] adoption always stood firm, still its efficacy was restricted to the elect part of them, so that God, without breaking his covenant, might reject the general body. *Four Last Bks of Moses IV:340.*

The decree of adoption, by which their eternal blessedness is secured is called the book of life. *Is. I:156.*

God has adopted [the godly] on the condition of directing themselves and their whole life to obedience to him. *Is. III:284.*

To believers a persuasion of God's fatherly love is more delightful than all earthly enjoyments. *Is. IV:395.*

Our heavenly Father holds forth in Christ a mirror of our eternal adoption. [Antidote to the Council of Trent] *Tracts III:135.*

Adoption . . . was the foundation of the covenant; and then Christ was the earnest and pledge of the covenant. *Jer. IV:250.*

[God] declares his election when he regenerates his elect by his Holy Spirit, and thus inscribes them with a certain mark, while they prove the reality of their sonship by the whole course of their lives, and confirm their own adoption. *Dan. II:372.*

It was . . . the adoption of God alone that prevented the total destruction of the Jews. *Mic.-Nah. 390.*

[God's] Book (*Dan. 12:2*) is that eternal counsel which predestinates us to himself, and elects us to the hope of eternal salvation . . . Our calling, which is his outward testimony to it, follows that gratuitous adoption which is hidden within himself. *Dan. II:373.*

[A Prayer of Calvin] Grant . . . that the certain testimony to our gratuitous adoption may appear in our life . . . that we may so prove ourselves to be sons . . . *Ezek. I:249.*

AFFLICTIONS

The disciples of Christ must walk among thorns, and march to the cross amidst uninterrupted afflictions. *Harmony of Gosp. I:388.*

[On Gen. 3:19] For God does not consider, in chastening the faithful, what they deserve; but what will be useful to them in future; and fulfils the office of a physician rather than of a judge. *Gen. I:178.*

[God's purpose in our afflictions] God partly invites us to repentance, partly instructs us in humility, and partly renders us more cautious and more attentive in guarding against the allurements of sin for the future. *Gen. I:179.*

Many crosses spring forth to us from the root of God's favour. *Gen. II:266.*

When visited with affliction, it is of great importance that we should consider it as coming from God, and as expressly intended for our good. *Ps. II:472.*

The best fruit of afflictions is, when we are brought to purge our minds from all arrogance, and to bend them to meekness and modesty. *Ps. III:201.*

Our afflictions prepare us for receiving the grace of God. *Is. II:333.*

Adversity does not fall out to us by chance, but is the method by which God arouses us to repentance. *Is. III:107.*

[3]

[On Is. 54:8] The afflictions of the Church are always momentary, when we raise our eyes to its eternal happiness. *Is. IV:141.*

Afflictions are not evils, because they have glory annexed to them . . . We are not afflicted by chance, but through the infallible providence of God. *Gen. Epp. 43.*

All afflictions derive their origin from sin. *Gen. Epp. 138.*

There is nothing in afflictions which ought to disturb our joy. *Gen. Epp. 279.*

Afflictions ought ever to be estimated by their end. *Gen. Epp. 352.*

Through God's marvellous provision it comes to pass, that to believers [adversities] are exercises of their faith and proofs of their patience. *Four Last Bks of Moses IV:357.*

ALLEGORY

[On allegorical interpretations of Gen. 49:11] I do not choose to sport with such great mysteries of God. *Gen. II:461.*

Allegories ought to be extended no further than they are supported by the authority of Scripture; for they are far from affording of themselves a sufficient foundation for any doctrines. *Inst. II:v.19.*

[On Aaron and Hur] I know how plausible such allegories are. *Four Last Bks of Moses I:293.*

In our natural vanity, most men are more delighted by foolish allegories, than by solid erudition. *Four Last Bks of Moses II:130.*

[The Tabernacle] It was by no means the intention of God to include mysteries in every hook and loop . . . It is better to confess our ignorance than to indulge ourselves in frivolous conjectures. *Four Last Bks of Moses II:172.*

Allegories tend . . . to hold up the Scriptures to ridicule. *Syn. Gosp. II:272.*

They turn dogs into men, trees into angels, and . . . all Scripture into a laughing-stock. *I Cor. 294.*

Many of the Ancients recklessly played with the sacred word of God [in allegorizing]. *II Cor. 175.*

[Allegorizing] a contrivance of Satan to undermine the authority of Scripture. *Gal. 135.*

AMBITION

How deadly a plague ambition is! *Syn. Gosp. II:423.*

The Church of God has always been infected by this disease . . . the mother of all errors, of all disturbances and sects. *Four Last Bks of Moses IV:42.*

[On Korah's rebellion, Num. 15:32] Jealousy . . . first a quarrel, then a tumult . . . There never was any more deadly or abominable plague in the Church of God, than ambition. *Four Last Bks of Moses IV:99.*

Ambition deludes men so much that by its sweetness it not only intoxicates but drives them mad. *Is. III:187.*

Teachers [ministers] have no plague more to be dreaded than ambition. *Syn. Gosp. I:269.*

Ambition is almost always connected with hypocrisy. *Syn. Gosp. III:87.*

Ambition is the mother of all heresies. *Acts II:258.*

There is nothing less tolerable in the servants of Christ than ambition and vanity. *Acts II:240.*

Greed and ambition . . . the two sources from which stems the corruption of the whole of the ministry. *I Thess. 343.*

The Gospel is heavenly wisdom, but our mind grovels on the earth. *John I:333.*

Ambition is evermore envious and malicious . . . All those are condemned of ungodliness and malice who envy other men's labours, and are grieved when they see the same have good success. *Acts I: 469, 470.*

No man can faithfully discharge the office of teacher in the Church, unless he be void of ambition, and resolve to make it his sole object to promote . . . the glory of God. *John I:292.*

The mother of all these evils is ambition. *I Cor. 124.*

Ambition is blind – man's favour is blind – the world's applause is blind. *I Cor. 138.*

We are dead in Christ, in order that all ambition and eagerness for distinction may be laid aside. *II Cor. 231.*

Ambition is almost invariably the mother of dissensions . . . a door for new and strange doctrines. *Philipp. 21.*

Inquisitive and ambitious persons are always in a diseased state. *Past. Epp. 32 (fn.).*

ANGELS

Christ, who is the living image of the Father, often appeared to the fathers under the form of an angel, while, at the same time, he yet had angels, of whom he was the head, for his attendants. *Gen. I:472.*

[On Gen. 19:13] Angels are the ministers of God's wrath, as well as of his grace. *Gen. I:504.*

They who think that each of us is defended by one angel only, wickedly depreciate the kindness of God. *Gen. II:186.*

Our salvation, being defended by such guardians, is beyond the reach of danger. *Heb. 50.*

[The Angel of the Lord, Ex. 23:20] No common angel is designated, but the chief of all angels, who has always been also the Head of the Church. *Four Last Bks of Moses I:403.*

[6]

[On Is. 37:36] Nor is it a new thing for the Lord to make use of the ministrations of angels to promote the safety of believers, for whose advantage he appointed all the armies of heaven. *Is. III:145.*

[On Is. 63:9] Angels can do nothing of themselves, and give no assistance, except so far as the Lord commissions them 'to be ministers of our salvation' (*Heb. 1:14*). *Is. IV: 347.*

[On Ezek. 1:9] Under the image of angels the government of the whole world is signified . . . because they are, as it were, the hands of God. *Ezek. I:73, 74.*

Angels are ministers of this grace, because they watch over the safety of the faithful, as Scripture everywhere testifies (*Ps. 91:11, 12 etc*). *Ezek. I:306.*

Under Christ, as the head, angels are the guardians of the Church. *Dan. II:368.*

Angels are united to us, but only through Christ. *Zech.-Mal. 39.*

How dear to God are the faithful, in whose favour he thus employs all his angels. *Zech.-Mal. 61.*

[On Matt. 4:6] That guardianship of angels . . . is only promised to the children of God, when they keep themselves within their bounds, and walk in their ways. *Syn. Gosp. I:219.*

ANGER

Anger . . . a disease which it is difficult to cure. *Ps. II:24.*

Intemperate anger deprives men of their senses. *Gen. II:229.*

Anger is usually inexhaustible. *Ezek. II:294.*

Hatred is nothing more than inveterate anger. *Inst. II:viii.39.*

ANTICHRIST

The name Antichrist does not designate a single individual, but a single kingdom, which extends throughout many generations. *II Thess. 403, 404.*

To recognize Antichrist we must see him in diametrical opposition to Christ. *II Thess. 400.*

When Scripture speaks of Antichrist, it includes the whole duration of his reign. *Is. I:448.*

[The Letter of Pope Paul III to the Emperor Charles V proves the Pope] to be Antichrist, the head of all the wicked. *Tracts I:263.*

['Pope'] . . . Antichrist is everything but a father. *Jer. III:130.*

Antichrist . . . has now for ages exercised dominion in God's sanctuary. *Joel 138.*

Antichrist and his horned bishops. *Gen. I:303, 304.*

APOSTLES AND APOSTOLIC SUCCESSION

The Apostles . . . the first architects of the Church. *Inst. IV:iii.4.*

[Jesus chose twelve] Christ had chosen that sacred number. *John I:280.*

[On John 20:21] The Apostles were now, for the first time, appointed to be ordinary ministers of the Gospel . . . He bids them succeed to that office which he had received from his Father, places them in his room, and bestows on them the same authority. *John I:266.*

[On John 20:22, 'He breathed on them'] The Spirit was given to the Apostles on this occasion in such a manner, that they were only sprinkled by his grace, but were not filled with full power; for, when the Spirit appeared on them in tongues of fire, (*Acts 2:3*), they were entirely renewed. *John II:268, 269.*

The writings of the apostles contain nothing else than a simple and natural explanation of the Law and the Prophets. *Past. Epp. 251.*

Wherein does Succession consist, if it be not in perpetuity of doctrine? [The True Method of Reforming the Church] *Tracts III:265.*

[On Matt. 16:18, 19] The commendations that follow relate to the Apostolic office . . . nothing is here said to Peter which does not apply equally to the others who were his companions. [Calvin quotes Cyprian] 'Christ spake to all in the person of one man'. [Peter] does not receive permission to give anything to his successors. So then the Papists make him bountiful with what is not his own. *Syn. Gosp. II:296, 297.*

As Matthias succeeded Judas, . . . so some Judas might succeed Peter. *I Cor. 292.*

ASCENSION OF CHRIST

Christ . . . ascended to the Father; first, to subdue all powers to himself, and to render angels obedient; next, to restrain the devil and to protect and preserve the Church by his help, as well as all the elect of God the Father. *Dan. II:44.*

The body of our Lord in heaven [is] the same as that which he had on earth . . . Scripture everywhere teaches us, that, as the Lord on earth took our humanity, so he has exalted it to heaven, withdrawing it from mortal condition, but not changing its nature. [Short Treatise on the Lord's Supper] *Tracts II:187.*

[His ascension was] . . . from the Mount of Olives, . . . whence he had descended to undergo the ignominy of the cross, [that] he might ascend the heavenly throne . . . the King of glory and the Judge of the world. *Syn. Gosp. III:392, 393.*

Christ was taken up into heaven, not to enjoy blessed rest at a distance from us, but to govern the world for the salvation of all believers. *Syn. Gosp. III:393.*

The Ascension of Christ . . . is one of the chief points of our faith. *Acts I:49.*

[On Acts 7:56, Stephen] seeth Christ reigning in that flesh wherein he was abased. *Acts I:315.*

[Christ's] ascension into heaven was the real commencement of his reign. *Inst. II:xvi.14.*

He appears there before God to defend us by his advocacy. *Heb. 216.*

[9]

Since [Christ] entered [heaven] in our own nature, and as it were in our names, . . . we not only hope for heaven, but already possess it in our Head. *Inst. II:xvi.16.*

ASSURANCE OF SALVATION

The furnishing of the heart with assurance [is] more difficult than the communication of knowledge to the understanding. *Inst. III:640.*

It is the peculiar privilege of the faithful who have once embraced the covenant offered to them in Christ, that they feel assured that God is propitious to them. *Heb. 190.*

In order to attain an assurance of our salvation we ought to begin with the word, and . . . with it our confidence ought to be satisfied, so as to call upon God as our Father. *Inst. III:xxiv.3.*

The true conviction which believers have of the word of God, of their own salvation, and of religion in general, does not spring from the judgment of the flesh, or from human and philosophical arguments, but from the sealing of the Spirit, who imparts to their consciences such certainty as to remove all doubt. *Eph. 208.*

The doctrine of the Gospel cannot be understood otherwise than by the testimony of the Holy Spirit . . . Those who have a testimony of this nature from the Holy Spirit, have an assurance as firm and solid, as if they felt with their hands what they believe. *I Cor. 111.*

It is the word of God alone which can first and effectually cheer the heart of the sinner. There is no true or solid peace to be enjoyed in the world except in the way of reposing upon the promises of God. *Ps. II:295.*

[On God's covenant of grace] We may not seek the certainty of our salvation anywhere else. *Ps. III:444.*

[On Gen. 25:7. Abraham] contented, both in life and death, with the bare promise of God. *Gen. II:36.*

Let us not seek any other ground of assurance than [God's] own testimony. *Jer. II:252.*

[10]

The certainty which rests on God's word exceeds all knowledge. *Zech.-Mal. 73.*

[On 1 Thess. 5:9] There is no better assurance of salvation to be
found anywhere than can be gained from the decree of God.
Thess. 370.

Those men who at this day obscure, and seek, as far as they can,
to extinguish the doctrine of election, are enemies to the human
race; for they strive their utmost to subvert every assurance of
salvation. *Zech.-Mal. 84, 85.*

When we are about assurance of salvation, then must we call to
mind the free adoption alone, which is joined with the purging
[expiation] and forgiveness of sins. *Acts II:60.*

. . . that diabolical doctrine of the Sophists as to a constant
hesitancy on the part of believers. For they require all believers
to be in doubt, whether they are in a state of grace or not. *I Cor.
112.*

The assurance of faith is not subject to men. *I Cor. 117.*

There are two operations of the Spirit in faith, . . . as it
enlightens and as it establishes the mind. *Eph. 208.*

When we have received the Spirit of God, his promises are
confirmed to us, and no dread is felt that they will be
revoked . . . Until we are supported by the testimony of the
Holy Spirit, we never rest upon them with unshaken confidence. *Eph. 209.*

Everyone is made sure of his own election by the testimony of
the Spirit . . . so he can know nothing certain of others. *Gen.
Epp. 24.*

Assurance of faith remains inwardly shut up, and does not
extend itself to others. *Philipp.-Col. 26.*

The Spirit of Christ never regenerates, but that he becomes also
a witness and an earnest of our divine adoption, so as to free our
hearts from fear and trembling. *Gen. Epp. 298.*

[11]

The certainty of faith depends on the grace of Christ alone . . . For God is not known by a naked imagination, since he reveals himself inwardly to our hearts by the Spirit. *Gen. Epp. 175.*

ASTROLOGY

This diabolical error. *Jer. II:11.*

Since [God] forbade it without exception, he showed that it contains nothing but absolute delusion, which all believers ought to detest. *Is. III:387.*

They who think that the stars control the life of men, immediately become hardened to the imagination of destiny, so that they now leave nothing to God. The tribunals of God are buried, piety is extinguished, and calling on God is at an end. *Is. III:387.*

ATONEMENT (see the Blood of Christ)

It is our wisdom to have a clear understanding of how much our salvation cost the Son of God. *Inst. II:xvi.12.*

By [Christ's] obedience, he has wiped off our transgressions; by his sacrifice, appeased the divine anger; by his blood, washed away our stains; by his cross, borne our curse; and by his death, made satisfaction for us. [Calvin's Reply to Cardinal Sadoleto] *Tracts I:42.*

In his death we ought chiefly to consider his atonement, by which he appeased the wrath and curse of God. *John II:32.*

The principal hinge on which our salvation turns . . . [is] that the sacerdotal dignity belongs exclusively to Christ, because, by the sacrifice of his death, he has abolished our guilt, and made satisfaction for our sins. *Inst. II:xv.6.*

The species of death which [Christ] suffered, is fraught with a peculiar mystery. The cross was accursed, not only in the opinion of men, but by the decree of the Divine law. *Inst. II:xvi.6.*

[Christ] suffered in his soul the dreadful torments of a person condemned and irretrievably lost. *Inst. II:xvi.10.*

If [Christ's] soul had experienced no punishment, he would have been only a Redeemer for the body. *Inst. II:xvi.12.*

Nor must we conceive that [Christ] submitted to a curse which overwhelmed him, but, on the contrary, that by sustaining it, he depressed, broke and destroyed all its power. Wherefore faith apprehends an absolution in the condemnation of Christ, and a benediction in his curse. *Inst. II:xvi.6.*

[Christ's] voluntary submission is the principal circumstance, even in his death. *Inst. II:xvi.5.*

[Heb. 5:7] points out two causes why it behoved Christ to suffer. The proximate was, that he might learn obedience; and the ultimate, that he might be thus consecrated a priest for our salvation. *Heb. 120.*

There are . . . two parties who find this Epistle [to the Hebrews] in no way favourable to them – the Papists and the Socinians. The Sole Priesthood of Christ, and his Sole Sufficient Sacrifice are here so distinctly stated. *Preface to Ep. to Heb. 5.*

AUTHORITY IN THE CHURCH

Whatever authority is exercised in the Church ought to be subjected to this rule – that God's law is to retain its own preeminence, and that men blend nothing of their own, but only define what is right according to the Word of the Lord. *Hab.-Hagg. 368, 369.*

Ours the Church, whose supreme care it is humbly and religiously to venerate the word of God, and submit to its authority. [Calvin's Reply to Sadoleto] *Tracts I:50.*

A soul, . . . when deprived of the word of God, is given up unarmed to the devil for destruction. Now then, will not the first machination of the enemy be to wrest the sword from the soldier of Christ? And what the method of wresting it, but to set him a doubting whether it be the word of the Lord that he is leaning upon, or the word of man? Christian faith must not be founded on human testimony, not propped up by doubtful opinion, not reclined on human authority, but engraven on our

[13]

hearts by the finger of the living God, so as not to be obliterated by any colouring of error. [Calvin's Reply to Sadoleto] *Tracts I:53.*

Though the whole world should condemn us, it is sufficient to free us from all blame, that we have the authority of God. *Josh. 170.*

[On Is. 8:20, 'To the law and to the testimony . . .'] Everything which is added to the word must be condemned and rejected. It is the will of the Lord that we shall depend wholly on his word, and that our knowledge shall be confined within its limits . . . Everything that is introduced by men on their own authority will be nothing else than a corruption of the word. *Is. I:290.*

God cannot approve of anything that is not supported by his word. *Is. II:27.*

We may allow ourselves to be taught by the pure word of God, and, relying on his authority, may freely and boldly condemn all that the world applauds and admires. *Is. II:76.*

It is a pernicious evil to exercise an arbitrary control over the conscience. *Hab.-Hagg. 368.*

God wills this honour to be conceded to him alone, – to be heard in his own Church. *Jer. I:43.*

All the authority that is possessed by pastors, . . . is subject to the word of God . . . We must beware of giving any authority to men, as soon as they depart from the word of God. *John I:315.*

. . . as if the unity of the Church were itself founded on anything else than the authority of Scripture. *John II:230.*

This is the best way to maintain and avouch the opinions of faith, that the authority of God go foremost; and that then the consent of the Church come next. *Acts II:374.*

The Church cannot follow God as its guide, except it observes what the word prescribes. *Gen. Epp. 388.*

The faithful, inwardly illuminated by the Holy Spirit, acknowledge nothing but what God says in his word. *Gen. Epp. 390.*

[14]

It has been the design of the Holy Spirit, in everything relating to the government of the Church, to guard against any dreams of principality or dominion. *Inst. IV:iv.4.*

The only way to edify the Church is for the ministers themselves to study to preserve to Jesus Christ his rightful authority. *Inst. IV:viii.1.*

There is nothing holier, or better, or safer, than to content ourselves with the authority of Christ alone. *Inst. IV:xv.19.*

[The RC doctrine of the infallibility of the Church] They ascribe to the Church an authority independent of the word; we maintain it to be annexed to the word, and inseparable from it. *Inst. IV:viii.13.*

How will the impious ridicule our faith, and all men call it in question, if it be understood to possess only a precarious authority depending on the favour of men! *Inst. I:vii.1.*

Whatever authority and dignity is attributed by the Holy Spirit, in the Scripture, either to the priests and prophets under the law, or to the apostles and their successors, it is all given, not in a strict sense to the persons themselves, but to the ministry over which they were appointed, or, to speak more correctly, to the word, the ministration of which was committed to them. *Inst. IV:viii.2.*

BACKSLIDING

Hardly one in ten of those who once made a profession of Christ, retains the purity of the faith to the end. *Gen. Epp. 394.*

We see how many there are every day, that throw away their spears, who formerly made a great show of valour. *Past. Epp. 210.*

The more anyone excels in grace, the more ought he to be afraid of falling. *Ps. I:241.*

Ingratitude is very frequently the reason why we are deprived of the light of the gospel, as well as of other divine favours. *Philipp.-Col. 179.*

It is an extreme curse, when God gives us loose reins, and suffers us, with unbridled liberty, to rush as it were headlong into evils, as though he had delivered us up to Satan, to be his slaves. *Jon.-Nah. 196.*

[On Ps. 73:23] God is always near his chosen ones; for although they sometimes turn their backs upon him, he nevertheless has always his fatherly eye turned towards us. *Ps. III:152.*

BAPTISM

Baptism – a pledge of eternal life before God . . . an outward sign of faith before men. *Syn. Gosp. III:385.*

Everyone profiteth so much in baptism as he learneth to look unto Christ . . . The whole strength of baptism is contained in Christ. *Acts I:120.*

Baptism, viewed in regard to us, is a passive work: we bring nothing to it but faith; and all that belongs to it is laid up in Christ. *Gal. 150.*

Baptism testifies to us our purgation and ablution; the eucharistic supper testifies our redemption. Water is a figure of ablution, and blood of satisfaction. *Inst. IV:xiv.22.*

It is [Christ] who 'sprinkles the conscience' with his blood. It is he who mortifies the old man, and bestows the Spirit of regeneration. The word 'fire' is added . . . because [the Spirit] takes away our pollutions, as fire purifies gold. *Syn. Gosp. I:199.*

Roman Catholic Baptism

[Calvin answered John Knox on the question whether the child of R.C. parents should be baptized]. Offspring descended from holy and pious ancestors, belong to the body of the church, though their fathers and grandfathers may have been apostates . . . God's promise comprehends not only the off-spring of every believer in the first line of descent, but extends to thousands of generations. *Calvin's Letters 215.*

As soon as infants are born among them, the Lord signs them with the sacred symbol of baptism; they are therefore, in some sense, the people of God. *Hos. 161, 162.*

Our baptism does not need renewal because . . . a Church is among them. *Ezek. II:120.*

Baptism of Infants of Believers

The offspring of believers is born holy, because their children, while yet in the womb . . . are included in the covenant of eternal life . . . Nor . . . are they admitted into the Church by baptism on any other ground than that they belonged to the body of Christ before they were born. [Antidote to Council of Trent] *Tracts III:275.*

The salvation of infants is included in the promise in which God declares to believers that he will be a God to them and to their seed . . . Their salvation, therefore, has not its commencement in baptism, but being already founded on the word, is sealed by baptism. [Antidote to Council of Trent] *Tracts III:109, 110.*

[The children of believers] do not become the sons of God through baptism; but because, in virtue of the promise, they are heirs of adoption, therefore the Church admits them to baptism. [Antidote to Articles of Faculty of Paris] *Tracts I:74.*

[God] was pleased from the first, (Gen. 17:12), that in his Church children should receive the sign of circumcision, by which he then represented all that is now signified to us by baptism. [Form of Administering Baptism, Geneva] *Tracts II:115.*

Those who were baptized when mere infants, God regenerates in childhood or adolescence, occasionally even in old age. [Mutual Consent, as to the Sacraments] *Tracts II:218.*

Infants are renewed by the Spirit of God, according to the capacity of their age, till that power which was concealed within them grows by degrees, and becomes fully manifest at the proper time. *Syn. Gosp. II:390.*

Christ . . . could not present the infants solemnly to God without giving them purity . . . They were renewed by the Spirit to the hope of salvation . . . [and] reckoned by Christ among his flock. *Syn. Gosp. II:391.*

[17]

The children of the godly are born the children of the Church, and . . . they are accounted members of Christ from the womb, because God adopteth us upon this condition, that he may be also the Father of our seed. *Acts I:363.*

To this end doth Christ admit infants by baptism, that as soon as the capacity of their age shall suffer, they may addict themselves to be his disciples, and that being baptized with the Holy Ghost, they may comprehend, with the understanding of faith, his power which baptism doth prefigure. *Acts I:364.*

[Circumcision, on Gal. 5:3] After the coming of Christ, it ceased to be a Divine institution, because baptism had succeeded in its room. *Gal. 150.*

[Paul] expressly substitutes baptism for circumcision (Col. 2:11). *Gen. I:456.*

Whoever, having neglected baptism, feigns himself to be contented with the bare promise, tramples as much as in him lies, upon the blood of Christ, or at least does not suffer it to flow for the washing of his own children. Therefore just punishment follows the contempt of the sign, in the privation of grace . . . because . . . the covenant of God is violated. *Gen. I:458.*

BIBLE

God's Word

[The Scripture] obtains the same complete credit and authority with believers, when they are satisfied of its divine origin, as if they heard the very words pronounced by God himself. *Inst. I:vii.1.*

When the Church receives it [the Scripture], and seals it with her suffrage, she does not authenticate a thing otherwise dubious or controvertible; but, knowing it to be the truth of her God, performs a duty of piety, by treating it with immediate veneration. *Inst. I:vii.2.*

Nothing is more precious to [God] than his own truth. *Inst. III:ii.8.*

The infallible rule of his holy truth . . . the unchangeable oracles of our Heavenly Master. [Calvin's Dedication of his Commentary on the Ep. to the Hebrews to Sigismund, King of Poland] *Heb. xxi.*

Every addition to His word . . . is a lie. [Necessity of Reforming the Church] *Tracts I:129.*

It is of great consequence that we be established in the belief of God's word. *Ps. II:429.*

[On Heb. 3:7, 'as the Holy Ghost says'] The words adduced from the books of the prophets are those of God and not of men. *Heb. 83.*

Believers embrace and revere every part of the Divine word. *Inst. III:ii.29.*

Take away the word . . . and there will be no faith left. *Inst. III:ii.6.*

The Holy Spirit has so regulated the writings which he has dictated to the Prophets and the Apostles, that he detracts nothing from the order instituted by himself. *Heb. 358.*

Our wisdom ought to consist in embracing with gentle docility, and without any exception, all that is delivered in the sacred Scriptures. *Inst. I:xviii.4.*

As all Divine revelations are justly entitled *the word of God*, so we ought chiefly to esteem that substantial Word the source of all revelations. *Inst. I:xiii.7.*

The Word of God . . . is . . . to be understood of the eternal wisdom residing in God, whence the oracles, and all the prophecies, proceeded. *Inst. I:xiii.7.*

The Scripture, in consideration of the ignorance and dullness of the human understanding, generally speaks in the plainest manner. *Inst. I:xi.1.*

The truths of revelation are so high as to exceed our comprehension, but, at the same time, the Holy Spirit has accommodated them so far to our capacity, as to render all Scripture profitable for instruction. *Ps. II:239.*

[19]

I do not venture to make any assertion where Scripture is silent. *Is. I:203.*

It is the highest virtue to ask nothing beyond the word of God. *Is. I:240.*

God cannot approve of anything that is not supported by his word. *Is. II:27.*

The power of the word of God is perpetual. *Is. II:336.*

As soon as he 'who cannot lie' (Tit. 1:2) has spoken, we ought to embrace and kiss his word as if the result were . . . certain. *Is. III:142.*

The power which is hid in God is revealed to us by the word. *Is. III:213.*

We should yield this honour to the word, to believe what is otherwise incredible. *Is. III:336.*

There is a kind of preparation for faith by which God procures reverence for his word. *Is. III:331.*

Whenever faith is mentioned, let us remember that it must be joined to the word. *Is. IV:160.*

The word is eternal, unchangeable and incorruptible and cannot, like the rain, vanish away. *Is. IV:171.*

Our whole happiness lies in obeying the word of God . . . There is no hope of salvation if we do not obey God and his word. *Is. IV:159, 160.*

To 'hear' the Lord is to obey his word. *Is. IV:393.*

There is no obedience without faith; and there is no faith without the word. *Is. IV:390, 391.*

God is not to be separated from his word. *Jer. I:45.*

God so shines forth in his word, that he does not appear as God, except his word remains safe and uncorrupted. *Jer. III:27.*

How precious to God is the honour of his word! *Jer. III:208.*

[On Jer. 36:2] To 'diminish' . . . was to soften what appeared sharp, or to suppress what might have offended, or to express indirectly or coldly what could not produce effect without being forcibly expressed. *Jer. III:308.*

There must be docility, in order that God's word may obtain credit, authority, and favour among us. *Jer. III:211.*

The first and . . . natural use of God's word is to bring salvation to men; and hence it is called food; but it turns into poison to the reprobate. *Jer. III:199.*

God's word ever retains its own dignity . . . It cannot . . . be deprived of its vigour and efficacy. *Jer. III:199.*

Scripture will not have us to feed on frivolous and unprofitable notions; it teaches only what avails to promote true religion. *Jer. III:189.*

It is the foundation of all true religion to depend on the mouth or word of God; and it is also the foundation of our salvation. *Jer. III:460.*

Then only he will be propitious to us, when we lean on his word. *Jer. IV:249.*

His word is ever good and right, though it may not be pleasant. *Jer. IV:248.*

How then is religion to remain pure? Even by depending on God's mouth, by subjecting ourselves to his word, and by putting a bridle on ourselves, so as not to introduce anything except what he commands and approves. *Jer. IV:543.*

God will not and cannot have himself separated from his word. *Jer. IV:542.*

Men never acquiesce in God's word, as they ought to do. *Jer. V:93.*

[We] can never lay hold on his mercy except through his word. *Jer. V:408.*

God wishes that reverence which he exacts from us to be given to his own word. *Ezek. I:359.*

The word partakes of the nature of God himself, from whom it has proceeded. *Amos-Obad. 324.*

We ought to have such reverence for God's word as to deem it sufficient for us to hear his voice. *Hab.-Hagg. 61.*

When we submit to God and to his word, it is . . . to enter on the work of worshipping him aright. *Hab.-Hagg. 262.*

The beginning of religion . . . humbly and soberly to submit to God's word. *Zech.-Mal. 229.*

Testimony of the Spirit

The Testimony of the Holy Spirit Necessary to Confirm the Scripture, in Order to the Complete Establishment of its Authority. [Heading to Chap. 7, Bk I, Institutes] *Inst. I:vii.1.*

They who have been inwardly taught by the Spirit, feel an entire acquiescence in the Scripture, and that it is self-authenticated, carrying with it its own evidence, and ought not to be made the subject of demonstration and arguments from reason . . . We feel the firmest conviction that we hold an invincible truth. *Inst. I:90, 91.*

The testimony of the Spirit is superior to all reason . . . The word will never gain credit in the hearts of men, till it be confirmed by the internal testimony of the Spirit. *Inst. I:vii.4.*

[On Is. 8:16, 'seal the law'] He compares the doctrine of the word to a *sealed* letter . . . The word is . . . sealed to those who derive no advantage from it, and is *sealed* in such a manner that the Lord unseals and opens it to his own people by the Spirit. *Is. I:282, 283.*

The Spirit will only thus guide us to a right discrimination, when we render all our thoughts subject to God's word. *Gen. Epp. 231.*

What God pronounces through men [in Scripture], he seals on our hearts by his Spirit. *Gen. II:491.*

Until God seal within us the certainty of his word, our belief of its certainty will be continually wavering . . . When God shines into us by his Spirit, he at the same time causes that sacred truth which endures for ever to shine forth in the mirror of his word. *Ps. V:29.*

The truth of God, sealed by the Holy Spirit on our hearts, despises and defies all that is in the world . . . This single Witness powerfully drives away, scatters, and overturns, all that the world rears up to obscure or crush the truth of God. *John II:130.*

The doctrine of the Gospel cannot be understood otherwise than by the testimony of the Holy Spirit, . . . Those who have a testimony of this nature from the Holy Spirit have an assurance as firm and solid, as if they felt with their hands what they believe. *I Cor. 111.*

[On 2 Cor 1:21, 'anointing'] God, by pouring down upon us the heavenly grace of the Spirit, does, in this manner, *seal* upon our hearts the certainty of his own word. *II Cor. 140.*

As an assurance of this nature is a thing that is above the capacity of the human mind, it is the part of the Holy Spirit to confirm within us what God promises in his word. *II Cor. 141.*

The true conviction which believers have of the word of God, of their own salvation, and of religion in general, does not spring from the judgment of the flesh, or from human and philosophical arguments, but from the sealing of the Spirit, who imparts to their consciences such certainty as to remove all doubt . . . There are two operations of the Spirit in faith . . . it enlightens and it establishes the mind. *Eph. 208.*

When we have received the Spirit of God, his promises are confirmed to us, and no dread is felt that they will be revoked . . . Until we are supported by the testimony of the Spirit, we never rest upon them with unshaken confidence. *Eph. 209.*

The Spirit, who is the only fit . . . approver of doctrine . . . seals it on our hearts, so that we may certainly know that God speaks. *Gen. Epp. 200.*

The inward testimony of conscience, the sealing of the Spirit . . . far exceeds all the evidence of the senses. *Gen. Epp. 383.*

[23]

The faithful, inwardly illuminated by the Holy Spirit, acknowledge nothing but what God says in his word. *Gen. Epp. 390.*

[On Ezek. 2:2] God indeed works efficiently by His own words, but we must hold that this efficacy is not contained in the words themselves, but proceeds from the secret instinct of the Spirit . . . This work of the Spirit . . . is joined with the word of God . . . The external word is of no avail by itself, unless animated by the power of the Spirit . . . The Holy Spirit penetrates our hearts, and thus enlightens our minds. All power of action . . . resides in the Spirit himself, and thus all praise ought to be entirely referred to God alone. *Ezek. I:108, 109.*

Word and Spirit

The Fanaticism which Discards the Scripture, under the Pretence of Resorting to Immediate Revelations, Subversive of every Principle of Piety [Heading to Bk I, Chap. 9 of Institutes] *Inst. I:ix.1.*

Well . . . does Chrysostom admonish us to reject all who, under the pretence of the Spirit, lead us away from the simple doctrine of the gospel – the Spirit having been promised not to reveal a new doctrine, but to impress the truth of the gospel on our minds . . . For when they boast extravagantly of the Spirit, the tendency certainly is to sink and bury the Word of God, that they may make room for their own falsehoods. [Calvin's Reply to Sadoleto] *Tracts I:36.*

God does not bestow the Spirit on his people, in order to set aside the use of his word, but rather to render it fruitful. *Syn. Gosp. III:375.*

[On Is. 59:21] The 'Spirit' is joined with the word, because, without the efficacy of the Spirit, the preaching of the gospel would avail nothing, but would remain unfruitful. In like manner 'the word' must not be separated from 'the Spirit', as fanatics imagine, who, despising the word, glory in the name of the Spirit, and swell with vain confidence in their own imaginations. It is the spirit of Satan that is separated from the word, to which the Spirit of God is continually joined. *Is. IV:271.*

Limits of Rational Proofs of Scripture

It is acting a preposterous part, to endeavour to produce sound faith in the Scripture by disputations. *Inst. I:vii.4.*

God always secured to his word an undoubted credit, superior to all human opinion. *Inst. I:vi.2.*

Those human testimonies, which contribute to [Scripture's] confirmation, will not be useless, if they follow that first and principal proof, as secondary aids to our imbecility. *Inst. I:viii.13.*

God proves by facts which he has testified in his word. *Hab.-Hagg. 338.*

When God's works have the appearance of being unreasonable, we ought humbly to admire them, and never judge them according to our computation. *Jer. V:192.*

Christ commends faith on this ground, that it acquiesces in the bare word, and does not depend on carnal views or human reason. *John II:278.*

The light of human reason differs little from darkness. *Eph. 290.*

The gospel can be understood by faith alone – not by reason, nor by the perspicacity of the human understanding. *Philipp.-Col. 174.*

And Unbelief

Adam had never dared to resist the authority of God, if [Satan] had not discredited his word. *Inst. II:i.4.*

They belong not at all to Christ, who turn aside from his word. *Heb. 70.*

[On Heb. 3:17] The contempt of his word ever led [Israel] to sin. *Heb. 92.*

Whenever [men] slander God's word . . . they show that they feel within its power, however unwillingly and reluctantly. *Heb. 105.*

The mainspring of their ungodliness, they had cast the Word of God behind their back. *Ps. II:276.*

This is the distinction between the elect and the reprobate, that the elect simply rely on the word . . . while ungodly men scorn and disdain the word, though God speak a hundred times. *Is. I:185.*

[On Is. 30:9] The source of all evils, namely, contempt of the word. *Is. II:357.*

Men are fools till they submit to the word of God. *Is. III:18.*

By his word he has . . . armed his elect for certain victory . . . Whoever has profited . . . by heavenly doctrine, will easily repel all the tricks of Satan by steadfast and victorious faith. *Is. III:270.*

Our guilt will be double when we come to the judgment-seat of God, if we . . . shut our ears when he teaches by his word. *Is. III:308.*

They who wish to build the Church by rejecting the doctrine of the word, build a hog's sty, and not the Church of God. *Is. IV:148.*

They carry on war with [God] by attacking and rejecting his word and treating it as a fable. *Is. IV:199.*

'Trembling at the word' [Is. 66:2] Many boast that they reverence and fear God; but, by disregarding his word, they . . . shew that they are despisers of God. *Is. IV:413, 414.*

In the present day what reverence is manifested anywhere for God's word? . . . to what extent of audacity and madness men will break forth when they begin to discredit God's word? *Jer. I:281.*

God cannot endure the contempt of his word. *Jer. I:345.*

The majority of men at this day set up their own fictions against God's word. *Jer. I:398.*

Whosoever does not believe [God's] word, he robs him of his glory. *Jer. II:177.*

[26]

As soon as men depart even in the smallest degree from God's word, they cannot preach anything but falsehoods, vanities, impostures, errors and deceits. *Jer. II:226, 227.*

The truth of God ought not to bend to the will of men; for God changes not, and so his word admits of no change. *Jer. II:297.*

God is forsaken as soon as men turn aside from his pure word. *Jer. II:438.*

The devil by his artifice fascinates the reprobate, when he renders God's word either hateful or contemptible. *Jer. III:205.*

Men are more ready to receive error and vanity, than to receive the word of God. *Jer. III:362.*

As his truth is precious to God, so it is a sacrilege that he cannot bear, when his truth is turned into falsehood. *Jer. III:450.*

The more audacious a man becomes, the farther God withdraws from him. *Jer. V:429.*

Numberless fallacies of the devil will meet us immediately, unless the word holds us in strict obedience. *Dan. I:392.*

Men, when they have begun to turn aside from the pure word of God, continually invent various kinds of trifles. *Amos-Obad. 289.*

God will allow nothing that proceeds from the inventions of men to be joined to his word. *Mic.-Nah. 165.*

We shall abominate every error when we are fully persuaded that we forsake the true God whenever we obey not his word. *Mic.-Nah. 89.*

[On our Lord's first temptation] The single object which [Satan] has in view, is to persuade Christ to depart from the word of God, and to follow the dictates of infidelity. *Syn. Gosp. I:213.*

[On Matt. 4:6] Satan profanes the word of God, and endeavours to torture it for our destruction. *Syn. Gosp. I:218.*

The highest dishonour that can be done to God is unbelief and contempt for his word. *Syn. Gosp. I:319.*

[27]

The Jews . . . laboured under an hereditary disease of obstinacy . . . they . . . try to find a subterfuge for not obeying his word. *Syn. Gosp. II:93, 94.*

The human mind has a natural inclination towards vanity and errors . . . Nothing is more easy than to depart from the true and simple purity of the word of God. *Syn. Gosp. II:280.*

All who mingle their own inventions with the word of God, or who advance anything that does not belong to it, must be rejected, how honourable soever may be their rank. *Syn. Gosp. II:284.*

All who forsake the word fall into idolatry. *John I:160.*

Unbelief . . . is always proud . . . [It] will never understand anything in the words of Christ, which it despises and disdains . . . This arises from the depravity of men. *John I:275.*

All who boast of the name of God without the word of God are mere liars. *John I:359.*

[On the doubt of Thomas, John chap. 20] When we render to the word of God less honour than is due to it, there steals upon us, without our knowledge, a growing obstinacy, which brings along with it a contempt of the word of God, and makes us lose all reverence for it. *John II:275.*

. . . drowned in the huge sink of errors; which punishment God in justice layeth upon men which refuse to obey his word. *Acts I:294.*

. . . the word of God . . . cannot be more grievously blasphemed than when men refuse to believe it. *Acts I:555.*

[On Acts 18:6] God is sorer displeased with contempt of his word than with any wickedness. *Acts II:184.*

There is no end of erring, when we depart from the word of God. *Acts II:217.*

Retribution always follows contempt of the word. *Cor. II:247.*

It is a most righteous punishment of human arrogance, that they who swerve from the purity of Scripture become profane. *Past. Epp. 175.*

A prayer of Calvin:

O grant, that being ruled by thy Spirit, we may surrender ourselves altogether to thee, and so acquiesce in thy Word alone, that we may not deviate either to the right hand or to the left, but allow thee alone to be wise, and that acknowledging our folly and vanity, we may suffer ourselves to be taught by thy Word . . . [Prayer concluding Lecture 36 on Jeremiah] *Jer. I:484.*

Bible Study

[On Acts 8:30, the Ethiopian eunuch] Thus must we also read the Scriptures. We must greedily, and with a prompt mind, receive those things which are plain, and wherein God openeth his mind. As for those things which are hid from us, we must pass them over until we see greater light. And if we be not wearied with reading, it shall at length come to pass that the Scripture shall be made more familiar by continual use. *Acts I:354.*

God grants to us the taste of his heavenly doctrine on the express condition, that we feed on it abundantly from day to day. *Syn. Gosp. II:105.*

That man has made great proficiency in the word of God, who does not fail to admire whatever he reads or hears every day, that contributes to his unceasing progress in faith. *Syn. Gosp. I:146.*

Let us . . . become submissive to God, and then he will convey to us by his word, nothing but sweetness, nothing but delights. *Mic.-Nah. 201.*

It is meditation upon the Divine Law which furnishes us with armour to resist. *Ps. I:283.*

The Psalmist . . . designates godliness by *the study of the law* . . . God is only rightly served when his law is obeyed. *Ps. I:4.*

In meditating on the works of God, they must bring with them a sober, docile, mild and humble spirit. *Gen. I:57.*

Continual meditation on the word is not ineffectual . . . God, by one and another promise, establishes our faith. *Gen. I:265.*

For want of daily exercising ourselves in the holy Scriptures, the truth which we had known little by little drops away, till at length it totally disappears. [Calvin to the Queen of Navarre on 16 January 1561] *Letters 231.*

Interpretation

As the Spirit of understanding is given to anyone from heaven, he will become a proper and faithful interpreter of God. *Gen. II:323.*

I am against all refined renderings. *Ps. IV:60.*

The true meaning of Scripture is the natural and obvious meaning. *Gal. 136.*

I do not love strained meanings. *Hos. 328.*

[On Dan. 12:11, 12] In numerical calculations I am no conjuror. *Dan. II:391.*

We ought to guard against violent and forced interpretations. *Is. III:483.*

[On 1 Cor. 2:15] The Spirit of God, from whom the doctrine of the gospel comes, is its only true interpreter. *Cor. I:117.*

BLOOD OF CHRIST (*see also* THE ATONEMENT)

It is . . . to the blood of Christ alone that we must look for the atonement of our sins; but we are creatures of sense, who must see with our eyes, and handle with our hands; and it is only by improving the outward symbols of propitiation that we can arrive at a full and assured persuasion of it. *Ps. II:294.*

It is the peculiar work of the Holy Spirit to sprinkle our consciences inwardly with the blood of Christ, and, by removing the sense of guilt, to secure our access into the presence of God. *Ps. II:295.*

[On the passover. God] taught that no advantage was to be expected from the blood poured forth, without the sprinkling. *Four Last Bks of Moses I:222.*

[The Israelites] could not be protected from God's wrath, except by holding up against it the shield of the blood. *Four Last Bks of Moses I:461.*

The eating of blood is here prohibited because it was consecrated to God in order to make expiation. *Four Last Bks of Moses II:335.*

Whenever we take the sacred books into our hands, the blood of Christ ought to occur to our minds, as if the whole of its sacred instruction were written therewith. *Four Last Bks of Moses III:320.*

The blood of Christ is not only the pledge of our salvation, but also the cause of our calling. *Gen. Epp. 50.*

This Spirit sprinkles our souls with the blood of Christ. *Rom. 156.*

[On John 16:26] The value of his sacrifice . . . is always powerful and efficacious; the blood . . . is a continual intercession for us. *John II:158.*

[The O.T. ritual] Faith in every case looked for an intervening blood. *Heb. 210.*

[God] is pacified towards us through the blood of Christ . . . Where Christ does not appear with his blood, we have nothing to do with God. *Heb. 210, 211.*

The promises of God are . . . only profitable to us when they are confirmed by the blood of Christ . . . His blood like a seal is engraven on our hearts . . . When the Gospel is preached, his sacred blood distils together with the voice. *Heb. 212.*

Christ employs his Spirit to sprinkle us in order to wash us by his own blood when he leads us to true repentance, when he purifies us from the depraved lusts of our flesh, when he imbues us with the precious gift of his own righteousness. *Heb. 213.*

[On Heb. 10:19, 'by the blood of Jesus'] It is a perpetual consecration of the way, because the blood of Christ is always in a manner distilling before the presence of the Father, in order to irrigate heaven and earth. *Heb. 235.*

[31]

Our faith looks not on the naked doctrine, but on the blood by which our salvation has been ratified. *Heb. 248.*

[On Heb. 13:20] God raised up his own Son, but in such a way that the blood he shed once for all in his death is efficacious after his resurrection for the ratification of the everlasting covenant, and brings forth fruit the same as though it were flowing always. *Heb. 357.*

The faith of Abram was directed to the blood of Christ. *Gen. I:355.*

This eternal justice depends upon the enduring effect of the death of Christ, since the blood of Christ flowed as it were before God, and while we are daily purged and cleansed from our pollution, God is also daily appeased for us. *Dan. II:217.*

BURIAL

The human body is formed for immortality . . . By sinking into death it does not utterly perish. *Gen. II:245.*

[Jacob's death, Gen. 49:33] The aged saint gave directions respecting the disposal of his body, as easily as healthy and vigorous men are wont to compose themselves to sleep. *Gen. II:473.*

To embalm corpses . . . was done as a public symbol of future incorruption. *Gen. II:477.*

The sacred rite of burial descended from the holy fathers, to be a kind of mirror of the future resurrection. *Gen. II:477.*

[On Gen. 23:1] Moses, who relates the death of Sarah in a single word, uses so many in describing her burial . . . The sepulchre cried aloud, that death formed no obstacle to their entering on the possession . . . Abraham by faith looked up to heaven. *Gen. I:575, 579.*

Religion carries along with it the care of burial . . . a sense [God] has never suffered to perish, in order that men might be witnesses to themselves of a future life. *Gen. I:578, 579.*

[Of the patriarchs] Their burying the dead [was] . . . a lively symbol of the future resurrection. *Gen. II:245.*

God watches over the scattered dust of his own children, gathers it again, and will suffer nothing of them to perish. *Ps. II:442.*

[On Deut. 21:23] The rights of sepulture are ordained for man, both as a pledge and symbol of the resurrection, and also to spare the eyes of the living. *Four Last Bks of Moses III:47.*

The rites of burial arouse us to the hope of resurrection and everlasting life. *Four Last Bks of Moses III:248.*

Burial . . . the symbol of the last resurrection, which we still look for . . . As the earth supports the living, so it covers the dead, and keeps them till the coming of Christ. *Is. I:449, 450.*

Burying has been held as a sacred custom in all ages; for it was a symbol of the last resurrection. *Jer. I:416.*

Burial is . . . a pledge . . . of immortality . . . a mirror of a future life. *Jer. III:108.*

[On Matt. 26:12. Christ] wished to testify by this symbol, that his grave would yield a sweet odour, as it breathed life and salvation through the whole world. *Syn. Gosp. III:191.*

Christ, in departing from the sepulchre, perfumed not one house, but the whole world, by the quickening odour of his death. *Syn. Gosp. III:191.*

Theodore Beza records that Calvin was buried in the common cemetery in Geneva, with no extraordinary pomp, and, as he had commanded, without any gravestone. *Tracts I:97.*

CEREMONIES

Ceremonies . . . have been abrogated, not as to their effect, but only as to their use. *Inst. II:vii.16.*

The devil has introduced the fashion of celebrating the Supper without any doctrine, and for doctrine has substituted ceremonies . . . pure apishness and buffoonery. [Short Treatise on the Supper of our Lord, 1540] *Tracts II:190.*

To return to the ceremonies which are abolished, is to repair the vail of the temple which Jesus Christ rent on his death . . . A multitude of ceremonies in the Mass is a form of Judaism quite contrary to Christianity. *Tracts II:192.*

God enjoined ceremonies that their outward use might be temporal, and their meaning eternal. *Syn. Gosp. I:280.*

We ought . . . to beware lest the unity of faith be destroyed, or the bond of charity broken, on account of outward ceremonies . . . Every man would willingly compel the whole world to copy his example. *Syn. Gosp. I:405, 406.*

CHARACTER

The greater part of the world rashly embrace whatever they meet with, and also ramble from one thing to another; but piety, in order to walk with a steady step, collects itself within its proper limits. *Inst. I:xii.1.*

Show me, if you can, a single individual, who, unless he has renounced himself according to the command of the Lord, is voluntarily disposed to practise virtue among men. *Inst. III:vii.2.*

Lighter is the loss of money than of character. *Gen. II:285.*

The chief part of the service of God . . . to have a pure and upright heart. *Is. IV:346.*

If we would judge rightly of any man we must see how he bears good and bad fortune. *Hab.-Hagg. 36.*

Nothing is more difficult than to counterfeit virtue. *Syn. Gosp. I:364.*

It is integrity of heart before God, and uprightness before men, that makes a Christian. *John I:78.*

There is a certain secret majesty in holy discipline and in sincere godliness. *Acts I:205.*

He who lives otherwise than as befits a child of God deserves to be expelled from the household of faith. *Thess. 346.*

[34]

CHARISMATIC GIFTS

All the gifts and power which men seem to possess are in the hand of God, so that he can, at any instant, . . . deprive them of the wisdom which he has given them. *Ps. III:198.*

[On Is. 11:2. Messiah's] whole strength, power, and majesty is here made to consist in the gifts of the Spirit . . . As he took upon him our flesh, it was necessary that he should be enriched with them . . . He received the gifts of the Spirit that he might bestow them upon us. *Is. I:374.*

Christ causes his heavenly anointing to flow over the whole body of his Church . . . Whenever . . . we feel that we are in want of any of these gifts, let us blame our unbelief . . . We ought to ask all blessings from Christ alone. *Is. I:376.*

[On Is. 30:1] Two things are here connected, the word and the Spirit of God, in opposition to fanatics, who aim at oracles and hidden revelations without the word. *Is. II:347.*

[On Is. 59:21] 'The word' must not be separated from 'the Spirit', as fanatics imagine, who, despising the word, glory in the name of the Spirit, and swell with vain confidence in their own imaginations. It is the spirit of Satan that is separated from the word, to which the Spirit of God is continually joined. *Is. IV:271.*

It is notorious that the Gifts of the Spirit, which were then given by the laying on of hands, some time after ceased to be conferred. [Antidote to the Council of Trent, 1547] *Tracts III:287.*

All know that the gift of healing was not perpetual . . . The anointers of this day are no more ministers of the grace of which James speaks than the player who acted Agamemnon on the stage was a king. *Tracts III:290.*

The reprobate are sometimes endued by God with the gifts of the Spirit, to execute the office with which he invests them. *John II:64.*

Frantic men require inspirations and revelations from heaven, and . . . contemn the minister of God, by whose hand they ought to be governed. *Acts I:355.*

The gift of the tongues, and other such things, are ceased long ago in the Church. *Acts I:452.*

[On 1 Cor. 12:1] The Corinthians abused the gifts of God for ostentation and show. *Cor. I:395.*

[On 1 Cor. 12:28] Tongues . . . comprehends both the knowledge of languages, and gift of interpretation . . . Foreign languages (14:2). *Cor. I:417.*

Many foolishly imagine that Christ taught only so as to lay down the first lessons, and then to send the disciples to a higher school . . . They substitute the Spirit in his place . . . As soon as the Spirit is separated from the word of Christ, the door is open to all kinds of delusions and impostures . . . a new theology . . . of revelations . . . Nothing . . . is bestowed on us by the Spirit apart from Christ, but he takes it from Christ, that he may communicate it to us . . . The Spirit enriches us with no other than the riches of Christ, that he may display his glory in all things . . . The grace of the Spirit is a mirror, in which Christ wishes to be seen by us. *John II:145–148.*

Those who are not satisfied with Christ are exposed to all fallacies and deceptions. *Philipp.-Col. 176.*

CHASTENING

All whom the Lord has chosen and honoured with admission into the society of his saints, ought to prepare themselves for a life, hard, laborious, unquiet and replete with numerous and various calamities. It is the will of their heavenly Father to exercise them in this manner, that he may have a certain proof of those that belong to him. *Inst. III:viii.1.*

God is wonderfully angry with his children, whom he ceases not to love . . . because he designs to terrify them with a sense of his wrath, to humble their carnal pride, to shake off their indolence, and to excite them to repentance. *Inst. III:ii.12.*

In every affliction we ought immediately to recollect the course of our past life. *Inst. III:viii.6.*

When God chastises his people, he promotes their future advantage. *Is. III:177.*

Every chastisement is a call to repentance. *Is. II:123.*

Chastisements . . . cure us of the fearfully dangerous disease of apostasy. *Is. II:25.*

Though the chastisements of the godly and ungodly appear to be the same, yet the reasons of them are exceedingly different. *Is. I:399.*

Chastisements are common to the elect and the reprobate. *Ezek. I:229.*

[God] tames his children with cords when they will not profit by his word. *Dan. I:317.*

[On Hos. 2:17] The Church cannot be rightly reformed except it be trained to obedience by the frequent scourges of God. *Hos. 108.*

All the chastisements which God by his own hand inflicts on us, have this as the object – to heal us of our vices. *Hos. 269.*

The scourges by which God chastises his children are testimonies of his love. *Hab.-Hagg. 139.*

None but those whose minds have been raised above the world by a taste of heavenly life really experience this perpetual and uninterrupted manifestation of the divine favour, which enables them to bear their chastisements with cheerfulness. *Ps. I:489.*

God, although he visit his children with temporary chastisements of a severe description, will ultimately crown them with joy and prosperity. *Ps. II:473.*

This fatherly chastisement then, which operates as medicine, holds the medium between undue indulgence . . . and extreme severity. *Ps. III:442.*

[37]

The Lord blesses us more by punishing us, than he would have done by sparing us. *Gen. II:472.*

In the darkness of our miseries, the grace of God shines more brightly. *Gen. II:302.*

CHILDREN

Because all offspring flows from the kindness of God . . . the Lord is said . . . to visit those, to whom he gives children . . . The birth of every child is rightly deemed the effect of divine visitation. *Gen. I:537.*

The fruit of the womb is not born by chance, but is to be reckoned among the precious gifts of God . . . But there are few who heartily acknowledge that their seed has been given them by God. *Gen. II:425.*

God is so kind and liberal to his servants, as, for their sakes, to appoint even the children who shall descend from them to be enrolled among his people. *Inst. IV:xvi.15.*

In [Isaac's] very birth God has set before us a lively picture of his Church. *Gen. I:537.*

God pronounces that he adopts our infants as his children, before they are born, when he promises that he will be a God to us, and to our seed after us. This promise includes their salvation. *Inst. IV:xv.20.*

The mere promise of God ought to be sufficient to assure us of the salvation of our children. *Inst. IV:xvi.9.*

Children are given to men on the express condition, that [they] . . . transmit the name of God to posterity. *Is. III:179.*

How far do men derive advantage from the faith of others? . . . To all believers . . . by their faith, the grace of God is extended to their children, and their children's children even before they are born. *Syn. Gosp. I:393.*

The children of the faithful which are born in the Church are from their mother's womb of the household of the kingdom of God. *Acts I:454.*

[On Acts 11:17] Those men make war against God who are set against the baptizing of infants; because they most cruelly exclude those out of the Church whom God hath adopted into the Church. *Acts I:463.*

Fellowship with Christ is communicated to infants in a peculiar way. They have the right of adoption in the covenant, by which they come into communion with Christ. *Rom. 117.*

CHRIST

Two stanzas of Calvin's hymn, *Salutation to Jesus Christ*, first discovered in an old Genevese prayer-book and published in 1868. The English translation from the French is by Mrs H. B. Smith of New York, 1868. The full hymn of eight verses appears in Philip Schaff's *Christ in Song*, 1879, pp. 549–551.

> I greet Thee, who my sure Redeemer art,
> My only Trust, and Saviour of my heart!
> Who so much toil and woe
> And pain didst undergo,
> For my poor, worthless sake;
> And pray Thee, from our hearts,
> All idle griefs and smarts,
> And foolish cares to take.
>
> Thou art the King of mercy and of grace,
> Reigning omnipotent in every place;
> So come, O King! and deign
> Within our hearts to reign,
> And our whole being sway;
> Shine in us by Thy light,
> And lead us to the height
> Of Thy pure, heavenly day.

Person of Christ

If we seek salvation, we are taught by the name of JESUS, that it is in him; if we seek any other gifts of the Spirit, they will be found in his unction; strength, in his dominion; purity, in his conception; indulgence discovers itself in his nativity, by which he was made to resemble us in all things, that he might learn to condole with us; if we seek redemption, it will be found in his passion; absolution, in his condemnation; remission of the curse, in his cross; satisfaction, in his sacrifice; purification, in his blood; reconciliation, in his descent into hell; mortification of the flesh, in his sepulchre; newness of life and immortality, in his resurrection; the inheritance of the celestial kingdom, in his entrance into heaven; protection, security, abundance, and enjoyment of all blessings, in his kingdom; a fearless expectation of the judgment, in the judicial authority committed to him . . . Let us draw from his treasury, and from no other source. *Inst. II:xvi.19.*

In treating of things respecting Christ, such reverence ought to be observed as not to know anything but what is written in the Word of the Lord . . . It is not lawful for us to allege anything of Christ from our own thoughts. *Heb. 157, 158.*

[Christ's pre-existence] Since they cannot openly rob him of his divinity, [they] secretly steal from him his eternity. *Inst. I:146.*

[The angel of the Lord, Exod. 23:20] No common angel is designated, but the chief of all angels, who has always been also the Head of the Church (1 Cor. 10:9). *Four Last Books of Moses I:403.*

[Quoting Augustine] Christ, considered in himself, is called God; but, with relation to the Father, he is called the Son. *Inst. I:xiii.19.*

[The Virgin Birth] We do not represent Christ as perfectly immaculate, merely because he was born of the seed of the woman unconnected with any man, but because he was sanctified by the Spirit, so that his generation was pure and holy, such as it would have been before the fall of Adam. *Inst. II:xiii.4.*

Christ is the temple of Godhead. *Zech.-Mal. 75.*

The name Jehovah is appropriated to Christ, and . . . there is no difference between the Father and the Son as to essence . . . Whenever . . . Christ announces his own divinity, he takes the name Jehovah. *Zech.-Mal. 74, 75.*

[Christ] voluntarily took upon him everything that is inseparable from human nature. *Syn. Gosp. I:167.*

[On Matt. 16:16] The designation *Christ*, or *Anointed*, includes both an everlasting Kingdom and an everlasting Priesthood. *Syn. Gosp. II:289.*

Christ is the ladder by which we ascend to God the Father. *Syn. Gosp. I:436.*

[Christ is] the conqueror of death and the Lord of life. *Syn. Gosp. II:14.*

By Christ Man we are conducted to Christ God. *John II:277.*

He who . . . does not perceive Christ to be God . . . is blind amidst the brightness of noonday. *John II:282.*

To search for wisdom apart from Christ means not simply foolhardiness, but utter insanity. *Rom. 15.*

There was never since the beginning any communication between God and men, save only by Christ; for we have nothing to do with God, unless the Mediator be present to purchase his favour for us. *Acts I:276.*

Christ with his gospel has been promised and always expected from the beginning of the world. *Rom. 15.*

The whole gospel is contained in Christ. *Rom. 15.*

All the blessings of God come to us through Christ. *Rom. 19.*

Every doctrine of the law, every command, every promise, always points to Christ. *Rom. 221.*

Whoever wishes to have the half of Christ, loses the whole. *Gal. 148.*

Christ is the beginning, middle and end . . . nothing is, or can be found, apart from him. *Col. 146.*

There is nothing necessary for salvation which faith finds not in Christ. *Gen. Epp. 244.*

Those are out of danger who remain in Christ, but . . . those who are not satisfied with Christ are exposed to all fallacies and deceptions. *Col. 176.*

Christ is the mirror in which it behoves us to contemplate our election. *Inst. III:xxiv.5.*

It is a fixed maxim with us, that whenever the Scripture mentions the purity of Christ, it relates to a real humanity. *Inst. II:xiii.4.*

Christ was sanctified from his earliest infancy that he might sanctify in himself all his elect, of every age, without any difference. *Inst. IV:xvi.18.*

Christ is that image in which God presents to our view not only his heart, but also his hands and his feet. I give the name of his *heart* to that secret love with which he embraces us in Christ. *Gen. I:64.*

God always acts by the hand of his Son. *Gen. I:513.*

Christ derives no glory from his ancestors . . . By his infinite purity they were all cleansed. *Gen. II:278.*

Christ liveth for us, not for himself . . . Nor has Christ any thing which may not be applied to our benefit. *Heb. 175.*

[On Is. 11:2. Messiah's] whole strength, power and majesty is here made to consist in the gifts of the Spirit . . . As he took upon him our flesh, it was necessary that he should be enriched with them . . . He received the gifts of the Spirit that he might bestow them upon us. *Is. I:374.*

Christ, the only light of truth, the soul of the law, the end of all the prophets. *Is. II:322.*

[On Is. 7:14] The prophets, when they promise anything hard to be believed, are wont immediately afterwards to mention Christ; for in him are ratified all the promises . . . (2 Cor. 1:20). *Is. III:283.*

Christ ought not to be regarded as a private individual, but as holding the office to which the Father has appointed him . . . Whatever he affirms concerning himself we ought to understand as belonging to us also. *Is. IV: 106, 107.*

God's goodness . . . is so exhibited to us in Christ, that not a particle of it is to be sought for anywhere else: for from this fountain must we draw whatever refers to our salvation and happiness of life. *Hos. 135.*

It has ever been the office of the Mediator to preserve in safety the Church of God. *Hab.-Hagg. 163.*

In the whole of the legal priesthood, in the sacrifices, and in the form of the sanctuary, we ought to seek Christ. *Syn. Gosp. III:360, 361.*

Faith ought not to be fixed on the essence of Christ alone . . . but ought to attend to his power and office. *John I:79.*

Moses had no other intention than to invite all men to go straight to Christ. *John I:217.*

They who imagine whatever they choose concerning Christ will ultimately have nothing instead of him but a shadowy phantom. *John I:218.*

No one will ever come to Christ as God, who despises him as man. *John I:268.*

[Christ] . . . continues, and will eternally continue to be, the only Teacher of the Church . . . He alone keeps possession of the whole power, while they [the apostles] claim nothing for themselves but the ministry. *John II:267.*

Christ is . . . spread abroad everywhere by the power of his Spirit, not by the substance of his flesh. *Acts I:53.*

There is so great a unity between Christ and his members, that the name of Christ sometimes includes the whole body, as in 1 Cor. 12:12. *Philipp.-Col. 164.*

The only way of retaining, as well as restoring pure doctrine – to place Christ before the view such as he is with all his blessings, that his excellence may be truly perceived. *Col. 146.*

[*Contrasted views of Christ*] We differ from Papists, that while we are both of us called Christians, and profess to believe in Christ, they picture to themselves one that is torn, disfigured, divested of his excellence, denuded of his office . . . a spectre rather than Christ himself; we, on the other hand, embrace him such as he is here described by Paul – loving and efficacious. [Colossians] distinguishes the true Christ from a fictitious one. *Philipp.-Col. 134.*

Work of Christ

There is no part in our salvation which may not be found in Christ. *Acts II:247.*

Christ . . . the chief governor, in accomplishing the salvation of the Church. *Acts I:284.*

All the wisdom of believers is comprehended in the cross of Christ. *Cor. I:74.*

Our salvation consists in the doctrine of the cross (1 Cor 1:23). *Syn. Gosp. III:274, 275.*

The Son of God stood, as a criminal, before a mortal man . . . that we may stand boldly before God. *Syn. Gosp. III:275.*

Christ . . . was at that time silent, that he may now be our advocate. *Syn. Gosp. III:277.*

On the cross, as in a magnificent chariot, he triumphed over his enemies and ours. *Syn. Gosp. III:285.*

Our filthiness deserves that . . . all the angels should spit upon us; but Christ, in order to present us pure and unspotted in presence of the Father, resolved to be spat upon. *Syn. Gosp. III:290.*

Whoever . . . in dying, shall commit to Christ, in true faith, the keeping of his soul . . . Christ will meet his prayer. *Syn. Gosp. III:313.*

God determined that his own Son should be stripped of his raiment, that we, clothed with his righteousness . . . may appear with boldness in company with the angels. *Syn. Gosp. III:298.*

Christ . . . permitted his garments to be torn in pieces like a prey, that he might enrich us with the riches of his victory. *Syn. Gosp. III:298, 299.*

[The dying thief] drawn from hell itself to heaven . . . admitted to heaven before the apostles . . . a distinguished teacher of faith and piety to the whole world . . . He adores Christ as a King while on the gallows, and declares him, when dying, to be the Author of life . . . He beheld life in death, exaltation in ruin, glory in shame, victory in destruction, a kingdom in bondage. *Syn. Gosp. III:308, 309, 311.*

In order that Christ might satisfy for us, it was necessary that he should be placed as a guilty person at the judgment-seat of God . . . actually to undergo in our room the judgment of God. *Syn. Gosp. III:318.*

The burial of Christ . . . an intermediate transition from the ignominy of the cross to the glory of the resurrection. *Syn. Gosp. III:330.*

[Christ's] humiliation and descent into hell raised us to heaven. *John I:267.*

[On Heb. 7:1. As] King of righteousness [Christ] communicates to us the righteousness of God, partly when he makes us to be counted righteous by a gratuitous reconciliation, and partly when he renews us by his Spirit, that we may lead a godly and holy life. *Heb. 156.*

[King of peace] This peace . . . is the fruit of that righteousness . . . yet I prefer to understand it here of that inward peace which tranquillizes the conscience and renders it confident before God. *Heb. 157.*

The death of Christ became the life of the world . . . He died on earth, but the virtue and efficacy of his death proceeded from heaven. *Heb. 180, 182.*

Christ was the earnest and pledge of the covenant. *Jer. IV:250.*

Cross of Christ

There is no tribunal so magnificent, no throne so stately, no show of triumph so distinguished, no chariot so elevated, as is the gibbet on which Christ has subdued death and the devil. *Philipp.-Col. 191.*

His whole life was nothing but a kind of perpetual cross. *Inst. III:viii.1.*

The form and beauty of Christ is especially disfigured by the cross. *Heb. 119.*

Our salvation consists in the doctrine of the cross. *Syn. Gosp. III:274, 275.*

Nothing . . . can raise us up to God, until Christ shall have instructed us in his school. Yet this cannot be done, unless we, having emerged out of the lowest depths, are borne up above all heavens, in the chariot of his cross. *Gen. I:63.*

The cross will be . . . a chariot, by which he shall raise all men, along with himself, to his Father. *John II:37.*

In the cross of Christ, as in a magnificent theatre, the inestimable goodness of God is displayed before the whole world . . . The honour which . . . belongs to the death of Christ, is the fruit which sprung from it for the salvation of men. *John II:73, 74.*

Whoever builds an altar for himself subverts the cross of Christ, on which he offered the only true and perpetual sacrifice. *Zech.-Mal. 501.*

The cross of Christ always contains in itself the victory. *John II:150.*

All the wisdom of believers is comprehended in the cross of Christ. *Cor. I:74.*

Bearing the Cross

They are a blessed people whom God exercises with the cross. *Ps. IV:20.*

All who seek exemption from the cross do as it were withdraw themselves from the number of his children. *Heb. 317.*

The discipline of the cross is necessary, so that earnest prayer may become vigorous in us. *Zech.-Mal. 403.*

Those are the truly blessed whom God has habituated through his word to the endurance of the cross, and prevented from sinking under adversity by the secret support and consolations of his own Spirit. *Ps. IV:21.*

The glory of the gospel was always joined with the cross and divers troubles. *Acts I:240.*

The Son of God is partner with them of the cross . . . He, as it were, put under his shoulders, that he may bear some part of the burden. *Acts. I:370.*

The endurance of the cross is the gift of God . . . Even the sufferings themselves are evidences of the grace of God. *Philipp.-Col. 48.*

A dread of the cross led them [the Galatians] to corrupt the true preaching of the cross. *Gal. 182.*

[God's] will is to exercise them with various trials, so that they may spend their whole life under the cross . . . They should lovingly kiss the cross rather than dread it. *Heb. 63.*

Christ leads his disciples by the hand to the cross, and thence raises them to the hope of the resurrection. *Syn. Gosp. III:211.*

In bearing the cross we are the companions of Christ. *Syn. Gosp. III:472.*

[On Mark 10:30, 'with persecutions'] The cross . . . is attached to their back, yet so sweet is the seasoning of the grace of God . . . that their condition is more desirable than the luxuries of kings. *Syn. Gosp. II:408.*

Whoever shall revolt at and shrink from the cross will always be ashamed of the gospel. *Past. Epp. 193.*

[We] ought by a long meditation to have been previously prepared to bear the cross. *Gen. Epp. 133.*

The chief virtue of the faithful . . . is a patient endurance of the cross and mortification by which they calmly submit themselves to God. *Ps. V:42.*

Christ's Kingly Rule

Under the person of David, the Prophets exhibited Christ. *Jer. IV:251.*

Christ's kingdom . . . is set forth under the image of an earthly and civil government. *Jer. IV:253.*

The word . . . Christ's royal sceptre. *Is. I:379.*

[47]

The preaching of the gospel, which is committed to [the Church], is the spiritual sceptre of Christ, by which he displays his power. *Is. III:414.*

[Christ] did not commence his reign till he was publicly ordained the Master and Redeemer of his people. *Dan. II:214.*

Christ is to us the fulness of a blessed life, because he is a king and a priest. *Hos. 283.*

[Matt. 28:18–20] extolled in magnificent language the reign of Christ over the whole world. *Syn. Gosp. III:391.*

[Christ's] regal unction . . . is not represented to us as composed of oil and aromatic perfumes . . . The kingdom of Christ consists in the Spirit, not in terrestrial pleasures or pomps . . . In order to be partakers of it, we must renounce the world. *Inst. II:xv.5.*

It is for us that he reigns for ever and ever. *Ps. I:154.*

Christ can only obtain a tranquil kingdom by fighting. *Ps. I:295.*

These two things, his offspring and his throne, are conjoined. *Ps. III:446.*

Christ's kingdom is inseparable from his priesthood. *Ps. V:157.*

The whole world became an enlarged Mount Zion upon the advent of Christ. *Ps. V:158.*

God would never allow [the Church] to be altogether destroyed since upon the event of its destruction he would cease to be a king. *Ps. V:179.*

Why is the preaching of the gospel so often styled the kingdom of God, but because it is the sceptre by which the heavenly king rules his people? [Calvin's Reply to Sadoleto] *Tracts I:36.*

God is properly said to rule or reign among the faithful, whom he governs by his Spirit. So God's kingdom begins and has its origin when regeneration takes place. *Jer. V:119.*

[48]

The kingdom of God among men is nothing else than a restoration to a happy life . . . true and everlasting happiness . . . 'newness of life' (Rom. 6:4). *Syn. Gosp. I:178.*

'The kingdom of heaven' means the renovation of the Church. *Syn. Gosp. I:279.*

The kingdom of God is continually growing and advancing to the end of the world. *Syn. Gosp. I:320.*

The kingdom of heaven and the kingdom of God denote the new condition of the Church . . . for it was promised that at the coming of Christ all things would be restored. *Syn. Gosp. II:14.*

The kingdom of God is . . . nothing else than the inward and spiritual renewal of the soul. *Syn. Gosp. II:212.*

The kingdom of Christ is strengthened more by the blood of the martyrs than by the aid of arms. *John II:211.*

The kingdom of Christ is only begun, and the perfection thereof is deferred until the last day. *Acts I:153.*

The kingdom of God is grounded and contained in the knowledge of the redemption purchased by Christ. *Acts II:431.*

In spite of the opposition of the world, [the kingdom of Christ] is erected in an astonishing manner by the invisible power of God . . . All that was accomplished in the person of Christ extends to the gradual development of his kingdom, even until the end of the world. *Ps. IV:393, 394.*

God reigns when men, renouncing themselves and despising the world and the present state, submit themselves to his righteousness, so as to aspire to the heavenly state. Thus this kingdom consists of two parts; the one, God's correcting by the power of his Spirit all our carnal and depraved appetites, which oppose him in great numbers; the other, his forming all our powers to an obedience to his commands. *Inst. III:xx.42.*

Kingdom of Christ

The whole of Satan's kingdom is subject to the authority of Christ. *Syn. Gosp. I:430.*

Satan endeavours, by every possible method, to take anything from Christ. *John I:31.*

[Christ] proclaims war against Satan in our behalf. *Zech.-Mal. 84.*

[On Zech. 3:1–2] Christ never performs the work of the priesthood, but . . . Satan stands at his side, that is, devises all means by which he may remove and withdraw Christ from his office. *Zech.-Mal. 82.*

[On the temptations of Christ] God intended . . . to exhibit in the person of his Son, as in a very bright mirror, how obstinately and perseveringly Satan opposes the salvation of men . . . By his victory he obtained a triumph for us . . . tempted as the public representative of all believers . . . The Spirit of God presides over our contests as an exercise of our faith. *Syn. Gosp. I:210.*

No war was ever carried on so continuously and professedly against the Church, as those which occurred after the Caesars arose, and after Christ was made manifest to the world . . . The wrath of Satan was excited against all God's children on account of the manifestation of Christ. *Dan. II:57.*

CHURCH

The source and origin of the Church is the free love of God. *Ps. II:154.*

The work of restoring and establishing the Church is not without reason everywhere assigned in Scripture to God. *Heb. xxiv.*

[On Ps. 65:5] It is in no common or ordinary manner that God has preserved his Church, but with terrible majesty. *Ps. II:459.*

The Church is a distinguished theatre on which the divine glory is displayed. *Ps. III:194.*

The Church, which God has selected as the great theatre where his fatherly care may be manifested. *Ps. III:12.*

In the whole world there is nothing enduring but the Church . . . Her happiness must be considered as consisting principally in this, that she has reserved for her an everlasting state in heaven. *Ps. III:394.*

A right judgment cannot be formed of the happiness of the Church, except when we estimate it according to the standard of God's word. *Ps. III:399.*

If we do not prefer the Church to all the other objects of our solicitude, we are unworthy of being accounted among her members. *Ps. IV:100.*

The sadder the desolation is to which the Church has been brought, the less ought our affections to be alienated from her. *Ps. IV:112.*

The Church . . . a mirror of the grace and justice of God. *Ps. IV:315.*

The state or kingdom of the Church constitutes the principal and august theatre where God presents and displays the tokens of his wonderful power, wisdom, and righteousness. *Ps. IV:335.*

The welfare of the Church is inseparably connected with the righteousness of God. *Ps. V:124.*

The whole world is a theatre for the display of the divine goodness, wisdom, justice, and power, but the Church is the orchestra . . . the most conspicuous part of it. *Ps. V:178.*

[On Ps. 147:2] It was no less properly God's work to raise up his Church when ruined and fallen down, than to found it at first . . . The Church, which is daily distracted, will be restored to its entireness; for God will not suffer his work to fail . . . Though it may not always be in a flourishing condition [it] is ever safe and secure, and . . . God will miraculously heal it. *Ps. V:293, 294.*

God exalts His Church to preeminence by ways and means unknown to men, in order that His power may be magnified in this weakness. *Four Last Bks of Moses IV:253.*

We are wont always to desire a multitude, and to estimate by it the prosperity of the Church. On the contrary, we should rather desire to be few in number, and that in all of us the glory of God may shine brightly. *Is. I:155.*

What is the Church? The body and society of believers whom God hath predestined to eternal life [Calvin's Catechism of 1536 and 1541] *Tracts II:50.*

We cannot become acceptable to God without being united in one and the same faith, that is, without being members of the Church. *Is. II:45.*

No difficulties can prevent the Lord from delivering and restoring his Church whenever he shall think fit. *Is. III:205.*

An assembly in which the preaching of heavenly doctrine is not heard does not deserve to be reckoned a Church. *Is. III:213.*

There will always be left a Church among the elect people, because God refuses to be deprived of his rightful possession. *Is. III:319.*

[On Is. 43:10] The Lord has chosen his Church in order to bear testimony to his truth. *Is. III:330.*

The Church, so long as she is a pilgrim in this world, is subjected to the cross, that she may be humble, and may be conformed to her Head . . . Her highest ornament and lustre is modesty. *Is. IV:42.*

The grace of God, which he displays in the preservation of his Church, surpasses all his other works. *Is. IV:72.*

All that relates to the full and perfect happiness of the Church is absolutely the gift of God. *Is. IV:219.*

Christ possesses nothing separate from his Church. *Is. IV:310.*

The outward face of the Church does not always appear, but it is sometimes hid. *Jer. IV:357.*

We may learn not to estimate the state of the Church by the common opinion of mankind. *Ezek. I:363.*

God's glory and the salvation of the Church are things almost inseparably united. *Ezek. II:294.*

Christ is the Church's sole master. *Cor. I:146.*

Christian households . . . so many little churches. *Philipp.-Col. 230.*

We know by experience what great force principal churches have to keep other lesser churches in order [Calvin, reflecting his experience in Geneva] *Acts II:85.*

Church in the Old Testament

God has been its perpetual Guard and Ruler, yet in such a way as to exercise it in the warfare of the cross. *Gen. I:66.*

Moses traces the offspring of Adam only through the line of Seth, to propose for our consideration the succession of the Church. *Gen. I:228.*

[From Noah to Abraham] The Church, in an ignoble and despised condition . . . is yet divinely preserved. *Gen. I:315.*

The calling of [Abram] . . . the renovation of the Church. *Gen. I:333.*

[On Gen. 15:17] The condition of the Church could not be painted more to the life, than when God causes a burning torch to proceed out of the smoke. *Gen. I:420.*

Sarah . . . the mother of the Church. *Gen. I:477.*

Substantial perpetuity may remain only in the Church. *Gen. II:39.*

The Church was produced and increased by divine power and grace, and not by merely natural means. *Gen. II:41.*

The glory of the Church, being covered with a sordid veil, is an object of derision to the wicked. *Gen. II:209.*

[Jacob] the father of the fathers of the Church. *Gen. II:420.*

The redemption from Egypt may be regarded as having been the first birth of the Church; because the people were gathered into a body, and the Church was established. *Is. III:341.*

The infancy of the Church lasted to the end of the Law, but, as soon as the Gospel had been preached, it immediately arrived at manhood. *John I:173.*

The Church only attained to her perfect age at his [Christ's] coming. *Ps. IV:120.*

Marks of the Church

Wherever we find the word of God purely preached and heard, and the sacraments administered according to the institution of Christ, there . . . is a Church of God. *Inst. IV:i.9.*

The Lord acknowledges no place as his temple, where his word is not heard and devoutly observed. *Inst. IV:ii.3.*

As soon as falsehood has made a breach in the fundamentals of religion, and the system of necessary doctrine is subverted, and the use of the sacraments fails, the certain consequence is the ruin of the Church, *Inst. IV:ii.1.*

There are three things on which the safety of the Church is founded, namely, doctrine, discipline and the sacraments. [Calvin's Reply to Sadoleto] *Tracts I:38.*

Ours the Church, whose supreme care it is humbly and religiously to venerate the word of God, and submit to its authority. [Calvin's Reply to Sadoleto] *Tracts I:50.*

The uniform characteristics of a well-ordered Church are the preaching of sound doctrine, and the pure administration of the Sacraments . . . A Church which, from incorruptible seed, begets children for immortality, and, when begotten, nourishes them with spiritual food, (that seed and food being the Word of God), and which, by its ministry, preserves entire the truth which God deposited in its bosom . . . This . . . is the mark which God himself impressed upon his Church . . . Wherever it. exists not, no face of a Church is seen. [The Necessity of Reforming the Church, 1544] *Tracts I:214.*

Church and the Word

The Church maintains the truth, because by preaching the Church proclaims it. *Past. Epp. 91.*

[God] hath committed his word to the care of the Church, that by her ministrations it may be published throughout the whole world. *Is. IV:12.*

The Lord will assist his Church, and will take care of it, so as never to allow it to be deprived of doctrine. *Is. IV:272.*

God wills this honour to be conceded to him alone, – to be heard in his own Church. *Jer. I:43.*

Nothing is more ruinous to the Church than for God to take away faithful pastors. *Jer. I:181.*

There is no other way of raising up the Church of God than by the light of the word . . . There is no Church, except it be obedient to the word of God, and be guided by it. *Jon.-Nah. 257.*

The peculiar government of God is that of his Church only, where, by his word and Spirit, He bends the hearts of men to obedience, so that they follow him voluntarily and willingly, being taught . . . inwardly by the influence of his Spirit, – outwardly by the preaching of the word. *Jon.-Nah. 261.*

The Church of God differeth from all profane sects in this, because it heareth him speak alone, and is governed by his commandment. *Acts II:425.*

[On 1 Cor. 3:13] God will have his Church trained up by the pure preaching of his own word, not by the contrivances of men. *Cor. I:137.*

As soon as we are tinctured with the contrivances of men, the temple of God is polluted. *Cor. I:143.*

Purity of the Church

Although it may not be in our power to cleanse the Church of God, it is our duty to desire her purity. *Ps. I:382.*

I see no reason why a Church, however universally corrupted, provided it contain a few godly members, should not be denominated, in honour of this remnant, the holy people of God. *Ps. II:263.*

Purity of doctrine preserve[s] the unity of the Church. [The Necessity of Reforming the Church] *Tracts I:174.*

The purification of the Church is God's own work. *Is. I:80.*

[On Is. 1:28] Hypocrites have always been mingled with the Church. *Is. I:83.*

To pastors and ministers the Lord commits his Church as his beloved wife. *Is. I:163.*

The Church was always like a barn (Matt. 3:12) in which the chaff is mingled with the wheat, or rather, the wheat is overpowered by the chaff. *Is. II:211.*

God cannot become propitious to his Church, to keep and make her safe, until he purges her from her filth. *Jon.-Nah. 323.*

The Church cannot be rightly formed, until all superstitions be rejected and banished. *Zech.-Mal. 379.*

Every Christian should have his Church inclosed within his heart, and be affected with its maladies, as if they were his own, – sympathize with its sorrows, and bewail its sins. *Cor. II: 389, 390.*

The purest [Churches] have their blemishes; and some are marked, not by a few spots, but by general deformity. *Gal. 25.*

Very many, under the pretext of zeal, are excessively displeased, when everything is not conducted to their wish, and, because absolute purity is nowhere to be found, withdraw from the Church in a disorderly manner, or subvert and destroy it by unreasonable severity. *Syn. Gosp. II:119.*

Christ will put the last hand to the cleansing of the Church by means of angels, but he now begins to do the work by means of pious teachers. *Syn. Gosp. II:123.*

God has graciously restored to us uncontaminated purity of doctrine, religion in its primitive state, the unadulterated worship of God, and a faithful administration of the sacraments. [A picture of Calvin's Geneva] *John I:17.*

Unity of the Church (see also Unity)

A departure from the Church is a renunciation of God and Christ . . . criminal dissension . . . Nor is it possible to imagine a more atrocious crime. *Inst. IV:i.10.*

[On Ps. 122:3] The Church can only remain in a state of safety when unanimity prevails in her, and when, being joined together by faith and charity, she cultivates a holy unity. *Ps. V:73.*

The Church . . . is the society of all the saints, . . . spread over the whole world, and existing in all ages, yet bound together by one doctrine, and the one Spirit of Christ, cultivates and observes unity of faith and brotherly concord. [Calvin's Reply to Sadoleto] *Tracts I:37.*

The last and principal charge which they bring against us is, that we have made a schism in the Church . . . and . . . that, in no case is it lawful to break the unity of the Church . . . But judgment must be used to ascertain which is the true Church, and what is the nature of its unity . . . and . . . to beware of separating the Church from Christ its Head. [The Necessity of Reforming the Church] *Tracts I:211, 213.*

The unity of the Church, such as Paul describes it, we protest we hold sacred, and we denounce anathema against all who in any way violate it . . . A holy unity exists amongst us, when, consenting in pure doctrine, we are united in Christ alone. [The Necessity of Reforming the Church] *Tracts I:214, 215.*

The disagreement of members within the Church can lead to nothing else than the ruin and consumption of the whole body. *Gal. 162.*

Reproach of the Church

[On the sin of Achan] How grievous a crime is it to disturb the Church of God. *Josh. 119.*

The Church of God has always been infested by this disease [ambition], than which none is worse; the mother of all errors, of all disturbances, and sects. *Four Last Bks of Moses IV:42.*

[On Ps. 120:5, 'an exile in Mesech'] No sin is more detestable to God, by whose Spirit David spake, than the false accusations which shamefully deface the beauty of God's Church, and lay it waste . . . where the uprightness of good men is overwhelmed by the criminations of lying lips . . . *Ps. V:60.*

[57]

The curse of God rests upon all such as afflict the Church, or plot and endeavour by any kind of mischief to accomplish its destruction. *Ps. V:77.*

The Lord's people, while they mourn under personal trials, should be still more deeply affected by public calamities which befall the Church . . . The zeal of God's house should have the highest place in our hearts. *Ps. V:195.*

The ungodly exalt themselves against God whenever they attack his Church. *Is. I:445.*

The salvation of his Church is so precious in the sight of God, that he regards the wrong done to the faithful as done to himself. *Jer. V:146.*

The Church . . . has had no enemies more inveterate than the members of the Church. *John II:66.*

Chastening of the Church

[On Hos. 2:17] The Church cannot be rightly reformed except it be trained to obedience by the frequent scourges of God. *Hos. 108.*

God in chastising his Church ever observes certain limits, as he never forgets his covenant. *Joel-Obad. 439.*

God wonderfully delivers his Church from death by death. *Gen. Epp. 22.*

Apostasy of the Church

The Church is dead, and is like a maimed body, when separated from its head. *Jer. V:485.*

Nothing can be sadder to the godly than when God leaves his dwelling and makes it desolate, in order to terrify all who may see it. *Jer. V:510.*

God cannot dwell in a profane place . . . When men introduce their inventions it immediately causes God to depart. *Ezek. I:284.*

[58]

Church and the Remnant

[Calvin, writing in 1551] True, we are almost none, and a wretched church is concealed in a few corners. *Is. II:33.*

God always preserves a hidden seed, that the Church should not be utterly extinguished . . . but sometimes it is preserved miserably, as it were in a sepulchre. *Ezek. II:165.*

Although the Devil has long reigned in the papacy, yet he could not altogether extinguish God's grace; nay, a Church is among them. *Ezek. II:120.*

The remnant abide in God's Church for no other reason but that the Lord has called them. *Joel-Obad. 111.*

Invincibility of the Church

Whenever we hear that Christ is armed with eternal power, let us remember, that this is the bulwark which supports the perpetuity of the Church. *Inst. II:xv.3.*

It is impossible for the devil, with all the assistance of the world, ever to destroy the Church, which is founded on the eternal throne of Christ. *Inst. II:xv.3.*

All those who undertake to promote the doctrine of salvation and the well-being of the Church must be armed with invincible firmness . . . We have such an invincible Leader, that the more he is assailed the greater will be the victories and triumphs gained by his power. *Heb. xxiv.*

He preserves the Church by unknown methods and without the assistance of men. *Is. I:90.*

Amidst the mad outcry and violent attacks of enemies, the kingdom of Christ stands firm through the invincible power of God. *Is. I:313.*

The Church will always rise again, and be restored to her former and prosperous condition, though all conclude that she is ruined. *Is. I:464.*

[The oppressed Church] shall stand erect . . . being renewed and multiplied from age to age by various resurrections. *Is. III:134.*

[On Is. 44:27] Let us not doubt that there will always be a Church; and when it appears to be in a lamentably ruinous condition, let us entertain good hope of its restoration. *Is. III:389.*

[On Is. 49:11] When the Church is about to be completely restored, no obstructions, however great and formidable, can hinder God from being finally victorious. *Is. IV:27.*

There are no raging billows which God cannot allay and calm in order to deliver his Church. *Is. IV:81.*

We must not . . . judge of the Church from the present condition of things . . . but from the purpose of God, which will not suffer it to be overturned or destroyed. *Is. IV:388.*

God can work in weakness, so that the Church shall nevertheless remain safe. *Ezek. I:363.*

His Church . . . can no more be destroyed than the very truth of God . . . Judge not of the safety of the Church by sight, but stand and rely on the word of God. *Joel-Obad. 108, 109.*

[On Mic. 4:6, 7] The Church is so preserved in the world, that it sometimes rises again from death: in short, the preservation of the Church, almost every day, is accompanied with many miracles . . . many resurrections. *Jon.-Nah. 275.*

The preservation of the Church depends on the mere favour of God . . . There is no need of any earthly aids. *Jon.-Nah. 313.*

Growth of the Church

God begets and multiplies his Church only by means of his word. It is by the preaching of the grace of God alone that the Church is kept from perishing. *Ps. I:388, 389.*

I see no reason why a Church, however universally corrupted, provided it contain a few godly members, should not be denominated, in honour of this remnant, the holy people of God. *Ps. II:263.*

The peace of the Church is founded in his eternal and unchangeable purpose . . . the heavenly decree. *Is. II:213.*

[60]

In nothing does the glory of God shine more conspicuously than in the increase of the Church. *Is. II:232.*

[Mount Zion, Is. 28:17] No, at the present time [1550] 'Mount Zion' is everywhere; for the Church has spread to the ends of the world. *Is. II:292.*

Although the Church does not make professions of towering greatness . . . yet the Lord imparts a secret vigour which causes it to spring up and grow beyond human expectation. *Is. III:140.*

God would overcome all those impediments, which Satan and the whole world may throw in the way, when it is his purpose to restore his Church. *Hab.-Hagg. 386.*

The more the Church is diminished, it may the more increase through the heavenly blessing. *Acts I:495.*

Triumph of the Church

[On Is. 44:24] God should at length collect under one head a Church taken out of the whole world. [French: His Church composed of all the nations in the world] *Is. III:384.*

[On Is. 54:8] The afflictions of the Church are always momentary, when we raise our eyes to its eternal happiness. *Is. IV:141.*

The Church doth always overlive her enemies. *Acts I:495.*

We will die, but in death be more than conquerors, not only because through it we shall have a sure passage to a better life, but because we know that our blood will be as seed to propagate the Divine truth which men now despise. [Calvin's closing words, in his address to the Emperor Charles V at the Diet of Spires, 1544, on The Necessity of Reforming the Church] *Tracts I:234.*

CONSCIENCE

A happy life depends on a good conscience. *Ps. I:7.*

There is no theatre more beautiful than a good conscience. [Calvin, quoting a common proverb of his time] *Ps. I:583.*

The fountain of that good and honest conscience, whereby we cultivate fidelity and justice towards men, is the fear of God. *Gen. II:343.*

Conscience is . . . the fountain of modesty. *Gen. II:268.*

Should the whole world refuse to hear us, we must learn . . . to rest satisfied with the testimony of a good conscience, and with appealing to the tribunal of God. *Ps. II:369.*

God has taken the consciences of the godly under the government of his word, and claims this as his right. [Antidote to the Council of Trent] *Tracts III:181.*

All are rendered inexcusable, as they carry in their hearts a law which is sufficient to make them a thousand times guilty. *Hab.-Hagg. 51.*

Guilty consciences are so disturbed by blind and unreasonable fears, that they . . . voluntarily become their own tormentors. *Gen. II:482.*

Conscience is as a thousand witnesses. *Inst. III:xix.15.*

[Conscience] – their internal executioner. *Syn. Gosp. II:219.*

[God] always punishes bad consciences by secret torments. *Syn. Gosp. III:336.*

There is no greater torment than an evil conscience. *Acts II:123.*

Those build for hell who build against their conscience. *Cor. I:280.*

How miserable and wretched is a doubting conscience . . . Hell reigns where there is no peace with God . . . We . . . carry always a hell within us. *Gen. Epp. 167.*

The Law was given to cite slumbering consciences to the judgment-seat, that, through fear of eternal death, they might flee for refuge to God's mercy. *Four Last Bks of Moses I:327.*

Our consciences will never enjoy peace till they rest on the propitiation for sins. *Eph. 230.*

It is a pernicious evil to exercise an arbitrary control over the conscience. *Hab.-Hagg. 368.*

CONSTANCY

Firmness is rare in men. *Acts II:85.*

Our stability is to depend only on the aid of God. *Hab.-Hagg. 258.*

How pleasing our constancy is to God, though it may not produce any immediate fruit before the world. *Dan. I:227.*

If we would judge rightly of any man we must see how he bears good and bad fortune. *Hab.-Hagg. 36.*

Dominus fortitudo mea. [Calvin's Latin trans. of Hab. 3:19, The Lord is my strength] *Hab.-Hagg. 175.*

The greater part of the world rashly embrace whatever they meet with and also ramble from one thing to another; but piety, in order to walk with a steady step, collects itself within its proper limits. *Inst. I:xii.1.*

This is the true trial of faith; when relying on the word of God alone, although tossed on the waves of the world, we stand as firmly as if our abode were already fixed in heaven. *Gen. II:107, 108.*

CONTROVERSY

All who are sent to teach the word are sent to carry on a contest. It is therefore not enough to teach faithfully what God commands, except we also contend . . . We have a contest with the devil, with the world, and with all the wicked. *Jon.-Nah. 234, 235.*

This 'power' of the prophets [Micah divides] into two kinds, even into wisdom or judgment, and into courage . . . Let them excel in doctrine; and . . . let them not bend . . . to please the world. *Jon.-Nah. 233.*

[On Mic. 3:8] When anyone is drawn into arduous and difficult struggles, he is at the same time especially strengthened by the Lord. *Jon.-Nah. 232.*

[63]

We ought not always to contend with wicked men when they reproach and tear in pieces the name of God; for amidst strife and confused noise the truth will not be heard. *Is. III:101.*

[On Jer. 16:19] Satan hunts for nothing more than to involve us in various and intricate disputes, and he is an acute disputant. *Jer. II:329.*

Boldness in disputing . . . is the mother of unbelief. *Syn. Gosp. I:46.*

[On Peter, in Matt. 26:51] We are much more courageous and ready for fighting than for bearing the cross. *Syn. Gosp. III:243.*

We must be courageous in defence of true doctrine, not stubborn nor rash. *Acts II:39.*

Oftentimes the immoderate heat of the pastors . . . does no less hurt than their sluggishness. *Acts II:85.*

The name of peace is plausible and sweet, but cursed is that peace which is purchased with so great a loss, that we suffer the doctrine of Christ to perish. *Acts II:38.*

We may learn to moderate our desire, even in the best causes, lest it pass measure and be too fervent. *Acts II:89.*

Faith can be grounded nowhere else than in the word of the Lord, so we must only stand to the testimony thereof in all controversies. *Acts II:130.*

Satan knoweth that nothing is more fit to lay waste the kingdom of Christ, than discord and disagreement among the faithful. *Acts II:276.*

Let us beg of God the Spirit of moderation, that he may keep us always in the right mean. *Acts II:413.*

[On Rom. 15:6] God sets so high a store on the unity of His servants, that He will not allow His glory to be sounded amid discord and controversy. *Rom. 306.*

We must . . . see to it that the pulling down of error is followed by the building up of faith. *Thess. 339.*

[64]

Accursed is that peace of which revolt from God is the bond, and blessed are those contentions by which it is necessary to maintain the kingdom of Christ. *Cor. I:466.*

He who . . . seems brilliant with some outward show of sanctity, will set himself off by defaming others, and this under the pretence of zeal, but really through the lust of slandering. *Gen. Epp. 298.*

. . . to seek reputation by blaming others . . . That immoderate desire to condemn . . . proceeds from ambition and pride. *Gen. Epp. 318.*

It usually happens, that in condemning the wicked, the contagion of their malice insinuates itself into our minds when we are not conscious of it. *Ps. II:8.*

[On Abraham and Lot] Let us beware of contentions, which will deliver us over to Satan to be destroyed. *Gen. I:371.*

[On Athanasius] Who can dare to censure those good men, as quarrelsome and contentious, for having kindled such a flame of controversy, and disturbed the peace of the Church on account of one little word? That little word distinguished Christians, who held the pure faith, from sacrilegious Arians. *Inst. I:xiii.4.*

The Genevan Church used common (not unleavened) bread in The Lord's Supper. Lausanne, urged by Berne, had decided in favour of unleavened bread and influenced Geneva [in Calvin's absence] to fall in line. Later Calvin, to avoid dispute over non-essentials, let the matter stand. [Beza's Life of Calvin] *Tracts I:xxxiii.*

Godly teachers must take heed, first, that they favour not the affections of the flesh too much under the colour of zeal; secondly, that they break not out with headlong and unseasonable heat where there is yet place for moderation; thirdly, that they give not themselves over to foolish and uncomely railing. *Acts I:509.*

Calvin's Last Will and Testament, dated 25 April 1564, recited: In all the disputes I have had with the enemies of truth, I have never made use of subtle craft nor sophistry, but have gone to work straightforwardly in maintaining his [God's] quarrel. *Letters of Calvin 250.*

CONVERSION

The true preparation for conversion [is] when the sinner is slain . . . acknowledges himself liable to the judgment of God, and takes a formidable view of his wrath. *Ezek. II:43.*

Conversion . . . is a mark of God's free favour. *Syn. Gosp. II:109.*

When God designs to forgive us, he changes our hearts and turns us to obedience by his Spirit. *Zech.-Mal. 216.*

The conversion of the heart is the peculiar gift of the Holy Spirit. *Zech.-Mal.602.*

It is a true conversion when men seriously acknowledge that they are at war with God, and that he is their enemy until they are reconciled; for except a sinner sets himself in a manner before God's tribunal, he is never touched by a true feeling of repentance. *Zech.-Mal. 364.*

The Lord raises us from the dead, and brings us, as it were, out of the grave, stretching out his hand to us from heaven, to rescue us even from hell. *Is. II:193.*

[On Is. 53:1] No man can come to God but by an extraordinary revelation of the Spirit. *Is. IV:112.*

Freewill assents to God calling and exciting it . . . God acts within, holds our hearts, moves our hearts, and draws us by the inclinations which he has produced in us. [Antidote to the Council of Trent] *Tracts III:147, 148.*

Freewill . . . putting conversion in the power of man. *Jer. III:229.*

God anticipates us by his grace, and also calls us to himself . . . We do not turn through our own efforts, but it is the Holy Spirit's work. *Jer. III:233.*

Conversion cannot be separated from prayer. *Jer. IV:332.*

[66]

God must put forth violence when he wishes to attach us entirely to himself. *Ezek. I:91.*

No one comes to the true God, unless impelled by necessity. *Dan. I:251.*

It is not in the power of men to fix for themselves, as they please, the season for mercy. *Joel-Obad. 56.*

Men come not to Christ except through the wonderful agency of God . . . It is first necessary to shake men, that they may unlearn their whole character . . . Our disposition is changed and we receive willingly the yoke of Christ. *Hab.-Hagg. 359, 360.*

Conversion . . . is the renewal of the mind and heart. *Jer. IV:102.*

The beginning of our conversion to God . . . is when he enlightens the hearts. *John II:44.*

We are led [in conversion] from Adam to Christ. *Eph. 225.*

A conviction of the divine goodness is the entrance of faith. *Syn. Gosp. I:33.*

[On Matt. 12:43] The devil is justly said to *go out of* those men to whom Christ exhibits himself as a Redeemer. *Syn. Gosp. II:83.*

Meditation on the heavenly life begins at conversion. *Past. Epp. 319.*

In the conversion of man, the properties of our original nature remain entire. *Inst. II:iii.6.*

[Repentance is] . . . a true conversion of our life to God, proceeding from a sincere and serious fear of God, and consisting in the mortification of our flesh and of the old man, and in the vivification of the Spirit. *Inst. III:iii.5.*

[On Zaccheus] Before revealing Himself to men, the Lord frequently communicates to them a secret desire, by which they, are led to Him, while He is still concealed and unknown . . . drawn to Him by a secret movement of the Spirit . . . He is never sought in vain by those who sincerely desire to know Him . . . This . . . must be regarded as the beginning of faith. *Syn. Gosp. II:434.*

[On the dying thief] . . . drawn from hell itself to heaven . . . admitted to heaven before the apostles . . . a distinguished teacher of faith and piety to the whole world . . . He adores Christ as *King* while on the gallows; . . . and declares him, when dying, to be the Author of Life . . . He beheld life in death, exaltation in ruin, glory in shame, victory in destruction, a *kingdom* in bondage. *Syn. Gosp. III:308–311.*

True conversion is proved by the constant tenor of the life. *Four Last Bks of Moses III:286.*

Calvin's conversion:

I was withdrawn from the study of philosophy, and was put to the study of law. . . . But God, by the secret guidance of his providence, at length gave a different direction to my course. And first, since I was too obstinately devoted to the superstitions of Popery to be easily extricated from so profound an abyss of mire, God by a sudden conversion subdued and brought my mind to a teachable frame . . . *Ps. I:xl.*

CONVICTION OF SIN

Shame, like sorrow, is a useful preparation for a hatred of sin. *Thess. 422.*

God . . . has assigned to his word the office of penetrating even into our inmost thoughts. *Heb. 105.*

There is not a man who knows the hundredth part of his own sins. *Ps. I:328.*

He who feels the most consternation, from a consciousness of his own calamity, poverty, nakedness, and ignominy, has made the greatest proficiency in the knowledge of himself. *Inst. II:ii.10.*

None are admitted to a participation of the blessings of God, but those who are pining away with a sense of their own poverty. *Inst. II:ii.10.*

The conscience cannot sustain the load of iniquity, without an immediate discovery of the divine judgment. *Inst. II:viii.3.*

We must seek for peace only in the terrors of Christ our Redeemer. *Inst. III:xiii.4.*

The very beginning of repentance is grief felt on account of sin, together with self-condemnation. *Gen. II:96.*

He who inflicts wounds on us, can alone heal us. *Jer. IV:34.*

Men never entertain a real hatred towards sin, unless God illuminates their minds and changes their hearts. *Jer. IV:102.*

Without hatred of sin and remorse for transgressions, no man will taste the grace of God. *Syn. Gosp. I:179.*

God does not forgive the sins of any but those who are dissatisfied with themselves. *Syn. Gosp. II:109.*

It is the special work of God to turn to himself the hearts of men by the secret influence of his Holy Spirit. *Ps. III:235.*

It is always profitable that the sense of sin should remain. *Gen. II:377.*

COURAGE

There can be no courage in men, unless God supports them by his word. *Zech.-Mal. 204.*

Courage is not only a special gift, but it is also necessary that God should daily and constantly strengthen those whom he has once made brave; otherwise they . . . will soon lose their valour. *Jer. V:46.*

None will ever be courageous and steady in acting properly, unless they depend solely on the will of God. *Syn. Gosp. III:189.*

[Of Stephen, in Acts 7] Courage in defending the doctrine of godliness is a sweet-smelling sacrifice to God. *Acts I:312.*

[On Matt. 26:23]Our Lord intended to admonish his followers in all ages, not to be discouraged or faint on account of intimate friends proving to be traitors. *Syn. Gosp. III:199.*

The invincible courage which overcomes all temptations resides in the fatherly favour of God. *Rom. 183.*

[69]

COVENANT OF GRACE

Covenant . . . This word is limited to those 'contracts' by which the Lord, who adopted his people, promised that he would be their God . . . The chief part of the word consists of promises, by which he adopts and receives us as his own people. *Is. II:170.*

Whenever . . . the word 'covenant' occurs in Scripture, we ought to remember the word 'grace'. *Is. IV:161.*

. . . A mutual stipulation; for God made a covenant with Abraham on this condition – that he should walk perfectly with him. *Jer. II:243.*

[God's] covenant was not made to depend on the merits of men. *Jer. V:343.*

The covenant was founded on Christ alone. *Jer. IV:249.*

Adoption was the foundation of the covenant; and then Christ was the earnest and pledge of the covenant. *Jer. IV:250.*

On the general covenant depended all particular promises. *Jer. IV:249.*

The new covenant . . . consists of two parts, even that God, in adopting us as his children, forgives us, and pardons all our infirmities, and then governs us by his Spirit. *Jer. IV:219.*

The new covenant so flowed from the old, that it was almost the same in substance, while distinguished in form. *Ezek. II:178.*

The new covenant does not destroy the old in substance, but only in form. *Four Last Bks of Moses I:463.*

[Moses] . . . having embraced God's covenant with both arms . . . had room for no objections. *Four Last Bks of Moses III:340.*

It was then registered as it were in public records, when the covenant was ratified by the written law. *Ps. III:231.*

The covenant of life is eternal, and the same which God made with his servants from the beginning until the end of the world. *Acts II:60.*

The covenant which God made with the fathers was founded on the Mediator. *Syn. Gosp. III:361.*

The covenant remains valid in the remnant. *Jer. III:132.*

We shall fail to seek God effectually, if we seek him apart from his covenant. *Zech.-Mal. 542.*

All the promises have been founded on a covenant . . . because God had adopted the people. *Joel-Obad. 137.*

The promises, which now and then occurred, were like streams which flowed from the first spring, even their gratuitous covenant. *Hab.-Hagg. 355.*

The relation . . . between God and his people, as to the covenant, is mutual. It is God's covenant, because it flows from him; it is the covenant of the Church, because it is made for its sake. *Zech.-Mal. 260.*

There is always a mutual relation between the covenant of God and the faith of men. *Syn. Gosp. III:215.*

[On John 10:16] The *door* of the fold was the gracious covenant of eternal life confirmed in Christ. *John I:406.*

[The Mediator's] expiation depended on the covenant. *Heb. xiii.*

[On Heb. 8:10] There are two main parts in this covenant; the first regards the gratuitous remission of sins; and the other, the inward renovation of the heart; there is a third which depends on the second, and that is the illumination of the mind as to the knowledge of God. *Heb. 188.*

It is the peculiar privilege of the faithful who have once embraced the covenant offered to them in Christ, that they feel assured that God is propitious to them. *Heb. 190.*

We may not seek the certainty of our salvation anywhere else. *Ps. III:444.*

There is always to be presupposed a mutual relation and correspondence between the covenant of God and our faith, in order that the unfeigned consent of the latter may answer to the faithfulness of the former. *Ps. III:254.*

[71]

The covenant of God is a secret which far exceeds human comprehension. *Ps. I:430.*

God's covenant was no less lovely than alarming . . . The Law was given to cite slumbering consciences to the judgment-seat, that, through fear of eternal death, they might flee for refuge to God's mercy. *Four Last Bks of Moses I:327.*

Since the greater part of men either despise or ridicule this divine covenant [they] deserve, by this single act of ingratitude, to be immersed in eternal fire. [Calvin is referring to Anabaptist objections] *Gen. I:297, 298.*

The Lord seals and sanctions by faith, those benefits which he promises us, so that they shall not fail. *Gen. II:427.*

[On Gen. 42, Jacob's sons. Jacob] seemed to be bringing up devils at home . . . How could the salvation of the world proceed from such a vicious offspring? *Gen. II:349.*

[Jacob, at Gen. 49:18, 'I have waited for thy salvation, O Lord'] The holy fathers were extremely solicitous that the gratuitous covenant of God should be remembered by themselves and by their children . . . [Jacob] exhibits the life-giving covenant of God to many generations, so as to prove his own confidence that, after his death, God would be faithful to his promise. *Gen. II:467, 464.*

DEATH

[Christ] . . . the conqueror of death and the Lord of life. *Syn. Gosp. II:14.*

[Believers] behold their death sanctified by his death [Psychopannychia] *Tracts III:436.*

If he leads us onwards to death, we must be assured it is best for us to die, and injurious for us to enjoy life any longer. *Dan. I:229.*

Whoever . . . in dying shall commit to Christ, in true faith, the keeping of his soul, . . . Christ will meet his prayer. *Syn. Gosp. III:313.*

[72]

When faith quickens the soul of a man, death already has its sting extracted, and its venom removed, and so cannot inflict a deadly wound. *John I:356, 357.*

The time of every man's death has been fixed by God . . . We are safe from all risk until God is pleased to call us away. *John I:301.*

Christ will have no discharged soldiers, but those who have conquered death itself. *Heb. 315.*

[For the Christian] death is a sort of emancipation from the bondage of death. *John I:436.*

[Christ's] death was a passage to the heavenly kingdom of God . . . This definition of death applies to the whole body of the Church. *John II:54.*

[On 2 Cor. 5:8] True faith begets not merely a contempt of death, but even a desire for it. *Cor. II:222.*

[Jonah, in Chap. 4] Let us learn so to love this life as to be prepared to lay it down whenever the Lord pleases: let us also learn to desire death, but so as to live to the Lord. *Jon.-Nah.129.*

[On Heb. 11:35] The victory of faith appears more splendid in the contempt of death than if life were extended to the fifth generation. *Heb. 305.*

The definition of this death is to be sought from its opposite. *Gen. I:127.*

The miseries and evils both of soul and body, are a kind of entrance into death. *Gen. I:127.*

The death of Adam had commenced immediately from the day of his transgression. *Gen. I:179.*

Nowhere in Scripture is the term sleep applied to the soul, when it is used to designate death. [Psychopannychia] *Tracts III:459.*

[On Gen. 47:30] It appears from this passage, that the word 'sleep', whenever it is put for 'die', does not refer to the soul, but to the body. *Gen. II:417.*

The human body is formed for immortality . . . By sinking into death it does not utterly perish. *Gen. II:245.*

The ceremony of mourning over the dead arose from a good principle; namely, that the living should meditate on the curse entailed by sin upon the human race. *Gen. II:476.*

The mitigation of sorrow is chiefly to be sought for, in the hope of a future life. *Gen. II:477.*

No man has made any good proficiency in the school of Christ, but he who joyfully expects both the day of death and that of the final resurrection. *Inst. III:ix.5.*

We sojourn in the world . . . held wrapped in the shadow of death, until our real life be manifested. *Gen. II:208.*

Men cannot be humbled otherwise than by placing death before them. *Ezek. II:43.*

. . . the reprobate and abandoned, who do not acknowledge God except in death. *Ezek. I:403.*

To nothing are we more prone than to the dream of immortality on earth, unless death is frequently brought before our eyes. *Gen. I:230.*

Death makes the great distinction between the reprobate and the sons of God, whose condition in the present life is commonly one and the same, except that the sons of God have by far the worst of it. *Gen. I:417.*

Out of Christ there is no life-giving light in the world, but everything is covered by the appalling darkness of death. *Syn. Gosp. I:77.*

[Jacob's death, Gen. 49:33] The aged saint gave directions respecting the disposal of his body, as easily as healthy and vigorous men are wont to compose themselves to sleep. *Gen. II:473.*

In order that a good conscience may lead us peacefully and quietly to the grave, it is necesssary to rely upon the resurrection of Christ; for we then go willingly to God. *Gen. II:473.*

DECEPTION

As soon as ever we depart from Christ there is nothing . . . respecting which we are not necessarily deceived. *Gen. I:64.*

Everything is a deceit which has not God himself as its author. *Jer. III:193.*

We are by nature prone to what is false and vain. *Jer. III:425.*

Satan as we know deludes men's senses with his prodigies and his wonderful arts of fascination; for it happens that the children of God are sometimes deluded. *Ezek. I:280.*

The heart of man has so many recesses of vanity, and so many retreats of falsehood, and is so enveloped with fraudulent hypocrisy, that it frequently deceives even himself. *Inst. III:ii.10.*

DECREES OF GOD
(*see also* Election, Predestination and Reprobation)

God does not deliberate or consult, but has once for all decreed before the creation of the world what he will do. *Jer. V:92.*

Those things which seem contingent, are yet ruled by the certain providence of God . . . Nothing is contingent, for everything that takes place flows from the eternal and immutable counsel of God. *Jer. V:428.*

How small is the measure of our intelligence; for God's judgments are a profound abyss (Ps. 36:6). *Ezek. II:60, 61.*

God will always find a way through the most profound abyss, to the accomplishment of what he has decreed. *Gen. II:266.*

The only remedy for soothing the griefs of the godly is, to cast their eyes on the result, by which God distinguishes them from the reprobate. *Is. II:237.*

[On 1 Thess. 5:9] There is no better assurance of salvation to be found anywhere than can be gained from the decree of God. *I Thess. 370.*

The preaching of Christ among them [the Ephesians] was nothing else than the announcement of that eternal decree. *Eph. 193.*

It was not at random that the doctrine of the gospel was preached to all nations, but by the decree of God, by whom it had been long ago ordained. *Is. III:425.*

DEFAMATION

Let us learn . . . to be prepared, though we do well, to be evil spoken of. *Four Last Bks of Moses IV:102.*

We are by nature hypocrites, fondly exalting ourselves by calumniating others. *Gen. Epp. 337.*

. . . that immoderate desire to condemn, which proceeds from ambition and pride. *Gen. Epp. 318.*

He who . . . seems brilliant with some outward show of sanctity, will set himself off by defaming others, and this under the pretence of zeal, but really through the lust of slandering. *Gen. Epp. 298.*

DEPRAVITY OF MAN

The Holy Spirit teaches us in Scripture, that our mind is smitten with so much blindness, that the affections of our heart are so depraved and perverted, that our whole nature is so vitiated, that we can do nothing but sin, until he forms a new will within us. [In the Dedication of Commentary on the General Epistles to King Edward VI of England, 1551] *Gen. Epp. xvii.*

[We] . . . are born lions, tigers, wolves and bears, until the Spirit of Christ tames us, and from wild and savage beasts forms us to be mild sheep. *John I:399.*

[Men] are born of Adam, they are depraved creatures, and therefore can conceive only sinful thoughts, until they become the new workmanship of Christ, and are formed by His Spirit to a new life. *Gen. I:284.*

According to the constitution of our nature, oil might be extracted from a stone sooner than we could perform a good work. *Inst. III:xiv.5.*

The human mind is unable, through its imbecility, to attain any knowledge of God without the assistance of his sacred word. *Inst. I:vi.4.*

From a purified root, therefore, have sprung putrid branches, which have transmitted their putrescence to remoter ramifications. *Inst. II:i.7.*

This depravity never ceases in us, but is perpetually producing new fruits . . . like . . . the streams of water from a never failing spring. *Inst. II:i.8.*

Nor can we pretend to excuse ourselves by a want of ability, like insolvent debtors. For it is improper for us to measure the glory of God by our ability, for whatever may be our characters, he ever remains like himself, the friend of righteousness, the enemy of iniquity. *Inst. II:viii.2.*

All the desires of men are evil; and we consider them to be sinful, not as they are natural but because they are inordinate; and we affirm that they are inordinate because nothing pure and immaculate can proceed from a corrupted and polluted nature. *Inst. III:iii.12.*

Our inability is our own fault . . . the criminality of which is within ourselves, and must be imputed to us. *Inst. II:viii.2.*

[Ps. 51:5] . . . intimates that we are cherished in sin from the first moment that we are in the womb . . . born into the world with the seed of every iniquity . . . Sin . . . exists within us as a disease fixed in our nature. *Ps. II:290.*

We have no adequate idea of the dominion of sin, unless we conceive of it as extending to every part of the soul . . . Both the mind and heart of man have become utterly corrupt. *Ps. II:291.*

Being full of blindness, nothing is more easy than for us to be greatly deceived by error. *Ps. IV:422.*

Every sin should convince us of the general truth of the corruption of our nature. *Ps. II:290.*

[77]

By *the workers of iniquity*, he means man wholly addicted to wickedness. *Ps. I:468.*

[God] has surrounded the human race with rottenness, in order that everywhere our eyes should light on the punishment of sin. *Four Last Bks of Moses II:18.*

There is no look of the eyes, no motion of the senses, no thought of the mind, unmingled with vice and depravity. *Ps. IV:428.*

Such blinding and hardening . . . must be ascribed exclusively to the depravity of man. *Is. I:217.*

The depravity of the human mind is such that it obscures the divine majesty, and places above it those things which ought to have been subject to God. *Is. III:221.*

Unbelief . . . is always proud . . . [It] will never understand anything in the words of Christ, which it despises and disdains . . . This arises from the depravity of men. *John I:275.*

[Babel] . . . a truly memorable history, in which we may perceive the greatness of men's obstinacy against God, and the little profit they receive from his judgments. *Gen. I:323.*

It is the folly of the human mind to gather to itself leaders and teachers of error. *Gen. II:319.*

The depravity of our nature is so great, that we cannot bear prosperity without some wantonness of the flesh . . . and without becoming even arrogant against Thee. [*Calvin's Prayer at close of Lecture 126, on Habakkuk, Zephaniah and Haggai, p.298*].

DIFFICULTIES IN THE SCRIPTURES

That the revealed will of God ought to be reverently acquiesced in, we will receive, without disputation, those mysteries which offend either the proud, or such as would be over-careful to remove the difficulties. *Ps. IV:194.*

We are permitted to pour into [God's] bosom the difficulties which torment us, in order that He may loosen the knots which we cannot untie. *Gen. I:489.*

I do not willingly follow uncertain conjectures; I leave the question undecided. *Gen. II:12.*

The things related in Scripture are not always proper to be imitated. *Gen. II:21.*

[On John 6:60] Out of the word of God the reprobate are accustomed to form stones to dash themselves on. *John I:270.*

God does not in every way untie all the knots by which we are entangled. *Ezek. I:316.*

Every truth that is preached of Christ is quite paradoxical to human judgment. *Rom. 121.*

The wisdom of the flesh is always exclaiming against the mysteries of God. *Rom. 131.*

Where the Lord closes His holy mouth, let us also stop our minds from going on further. *Rom. 203.*

All the articles of true doctrine are not of the same description. *Inst. IV:i.12.*

Let us . . . hold to this rule, even to seek from the Law and the Prophets, and the Gospel, whatever we desire to know respecting the secret judgments of God . . . Let us . . . learn to bridle all curiosity when we speak of God's secret judgments, and instantly to direct our minds to the word itself. *Jer. V:377.*

DISCIPLESHIP

Whosoever desires to be God's disciple must necessarily be conscious of his own folly, that is, he must come free from a conceit of his own acumen and wisdom, and be willing to be taught by God. *Zech.-Mal. 109.*

Christ hath no disciples where he is not counted the only master. *Acts II:260.*

The disciples of Christ must learn the philosophy of placing their happiness beyond the world, and above the affections of the flesh. *Syn. Gosp. I:260.*

No man is qualified to be a disciple of Christ until he has been divested of self. *John I:392.*

No one is a fit teacher in the Church who has not been a disciple of the Son of God, and rightly instructed in his school, since his authority alone ought to prevail. *Gen. Epp. 158.*

No man is fit to be a teacher in the Church, save only he who willingly submits himself, that he may be fellow-disciple with other men. *Acts I:390.*

We must become fools if we desire to be God's disciples. *Is. I:187.*

Hardly one in ten of those who have once made a profession of Christ, retains the purity of faith to the end. *Gen. Epp. 394.*

In order to increase in faith, we must be instant in prayer, and maintain our calling by love. *Gen. Epp. 447.*

DISCIPLINE IN THE CHURCH

Beza's *Life of Calvin* records that Calvin endorsed and quoted John Chrysostom's well-known words, 'I will die sooner than this hand shall stretch forth the sacred things of the Lord to those who have been judged despisers.' *Tracts I:xiii.*

The body of the Church, to cohere well, must be bound together by discipline as with sinews. [Calvin's Reply to Sadoleto] *Tracts I:55.*

Discipline consists of two parts, the one relating to the clergy, the other to the people. [On the Necessity of Reforming the Church] *Tracts I:202, 203.*

Excommunication, that best nerve of discipline. [On the Necessity of Reforming the Church] *Tracts I:205.*

St Paul does not command us to examine others, but each to examine himself. [Short Treatise on the Supper] *Tracts II:181.*

The punishments inflicted by God on his servants are only temporary and limited, and intended as medicine. *Jer. V:75.*

Christ will put the last hand to the cleansing of the Church by means of angels, but he now begins to do the work by means of pious teachers. *Syn. Gosp. II:123.*

Those who proceed, with undue haste, to root out whatever displeases them, prevent, as far as lies in their power, the sentence of Christ, deprive angels of their office, and rashly take that office on themselves. *Syn. Gosp. II:123.*

Purity of doctrine is the soul of the Church . . . discipline . . . the sinews. *Acts I:xxi.*

Under colour of zeal for discipline, a Pharisaical rigour creeps in. *Cor. II:153.*

Christ has given the commandment as to *loosing* before that of *binding*. *Cor. II:325.*

We ought to avoid the cruelty of condemning our brethren, or an extreme rigour in despairing of their salvation. *Gen. Epp. 268.*

As doctrine is the soul of the Church for quickening, so discipline and the correction of vices are like the nerves to sustain the body in a state of health and vigour. [Calvin's Letter to the Duke of Somerset] *Letters 103.*

Provided religion continue pure as to doctrine and worship, we must not be . . . stumbled at the faults and sins which men commit, as on that account to rend the unity of the Church. *Ps. I:204.*

God's sacred barn-floor will not be perfectly cleansed before the last day. *Ps. I:205.*

As a general . . . enrols the names of his soldiers . . . and as a schoolmaster writes the names of his scholars . . . so has God written the names of his children in the book of life, that he may retain them under the yoke of his discipline. *Ps. II:103.*

It belongs to God alone to forgive sins . . . to man . . . to be the witness and herald of the grace which He confers . . . Absolution is not in the power or will of man . . . Whosoever has been once cast out of the holy congregation by public authority, must not be received again except upon professing penitence and a new life. *Four Last Bks of Moses II:25.*

[81]

We must abstain from violent remedies which surpass the evil we desire to correct. *Gen. II:221*.

The keys are inseparably connected with the word. *Inst. IV:ii.10*.

The severity becoming the Church must be tempered with a spirit of gentleness [lest] a remedy . . . become a poison. *Inst. IV:xii.8*.

DOCTRINE

Sound doctrine

A holy unity exists amongst us, when, consenting in pure doctrine, we are united in Christ alone. [The Necessity of Reforming the Church] *Tracts I:215*.

[Calvin and Farel] 'studied sincere perspicuity, free from all gloss and cunning'. [Mutual Consent in regard to the Sacraments] *Tracts II:201*.

The chief ground of gladness and joy is, when God restores to us pure and sound doctrine; for no scarcity of wheat ought to terrify and alarm us so much as a scarcity of the word. *Is. II:371*.

We are all agreed that peace is not to be purchased by the sacrifice of truth. *Tracts II:222*.

We do not understand spiritual doctrine, in consequence of possessing an acute understanding, or having received a superior education . . . *Is. II:322, 323*.

The Lord will assist his Church, and will take care of it, so as never to allow it to be deprived of doctrine. *Is. IV:272*.

Nothing is more to be dreaded, than that the Lord should extinguish the light of sound doctrine, and suffer us to go astray in darkness. *Joel-Obad. 270*.

God's doctrine is precious to himself . . . He cannot bear us to despise it. *Ezek. I:119*.

Purity of doctrine is the soul of the Church . . . discipline . . . the sinews. *Acts I:21*.

[82]

Faith is the soul of the Church, nothing is more proper to faith than agreement, nothing more contrary than sects. *Acts II:321.*

Would you then be reckoned as belonging to Christ's flock? Do not deviate a nail's-breadth from purity of doctrine. *Col. 180.*

The use of doctrine is, not only to initiate the ignorant in the knowledge of Christ, but also to confirm those more and more who have been already taught. *Gen. Epp. 264.*

There ought to be an explicit summary of doctrine which all ought to preach . . . and no one should be received . . . who does not promise to preserve such agreement. [Calvin's letter to the Duke of Somerset] *Letters 96.*

Next, that they have a common *formula* of instruction for little children and for ignorant persons . . . The Church of God will never preserve itself without a catechism. *Letters 96.*

Drawn from Scripture

How then is religion to remain pure? Even by depending on God's mouth, by subjecting ourselves to his word . . . and by putting a bridle on ourselves, so as not to introduce anything except what he commands and approves. *Jer. IV:543.*

God's doctrine is precious to himself . . . He cannot bear us to despise it. *Ezek. I:119.*

No doctrine is to be allowed, except what he himself has revealed. *Zech.-Mal. 532.*

[On Acts 8:6] The very doctrine which is contained in [God's] word shall purchase authority for itself. *Acts I:330.*

No man can have the least knowledge of true and sound doctrine, without having been a disciple of the Scripture. *Inst. I:vi.2.*

Centres on Christ

The principal point of all spiritual doctrine, on which souls are fed, consists in Christ. *John I:397.*

The only means of retaining as well as restoring pure doctrine – to place Christ before the view such as he is with all his blessings, that his excellence may be perceived. *Col. 146.*

Our faith looks not on the naked doctrine, but on the blood by which our salvation has been ratified. *Heb. 248.*

Bears good fruit

Prayers flow from doctrine. *Is. III:111.*

Doctrine . . . the seed of spiritual life, by which the children of the Church are begotten (1 Pet. 1:23). *Is. IV:37.*

The chief point in preserving charity is to maintain faith sacred and entire. [Calvin's Preface to Psychopannychia] *Tracts III:416.*

The true love of Christ . . . is regulated by the observation of his doctrine as the only rule. *John II:91.*

True and sound doctrine . . . is represented as being sufficient to put an end to all ungodliness . . . to be victorious over all the devices of Satan. *Thess. 405.*

The design of Christian doctrine is, that believers should exercise themselves in good works. *Past. Epp. 338.*

As the saving doctrine of Christ is the soul of the Church, so discipline forms the ligaments which connect the members together, and keep each in its proper place . . . a most excellent preservative of health, foundation of order, and bond of unity. *Inst. IV:xii.1.*

Power of sound doctrine

[On Mic. 4:2] The truth of God is not . . . speculative, but full of energizing power. *Mic.-Nah. 258.*

Doctrine has no power, if efficacy be not imparted to it from above. *John II:163.*

Unless he teach us inwardly by his Spirit, the outward doctrine shall always wax cold. *Acts II:390.*

[On 1 Thess. 5:20] Since the Spirit of God enlightens us most of all by means of doctrine, those who do their utmost to deny doctrine its proper place *quench the Spirit. Thess. 376.*

Any doctrine is useless until God engraves it with his finger on our hearts. *Thess. 379.*

Doctrine is the soul of the Church for quickening. [Calvin to Duke of Somerset] *Letters 103.*

Doctrine without zeal is either like a sword in the hand of a madman, or . . . it serveth for vain and wicked boasting. *Acts II:201.*

No doctrine can strike firm and perpetual roots in men's hearts, if it be accompanied with any doubt. *Gen. Epp. 154.*

Purity of doctrine is preserved unimpaired in the world, and propagated by the ministry of pastors, whilst piety would soon decay if the living preaching of doctrine should cease. *Four Last Bks of Moses II:230.*

Ruinous effects of unsound doctrine

As soon as falsehood has made a breach in the fundamentals of religion, and the system of necessary doctrine is subverted . . . the certain consequence is the ruin of the Church. *Inst. IV:ii.1.*

If we deviate from it . . . though we run with the utmost celerity, yet, being out of the course, we shall never reach the goal. *Inst. I:vi.3.*

Scripture compares strange doctrines to leaven. [On Matt. 16:11] *Four Last Bks of Moses II:49.*

If you once give entrance to [false doctrines], they spread till they have completed the destruction of the Church. *Past. Epp. 224.*

There is a weariness as to simple doctrine, which produces innumerable prodigies of errors, when everyone gapes continually for new mysteries. *Gen. Epp. 178.*

Nothing is more pestilential than corrupt doctrine and profane disputations, which draw us off, even in the smallest degree, from a right and simple faith. *Cor. II:43.*

[85]

How dangerous to the Church is that knowledge which leads to debates . . . disregards piety, and tends to ostentation. *Past. Epp. 220.*

Philosophy is nothing else than a persuasive speech, which insinuates itself into the minds of men by elegant and plausible arguments . . . a corruption of spiritual doctrine. *Col. 180, 181.*

Wicked doctrines cannot be driven away by any other method than by the gospel. *Is. I:380, 381.*

Whatever is contrary to sound doctrine, is a sinful device, a fallacy of Satan, and, in a word, the impiety of a corrupt heart. *Jer. II:405.*

When divine truth is avowedly attacked we must not tolerate the adulteration of one *iota* of it [Psychopannychia] *Tracts III:418.*

There are so many Pilates . . . who scourge Christ, not only in his members, but also in his doctrine. *John II:215.*

Nothing is more difficult than to restore [doctrine] to its purity after having been once corrupted. *John II:215.*

We learn how greatly a servant of Christ should labour to maintain and defend the purity of doctrine, and not only while he lives, but as long as his care and labour can extend it. *Past. Epp. 209.*

DOUBT

We know our great propensity to doubt. *Ezek. I:337.*

. . . our great licence in posing inquisitive questions. *Rom. 252.*

How shockingly do they insult God, when they doubt his truth! What do you leave to God if you take that from him? *Is. I:240.*

Fear, proceeding from unbelief, cannot be otherwise dissipated but by God's promises made to us, which chase away all doubts. *Zech.-Mal. 213.*

[On Thomas' doubt] When we render to the word of God less honour than is due to it, there steals upon us, without our knowledge, a growing obstinacy, which brings along with it a contempt of the word of God, and makes us lose all reverence for it. *John II:275.*

Distrust is cured by meditating upon the promises of God. *Acts I:46.*

If . . . we have resolved to allow ourselves to be directed by the word of God, and always seek in it the rule of life, God will never suffer us to remain in doubt. *Is. II:348.*

Whenever thoughts creep into our minds, which toss us here and there, we ought to flee to prayer. For many increase their anxieties by fomenting them. *Jer. IV:168.*

No doctrine can strike firm and perpetual roots in men's hearts, if it be accompanied with any doubt. *Gen. Epp. 154.*

How miserable and wretched is a doubting conscience! . . . Hell reigns where there is no peace with God . . . We . . . carry a hell within us. *Gen. Epp. 167.*

A great many coin mere dross in their own brain, by which to efface or obscure the brightness which shines in the word of God. *Ps. I:178.*

Our prayers . . . are worthless when they are agitated with doubts. *Ps. IV:343.*

Satan . . . wished to inject into the woman [Eve] a doubt . . . She begins to give way, by inserting the adverb 'perhaps'. *Gen. I:148, 149.*

The reason why we doubt of God's promises is, because we sinfully detract from his power. *Gen. I:476.*

Faith is never so absolutely perfect in the saints as to prevent the occurrence of many doubts. *Gen. II:20.*

How comes it that we have any doubts about the word, but because we do not ascribe to God that power which belongs to him, or because we are not convinced of his power? These are the only two causes of our unbelief . . . We ought to believe, first, that God is *true*, and, secondly, that he is *powerful*. *Is. I:460.*

[87]

EFFECTUAL CALLING

No one will dedicate himself to God till he be drawn by his goodness, and embrace him with all his heart. He must therefore call us to him before we call upon him. *Is. II:74.*

This calling of Abram is a signal example of the gratuitous mercy of God . . . He was plunged in the filth of idolatry . . . God deigns to open his sacred mouth, that he may show to one, deceived by Satan's wiles, the way of salvation. *Gen. I:343.*

Abram was justified many years after he had been called by God . . . We are not told when. *Gen. I:408.*

In the elect we consider calling as an evidence of election, and justification as another token of its manifestation, till they arrive in glory, which constitutes its completion. *Inst. III:xxi.7.*

This internal call . . . is a pledge of salvation, which cannot possibly deceive. *Inst. III:xxiv.2.*

We can only begin an upright course of life when God of his good pleasure adopts us into his family, and in effectual calling, anticipates us by his grace. *Ps. I:280.*

The external call alone would be insufficient, did not God effectually draw to himself those whom he has called. *Ps. III:322.*

There is this difference in the calling of God, that he invites all indiscriminately by his word, whereas he inwardly calls the elect alone (John 6:37). [Antidote to the Council of Trent] *Tracts III:155, 156.*

On our calling is our salvation founded. *Jer. V:64.*

God prepares his elect for hearing, and gives them ears for that purpose. *Ezek. I:139.*

[On Hos. 1:10] The beginning of our salvation is God's call. *Hos. 67.*

There is . . . an inward call, which dwells in the secret counsel of God; and then follows the call, by which he makes us really the partakers of his adoption. *Joel-Obad. 111.*

The impulse by which God moves his elect to betake themselves to the fold of Christ is supernatural. *Hab.-Hagg. 359.*

[John 6:65] There is no other reason why God draws than because, out of free grace, he loves us. *John I:276.*

The gift of believing is a special gift . . . God effectually calls all whom he has elected, so that the sheep of Christ are proved by their faith. *John I:414, 415.*

Though our heavenly Father inviteth all men unto the faith by the external voice of man, yet doth he not call effectually by his Spirit any save those whom he hath determined to save. *Acts I:556.*

As his eternal election is free, so his calling is also free which flows thence. *Acts II:97.*

He places the certainty of salvation in the calling. *Past. Epp. 194.*

The effectual cause of faith is not the perspicacity of our mind, but the calling of God. *Gen. Epp. 369.*

The effect of calling in the elect, is to restore to them the glorious image of God, and to renew them in holiness and righteousness. *Gen. Epp. 370.*

EGOTISM AND ENVY

Egotism

Nothing is more difficult than for men to strip themselves of their blind arrogance, whereby they detract some portion of the praise from God's mercies. *Four Last Bks of Moses I:379.*

We ought always to beware of making the smallest claim for ourselves. *Is. III:100.*

. . . such diabolical pride as to rob God and adorn ourselves with the spoils. *Is. III:100.*

Envy

Whoever are moved by envy to enter into contention with [God's] servants, endeavour . . . to overthrow his glory by obscuring the gifts of the Spirit. *Four Last Bks of Moses IV:48.*

It is between equals that envy is cherished. *Ps. IV:282.*

How pestilential a plague ambition is, from which envy springs up, and afterwards perfidy and cruelty! *Dan. I:353.*

All those are condemned of ungodliness and malice who envy other men's labours, and are grieved when they see the same have good success. *Acts I:470.*

Signal success commonly draws its companion envy along with it. *Gen. I:378.*

Envy or pride is the mother of almost all heresies. *Cor. I:366.*

It is no light good to live free from envy, tumults and strife. *Gen. II:65.*

ELECTION
(*see also* Predestination and Reprobation)

Election is . . . the parent of faith. *Inst. III:xxii.10.*

God, it is true, wrote the names of his children in the Book of Life before the creation of the world; but he enrols them in the catalogue of his saints, only when, having regenerated them by the Spirit of adoption, he impresses his own mark upon them. *Ps. III:403.*

Election depends on the promise of God. *Is. III:255.*

The wickedness of men cannot change the election of God. *Is. III:258.*

The gospel is preached indiscriminately to the elect and the reprobate; but the elect alone come to Christ, because they have been 'taught by God' *Is. IV:146.*

God acts as a Father towards his elect, and as a judge towards the reprobate. *Jer. II:66.*

There is this difference in the calling of God, that he invites all indiscriminately by his word, whereas he inwardly calls the elect alone . . . (John 6:39). [Antidote to the Council of Trent] *Tracts III:155, 156.*

Whatever God promises belongs to his elect . . . It does not appertain indiscriminately to all. *Jer. III:128.*

God's election is one single act, for it is eternal and immutable. *Zech.-Mal. 78.*

The election of God is anterior to Adam's fall. *Zech.-Mal. 477.*

We are believers, because we have been elected. *Zech.-Mal. 480.*

Take away faith, and election will be imperfect. *John I:254.*

Drawing some, and passing by others, he alone makes a distinction among men, whose condition by nature is alike. *Syn. Gosp. II:37.*

No man will remain steadfast, unless his salvation be secured by the election of God. *Syn. Gosp. II:258.*

He chooses from among his enemies those whose hearts he bends to the love of him. *John II:97.*

[On Acts 15:7] Seeing that the elect are illuminate into the faith by a peculiar grace of the Spirit, doctrine shall bring forth no fruit, unless the Lord show forth his power in his ministers, in teaching the minds of those inwardly which hear, and in drawing their hearts inwardly. *Acts II:46.*

[God's] secret election precedes adoption. *Rom. 239.*

Satan has no power to keep any whom God has chosen from being saved. *Thess. 409.*

The cause of our election

The origin [of election] is from the donation of the Father, that we are given into the custody and protection of Christ. *Inst. III:xxii.7.*

By an eternal and immutable counsel, God has once for all determined, both whom he would admit to salvation, and whom he would condemn to destruction. *Inst. III:xxi.7.*

The great and only object of our election is 'that we should be to the praise of' Divine 'grace'. *Inst. III:xxii.3.*

When we come to election, we see nothing but mercy on every side. *Inst. III:xxiv.1.*

Among men some perish, some obtain salvation; but the cause of this depends on the secret will of God. *Gen. II:47.*

Our dignity is hidden in the counsel of God alone . . . The primary source of election is his free good pleasure. *Gen. II:432.*

Faith flows from the secret election of God. [Calvin, in a letter to Melanchthon, dated 27/8/1554] *Letters 160.*

[On Ps. 33:12] It proceeds from the fountain of God's gracious electing love that we are accounted the people of God; . . . we have no interest in him at all unless he prevent us by his grace. *Ps. I:548.*

The difference which exists between the elect and the rest of the world [is] the mere good pleasure of God. *Ps. II:154.*

We are near [God], not as having anticipated his grace, and come to him of ourselves, but because, in his condescension, he has stretched out his hand as far as hell itself, to reach us . . . He first elects us, and then testifies his love by calling us. *Ps. II:457.*

By the word *chosen*, God calls us back to the consideration of his own free will. *Ps. III:433.*

[On Ps. 105:44] The end which God proposed in our election was, that he might have on the earth a people by whom he should be called upon and served. *Ps. IV:205.*

The whole world is governed by God for our salvation, . . . that those whom he has elected may be saved. *Is. I:434.*

By the word love [Jer. 2:2] God means in many other places the gratuitous election with which he had favoured the whole people [Israel]. *Jer. I:70.*

The beginning of all blessings . . . that it pleased him to choose the people for himself. *Jer. I:71.*

The preparation for receiving grace is the free election of God. [Antidote to the Council of Trent, quoting Augustine] *Tracts III:120.*

God prepares his elect for hearing, and gives them ears for that purpose. *Ezek. I:139.*

God, before he testifies his election to men, adopts them first to himself in his own secret counsel. *Joel-Obad. 111.*

It is the election of God alone which makes the difference between some and others. *Joel-Obad. 111.*

As his eternal election is free, so his calling is also free which floweth thence, and is not grounded in men. *Acts II:97.*

Our election is in Christ

Christ . . . is the mirror, in which it behoves us to contemplate our election. *Inst. III:xxiv.5.*

[On Heb. 2:13] Christ brings none to the Father, but those given him by the Father; and this donation, as we know, depends on eternal election. *Heb. 70.*

The fountain whence all the blessings God bestows on us flows is, that he hath chosen us in Christ. *Ps. I:473.*

It becomes all believers to be assured of their election, that they may learn to behold it in Christ as in a mirror. [Antidote to the Council of Trent] *Tracts III:155.*

The extent of God's election

[God] vouchsafes to the elect alone, the living root of faith, that they may persevere even to the end. *Inst. III:xvi.7.*

[On Ps. 47:4] The grace which God displays towards his chosen is not extended to all men in common, but is a privilege by which he distinguishes a few from the great mass of mankind. *Ps. II:210.*

He celebrates the sovereign grace of God, by which he chose for himself from amongst the lost race of Adam a small portion to whom he might show himself to be a father. *Ps. IV:173.*

[On John 12:38] He bestows the grace of his Holy Spirit on very few. *John II:41.*

Misrepresentation of election

. . . covering [election] with the veil of foreknowledge. *Inst.
III:xxii.1.*

[On Gen. 37:8, Joseph's brothers] The paternal favour of God
towards the elect, is like a fan to excite against them the enmity
of the world. *Gen. II:262.*

Those men who at this day obscure, and seek, as far as they can,
to extinguish the doctrine of election, are enemies to the human
race; for they strive their utmost to subvert every assurance of
salvation. *Zech.-Mal. 84, 85.*

Purpose of election

The object to be gained by election is, that they who were the
slaves of Satan may submit and devote themselves unreserved-
ly to God. *Is. III:255.*

The end of our election is, that we may show forth the glory of
God in every possible way. *Is. III:345.*

The beginning of our salvation . . . is God's election by free
grace; and the end of it is the obedience which we ought to
render to him. *Is. III:399.*

Obedience is the end of our calling. *Is. IV:164.*

Fruit of election

How diminutive and weak soever faith may be in the elect, yet,
as the Spirit of God is a certain pledge and seal to them of their
adoption, his impression can never be erased from their hearts.
Inst. III:ii.12.

All the virtue discovered in men is the effect of election. *Inst.
III:xxii.2.*

This doctrine ought to have a practical influence on our
prayers. *Inst. III:xxiv.5.*

Although this difference [between all Israel and the remnant]
flows from the fountain of gratuitous election, whence also faith
springs; yet, since the counsel of God is in itself hidden from us,

we therefore distinguish the true from the spurious children, by the respective marks of faith and of unbelief. *Gen. I:449.*

Whatever poison Satan produces, God turns it into medicine for his elect. *Gen. II: 488.*

The end of our election is, to be holy and unblamable in his sight (Col. 1:22). *Heb. 228.*

The godly are immediately led to consider their election, the confident belief of which cheers their hearts. *Is. I:435.*

In election we perceive the beginning of sanctification; salvation ought to be ascribed exclusively to his election, which is of free grace. *Is. IV:21.*

[God] declares his election when he regenerates his elect by his Holy Spirit and thus inscribes them with a certain mark, while they prove the reality of their sonship by the whole course of their lives, and confirm their own adoption. *Dan. II:372.*

Whatever blessings God confers on his own people proceed from eternal election, . . . a perpetual fountain. *Zech.-Mal. 52.*

[On John 13:18. Christ] ascribe[s] to election their perseverance . . . [and] the commencement of their piety. *John II:63.*

Every part of our salvation depends on election. *John II:64.*

Our holiness flows from the fountain of divine election, and . . . is the end of our caling. *Cor. I:53.*

Election . . . is the source and beginning of all good works. *Past. Epp. 195.*

Calvin's prayer [at close of Lecture 170 on the Minor Prophets] Grant, Almighty God, . . . that through our whole life we may strive to seal in our hearts the faith of our election . . . that having cast away and renounced all confidence in our own virtue, we may be led to Christ only as the fountain of thy election, in whom also is set before us the certainty of our salvation through thy gospel, until we shall at length be gathered into that eternal glory which He has procured for us by his own blood. Amen. *Zech.-Mal. 482.*

ERROR

Men are more ready to receive error and vanity, than to receive the word of God. *Jer. III:362.*

To assert the truth is only one-half of the office of teaching . . . except all the fallacies of the devil be also dissipated. *Jer. III:423.*

Men, when they have begun to turn aside from the pure word of God, continually invent various kinds of trifles. *Amos-Obad. 289.*

We shall abominate every error when we are fully persuaded that we forsake the true God whenever we obey not his word. *Jon.-Nah. 89.*

The greater part of the world ever seeks to be deceived. *Jon.-Nah. 367.*

When God comes forth with the teaching of his word, all the deceptions of Satan must necessarily be dissipated. *Zech.-Mal. 378.*

A good and faithful pastor ought . . . simply to assert what is true . . . to detect all corruptions . . . to recover men from the deceptions of Satan, and . . . to carry on a war with all superstitions. *Zech.-Mal. 379.*

Errors arise . . . when a loose rein is given to false teachers. *Zech.-Mal. 380.*

[On John 8:41] They separate God from his word, the Church from faith, and the kingdom of heaven from the Spirit. *John I:348.*

The most . . . deadly wound for killing the soul is *falsehood. John I:352.*

If we make the smallest departure from [the word], we shall be involved in strange labyrinths. *Is. III:212.*

Whenever [God] permitted false prophets to come among them, it was to try them to see what sort of people they were. (Deut. 13). *Jon.-Nah. 223.*

Diseases descend from the head to the whole body. *Joel-Obad. 259.*

Nothing is more to be dreaded than that the Lord should extinguish the light of sound doctrine, and suffer us to go astray in darkness. *Joel-Obad. 270.*

Satan's lies multiplied . . . because God repays a graceless . . . people with a just recompense . . . Error has a divine efficacy, when men prefer embracing a lie to the truth (2 Thess. 2:11,12). *Ezek. II:57.*

All who boast of the name of God without the word of God are mere liars. *John I:359.*

. . . drowned in the huge sink of errors; which punishment God in justice layeth upon men which refuse to obey his word. *Acts I:294.*

Obstinacy doth for the most part accompany error. *Acts I:457.*

There is no end of erring, when men depart from the word of God. *Acts II:217.*

[On 2 Thess. 2:3] When one [scholar] has gone astray, others, lacking judgment, followed in droves. *Thess. 399.*

Being full of blindness, nothing is more easy than for us to be greatly deceived by error. *Ps. IV:422.*

Falsehood . . . God's children must hate it with a deadly hatred. *Ps. V:39.*

It is the folly of the human mind to gather to itself leaders and teachers of error. *Gen. II:319.*

The majority of men, immersed in their errors, are blind amidst the greatest opportunities of seeing. *Inst. I:v.8.*

Errors can never be eradicated from the human heart, till the true knowledge of God is implanted in it. *Inst. I:vi.3.*

The best method of guarding against error is to consider the dangers which threaten us on every side. *Inst. II:ii.1.*

The human mind is naturally so prone to falsehood, that it will sooner imbibe error from one single expression, than truth from a prolix oration. *Inst. II:ii.7.*

EVIL

God is the author of the 'evil' of punishment, but not of the 'evil' of guilt. *Is. III:403.*

All who really serve and love God, ought . . . to burn with holy indignation whenever they see wickedness reigning without restraint among men, and especially in the Church of God. *Hab.-Hagg. 18.*

[On Is. 30:10] . . . the source of all evils . . . contempt of the word [of God]. *Is. II:357.*

The cause of all the evils we endure is our rebellion against God. *Is. I:219.*

I expect, with Paul, a reparation of all the evils caused by sin. *Inst. III:xxv.11.*

FAITH

Faith defined

A sure and steadfast knowledge of the paternal goodwill of God toward us, as he declares in the gospel that for the sake of Christ he will be our Father and Saviour. [Catechism of the Church of Geneva, being a form of instruction for children in the doctrine of Christ 1536, enlarged 1541] *Tracts II:53.*

Faith is obtained by us, only through the Spirit of God, and so is a peculiar gift which is given to the elect alone. [Calvin, Brief Confession of Faith] *Tracts II:132.*

Faith . . . the key which opens the gate that leads us to God. [Calvin's Confession of Faith, in the name of the Reformed Churches of France, 1542] *Tracts II:146.*

God includes faith in the word fear. *Jer. IV:218.*

The gospel contains nothing else but repentance and faith. *Ezek. II:174.*

Faith

Faith is the resurrection of the soul. [The True Method of Reforming the Church] *Tracts III:250.*

To trust . . . is nothing else than sincerely to embrace the favour which [God] offers in his word . . . to call on him with a pure heart and with a deep feeling of penitence. *Hab.-Hagg. 296.*

A conviction of the Divine goodness is the entrance of faith. *Syn. Gosp. I:33.*

In the act of believing we give our assent to God who speaks to us, and hold for certain what he has promised to us that he will do. *Syn. Gosp. I:51.*

No man can obtain faith by his own acuteness, but only by the secret illumination of the Spirit. *Syn. Gosp. II:39.*

Faith does not proceed from ourselves, but is the fruit of spiritual regeneration. *John I:43.*

Faith ought not to be fixed on the essence of Christ alone . . . but ought to attend to his power and office. *John I:79.*

Faith is . . . a warm embrace, of Christ, by which he dwells in us, and we are filled with the Divine Spirit. *Eph. 262.*

True faith confines its view so entirely to Christ, that it neither knows, nor desires to know, anything else. *Eph. 283.*

[Faith] is a steady and certain knowledge of the Divine benevolence towards us, which, being founded on the truth of the gratuitous promise in Christ, is both revealed to our minds, and confirmed to our hearts, by the Holy Spirit. *Inst. III:ii.7.*

[The assent] which we give to the Divine word . . . is from the heart, rather than the head, and from the affections, rather than the understanding. *Inst. III:ii.8.*

Faith we compare to a vessel; for unless we come empty with the mouth of our soul open to implore the grace of Christ, we cannot receive Christ. *Inst. III:xi.7.*

Faith and Obedience

Obedience is the source, not only of an absolutely perfect and complete faith, but of all right knowledge of God. *Inst. I:vi.2.*

To hear . . . generally means *to believe. Inst. III:ii.6.*

Holy is that timidity which is produced by the obedience of faith. *Gen. I:280.*

Faith is known by its promptitude. *Jer. III:242.*

There is no obedience without faith; and there is no faith without the word. *Is. IV:390, 391.*

Obedience . . . rests on faith, as faith does on the word. *Jon.-Nah. 257.*

The gate of faith is shut against all whose hearts are preoccupied by a vain desire of earthly glory. *John I:221.*

Faith and love . . . the sum total of godliness. *Thess. 354.*

It is the property of faith to rest upon God alone, without depending upon men. *Cor. I:101.*

Faith and the word

Take away the word . . . and there will be no faith left. *Inst. III:ii.6.*

Faith is a knowledge of the will of God respecting us, received from his word. And the foundation of this is a previous persuasion of the Divine veracity. *Inst. III:ii.6.*

We depend entirely upon the word of the Lord, and apprehend by faith that blessing which is not yet apparent. *Gen. II:59.*

Faith . . . confines us within Divinely-prescribed bounds, so that we attempt nothing except with God's authority or permission. *Gen. II:63.*

[On Heb. 11:4] He commends faith here on two accounts: . . . it undertakes nothing but what is according to the rule of God's word, and it relies on God's promises. *Heb. 267.*

It is one of the chief things which belong to faith, not to move a step except God's word shows us the way (Ps. 119:105). *Heb. 278.*

There is no faith without God's word. *Heb. 282.*

His faith continued shut up in the word of God. *Ps. I:399.*

Faith

[On Ps. 106:13] The touchstone of faith is when they spontaneously receive the word of God, and constantly continue firm in their obedience to it. *Ps. IV:216.*

Noah . . . embraced, by faith, the word in which salvation was contained. *Gen. I:273.*

It is the work of God alone to begin and to perfect faith . . . The word holds the chief place, and . . . signs are to be estimated by it. *Gen. I:299.*

Our faith is not rightly founded upon anything except the sole word of God . . . to prevent it from ever being shaken or overthrown by any devices whatever. *Gen. II:422.*

Religion is especially founded on faith, and faith is based on the word of God. *Jer. I:413.*

There is a kind of preparation for faith, by which God procures reverence for his word. *Is. III:331.*

Whenever faith is mentioned let us remember that it must be joined to the word. *Is. IV:160.*

Sobriety of faith is not only to acquiesce in the decision of God, and apprehend no more than his sacred lips have revealed, but also to attend diligently to the spirit of prophecy, and embrace a sound interpretation with meek docility. [Mutual Consent in regard to the Sacraments, 1554] *Tracts II:239.*

Our faith recumbs not on the opinion of men, but is sustained by thy word. *Hab.-Hagg. 39.*

There is no place for faith if we expect God to fulfil immediately what he promises. It is . . . the trial of faith to acquiesce in God's word . . . We have no faith except we are satisfied with God's word alone. *Hab.-Hagg. 68.*

Faith always springs from the word of God. *Syn. Gosp. II:263.*

This only is true of faith when we embrace not the one half of the Word of God alone, but subject ourselves wholly unto it. *Acts I:436.*

Faith is not of a right kind unless it is founded on the word of God . . . It ought to rest exclusively on the promises and word of God. *John II:279, 281.*

Christ commends faith on this ground that it acquiesces in the bare word, and does not depend on carnal views or human reason. *John II:278.*

The nature of faith is expressed, when there is a mutual relation made between it and the Word of God. *Acts II:402.*

Faith can bring us no more than it has received from the Word. *Rom. 100.*

Faith always connects the power of God with the word (Col. 1:29). *Past. Epp. 200.*

Faith and the promises

We make the foundation of faith to be the gratuitous promise; for on that faith properly rests. *Inst. III:ii.29.*

[On Gen. 15:4] The faith of Abraham was increased by the sight of the stars. *Gen. I:403.*

There is always to be presupposed a mutual relation and correspondence between the covenant of God and our faith, in order that the unfeigned consent of the latter may answer to the faithfulness of the former. *Ps. III:254.*

There is a mutual relation between God's promises and our faith. *Ps. I:494.*

Faith cannot stand unless it be founded upon the promises of God. *Gen. I:346.*

Faith, sustained by promises, elevates us above all the world. *Jer. IV:333.*

What faith properly looks to in the word of God is the free promises, and especially Christ, their pledge and foundation. [The True Method of Reforming the Church] *Tracts III:250.*

What benefit do God's promises confer on us, unless we embrace them by faith? *Dan. II:134, 135.*

Our faith answers to his promises. *Syn. Gosp. I:126.*

Faith

Faith dependeth upon the promises. *Acts I:450.*

Our faith should be borne up on wings by the promises of God. *Rom. 187.*

There are three stages in our progress. First, we believe the promises of God; next, by relying on them, we obtain that *confidence*, which is accompanied by holiness and peace of mind; and, last of all, comes *boldness*, which enables us to banish fear, and to come with firmness and steadiness into the presence of God. *Eph. 257.*

Faith and divine election

Faith . . . depends on God alone. *Hab.-Hagg. 73.*

[Christ] connects faith with the eternal predestination of God. *Syn. Gosp. II:40.*

The treasure of faith is not set before all promiscuously, but is offered peculiarly to the elect. *Acts II:301.*

. . . the science of faith, which the elect have received from God. *Cor. I:119, note.*

Faith leans on the sole promise of gratuitous adoption. *Gen. Epp. 36.*

Election is . . . the parent of faith. *Inst. III:xxii.10.*

. . . the faith of the gospel, by which we discover our interest in election. *Inst. III:xxiv.4.*

Faith flows from the secret election of God. [Letter to Melanchthon] *Letters 160.*

It is only by an assured faith of adoption that any of us can rest upon him. *Ps. V:287.*

Faith is the evidence of Divine adoption. [The True Method of Reforming the Church] *Tracts III:250.*

Faith's certainty

The true character of faith is to set the Lord always before our eyes; secondly, that faith beholds higher and more hidden things in God than what our senses can perceive; and, thirdly, that a view of God alone is sufficient to strengthen our weakness . . . to withstand all the assaults of Satan. *Heb. 298.*

. . . to fly on the wings of faith to the goodness of God . . . and . . . to perceive the same goodness in the thickest darkness. *Gen. II:428.*

Strong faith quietens the conscience and composes the spirit. *Ps. IV:363.*

The tranquillity of faith has no affinity with indolence. *Gen. II:355.*

. . . the special characteristic of faith, not to inquire curiously what the Lord is to do . . . but to cast all our anxious cares upon his providence. *Josh. 59.*

Faith ever brings us peace with God . . . because the will of God alone is sufficient to appease our minds. *Jer. I:342.*

Faith, having apprehended the love of God, has promises for the present life and the life to come, and a solid assurance of all blessings . . . such an assurance as may be derived from the Divine word. *Inst. III:ii.28.*

The inward joy which faith brings to us can overcome all fears, terrors, sorrows and anxieties. *Hab.-Hagg. 175.*

God is not properly worshipped but by the certainty of faith, which cannot be produced in any other way than by the word of God. *John I:160.*

Faith is by hearing (Rom. 10:17), and yet it derives its certainty from the *seal* and *earnest of the Spirit* (Eph. 1:13,14). *John II:131.*

Faith is not like mere opinion . . . but has a firm steadfastness, which can withstand all the machinations of hell. *Philipp.-Col. 160.*

The gospel can be understood by faith alone – not by reason, nor by the perspicacity of the human understanding. *Philipp.-Col. 174.*

To believe is . . . a firm, undoubting conviction, so that we may dare to subscribe to the truth as fully proved. *Gen. Epp. 157.*

Faith

Faith's humility

[On Ps. 51:17] Faith cannot be separated from the humility of which David speaks . . . a humility . . . unknown to the wicked. *Ps. II:306.*

It is the peculiar virtue of faith that we should willingly be fools, in order that we may learn to be wise only from the mouth of God. *Four Last Bks of Moses IV: 155, 156.*

Nothing is more contrary to faith than pride, as also humility is the true principle of faith. *Jer. III:374.*

Humility is the best preparation for faith, that there may be a submission to the word of God. *Jer. II:336.*

The beginning of faith . . . is humility, by which we yield our senses as captives to God. *Is. III:331.*

Faith, in order to please God, needs forgiveness. *Syn. Gosp. I:413.*

Temporary faith

[On Mark 4:17] Temporary faith . . . not so much a fruit of the Spirit of regeneration, as of a certain mutable affection. *Ps. IV:216.*

There is a great similarity and affinity between temporary faith and that which is living and perpetual. *Inst. III:ii.12.*

Weak faith

Faith, though halting and imperfect, is still approved by God. *Heb. 303.*

Some portion of unbelief is always mixed with faith in every Christian. *Inst. III:ii.4.*

Our faith is never perfect; . . . we are partly unbelievers. *Syn. Gosp. II:325.*

Nothing is more at variance with faith than the foolish and irregular desires of our flesh. *Syn. Gosp. II:326, 327.*

Justifying faith

The saints are justified freely even unto death . . . He counts them just, by imputation. *Gen. I:409.*

Abram was justified by faith many years after he had been called by God. *Gen. I:408.*

Faith . . . not . . . the efficient, but only the formal cause [of righteousness] *Gen. I:407.*

Satan has laboured at nothing more assiduously than to extinguish, or to smother, the gratuitous justification of faith. *Gen. I:405.*

The faith of Abraham was directed to the blood of Christ. *Gen. I:355.*

Faith does not justify us for any other reason, than that it reconciles us to God . . . not by its own merit; but because we receive the grace offered to us in the promises. *Gen. I:407.*

It is . . . faith alone which justifies, and yet the faith which justifies is not alone. [Antidote to the Council of Trent] *Tracts III:152.*

With respect to justification, faith is a thing merely passive, bringing nothing of our own to conciliate the favour of God, but receiving what we need from Christ. *Inst. III:xiii.5.*

[On Hab. 2:4] The just . . . brings nothing before God except faith. *Hab.-Hagg. 75.*

Faith and law are contrary, the one to the other; contrary as to the work of justifying. *Hab.-Hagg. 77.*

Faith does not make us clean . . . but because it receiveth that cleanness which is offered in Christ. *Acts II:50, 51.*

Christ is the mark whereat faith must aim. *Acts II:122.*

Faith the gift of God

It is the work of God alone to begin and to perfect faith. *Gen. I:299.*

Faith does not depend on miracles, or any extraordinary sign, but is the peculiar gift of the Spirit, and is produced by means of the word. *Syn. Gosp. II:193.*

Faith does not depend on the will of men . . . it is God who gives it. *John I:257.*

No man . . . can arrive at faith by his own sagacity; for all are blind, until they are illuminated by the Spirit of God. *John I:276.*

Faith does not proceed from the ordinary faculties of men, but is an uncommon and extraordinary gift of God. *John II:40.*

[On Lydia, Acts 16:14] Not faith alone, but all understanding and knowledge of spiritual things, is the peculiar gift of God. *Acts II:103.*

Faith itself . . . is a part of grace. *Rom. 217.*

There are two operations of the Spirit in faith . . . it enlightens, and . . . it establishes the mind. *Eph. 208.*

Faith . . . brings a man empty to God, that he may be filled with the blessings of Christ. *Eph. 227.*

It is the chief foundation of faith, to know that it has God for its author. *Past. Epp. 247.*

Faith's fragrance

[On Gen. 12:9] Abram perfumed [the land] with the odour of his faith. *Gen. I:357.*

All religious services which are not perfumed with the odour of faith, are of an ill-savour before God. *Gen. I:282.*

The faith of one proves the consolation of others. *Thess. 353.*

Faith and works

The merit of works ceases when righteousness is sought by faith. *Gen. I:407.*

Faith cannot remain inoperative in the heart . . . Here the Holy Spirit unites with a sacred bond, the faith of the heart with outward confession. *Ps. IV:366.*

The simplicity of faith is our spiritual chastity. *Jer. III:112.*

Faith is the evidence of divine adoption. [Antidote to Council of Trent] *Tracts III:250.*

Faith . . . the only ground-work of godliness. *Acts II:348.*

The power of faith

[God's] power is connected by a sacred bond with his grace, and with faith in his promises. *Gen. I:511.*

Faith is not only prompt and ready in obedience, but invigorates and quickens the whole man. *Four Last Bks of Moses IV:70.*

Faith is no idle feeling . . . but an energizing principle. *Dan. II:326.*

[Peter walking on the water] Without the wings of faith, he desires to fly at will. *Syn. Gosp. II:241.*

Faith should fix its whole attention on the power of God alone. *Rom. 100.*

Faith's testing

[God] . . . conceals his remedies until he has exercised our faith . . . They who fancy that faith is exempt from all fear, have had no experience of the true nature of faith. *Gen. II:189.*

Nothing is more improper, than to prescribe the time in which God shall help us; since he purposely, for a long season, keeps his people in anxious suspense, that . . . they may truly know what it is to trust him. *Gen. II:312.*

The faith which is more precious than gold and silver, ought not to lie idle, without trial. *Gen. I:564.*

[We are] to fly on the wings of faith to the goodness of God, and instead of being overwhelmed by a mass of evils, to perceive the same goodness in the thickest darkness. *Gen. II:428.*

It is a real and just trial of faith, when God bids us to depend on his word. *Zech.-Mal. 45.*

Faith has its silence to lend an ear to the Word of God. *Syn. Gosp. I:26.*

Faith

The test of faith lies in prayer. *Syn. Gosp. III:19.*

This is the true proof of faith, when we never suffer ourselves to be torn away from Christ, and from the promises. *John II:81.*

. . . the holy silence of faith. *Acts I:433.*

Faith and hope

True faith is ever connected with hope. *Heb. 146.*

Faith can be no more separated from patience than from itself. *Heb. 260.*

Faith, divesting us of our own wisdom, enables us hopefully and quietly to wait until God accomplish his own work. *Ps. IV:217.*

Faith and hope . . . are the wings by which our souls, rising above this world, are lifted up to God. *Ps. I:414.*

[On Is. 25:9] This *waiting* springs from faith, which is accompanied by patience and there is no faith without the word. *Is. II:202.*

Patience is the fruit and proof of faith. *Thess. 388.*

Faith is the mother of hope. *Cor. I:432.*

Our faith cannot stand otherwise than by looking to the coming of Christ. *Gen. Epp. 205.*

Faith and prayer

Faith . . . lies idle and even dead without prayer. *Ps. V:281.*

The chief work of faith is prayer to God . . . that primary exercise of faith. *Jer. IV: 67, 68.*

Faith gives us access to God. [Antidote to Council of Trent] *Tracts III:250.*

Prayer is the chief exercise of faith. *Dan. II:135.*

Our faith cannot be supported in a better way than by the exercise of prayer. *Hab.-Hagg. 133.*

Faith goes before all prayers in order and in time. *Syn. Gosp. I:352, 353.*

Faith . . . the mother of prayer. *Acts I:346*.

Faith will obtain anything from the Lord. *Syn. Gosp. II:269*.

The victory of faith

[On Heb. 11:35] The victory of faith appears more splendid in the contempt of death. *Heb. 305*.

[On Ps. 91:2] This holy species of boasting constitutes the very highest triumph of faith. *Ps. III:479*.

This is faith's true office, to see life in the midst of death. *Ps. V:204*.

How greatly opposed to faith is cowardice. *Four Last Bks of Moses IV:64*.

The valour of the godly rests on the word of God, and proceeds from true faith. *Is. I:272*.

Faith's vision

A godly confidence delights to look on God. *Gen. Epp. 201*.

If our faith does not ascend on heavenly wings . . . it will always stick fast in the mud of this world. *Rom. 96*.

Faith hath this property to set God always before it as a guide in all dangers and confused matters. *Acts I:104*.

Faith apprehends both God's pity and his judgments. *Dan. II:170*.

The lofty watch-tower of faith. *Is. II:209*.

Faith prepares us to perceive the operation of God. *Josh. 60*.

We are not allowed to transfer to men even the smallest part of our confidence, which must be placed in God alone . . . The trust that is put in the flesh shall at last be accursed. *Ps. IV:380, 381*.

Faith and knowledge

It is proper to distinguish between the knowledge which springs from faith and the knowledge which springs from experience. *Is. I:434*.

Faith

The feeling of faith is different from that of experience. *Is. IV:294.*

Faith . . . is not a bare knowledge . . . but it carries along with it a lively affection, which has its seat in the heart. [Antidote to the Council of Trent] *Tracts III:250.*

Faith's hunger

Faith alone is the mouth . . . and the stomach of the soul. *John I:268.*

Faith and worship

Faith is always connected with a seemly and spontaneous reverence for God. *Thess. 407.*

FALSE PROPHETS

False prophets described

[On Ezek. 13:1–3] God briefly defines who the false prophets are; namely, those who prophesy out of their own hearts . . . The Spirit of God pronounces every one who prophesies from his own heart to be an impostor . . . God puts a perpetual distinction between the human mind and revelation of his Spirit. *Ezek. II:7, 8.*

Whatever is contrary to sound doctrine, is a sinful device, a fallacy of Satan, and, in a word, the impiety of a corrupt heart. *Jer. II:405.*

The Church cannot stand, except false teachers be prevented from turning truth into falsehood, and from prating at their pleasure against the word of God. *Zech.-Mal. 380.*

All doctrines must be brought to the Word of God as the standard . . . in judging of false prophets. *Syn. Gosp. I:365.*

False prophets . . . divide God, as it were, in half, since they speak only of his freeness to forgive, and . . . are profoundly silent about repentance . . . They used his name falsely . . . for by the feint of speaking in God's name, they darkened men's minds. *Ezek. 11:13.*

False prophets, relying on their number, were on that account bolder. *Hab.-Hagg. 267.*

Man's readiness to listen to false prophets

The greater part of the world ever seeks to be deceived. *Jon.-Nah. 367.*

Satan thus hunts his prey when he soothes the people by his false teachers, and keeps them . . . asleep. *Hos. 329.*

False teachers . . . fascinated the people with their flatteries, so that every regard for sound and heavenly doctrine was almost extinguished. *Jer. III:200.*

We know how haughtily false teachers elevate themselves. *Jer. III:202.*

With the view of making themselves admired, they contrived a new method of teaching, at variance with the simplicity of Christ. *Cor. I:39.*

As there is an unsatiable longing for those things which are unprofitable and destructive . . . the devil has always at hand a sufficiently large number of such teachers as the world desires to have. *Past. Epp. 256.*

. . . the lofty vaunting of the false teachers, who wished to be deemed the organs of the Holy Spirit, and assumed to themselves all the authority of God. *Jer. III:203.*

All [Satan's] teachers in all ages have presented their poison, even all their errors and fallacies, in a golden cup. *Jer. I:85.*

God's purpose in this

It was God's will that many impostors should assume the prophetic name. *Jer. I:213.*

When [God] permits false prophets to work miracles to deceive, it is to prove men's hearts. *Four Last Bks of Moses I:149.*

[On Gal. 5:15] False doctrine was probably a judgment from heaven upon their ambition, pride, and other offences. *Gal. 161.*

FAMILY

[On Jer. 16:2] The law of man's creation, we know, was this, 'Increase and multiply' (Gen. 1:22; 8:17; 9:1, 7). *Jer. II:301.*

[On Ps. 127:3] The meaning . . . is, that children are not the fruit of chance, but that God, as it seems good to him, distributes to every man his share of them. *Ps. V:110.*

The offspring of believers is born holy, because their children, while yet in the womb . . . are included in the covenant of eternal life . . . Nor . . . are they admitted into the Church by baptism on any other ground than that they belonged to the body of Christ before they were born. [Antidote to the Council of Trent] *Tracts III:275.*

Piety towards parents is the mother of all virtues. *Gen. I:302.*

[On Ham] . . . in the hallowed sanctuary of God, among so small a number, one fiend was preserved. *Gen. I:302.*

[On Jacob's sons, Gen. 42. Jacob] seemed to be bringing up devils at home . . . How could the salvation of the world proceed from such a vicious offspring? *Gen. II:349.*

Every family of the pious ought to be a Church. *Gen. I:455.*

Christian households . . . so many little churches. *Philipp.-Col. 230.*

FASTING

The life of believers, indeed, ought to be so regulated by frugality and sobriety, as to exhibit, as far as possible, the appearance of a perpetual fast . . . This restriction consists in three things – in time, in quality, and in quantity of food. *Inst. IV:xii.18.*

Fasting . . . is an appendage to prayer . . . added to prayer by Christ himself (Matt. 17:21). It is not appointed . . . for its own sake. *Is. IV:232.*

Fasting does not of itself displease God; but it becomes an abomination to him, when it is thought to be a meritorious work, or when some holiness is connected with it. *Jer. I:348.*

[Zech. 8:18, 19] Fasting . . . the habit of criminals, when they desire to obtain pardon from God. *Zech.-Mal. 222.*

FATHERHOOD OF GOD

That most delightful name of Father. *Inst. III:xiii.5.*

The Church, which God has selected as the great theatre where his fatherly care may be manifested. *Ps. III:12.*

God is not a Father to any that are not members and brethren of his only-begotten Son. *Cor. II:138.*

The Father . . . loves none but in Christ. *John II:185.*

The Father cannot look upon his Son without having likewise before his eyes the whole body of Christ. *John II:189.*

Through the promises alone it is that we can have a taste of God's paternal goodness. *Jer. V:322.*

God, in the gospel, takes upon him the character of a nursing father. *Gen. II:238.*

God testifies his fatherly regard to his people by opposing all her enemies. *Is. II:143.*

God never was a Father, either to angels or to men, but with reference to his only-begotten Son. *Inst. II:xiv.5.*

FEAR

The fear of God

The *fear of the Lord* means a sincere desire to worship God. *Is. I:375.*

Fear is the true preparation for obedience. *Dan. II:116.*

God includes faith in the word *fear*. *Jer. IV:219.*

What else is God's fear than that reverence by which we show that we are submissive to his will, because he is a Father and a Sovereign? *Jer. III:335.*

Righteousness flows from only one principle – the fear of God. *Ezek. II:234.*

Fear – the whole service of God. *Four Last Bks of Moses IV:351.*

Faithful trust . . . is . . . always coupled with fear. *Josh. 59.*

True faith, while it reclines on God, keeps those who possess it in his fear. *Josh. 265.*

There is no wisdom but that which is founded on the fear of God. *Is. II:58.*

The hatred of sin proceeds from the fear of God. *Hab.-Hagg. 172.*

Under the *fear* of the Lord is included the whole of godliness and religion, and this cannot exist without faith. *Syn. Gosp. I:57.*

The fear of God – the highest of all virtues. *Gen. I:476.*

Nothing is more powerful to overcome temptation than the fear of God. *Gen. II:297.*

The fountain of that good and honest conscience, whereby we cultivate fidelity and justice towards men, is the fear of God. *Gen. II:343.*

[On Ps. 40:3] I understand fear in general to mean the feeling of piety which is produced in us by the knowledge of the power, equity, and mercy of God. *Ps. II:92.*

The fear of man

How greatly opposed to faith is cowardice! *Four Last Bks of Moses IV:64.*

When anyone goes astray through the fear of men, it is certain that he never has truly tasted the sweetness of the name of God. *Is. II:230.*

By an excessive fear of men we betray contempt of God. *Is. IV:78.*

Fear . . . a sign of hopeless unbelief. *Jer. IV:410.*

Guilty consciences are so disturbed by blind and unreasonable fears, that they . . . voluntarily become their own tormentors. *Gen. II:482.*

Wicked men . . . have fears on all sides. *Gen. II:179.*

The most audacious contemners of God are most alarmed, even at the noise of a falling leaf. *Inst. I:iii.2.*

All those who do not draw nigh to God sincerely and with all their heart . . . are compelled to stand before the judgment-seat of mortal man. *Gen. II:483.*

The beginning of infidelity is to be withheld by fear from obedience to God. *Four Last Bks of Moses IV:64.*

Fear in the Christian

We must beware lest *fear* take away our judgment . . . No higher affront can be offered to God than to give way to *fear. Is. I:277, 278.*

We are more terrified frequently by the empty mask of a single man than we are strengthened by all the promises of God. *Is. III:231.*

He walks in darkness who is not ruled by the fear of God. *Gen. Epp. 164.*

Confidence, founded on Christ, rises superior to all fear. *John II:23.*

The inward joy, which faith brings to us, can overcome all fears. *Hab.-Hagg. 175.*

Fear, proceeding from unbelief, cannot be otherwise dissipated but by God's promises made to us, which chase away all doubts. *Zech.-Mal. 213.*

They who fancy that faith is exempt from all fear, have had no experience of the true nature of faith. *Gen. II:189.*

Fear in the Ministry

[On 2 Tim. 1:7] God governs his ministers by *the Spirit of power,* which is the opposite of *cowardice. Past. Epp. 191.*

[On 1 Thess. 2:4] Paul compares pleasing God and pleasing men as opposites. *Thess. 342.*

No man can rightly handle the doctrine of godliness, unless the fear of God reign . . . in him. *Acts II:312.*

Nothing is more contrary to the pure and free preaching of the gospel than the straits of a faint heart. *Acts II:187.*

FLATTERY

Oftentimes the enemies of the truth assail [us] by flatteries . . . These things have often been said to us. *Joel-Obad. 345.*

The higher that every one of us shall be extolled, let him submit himself unto God with modesty and fear. *Acts I:238.*

[On Herod, Acts 12:23] . . . drunk with the false commendation and flattery of men as with deadly poison. *Acts I:494.*

FLESH

The term *flesh* is . . . employed to describe man's whole nature. *Cor. I:124.*

The flesh means the whole corrupt nature of man. *Gen. Epp. 187.*

'Flesh' is the designation applied to all men at birth and for as long as they retain their natural character. *Rom. 147.*

Flesh . . . includes all the endowments of human nature, and everything that is in man, except the sanctification of the Spirit. *Rom. 151.*

All our affections are so many soldiers of Satan. *Syn. Gosp. I:319.*

Our flesh will suggest to us various shifts and devices, and lead us into many errors in search of counsel. *Ps. II:62.*

[On Ps. 42:6] The soul of man serves the purpose . . . of a workshop to Satan in which to forge a thousand methods of despair. *Ps. II:137.*

[Intro. to Ps. 44] Christ . . . did not . . . appear, that the flesh should luxuriate in ease upon the earth, but rather that we should wage war under the banner of the cross, until we are received into the rest of the heavenly kingdom. *Ps. II:149.*

[On Gen. 6:3, 'carnal'] The Lord here seems to place his Spirit in opposition to the carnal nature of men . . . For since the soul of man is vitiated in every part, and the reason of man is not less blind than his affections are perverse, the whole is properly called carnal. *Gen. I:242.*

FORGIVENESS

The gratuitous pardon of sins is . . . daily offered to the faithful . . . All the saints have need of the daily forgiveness of sins. *Gen. Epp. 165.*

We never obtain forgiveness of sins without repentance. *Cor. II:275.*

God does not forgive the sins of any but those who are dissatisfied with themselves. *Syn. Gosp. II:109.*

God is irreconcileable to the impenitent. *Jon.-Nah. 422.*

In order that we may be partakers of ablution, it is necessary that each of us should offer Christ to the Father . . . We set Christ before God's face in order to propitiate him. *Four Last Bks of Moses II:39.*

In all the deliverances which God grants his people, there is an accompanying remission of their sins. *Ps. V:188.*

That blessing would forthwith be lost did he not confirm it in us by daily pardoning our sins . . . even to the close of [our] life. *Ps. IV:136.*

If we really desire absolution . . . we must institute a rigid and formidable scrutiny into the character of our transgressions. *Ps. II: 285.*

This pardon is promised to them, not for one day only, but to the very end of life, so that they have a daily reconciliation with God. *Heb. 190.*

FREE OFFER OF THE GOSPEL
(*see also* Preaching)

He calls all men to himself, without a single exception, and gives Christ to all, that we may be illumined by him. *Is. III:295.*

When we pray, we ought, according to the rule of charity, to include all. *Jer. II:248.*

God invites all indiscriminately to salvation through the Gospel. *Syn. Gosp. I:116.*

As no man is excluded from calling upon God, the gate of salvation is set open to all men; neither is there any other thing which keepeth us back from entering in, save only our own unbelief. *Acts I:92.*

Though it is offered to all for salvation, it does not yield this fruit in any but the elect. *Syn. Gosp. II:257.*

God . . . shows himself to be reconciled to the whole world, when he invites all men without exception to faith in Christ . . . For Christ is made known and held out to the view of all, but the elect alone are they whose eyes God opens, that they may seek him by faith. *John I:125.*

. . . the end and design of public teaching . . . that all should in common be called; but God's purpose is different; for he intends, according to his own secret counsel, to draw to himself the elect, and he designs to take away all excuse from the reprobate. *Joel-Obad. 252.*

Paul makes grace common to all men, not because it in fact extends to all, but because it is offered to all. *Rom. 117, 118.*

Christ . . . kindles for all indiscriminately the torch of his gospel; but all have not the eyes of their minds opened to see it, but on the contrary Satan spreads the veil of blindness over many. *Gen. Epp. 273, 274.*

God commands [the gospel] to be offered indiscriminately to all. *Gen. I:503.*

[God] . . . commands his threatenings to be proposed to the elect, and reprobate, in common. *Gen. I:255.*

[119]

God's mercy is offered for the worst of men. *Four Last Bks of Moses III:240.*

It is our duty to pray for all who trouble us; to desire the salvation of all men. *Ps. IV:283.*

FREE WILL

What *free will* is, though the expression frequently occurs in all writers, few have defined. Yet Origen appears to have advanced a position to which they all assented, when he calls it a power of *reason* to discern good and evil, of *will* to choose either. *Inst. II:ii.4.*

Man is not possessed of free will for good works, unless he be assisted by grace, and that special grace which is bestowed on the elect alone, in regeneration. *Inst. II:ii.6.*

Whatever deficiency of natural ability prevents us from attaining the pure and clear knowledge of God, yet, since that deficiency arises from our own fault, we are left without any excuse. *Inst. I:v.15.*

After the impious have wilfully shut their own eyes, it is the righteous vengeance of God upon them to darken their understandings, so that, seeing, they may not perceive. *Inst. I:iv.2.*

I . . . protest against those who attribute to us some degree of free will, by which we can prepare ourselves for receiving the grace of God. [Brief Confession of Faith] *Tracts II:131.*

Freedom of choice having been taken away after the fall of the first man, will alone was left; but so completely captive under the tyranny of sin, that it is only inclined to evil. [Antidote to the Council of Trent] *Tracts III:113.*

Free-will . . . putting conversion in the power of man. *Jer. III:229.*

Men by their own free will cannot turn to God, until he first change their stony hearts into hearts of flesh. *Ps. III:324.*

Freewill assents to God calling and exciting it . . . [God] acts within, holds our hearts, moves our hearts, and draws us by the inclinations which he has produced in us. [Antidote to the Council of Trent] *Tracts III:147, 148.*

The Papists, . . . speaking of repentance, hold that man, through his own free will, returns to God; and on this point is our greatest contest with them at this day. *Jer. IV:102.*

GIFTS

Whatever gifts are offered us in Christ, we receive by the agency of the Spirit. [Catechism of the Church of Geneva, 1536] *Tracts II:50.*

The gifts of the Spirit are not the gifts of nature. *Eph. 212.*

The gift of prophecy and all teaching is God's peculiar gift. *Ezek. I:274.*

We shall be enriched every now and then with new gifts of the Spirit, if we hold out unto God the lap of faith. *Acts I:220.*

[On John 7:38] The Holy Spirit is like a living and continually flowing fountain in believers . . . Everyone partakes of the gifts and grace of the Holy Spirit according to his faith. *John I:308.*

[Bezaleel and Aholiab] As God conferred this honour on the architects of the visible sanctuary, so he declares that their names shall be glorious in heaven who, being furnished with the illustrious gifts of the Spirit, faithfully employ their labours in the building of his spiritual temple. *Four Last Bks of Moses III:296.*

[On Exod. 4:16] The gifts of the Spirit, as well as our vocations, are distributed by him at his own good pleasure. *Four Last Bks of Moses I:96.*

[On Exod. 18:13] Let God's servants learn to measure carefully their powers . . . God has so arranged our condition that individuals are only endued with a certain measure. *Four Last Bks of Moses I:303.*

[On Exod. 40:9] . . . the anointing oil, a symbol of all the gifts of the Holy Spirit. *Four Last Bks of Moses III:404.*

Many are proud of the gifts of the Spirit. *Past. Epp. 325.*

Many men excel oftentimes in the gifts of the Spirit, who have an unclean heart. *Acts I:345.*

God has often so distributed the gifts of his Spirit that he has honoured with the prophetic office even the ungodly and unbelieving; for it was a special gift, distinct from the grace of regeneration. *Jon.-Nah. 334.*

GIVING

Liberality is estimated by God, not so much from the sum, as from the disposition. *Cor. II:309.*

By liberality of mind we make up for what is deficient in our coffers . . . In laying out our favours we are simply the dispensers of his favour . . . Christ has consecrated poverty in his own person, that believers may no longer regard it with horror. *Cor. II:285–287.*

'What riches you give away, those alone you shall always have' [Calvin, quoting the Roman writer Martial] *Cor. II:69.*

[On 2 Cor. 9:11] How few Macedonians are there in the present day . . . How many Corinthians you may find everywhere! *Cor. II:348.*

It was the design of Christ (Matt. 5:42; Luke 6:34) to make his disciples generous, but not prodigals. *Syn. Gosp. I:301.*

GOD

His Person

We ought to speak of God with the same religious caution, which should govern our thoughts of him. *Inst. I:xiii.3.*

[God's] essence . . . is rather to be adored than too curiously investigated. *Inst. I:v.9.*

Only fools . . . seek to know the essence of God. *Rom. 31.*

. . . the immensity and spirituality of the essence of God. *Inst. I:137.*

What I denominate a Person, is a subsistence in the Divine essence, which is related to the others, and yet distinguished from them by an incommunicable property. *Inst. I:xiii.6.*

'[God] alone', as Hilary says, 'is a competent witness for himself, being only known by himself.' *Inst. I:xiii.21.*

Whatever we think, and whatever we say of him, should savour of his excellence, correspond to the sacred sublimity of his name, and tend to the exaltation of his magnificence. *Inst. II:viii.22.*

The intention of Moses, in beginning his book with the creation of the world, is, to render God . . . visible to us in his works. *Gen. I:58.*

God – by other means invisible – clothes himself . . . with the image of the world . . . Let the world become our school if we desire rightly to know God. *Gen. I:60.*

We are accustomed to imagine God absent, except when we have some sensible experience of his presence. *Gen. I:276.*

God would have us to acknowledge him as the author of all our blessings. *Ps. I:111.*

God is sought in two ways, either by invocation and prayers, or by studying to live a holy and upright life. *Ps. I:120.*

[On Ps. 44:4] The faithful praise God alone as the guardian of their welfare to the exclusion of all others, and the renunciation of aid from any other quarter. *Ps. II:155.*

The ark . . . the beauty of God . . . a mirror in which he might be seen. *Ps. III:271.*

The true knowledge of God corresponds to what faith discovers in the written Word. *Ps. IV:133.*

[On Ps. 145:8] The Papists represent [God as] a dreadful God, from whose presence all must fly, whereas the proper view of him is that which invites us to seek after him. *Ps. V:275.*

Irreligious men idly and foolishly imagine a God according to their own pleasure. *Is. II:106.*

The majesty of God is . . . indissolubly connected with the public preaching of his truth . . . If his word is not allowed to have authority, it is the same as though its despisers attempted to thrust God from heaven, or denied his existence. *Jer. I:280.*

As soon . . . as we allow ourselves the liberty to worship God in this or in that way, or to imagine God to be such and such a being, we create gods for ourselves. *Jer. II:336.*

A mere fiction is every idea which men form of God in their minds, when they neglect that mirror in which he has made himself known. *Jer. III:27.*

It was ever a principle held by all nations, that there is some supreme Deity; for though they devised for themselves various gods, yet they all believed that there is one supreme God. *Jer. V:135.*

Man's mind conceiveth nothing of God but that which is gross and earthly. *Acts I:291.*

Let God be found true [Rom. 3:4] . . . the primary axiom of all Christian philosophy. *Rom. 60.*

God's name

The name of God is more excellent than anything in the whole world. *Jon.-Nah. 343, 344.*

It is . . . the extremity of evil, when men allow themselves to treat the awful name of God with scoffs. *Gen. Epp. 414.*

If God's name is rashly exposed to reproach or contempt, He will avenge it . . . [His] holy name is more precious than a hundred worlds. *Four Last Bks of Moses II:410, 411.*

God's glory

The proclaiming of [God's] glory on earth . . . the very end of our existence. *Ps. IV:358.*

God is called jealous, because He permits no rivalry which may detract from his glory. *Four Last Bks of Moses I:423.*

There is scarcely one among a hundred who makes the manifestation of God's glory his chief end. *Ps. IV:291.*

[124]

Whenever any image is made as a representation of God, the Divine glory is corrupted by an impious falsehood. *Inst. I:xi.1.*

[On Is. 42:8] The glory of God is chiefly visible in his fulfilment of what he has promised. *Is. III:296.*

[On Is. 43:8] His glory . . . is intimately connected with the salvation of his people. *Is. III:326.*

The end of our election is that we may show forth the glory of God in every possible way (Exod. 14:4, 17, 18) *Is. III:345.*

Men rob God of the glory which is due to him, and direct all their faculties towards distributing among the creatures that which belongs to him alone, so as to leave him nothing but a bare and empty name. *Is. III:473.*

It will not be lawful to transfer to man even the smallest portion of praise. *Is. IV:351.*

Our salvation is connected with his glory. *Is. IV:372.*

. . . the Church, the principal theatre of his glory. *Is. IV:424.*

Whoever does not believe God's word robs him of his glory. *Jer. II:177.*

The law was, as it were, the representation of the glory of God . . . a mirror before their eyes. *Jer. V:227.*

We always attribute something to pride, which renders our senses obtuse, so as to be incapable of the glory of God. *Ezek. I:81.*

God's glory and the salvation of the Church are things almost inseparably united. *Ezek. II:294.*

If anything is attributed to men, as springing from themselves, it so far detracts from the supreme power and empire of God. *Dan. I:297.*

[God's] chief glory is that vast and ineffable goodness by which he has once embraced us, and which he will show us to the end. *Hab.-Hagg. 305.*

[125]

The glory of God so shines in his word, that we ought to be so affected by it, whenever he speaks by his servants, as though he were nigh to us, face to face. *Hab.-Hagg. 343.*

All things ought to be referred to his glory and worship, otherwise every good thing he bestows on us is profaned. *Zech.-Mal. 90.*

The interest of the faithful is always annexed to the glory of God. *Acts I:403.*

There is no one of us who can take to himself the least jot of glory without sacrilegious robbing of God. *Acts I:495.*

All God's blessings, with which he favours us, are intended for this end, that his glory may be proclaimed by us. *Gen. Epp. 76.*

There is no duty more becoming the faithful than that of earnestly seeking for the advance of his glory. *Ps. IV:396.*

Attributes of God

When mention is made of God, it behoves us to apply our minds properly to those attributes of his nature which are specially fitted to establishing our faith, that we may not lose ourselves by vainly indulging in subtle speculations. *Ps. III:427.*

God cannot be rightly worshipped unless when he has his peculiar attributes acknowledged. *Four Last Bks of Moses I:422.*

Power: When men seek to comprehend the power of God it is like a fly attempting to devour all the mountains. *Jer. V:164.*

Since his power is infinite we are defended by an invincible fortress. *Ps. I:484.*

We only praise God aright when we are filled and overwhelmed with an ecstatic admiration of the immensity of his power. *Ps. V:273.*

There is power in God to lay prostrate the whole world, and to tread it under his feet, whenever it may please him. *Hab.-Hagg. 132.*

Life: [On Dan. 6:25–27] Darius calls [God] *the living God* not only because he has life in himself, but out of himself, and is also the origin and fountain of life. *Dan. I:392.*

By the sole bidding of God both nations and kingdoms are propagated, and are also abolished and destroyed. *Jon.-Nah. 446.*

Affection, Goodness, Mercy: No figures of speech can describe God's extraordinary affection toward us, for it is infinite and various. *Is. III:436.*

God's judgments are always founded on his goodness. *Jer. III:383.*

The jealousy of God is nothing else but the vehemence and ardour of his paternal love. *Joel-Obad. 75.*

Justice, Judgments: [On Jer. 9:24] Justice is to be taken for that faithful protection of God, by which he defends and preserves his own people; and judgment for the rigour which he exercises against the transgressors of the law. *Jer. I:501.*

These things are undivided, God's power and justice, though justice often does not appear. *Jer. V:193.*

What is God without his judgment? *Jer. V:426.*

Anger, Hatred: God, apart from Christ, is always angry with us. God does not hate us in his own workmanship . . . but he hates our uncleanness, which has extinguished the light of his image. *Rom. 76.*

When we contemplate God without a Mediator we cannot conceive of him otherwise than as angry with us. *Cor. II:237.*

God is no less worthy to be praised on account of his rigour, than on account of his mercy. *Ps. III:391.*

Righteousness: The righteousness of God is to be understood of his faithfulness, which he observes in maintaining and defending his own people. *Ps. II:229.*

The most remarkable instance of the righteousness of God is when he preserves, guards and delivers his people. *Is. III:447.*

Love: The love of God is not to be sought out of Christ. *Rom. 187.*

[God's] fatherly love, the fountain from whence everything else flows. *Cor. II:111.*

GOOD WORKS (*see also* Works)

There is nothing in which men resemble God more truly than in doing good to others. *Ps. I:487.*

God not only loves the faithful, but also their works. The grace of Christ, and not their own dignity or merit, is that which gives worth to our works. *Gen. I:266.*

[On Heb. 6:10] Reward . . . is reserved for works, not through merit, but through the free bounty of God alone, [and only if] we be first received into favour through the kind mediation of Christ . . . He recognises himself, and the work of his Spirit, in them. *Heb. 142.*

God never speaks except to render men fruitful in good works. *Four Last Bks of Moses IV:337.*

Outward works . . . the only testimonies to real repentance. *Dan. I:279.*

The design of Christian doctrine is that believers should exercise themselves in good works. *Past. Epp. 338.*

Election is the source and beginning of all good works. *Past. Epp. 195.*

In our good works nothing is our own. *Ezek. I:380.*

Our good works are pure gifts of God. [Calvin's Confession of Faith in the name of the Reformed Churches of France, 1542] *Tracts II:144.*

God alone does what is good in us, and all the good actions which men perform are from his Spirit. *John II:227.*

Not only do we receive righteousness by grace, through faith, but, as the moon borrows her light from the sun, so does the same faith render our works righteous. *Ps. IV:233.*

However defective the works of believers may be, they are nevertheless pleasing to God through the intervention of pardon . . . Reward is given to their efforts, even though imperfect, exactly as if they had fully discharged their duty. *Four Last Bks of Moses III:214.*

Works are just before God to the extent that we seek to render worship and obedience to him by them. *Rom. 69.*

Our works are counted righteous in the sight of God, because any imperfections in them are obliterated by the blood of Christ. *Rom. 73.*

The spots and blemishes of our works are covered by the purity of Christ. *Rom. 87.*

[On 2 Cor. 5:11] After he has received us into favour, he receives our works also by a gracious acceptance. *Cor. II:226.*

The contrite heart abjures the idea of merit, and has no dealings with God upon the principle of exchange. *Ps. II:306.*

Even after regeneration no work which men perform can please God unless he pardons the sin which mingles with it. *Ps. I:524.*

Our works, perfumed by the odour of Christ's grace, emit a sweet fragrance in God's presence, while otherwise they would have a fœtid smell. *Heb. 357.*

The merit of works ceases when righteousness is sought by faith. *Gen. I:407.*

All religious services which are not perfumed with the odour of faith, are of an ill-savour before God. *Gen. I:282.*

All things in men which please us under the colour of virtue, are like wine spoiled by the odour of the cask. *Gen. I:285.*

All works done before faith . . . were nothing but mere sins (being defiled from their root), and were offensive to the Lord. *Gen. I:195.*

Man is not possessed of free will for good works, unless he be assisted by grace, and that special grace which is bestowed upon the elect alone in regeneration. *Inst. II:ii.6.*

According to the constitution of our nature, oil might be extracted from a stone sooner than we could perform a good work. *Inst. III:xiv.5*

All our righteousnesses are odious in the Divine view, unless they are perfumed with the holiness of Christ. *Inst. III:xiv.16.*

Not only our persons, but even our works, are justified by faith alone. *Inst. III:xviii.10.*

Whatever is laudable in our works proceeds from the grace of God. *Inst. III:xv.3.*

In order that [the saints'] works may please God it is necessary that these works themselves should be justified by gratuitous imputation; but some evil is always inherent in them. *Gen. I:409.*

Whatever God grants to good works ought to be received as from grace. *Gen. I:572.*

While men are congratulating themselves on account of the external mask of righteousness which they wear, the Lord is at the same time weighing, in his own balance, the latent impurity of their hearts. *Inst. III:xii.5.*

It is easy for anyone in the cloisters of the schools to indulge himself in idle speculations on the merit of works to justify men; but when he comes into the presence of God he must bid farewell to these amusements, for there the business is transacted with seriousness, and no ludicrous logomachy practised. *Inst. III:xii.1.*

We cannot think of ourselves as we ought to think, without utterly despising everything that may be supposed an excellence in us. *Inst. III:xii.6.*

Looking for the reward of good works we must wait patiently till the last day, the day of resurrection. *Syn. Gosp. I:311.*

The best work that ever was, if brought by God to judgment, will be found stained by some blemish. [Antidote to the Council of Trent] *Tracts III:134.*

GOSPEL

Gospel (*euangelion*) means 'the glad and delightful message of grace exhibited to us in Christ'. *John I:20.*

The doctrine of the gospel is a heavenly mystery, which cannot be comprehended by the most learned and talented among men (1 Cor. 2:14) *Dan. I:155.*

The whole gospel is contained in Christ. *Acts I:15.*

Christ with his gospel had been promised, and always expected, from the beginning of the world (Rom. 1:1). *Acts I:15.*

Taking the word gospel in a large sense, it comprehends all those testimonies which God formerly gave to the fathers, of his mercy and paternal favour; but it is more eminently applicable to the promulgation of grace exhibited in Christ. *Inst. II:ix.2.*

The gospel contains nothing else than repentance and faith. *Ezek. II:174.*

Christ's gospel is the sceptre of his kingdom. *Syn. Gosp. I:447.*

The gospel in its very nature, breathes the odour of life; but if we are stubborn and rebellious, this grace will become a ground of terror, and Christ will convert the very doctrine of his salvation into a sword and arrows against us. *Ps. II:183.*

[On Gen. 3:15] In that sentence the remission of sins and the grace of eternal salvation is contained. *Gen. I:178.*

[On Is. 40:8] This passage comprehends the whole gospel in a few words. *Is. III:212.*

[On Is. 55:19] The principal end and use of the law [is] to invite men to God. *Is. III:421.*

The glory of the gospel was always joined with the cross and divers troubles. *Acts I:240.*

God, in the gospel, adds vehemence and sharp goads to the truth. *Jer. II:231.*

The gospel can be understood by faith alone – not by reason, nor by the perspicacity of the human understanding. *Philipp.-Col. 174.*

The gospel cannot be published without instantly driving the world to rage. *John II:123.*

The gospel is always a fruitful seed as to its power, but not as to its produce. *Syn. Gosp. II:114.*

By *another gospel* [Paul] means one to which the inventions of other men are added. *Gal. 34.*

GOVERNMENT

The two eyes in a true and legitimate government are the judges and the pastors of the Church. *Jer. IV:194.*

[On Dan. 5:25–28] God has prescribed a certain time for all kingdoms. *Dan. I:343.*

Without the sword laws are dead. *Syn. Gosp. I:195.*

Those who destroy political order are rebellious against God. *Syn. Gosp. III:45.*

There is no kind of government to which we ought not to submit. *Gen. Epp. 82.*

The magisterial office excels every other, because in governing mankind God himself is represented. *Gen. Epp. 401.*

The peculiar government of God is that of his Church only, where, by his word and Spirit, he bends the hearts of men to obedience, so that they follow him voluntarily and willingly, being taught inwardly and outwardly – inwardly by the influence of his Spirit; outwardly by the preaching of the word (Ps. 90). *Jon.-Nah. 261.*

GRACE OF GOD

That [God] pays any attention to us is entirely the result of his grace. *Is. III:474.*

The restoration of the Church proceeds only from the grace of God. *Is. II:420.*

Grace, properly speaking, is in God, and it is the effect of grace which is in us. *Rom. 115.*

Paul makes grace common to all men (Rom. 5:18) . . . not because it in fact extends to all, but because it is offered to all. *Rom. 117, 118.*

He who is the foundation of the covenant of grace, held also the highest rank in the giving of the law. *Gal. 102.*

None can require of [God] an equal distribution of grace, the inequality of which demonstrates it to be truly gratuitous. *Inst. III:xxi.6.*

Illustrations of God's grace

[On Gen. 6:8, *Noah found grace*] Whence did he attain this integrity but from the preventing grace of God? *Gen. I:251.*

The deliverance of Noah was a magnificent work of grace, and worthy of everlasting remembrance. *Gen. I:278.*

In Joseph a lively image of grace is presented . . . God of his mere grace conferred peculiar honour on the boy . . . He was ordained to be chief by the good pleasure of God. *Gen. II:261.*

The deliverance of God's people from Egypt . . . the archetype or original copy of the grace of God. *Ps. I:269.*

The holy people are blessed only though the grace of the Mediator. *Gen. I:349.*

[The sacraments] . . . mirrors, in which we may contemplate the riches of grace which God imparts to us. *Inst. IV:xiv.6.*

Grace and Faith

Nothing but pure grace is put before faith. *Rom. 94.*

Faith itself . . . is a part of grace. *Rom. 217.*

Grace and Works

Grace and reward are incompatible . . . Whatever God grants to good works, ought to be received as from grace. *Gen. I:572.*

Whenever the faithful vow to [God], they do not look to what they are able to do . . . but they depend upon the grace of God. *Ps. IV:480.*

The Lord . . . may manifest his free grace, by giving to some what they never deserve, while, by not giving to all, he declares the demerit of all. *Inst. III:xxiii.11.*

Whatever is laudable in our works proceeds from the grace of God. *Inst. III:xv.3.*

Grace and Election

[On Ps. 33:12] It proceeds from the fountain of God's gracious electing love that we are accounted the people of God . . . We have no interest in him at all unless he prevent us by his grace. *Ps. I:548.*

God vouchsafes to those whom he has determined to call to salvation special grace. *Ps. I:317.*

Grace and Conversion

God not only offers his grace in the outward preaching, but at the same time in the renewing of our hearts. *Hos. 116.*

God anticipates us by his grace, and also calls us to himself . . . We do not turn through our own will or efforts, but it is the Spirit's work. *Jer. III:233.*

No man is rescued from the tyranny of the devil . . . till the grace of God go before; for no man will redeem himself. *Is. III:73.*

The grace of God has no charms for men till the Holy Spirit gives them a taste for it. *Inst. III:xxiv.14.*

Grace maligned

The doctrine of grace has always been calumniated by the ungodly. *Gen. Epp. 170.*

Whatever mixture men study to add from the power of free will to the grace of God, is only a corruption of it; just as if anyone should dilute good wine with dirty or bitter water. *Inst. II:v.15.*

[Pelagians] . . . the enemies of the grace of God [and their] idol of free will. *Inst. II:v.11.*

GRATITUDE

The gifts which we receive from God's hand ought to be invitations to gratitude. *Ezek. II:111.*

Gratitude will have this effect upon us – that the will of God will be the grand sum of our desires. *Philipp.-Col. 120.*

The best means . . . of cherishing in us habitually a spirit of .gratitude towards God, is to expel from our minds this foolish opinion of our own ability. *Ps. II:153.*

[On Ps. 135:1] There is no sacrifice in which [God] takes greater delight than the expression of our gratitude. *Ps. V:171.*

Not even their gratitude was acceptable to [God] except through the sacrifice of the Mediator. *Four Last Bks of Moses II:295.*

GUIDANCE

God sustains us by his word in the deepest afflictions as upon a vast sea, and as long as his teaching remains to us we have, as it were, a chart of guidance which will bring us safely into harbour. *Ezek. I:273.*

Walk in the light of faith . . . within the limits of God's word. *Syn. Gosp. III:153.*

We cannot otherwise know the will of God save only by his word. *Acts I:122.*

[On Rom. 14:23] The first principle . . . of upright living . . . is to rest with confidence on the Word of God, and go wherever it calls us. *Rom. 302.*

[God's] will is not to be sought anywhere else than in his word. *Philipp.-Col. 142.*

The Spirit will only thus guide us to a right discrimination, when we render all our thoughts subject to God's word. *Gen. Epp. 231.*

One of the chief things which belong to faith, not to move a step except God's word shows us the way. *Heb. 278.*

It is a genuine proof of obedience when we simply obey God, however numerous the obstacles. *Jon.-Nah.24.*

It is better, with closed eyes, to follow God as our guide, than, by relying on our own prudence, to wander. *Gen. I:344.*

[Peter walking on the water] Now, without the wings of faith, he desires to fly at will. *Syn. Gosp. II:241.*

[On Peter's request] Let believers . . . beware of excessive haste. *Syn. Gosp. II:241.*

Satan always comes forth when we resolve to obey God. *Jon.-Nah. 30.*

Disordered then will be the whole course of our life, except God presides over and guides us, and raises up over us . . . his own banner. *Jon.-Nah. 28.*

HAPPINESS

A happy life depends on a good conscience. *Ps. 1:7.*

He who has God as his portion is destitute of nothing which is requisite to constitute a happy life. *Ps. I:226.*

Though men pray for blessings on each other, God declares himself to be the sole Dispenser of perfect happiness. *Gen. II:240.*

The highest and best part of a happy life consists in this, that God forgives a man's guilt, and receives him graciously into his favour. *Ps. I:521.*

The only way to walk through life happily, is to walk holily and harmlessly in the world, in the service and fear of God. *Ps. I:555.*

While all men seek after happiness, scarcely one in a hundred looks for it from God. *Ps. II:44.*

Whoever has obtained Christ wants nothing that is necessary to perfect happiness. *Syn. Gosp. II:290.*

The kingdom of God among men is nothing else than a restoration to a happy life . . . It is true and everlasting happiness . . . 'newness of life'. *Syn. Gosp. I:178.*

The full perfection of a happy life consists in the knowledge of God, which we obtain by faith. *Is. III:18.*

He who has God for his inheritance does not exult in fading joy, but . . . enjoys the solid happiness of eternal life. *Gen. I:407.*

Liberty . . . will be destructive to us, until God undertake the care of us, and prepares and forms us, that we may bear his yoke . . . When we obey God, we possess true and real happiness. *Jer. IV:15.*

The disciples of Christ must learn the philosophy of placing their happiness beyond the world, and above the affections of the flesh. *Syn. Gosp. I:260.*

They who desire to be happy in the world renounce heaven. *Syn. Gosp. I:333.*

All happiness is ruinous which does not flow from the fountain of God's gratuitous love . . . a cursed happiness. *Zech.-Mal. 46.*

The happiness and prosperity which the ungodly enjoy is only a mask or phantom. *Ps. II:25.*

Those who fear his name are not left to the poor privilege of rejoicing for a few days, but secured in a permanent heritage of happiness. *Ps. II:415.*

The true security for a happy life lies in being persuaded that we are under Divine government. *Ps. II:416.*

True happiness consists in our apprehending the Divine goodness which, filling our hearts with joy, may stir us up to praise and thanksgiving. *Ps. III:429.*

Man, without the knowledge of God, being the most miserable object that can be imagined, the discovery which God has been pleased to make to us in his Word, of his fatherly love, is an incomparable treasure of perfect happiness. *Ps. IV:132.*

HEALING

The first step of healing is repentance. *Is. I:219.*

[On Mark 9:17] Our diseases are effectually counteracted by heavenly medicine. *Syn. Gosp. II:323.*

The gift of healing was temporary. *Gen. Epp. 356.*

Christ bestowed on the Apostles the gift of healing, not as an inheritance which they should hand down to posterity, but as a temporary seal of the doctrine of the gospel. *Syn. Gosp. II:6.*

[On Is. 53:4] Christ . . . was appointed not to cure bodies, but rather to cure souls. *Is. IV:115.*

All diseases are . . . light punishments wherewith God doth punish us . . . In more grievous scourges he useth Satan as the minister of his wrath, and as it were an hangman. *Acts I:444.*

All know that the gift of healing was not perpetual . . . The anointers of this day are no more ministers of the grace of which James speaks than the player who acted Agamemnon on the stage was a king. [Antidote to the Council of Trent] *Tracts III:290.*

HEATHEN

The foolish heathen made for themselves as many gods as they saw stars in the heavens. There was scarcely an animal, indeed, which the Egyptians did not consider an image of God. *Inst. I:xi.1.*

The Lord afforded them [the heathen] . . . some slight sense of his Divinity, that they might not be able to plead ignorance as an excuse for impiety. *Inst. II:ii.18.*

Heathens shall indeed be punished, and no excuse of ignorance shall be of any avail to them; but far heavier shall be the punishment of those who shall abuse the grace of God. *Is. III:381.*

HEAVEN

Very few persons are concerned about the way that leads to heaven, but all are anxious to know, before the time, what passes there. *Inst. III:xxv.11.*

[On bold speculators] They leave not a corner of heaven unexplored. *Inst. III:xxv.11.*

The Lord almost always places the reward of labours and the crown of victory in heaven. *Inst. III:xv.4.*

If we believe heaven to be our country, it is better for us to transmit our wealth thither, than to retain it here, where we may lose it by a sudden removal. *Inst. III:xviii.6.*

Heaven won for God's people by Christ

[Christ's] humiliation and descent into hell raised us to heaven. *John I:267.*

Christ was sunk into the depths of ignominy, that he might obtain for us, by his humiliation, an ascent to the heavenly glory. *Syn. Gosp. III:282.*

[God] determined that his Son should be cast out of the city as unworthy of human intercourse, that he might admit us into his heavenly kingdom with the angels. *Syn. Gosp. III:296.*

Heaven and the Old Testament saints

The fathers under the Law embraced by faith, while they lived, that inheritance of the heavenly life unto which they were admitted at death. *Syn. Gosp. II:188.*

Abraham by faith had looked up to heaven. *Gen. I:579.*

[On Heb. 11:15. The fathers] in spirit, amid dark clouds, took a flight into the celestial country. *Heb. 284.*

[God] appointed the land of Canaan as a mirror and pledge to them of the celestial inheritance. *Gen. II:91.*

[Abraham's bosom] That quiet harbour at which believers arrive after the navigation of the present life. *Syn. Gosp. II:188.*

Meditation on heaven

Meditation on the heavenly life begins with regeneration. *Past. Epp. 319.*

Meditation . . . upon the heavenly life stirs up our affections both to the worship of God, and to exercises of love. *Philipp.-Col. 139.*

[On 2 Cor. 5] The true glory of Christians lies beyond this world . . . [We should] set ourselves with the whole bent of our mind to meditation on a blessed immortality. *Cor. II:105.*

If meditation on the heavenly life were the prevailing sentiment in our hearts, the world would have no influence in detaining us. *John II:30.*

[On Matt. 25:31] Believers, in order to encourage themselves to a holy and upright conduct, ought to contemplate with the eyes of faith the heavenly life which . . . will be manifested at the last coming of Christ. *Syn. Gosp. III:174.*

Whilst we travel through the world we ought always to erect our minds and senses towards heaven. *Ezek. I:254.*

If we would perceive the worthlessness of this fading life, we must be deeply affected by the view of the heavenly life. *Syn. Gosp. II:305.*

No man can meditate on the heavenly life unless he be dead to the world and to himself. *Is. IV:242.*

The link between earth and heaven

. . . this principle . . . that whatever benefits the Lord confers on the faithful in this life, are intended to confirm them in the hope of the eternal inheritance. *Hab.-Hagg. 76.*

The godly have no other reason for living here than that, being sojourners in the world, they may travel rapidly towards their heavenly country. *John I:241.*

The Lord, by calling us to heaven, withdraws us from the earth. *Past. Epp. 320.*

There is no place for us among God's children, except we renounce the world, and there will be no inheritance in heaven, except we become pilgrims on earth. *Heb. 285.*

We recumb on God when we cast our anchor in heaven. *Jer. III:144.*

Two prayers of John Calvin

May we be cast down in ourselves and be raised by hope and faith towards heaven; when prostrate before thy face, may we so conduct ourselves in the world, as in the interval to become free from all the depraved desires and passions of our flesh, and dwell mentally in heaven. Then at length may we be withdrawn from this earthly warfare, and arrive at that celestial rest which thou hast prepared for us, through the same Jesus Christ our Lord. Amen. [Close of Lecture 53 on Daniel] *Dan. II:246.*

Grant, Almighty God, that . . . we may stand fixed in our watch-tower . . . until at length we ascend, above all watch-towers, into that blessed rest, where we shall no more watch . . . but see, face to face, in thine image, whatever can be wished, and whatever is needful for our perfect happiness, through Christ our Lord. Amen. [Close of Lecture 109 on the Minor Prophets] *Hab.-Hagg. 69.*

HEAVENLY SESSION OF CHRIST

He appears there before God to defend us by his advocacy. *Heb. 216.*

Unless Christ were seated at the Father's right hand, and had obtained supreme dominion, causing every knee to bow before him, the Church could never exercise its power. *Dan. II:78.*

[On Heb. 10:19] It is a perpetual consecration of the way, because the blood of Christ is always in a manner distilling before the presence of the Father, in order to irrigate heaven and earth. *Heb. 235.*

HELL

Scripture's descriptions of hell

These forms of speech denote, in a manner suited to our feeble capacity, a dreadful torment which no man can now comprehend, and no language can express. *Syn. Gosp. I:201.*

There can be no doubt but that, by such modes of expression, the Holy Spirit intended to confound all our faculties with horror. *Inst. III:xxv.12.*

The reprobate will be delivered over into eternal fire with their bodies . . . the instruments of perpetrating evil. *Gen. I:166.*

No one will ever seriously resort to the mercy of God, but he who, having been touched with the threatening of God, shall dread that judgment of eternal death. *Gen. I:255.*

Men are seldom if ever drawn to repentance, except by the fear of punishment. *Gen. II:229.*

[Tophet] was in sight of the temple. *Jer. I:412.*

The fire through which the five cities perished was a type of the eternal fire . . . Whenever the prophets wished to designate some memorable and dreadful judgment of God, they painted it under the figure of sulphurous fire. *Gen. Epp. 436.*

Hell anticipated in a bad conscience

'Those build for hell who build against their conscience.' *Cor. I:280.*

Men . . . choose to seek their safety in hell itself, rather than in heaven, whenever they follow their own reason. *Gen. I:510.*

How miserable and wretched is a doubting conscience . . . Hell reigns where there is no peace with God . . . We . . . carry always a hell within us. *Gen. Epp. 167.*

The soul is exposed to innumerable evils, so that we find always a hell within us. *Gen. Epp. 204.*

HERESY

Its causes

Almost all corruptions of doctrine flow from the pride of men. *Acts II:258.*

Ambition is the mother of all heresies. *Acts II:258*
[On Tit. 3:10] Every person who, by his over-weening pride, breaks up the unity of the Church, is pronounced by Paul to be a 'heretic'. *Past. Epp. 341.*

Envy or pride is the mother of almost all heresies. *Cor. I:366.*

Its character

A heresy or sect and the unity of the Church – are things totally opposite to each other. *Past. Epp. 342.*

The perplexed and ambiguous phraseology of the heretics. *John I:28.*

If we would have peace with God, we must strive against those which contemn him. *Acts II:431.*

Some examples

[On the Arian heresy] Who can dare to censure those good men, as quarrelsome and contentious, for having kindled such a flame of controversy, and disturbed the peace of the Church on account of one little word? That little word distinguished Christians, who held the pure faith, from sacrilegious Arians. *Inst. I:xiii.4.*

[On the Trinity] To compose a catalogue of the errors, by which the purity of the faith has been attacked on this point of doctrine, would be too prolix and tedious. *Inst. I:xiii.22.*

[On the 'falling away', 2 Thess. 2:3] This we see accomplished in popery. The defection has . . . spread more widely, for since Mohammed was an apostate, he turned his followers, the Turks, from Christ. All heretics have destroyed the unity of the Church by their sects, and thus there have been as many secessions from Christ. *Thess. 399.*

[On Osiander's] monstrous notion of essential righteous-ness . . . This principle is like a cuttle-fish, which, by the emission of black and turbid blood, conceals its many tails . . .

[143]

There is a necessity for a vigorous opposition to it, unless we mean to submit to be openly robbed of that righteousness which alone affords us any confidence concerning our salvation. *Inst. III:xi.5.*

[In general] . . . those foolish and absurd notions, which were disseminated by Satan many years ago, and are frequently springing up afresh. *Inst. I:xiv.9.*

A warning

Nothing is more to be dreaded than that the Lord should extinguish the light of sound doctrine, and suffer us to go astray in darkness. *Joel-Obad. 270.*

HOLINESS

Its Origin in God

The calling of God brings holiness with it. *Hos. 255.*

When we hear any mention of our union with God, we should remember that holiness must be the bond of it. *Inst. III:vi.2.*

No one leads a holy life except he is united to God. *Gen. Epp. 164.*

Brought to us by God's Word

A strict adherence to the word of God constitutes spiritual chastity . . . The holiness, which is truly connected with the worship of God, comes from his word. *Ps. IV:240.*

It is not unusual in Scripture, to seek a description of a pious and holy life, from the Second Table of the Law. *Gen. I:482.*

Promises are necessary to us, to excite and encourage us to holiness of life, so threatenings are . . . necessary to restrain us by anxiety and fear. *Syn. Gosp. III:182.*

Imparted to us by Christ

We . . . are only a sweet smell unto God as being covered with the garment of Christ . . . Nothing proceeds from us pleasing to God except through the intervention of the grace of the

Mediator . . . Our very holinesses are so impure as to need pardon. *Four Last Bks of Moses II:201, 202.*

Fruitful in our own lives

A man is acceptable to God only if he brings Him holiness of heart. *Thess. 356.*

Holiness of life and rectitude on the part of Christians is the glory of the gospel. *Thess. 413.*

No man . . . is a believer who is not also a saint; . . . no man is a saint who is not a believer. *Eph. 196.*

There is . . . no part of our life which is not to be redolent with this good odour of holiness. *Gen. Epp. 47.*

Warnings

No man can rightly handle the doctrine of godliness, unless the fear of God reign . . . in him. *Acts II:312.*

There is nothing more opposed to holiness than the impurity of fornication, which corrupts the whole man. *Thess. 359.*

HOLY SPIRIT

His Personality

Afterwards arose Sabellius, who considered the names of Father, Son and Holy Spirit, as little more than empty sounds. *Inst. I:xiii.4.*

The Spirit of God, also, has an eloquence of his own. *Cor. I:77.*

The Spirit and the Word

It is incumbent on us diligently to read and attend to the Scripture, if we would receive any advantage or satisfaction from the Spirit of God. *Inst. I:ix.2.*

The Holy Spirit so adheres to his own truth, . . . that he only displays and exerts his power where the word is received with due reverence and honour. *Inst. I:ix.3.*

It is his [the Spirit's] determination to be connected with the word by an indissoluble bond; and this was declared by Christ when he promised him to his Church. *Inst. IV:viii.13.*

When God shines into us by his Spirit, he at the same time causes that sacred truth which endures for ever to shine forth in the mirror of his word. *Ps. V:29.*

When they boast extravagantly of the Spirit, the tendency certainly is to sink and bury the Word of God, that they may make room for their own falsehoods. [Calvin's Reply to Sadoleto] *Tracts I:36.*

The efficacy of the Spirit ought not to be separated from the preaching of the Gospel (2 Cor. 3:6) *Is. IV:39.*

[On Is. 59:21] The 'Spirit' is joined with the word, because, without the efficacy of the Spirit, the preaching of the gospel would avail nothing. *Is. IV:271.*

[God] bends the hearts of men to obedience, so that they follow him voluntarily and willingly, being taught . . . inwardly by the influence of the Spirit, outwardly by the preaching of the word. *Jon.-Nah. 261.*

God does not bestow the Spirit on his people, in order to set aside the use of his word, but rather to render it fruitful. *Syn. Gosp. III:375.*

Many foolishly imagine that Christ taught only so as to lay down the first lessons, and then to send the disciples to a higher school . . . They substitute the Spirit in his place . . . As soon as the Spirit is separated from the word of Christ, the door is open to all kinds of delusions and impostures. *John II:145.*

Many, to the end they may amplify the grace of the Spirit, feign to themselves certain inspired persons [Gk. *enthusiasmous*], that they may leave no use of the external word. *Acts II:103.*

The Spirit is given us, not that he may bring contempt of the word, but rather . . . instil into our minds, and write in our hearts the faith thereof. *Acts II:104.*

[146]

[On 2 Cor. 1:21, *anointing*] God, by pouring down upon us the heavenly grace of the Spirit, does, in this manner, *seal* upon our hearts the certainty of his own word. *Cor. II:140.*

What God demands from us by his word he likewise bestows by his Spirit, so that we are strengthened in the grace which he has given to us. *Past. Epp. 208.*

The Spirit and Christ

Christ employs his Spirit to sprinkle us in order to wash us by his own blood when he leads us to true repentance, when he purifies us from depraved lusts of our flesh, when he imbues us with the precious gift of his own righteousness. *Heb. 213.*

[On the burnt sacrifices] By the fire the efficacy of the Spirit is represented, on which all the profit of the sacrifices depends; for unless Christ had suffered in the Spirit, He would not have been a propitiatory sacrifice. Fire, then, was as the condiment which gave their true savour to the sacrifices, because the blood of Christ was to be consecrated by the Spirit. *Four Last Bks of Moses II:326.*

Whatever gifts are offered us in Christ, we receive by the agency of the Spirit. [Calvin's Catechism of the Church of Geneva, 1536, 1541] *Tracts II:50.*

The gift of the Spirit was a fruit of the resurrection of Christ. *Acts I:100.*

[On 1 Cor. 6:11] Christ . . . is the source of all blessings to us; but Christ himself, with all his blessings, is communicated to us by the Spirit . . . The Author of faith is the Spirit. *Cor. I:212.*

We are partakers of the Holy Spirit, in proportion to the intercourse we maintain with Christ; the Spirit will be found nowhere but in Christ. *Eph. 262.*

The Holy Spirit is the bond by which Christ efficaciously unites us to himself. *Inst. III:i.1.*

The Work of the Spirit

(a) in the world: The Holy Spirit . . . being universally diffused, sustains and animates all things in heaven and in earth. *Inst. I:xiii.14.*

(b) in the believer: Till the Spirit has become our instructor, all that we know is folly and ignorance. *Eph. 212.*

The increase, as well as the commencement, of everything good in us, comes from the Holy Spirit. *Eph. 261.*

[On 1 John 2:20 *an unction from the Holy One*] Men are not rightly made wise by the acumen of their own minds, but by the illumination of the Holy Spirit . . . and we are not otherwise made partakers of the Spirit than through Christ. *Gen. Epp. 194.*

The smallest drop of the Spirit . . . resembles an ever-flowing fountain, which never dries up. *Past. Epp. 335.*

The Spirit is a pledge of our adoption. *Gen. Epp. 203.*

[The Holy Spirit] ratifies the gospel to us. *Inst. III:ii.36.*

The Holy Spirit not only originates faith, but increases it by degrees, till he conducts us by it all the way to the heavenly kingdom. *Inst. III:ii.33.*

We have not a particle of vigour in us, but what we have received from the Holy Spirit, who has chosen his residence in Christ, that those heavenly riches, which we so greatly need, may from him be copiously distributed to us. *Inst. II:xx.5.*

Everyone's advancement in piety is the secret work of the Spirit. *Inst. III:xxiv.13.*

God gives us the Spirit, to be the director of our prayers, to suggest what is right, and to regulate our affections. *Inst. III:xx.5.*

The Spirit of God acts the part of a judge within us. *Gen. I:241.*

We come to the sanctuary under the leading of the Holy Spirit. *Ps. II:458.*

It is the peculiar work of the Holy Spirit to sprinkle our consciences inwardly with the blood of Christ, and, by removing the sense of guilt, to secure our access into the presence of God. *Ps. II:295.*

The reason . . . why we do not succumb, even in the severest conflicts, is nothing else than because we receive the aid of the Holy Spirit. *Ps. III:152.*

It is the special work of God to turn to himself the hearts of men by the secret influence of his Holy Spirit. *Ps. III:235.*

An unfeigned love of God's law is an undoubted evidence of adoption, since this love is the work of the Holy Spirit. *Ps. V:35.*

When anything grows in us, and our endowments manifest themselves more conspicuously, our progress is only derived from the continued operation of the Spirit. *Four Last Bks of Moses III:292.*

[On Is. 53:1] No man can come to God but by an extraordinary revelation of the Spirit. *Is. IV:112.*

It is not sufficient for us to be imbued once with the illumination of the Holy Spirit, unless God works in us daily . . . This gift [is] necessary for every act. *Ezek. I:352.*

The proper discrimination between truth and falsehood . . . does not arise from the sagacity of our own mind, but comes to us from the Spirit of wisdom. *Syn. Gosp. III:356.*

[On John 4:13] The Holy Spirit is a continually flowing fountain . . . which will never fail us. *John I:151.*

[On the outpouring of the Spirit on the day of Pentecost. Christ] baptiseth all the elect thus daily. *Acts I:40.*

The Spirit alone is to everyone a faithful and sure witness of his election, upon which perseverance depends. *Cor. I:59.*

There are two operations of the Spirit in faith; . . . it enlightens, and . . . it establishes the mind. *Eph. 208.*

When we have received the Spirit of God, his promises are confirmed to us, and no dread is felt that they will be revoked . . . Until we are supported by the testimony of the Spirit, we never rest upon them with unshaken confidence. *Eph. 209.*

[The day of Pentecost] All godly men since the beginning of the world were endued with the same spirit of understanding, of righteousness and sanctification, wherewith the Lord doth at this day illuminate and regenerate us. *Acts I:86.*

The gifts of the Spirit

We have nothing of the Spirit, except by regeneration. *Inst. II:iii.1.*

[The Holy Spirit] . . . may be justly called the key with which the treasures of the kingdom of heaven are unlocked to us; and his illumination constitutes our mental eyes to behold them. *Inst. III:i.4.*

None are called to obtain the riches of the Spirit but those who burn with desire of them. *John I:307.*

[On John 7:38] The Holy Spirit is like a living and continually flowing fountain in believers . . . Everyone partakes of the gifts and graces of the Holy Spirit according to the measure of his faith. *John I:308.*

If we will be enriched every now and then with new gifts of the Spirit, let us hold out unto God the lap of faith. *Acts I:220.*

The reprobate are sometimes endued by God with the gifts of the Spirit, to execute the office with which he invests them. . . . This is widely different from the sanctification of the Holy Spirit, which the Lord bestows on none but his own children. *John II:64.*

The gifts of the Spirit are not the gifts of nature. *Eph. 212.*

Sin against the Spirit

God . . . closes up the way of salvation against those who spurn the Holy Spirit, the only true guide. *Heb. 249.*

By detracting from the grace and power of God we make a direct attack on *the Spirit*, from whom they proceed, and in whom they are revealed to us. *Syn. Gosp. II:75.*

Blasphemy against the Spirit is a token of reprobation. *Syn. Gosp. II:76.*

No darkness is more dangerous for quenching the light of the Spirit than reliance on our own sagacity. *Syn. Gosp. III:375.*

A definition of the sin against the Holy Ghost, is first, . . . open rebellion against God in the transgression of the first table [of the Law]; secondly, . . . malicious rejection of the truth; lastly, *unbelief*; and malicious design. *Past. Epp. 36.*

HOPE

Faith is the mother of *hope. Cor. I:432.*

Hope has been appointed by God as the guardian of salvation. *Rom. 176.*

Hope is nothing else than perseverance in *faith. Cor. I:432.*

Hope is living and efficacious. *Gen. Epp. 422.*

True faith is ever connected with hope. *Heb. 146.*

[On Heb. 3:6] Hope is nothing else but the constancy of faith. *Heb. 81, 82.*

Faith and hope . . . are the wings by which our souls, rising above the world, are lifted up to God. *Ps. I:414.*

We derive alacrity from hope. *Gen. I:269.*

Hope is the foundation of patience. *Jer. V:419.*

By the word hope, [God] first requires faith, and then prayer, which arises from it, and thanksgiving, which necessarily follows. *Hos. 432.*

There would be no occasion for exercising hope, were our salvation complete. *Jer. V:413.*

[On Is. 30:19] Hope is nothing else than steadfastness of faith, when we wait calmly till the Lord fulfil what he has promised. *Is. II:368.*

[On Hab. 2:1] The tower . . . is patience, arising from hope . . . The tower is the recess of the mind, where we withdraw ourselves from the world . . . from the thoughts of the flesh. *Hab.-Hagg. 56.*

When hope animates us, there is a vigour in the whole body. *Hab.-Hagg. 303.*

[On Hagg. 2:20–23] God invites here the attention of the faithful to their election, so that they might hope for more than what the perception of the flesh could conceive or apprehend. *Hab.-Hagg. 388.*

It behoves us to ask . . . that [God] would increase our hope when it is small, awaken it when it is dormant, confirm it when it is wavering, strengthen it when it is weak, and raise it up when it is overthrown. *Ps. I:434.*

For hope, while it is silently expecting the Lord, restrains faith, that it may not be too precipitate; it confirms faith, that it may not waver in the Divine promises, or begin to doubt of the truth of them; it refreshes it, that it may not grow weary; it extends it to the farthest goal, that it may not fail in the midst of the course, or even at the entrance of it. *Inst. III:ii.42.*

HUMANITY OF CHRIST

No one will ever come to Christ as God, who despises him as man. *John I:268.*

[On Heb. 2:17] In Christ's human nature there are two things to be considered; the real flesh and the affections or feelings. *Heb. 74.*

Even during the time that he *emptied himself,* (Phil. 2:7) he continued to retain his divinity entire, though it was concealed under the veil of the flesh. *Syn. Gosp. II:317.*

Scripture everywhere teaches us, that as the Lord on earth took our humanity, so he has exalted it to heaven, withdrawing it from mortal condition, but not changing its nature. [Short Treatise on the Lord's Supper, 1540] *Tracts II:187.*

Christ derives no glory from his ancestors; . . . even . . . he himself has no glory in the flesh. . . . By his infinite purity, they were all cleansed. *Gen. II:278.*

[Christ] not only as God sanctifies us, but there is also the power of sanctifying in his human nature. *Heb. 64.*

[On Heb. 5:7] In this contest the Son of God had to engage . . .
because he sustained as a man in our flesh the judgment of God.
Heb. 122.

What was bestowed upon Christ's human nature was a free
gift . . . Whatever gifts he has received ought to be considered
as proceeding from the free grace of God . . . to be conferred
upon us. *Ps. I:104, 105.*

HUMILITY

Humility . . . a real annihilation of ourselves, proceeding from a
thorough knowledge of our own weakness, the entire absence of
lofty pretensions and a conviction that whatever excellence we
possess comes from the grace of God alone. *Syn. Gosp. II:165.*

[On Matt. 18:4] A short definition of humility. That man is
truly humble who never claims any personal merit in the sight
of God, nor proudly despises brethren, or aims at being thought
superior to them, but reckons it enough that he is one of the
members of Christ, and desires nothing more than that the
Head alone should be exalted. *Syn. Gosp. II:333.*

Whence comes true and genuine humility, except from a sense
of sin. *Hos. 486.*

Where God's Spirit does not reign, there is no humility, and
men ever swell with inward pride. *Hab.-Hagg. 52.*

True religion begins with teachableness; when we submit to
God and his word, it is really to enter on the work of
worshipping him aright. *Hab.-Hagg. 262.*

As we are extremely prone to arrogance and pride, we ought
carefully to seek to conduct ourselves in a meek and humble
manner, when favoured with God's singular benefits. *Hab.
-Hagg. 293.*

We cannot be formed and habituated to humility until we
submit to the yoke of God. *Zech.-Mal. 600.*

No man deserves to be reckoned one of Christ's flock, unless he
has made such proficiency under the teacher of humility, as to

claim nothing for himself, but condescend to cultivate brotherly love. *Syn. Gosp. II:424.*

Reverence always begets modesty. *John II:27.*

The higher any one of us shall be extolled, let him submit himself unto God with modesty and fear. *Acts I:238.*

[On 2 Cor. 12:1] It is humility alone, that can give stability to our greatness in the sight of God. *Cor. II:366.*

Humility . . . the mother of moderation . . . depends on a right estimate of God's gifts, and our own infirmities. *Philipp.-Col. 52–53.*

In meditating on the works of God, [the readers] must bring with them a sober, docile, mild, and humble spirit. [Introduction to Commentary on Genesis] *Gen. I:57.*

Ignorance of this principle [of election] evidently detracts from the Divine glory, and diminishes real humility . . . They who desire to extinguish this principle . . . pluck up humility by the roots. *Inst. III:xxi.1.*

How fitting it is that we should live and die humbly. *Gen. I:328.*

The whole human race is infected with the disease of pride; for by the gospel all the glory of the flesh is reduced to nothing . . . The doctrine of humility . . . is . . . confirmed by the precious blood of Christ. *Gen. II:264.*

The whole humility of man consists in the knowledge of himself. *Ps. I:133.*

Faith cannot be separated from the humility of which David speaks . . . a humility . . . unknown to the wicked. *Ps. II:306.*

Obedience . . . the mistress of humility. *Four Last Bks of Moses IV:78.*

That humility only is genuine which is framed in conformity to the Word of God. [Calvin's Reply to Sadoleto] *Tracts I:47.*

Nothing but the pure knowledge of God can teach us humility. *Is. III:97.*

[On Is. 40:11] God will be a shepherd to none but those who, in modesty and gentleness, shall imitate the sheep and the lambs. *Is. III:216.*

The godly, whose faith is . . . founded on humility . . . for it has for its guide and teacher the Spirit of God, that it may not go astray from the sure light of the word. *Is. III:270.*

The beginning of faith . . . is humility, by which we yield our senses as captives to God. *Is. III:331.*

The Church, so long as she is a pilgrim in this world, is subjected to the cross, that she may be humble and may be conformed to her Head . . . Her highest ornament and lustre is modesty. *Is. IV:42.*

Humility is the best preparation for faith, that there may be a submission to the word of God. *Jer. II:336.*

There must be docility, in order that God's word may obtain credit, authority, and favour among us. *Jer. III:211.*

Nothing is more contrary to faith than pride, as also humility is the principle of faith. *Jer. III:374.*

In prayer two things are necessary – faith and humility: by faith we rise up to God, and by humility we lie prostrate on the ground. *Jer. IV:332.*

Humility has its roots fixed deeply within . . . The root, which appears not on the surface, sustains the tree. *Jer. V:84.*

Humility is the beginning of true intelligence. *Ezek. I:81.*

No man is fit to be a teacher in the Church save only he who willingly submits himself that he may be a fellow-disciple with other men. *Acts I:390.*

Kneeling in time of prayer is a token of humility. *Acts I:402.*

Unity . . . to which humility is the first step. *Eph. 267.*

. . . such a consciousness of our weakness as produces humility and excites to prayer. *Syn. Gosp. III:125.*

Farewell, friendly reader; and if you have received any benefit from my labours, let me have the assistance of your prayers

[155]

with God our Father. [Closing words of Calvin's Preface to The
Institutes, Geneva, 1st August 1559] *Inst. I:19.*

Calvin's farewell words to the Senate of Geneva, when dying:
Your having borne patiently with my vehemence, which was
sometimes carried to excess; my sins, in this respect, I trust,
have been pardoned by God also . . . [Calvin] was buried in the
common cemetery of the city of Geneva, with no extraordinary
pomp, and, as he had commanded, without any grave-stone.
[Theodore Beza's Life of Calvin] *Tracts I: xc, xcvii.*

HYPOCRISY

[On Is. 1:28] Hypocrites have always been mingled with the
Church, and indeed are connected with it in the closest
manner. *Is. I:83.*

Where hypocrisy is, there can be no true calling on God. *Is.
I:61.*

The fervent devotion . . . of unbelievers, is their own executioner. *Is. III:373.*

Hypocrisy is never free from supercilious disdain and haughtiness. *Is. IV:383.*

Hypocrites are not ashamed to practise grosser impositions on
God than on men. *Syn. Gosp. I:190.*

Ambition is almost always connected with hypocrisy. *Syn. Gosp.
III:87.*

Hypocrites are so stupid that they do not feel their sores. *John
I:281.*

Hypocrisy is always proud and cruel. *John I:373.*

[On Ananias and Sapphira. God] declared by the visible
punishment of two, how horrible a judgment remaineth for all
hypocrites. *Acts I:199.*

Hypocrites . . . shroud themselves under zeal. *Acts I:243.*

. . . the intoxicating confidence in which hypocrites repose.
Rom. 144.

[156]

We are by nature hypocrites, fondly exalting ourselves by calumniating others. *Gen. Epp. 337.*

There is . . . no thicker darkness than that of unbelief, and hypocrisy is a horrible blindness. *Heb. 104.*

All who are not taught in the school of God are infected with deceit and hypocrisy. *Ps. V:40.*

IDOLATRY

Every one of us is, from his mother's womb, expert in inventing idols. *Acts II:413.*

How great is the leaning of the human soul to idolatry! *Four Last Bks of Moses II:121.*

Idols . . . so many masks under which the devil hides himself for the deception of the simple. *Four Last Bks of Moses IV:350.*

In the sight of God idolatry is a very base kind of fornication. *Is. IV:200.*

Feasting and play were two appendages of idolatry. *Cor. I:323.*

Among all nations a persuasion has existed concerning a supreme God who reigns alone. Afterwards they imagined inferior deities, and each fabricated a god for himself according to his taste. *Dan. I:133.*

Images are only the juggleries of Satan . . . the impostures of Satan . . . dead things. *Hab.-Hagg. 125, 126, 128.*

Such knowledge of God as now remains in men is nothing else than a frightful source of idolatry and of all superstitions. *John I:113.*

Though all men do not worship the same idols, they are all nevertheless in bondage to idolatry. *Rom. 338.*

Every statue, every image, by which foolish men seek to represent God, is a teacher of falsehood. *Jer. II:24.*

[157]

The remedy

The knowledge of the true God alone is sufficient for the abolishing of all idols . . . All is idolatry which men invent without his word. *Acts II:156.*

All who forsake the word fall into idolatry. *John I:160.*

The first difference between true worship and idolatry is this: when the godly take in hand nothing but what is agreeable to the Word of God. *Acts I:299.*

IGNORANCE

Its character

There is no greater darkness than ignorance of God. *Thess. 368.*

Nothing is so arrogant as ignorance. *Cor. I:274.*

Where pride is, *there* is ignorance of God. *Cor. I:274.*

That Platonic dogma is false, that ignorance alone is the cause of sin. *Gen. Epp. 46.*

Men sin more through insolence and pride than through ignorance. *Is. III:226.*

Ignorance always implies hypocrisy. *Is. III:426.*

Our ignorance is always accompanied by gross and shameful negligence. *Syn. Gosp. III:167.*

Its consequences

Ignorance of God . . . is a kind of madness which carries men headlong to every sort of impiety. *Jer. I:463.*

Ignorance is closely followed by obstinacy. *John II:57.*

A learned ignorance

To be ignorant of things which it is neither possible nor lawful to know, is to be learned. *Inst. III:xxiii.8.*

Nor let us be ashamed to be ignorant of some things relative to a subject [predestination] in which there is a kind of learned ignorance. *Inst. III:xxi.2.*

ILLUMINATION

A prayer of Calvin

Grant, Almighty God . . . that we may . . . distinguish between that common sense which thou hast bestowed upon us, and the illumination of thy Spirit, and the gift of faith . . . We entreat also from thee further progress and increase of the same faith, until at length thou bring us to the full manifestation of light. Then, being like thee, we shall behold thy glory face to face, and enjoy the same in Christ our Lord. Amen. [Prayer concluding Lecture 8 on Daniel] *Dan. I:161.*

There are three ways in which [God] acts the part of our teacher, instructing us by his word, enlightening our minds by the Spirit, and engraving instruction upon our hearts, so as to bring us to observe it with a true and cordial consent. *Ps. V:256, 257.*

The Spirit not merely . . . enlightens our minds, but as effectually influences the consent of our hearts, and as it were leads us by the hand. *Ps. V:257.*

[On Is. 8:16, *seal the law*] He compares the doctrine of the word to a *sealed* letter, which may . . . be felt and handled by many . . . but yet is read and understood by few, that is, by those to whom it is sent and addressed . . . The word is . . . *sealed* to those who derive no benefit from it, and is *sealed* in such a manner that the Lord unseals and opens it to his own people by the Spirit. *Is. I:282, 283.*

Spiritual illumination the gift of God

If God do not enlighten us with the spirit of discernment, we are not competent to behold the light which shines forth from his law, though it be constantly before us. *Ps. IV:410.*

As it belongs to [God] to give eyes to see, and to enlighten minds by the spirit of judgment and understanding, so he alone deprives us of all light, when he sees that . . . we . . . wish for darkness. *Is. II:320.*

The only thing which distinguishes the Elect from the Reprobate, is, that . . . [God] presents the former with new eyes . . . and inclines their hearts to obey his word. [The True Method of Reforming the Church] *Tracts III:253.*

It is [God's] peculiar office to illuminate our minds, so that we may comprehend heavenly mysteries. For although we are naturally endued with the greatest acuteness, which is also his gift . . . it does not reach to the heavens. *Dan. I:160.*

Out of Christ there is not even a spark of true *light* . . . [He is] *the life-giving light. John I:325.*

None believe but those whom God, of free grace, enlightens for his own good pleasure. *John II:42.*

The beginning of our conversion to God . . . is when he enlightens the hearts. *John II:44.*

In seeing without him we see not; it is he also which openeth the eyes of the mind. *Acts I:383.*

We are not wise, except when we are illuminated by God from above through his Spirit. *Gen. Epp. 325.*

Spiritual illumination is through the Holy Spirit

[The Holy Spirit] may be justly called the key with which the treasures of the kingdom of heaven are unlocked to us; and his illumination constitutes our mental eyes. *Inst. III:i.4.*

The understanding of spiritual things is a rare and singular gift of the Holy Spirit. *Dan I:148.*

No man can obtain faith by his own acuteness, but only by the secret illumination of the Spirit. *Syn. Gosp. II:39.*

The illumination of our minds by the Holy Spirit belongs to our renewal, and thus faith flows from regeneration as its source. *John I:44.*

As soon as any man begins to live by the Spirit, he is immediately endued with eyes to see Christ. *John II:95.*

There is a heavenly and secret wisdom that is contained in the gospel, which cannot be apprehended by any acuteness or perspicacity of intellect . . . but . . . by the revelation of the Spirit. *Cor. I:41.*

None but those who have been enlightened by the Holy Spirit have eyes to perceive what . . . is visible to the elect alone. *Past. Epp. 249.*

Men are not rightly made wise by the acumen of their own minds, but by the illumination of the Spirit. *Gen. Epp. 194.*

Spiritual illumination opens the Scriptures

[On Ps. 86:11] Having the law among his hands, he prays for the inward light of the Holy Spirit, that he may not labour in the unprofitable task of learning only the letter . . . Reading or hearing is not enough, unless God impart to us inward light by his Spirit. *Ps. III:387, 388.*

God gives light to us by his word . . . We do not receive the illumination of the Spirit of God to make us contemn the external word, and take pleasure only in secret inspirations, like many fanatics who . . . substitute their own wild speculations. *Ps. IV:413.*

In proportion to the spirit of knowledge given to us, our regard for the law of God, and our delight in meditating on it, ought to increase. *Ps. IV:420.*

[On Ps. 119:130] The light of the truth revealed in God's word, is so distinct that the very first sight of it illuminates the mind. *Ps. V·10.*

Only when God shines in us by the light of His Holy Spirit is there any profit from the Word. *Rom. 232.*

The spirit of discernment will be given us, who, as a faithful interpreter, will open to us the meaning of what is said in Scripture. *Gen. Epp. 237, 238.*

The Lord does not shine upon us except when we take the word as our light. *Gen. Epp. 388.*

The fruits of spiritual illumination

No man . . . can arrive at faith by his own sagacity; all are blind, until they are illuminated by the Spirit of God. *John I:276.*

[On Acts 15:7] Seeing that the elect are illuminate into the faith by a peculiar grace of the Spirit, doctrine shall bring forth no fruit, unless the Lord show forth his power in his ministers, in teaching the minds of those inwardly which hear, and in drawing their hearts inwardly. *Acts II:46.*

Whence cometh aptness to be taught, and a mind to obey, but from his Spirit? *Acts II:97.*

[On Lydia, Acts 16:14] Not faith alone, but all understanding and knowledge of spiritual things, is the peculiar gift of God. *Acts II:103.*

[Paul] speaks of the illumination of the Holy Spirit . . . to enlighten the mind by kindling it up with the light of truth, [and] transforming the whole man. *Philipp.-Col. 211.*

Warnings

Men never entertain a real hatred towards sin, unless God illuminates their minds and changes their hearts. *Jer. IV:102.*

No darkness is more dangerous for quenching the light of the Spirit than reliance on our own sagacity. *Syn. Gosp. III:375.*

All whom God does not enlighten with the Spirit of adoption are men of unsound mind; . . . while they are more and more blinded by the word of God, the blame rests wholly on themselves, because this blindness is voluntary. *Syn. Gosp. II:108.*

The effect of the habit of sinning is, that men grow hardened in their sins, and discern nothing, as if they were enveloped in thick darkness. *Ps. I:192.*

A prayer of Calvin

Grant, Almighty God, that as there is in us so little of right judgment . . . O grant that thy Spirit may always shine in us, and that being attentive to the light of thy word, we may also keep to the right way through the whole course of our pilgrimage . . . until [Christ] at length gathers us all into that celestial kingdom which he has purchased for us by his own blood. Amen. [Prayer concluding Lecture 113 on The Twelve Minor Prophets] *Hab.-Hagg. 124.*

IMAGE OF GOD

[God] . . . would have his image extant in us. For the soul wherein the image of God is properly engraven cannot be painted. *Acts II:171.*

The mind of man is [God's] true image. *Acts II:154.*

Nothing can bear the image of God but spirit, since God is a Spirit. [Psychopannychia] *Tracts III:424.*

. . . the rectitude and integrity of the whole soul, so that man reflects, like a mirror, the wisdom, righteousness, and goodness of God. *Col. 212.*

[Of fallen Adam] The image of God . . . has been miserably deformed, but . . . many excellent endowments . . . still remain. *Gen. Epp. 323.*

The [Old Testament] tabernacle was a sort of visible image of God. *Heb. 211.*

Spiritual regeneration, by which he creates anew his image in his elect. *Ps. IV:84.*

Since the image of God has been destroyed in us by the fall, we may judge from its restoration what it originally had been . . . Adam was endued with a right judgment, had affections in harmony with reason, had all his senses sound and well regulated, and truly excelled in everything good. Thus the chief seat of the Divine image was in his mind and heart. *Gen. I:94, 95.*

But now, although some obscure lineaments of that image are found remaining in us; yet are they so vitiated and maimed, that . . . no part is free from the infection of sin. *Gen. I:95.*

[God] appointed man . . . lord of the world . . . Thus man was rich before he was born. *Gen. I:96.*

[The soul] It is a brutish error . . . to despoil that part of us in which Divinity is eminently displayed. *Inst. III:xxv.6.*

No one can be injurious to his brother without wounding God himself . . . He deems himself violated in their person . . . He looks upon his own gifts in them. *Gen. I:295, 296.*

The face of Christ, dishonoured by spitting and blows, has restored to us that image which had been disfigured, and almost effaced, by sin. *Syn. Gosp. III:259.*

It was not . . . possible for God to act more liberally towards man, than by impressing his own glory upon him. *Gen. I:228.*

The image of God [in man] includes all the excellence in which the nature of man surpasses all the other species of animals. The term, therefore, denotes the integrity which Adam possessed, when he was endued with a right understanding, when he had affections regulated by reason, and all his senses governed in proper order, and when, in the excellency of his nature, he truly resembled the excellence of his Creator. And though the principal seat of the Divine image was in the mind and heart, or in the soul and its faculties, yet there was no part of man, not even the body, which was not adorned with some rays of its glory. *Inst. I:xv.3.*

Although we allow that the Divine image was not utterly annihilated and effaced in him, yet it was so corrupted that whatever remains is but horrible deformity. *Inst. I:xv.3.*

What holds the principal place in the renovation of the Divine image, must also have held the same place in the creation of it at first. *Inst. I:xv.4.*

We must not regard the intrinsic merit of men, but must consider the image of God in them, to which we owe all possible honour and love. *Inst. III:vii.6.*

IMMORTALITY (see Intermediate State)

[On Jer. 38:16] The word *chi* [Hebrew], when applied to God, denotes a life different from what is in men . . . God alone is immortal. *Jer. IV:405.*

[164]

By the 'soul' I understand an immortal, yet created essence, which is the nobler part of [man] *Inst. I:xv.2.*

Enoch, an example of immortality. *Gen. I:231.*

To nothing are we more prone than to dream of immortality on earth, unless death is frequently brought before our eyes. *Gen. I:230.*

It behoves us, with all the holy Fathers, to press towards the mark of a happy immortality. *Gen. I:66.*

Our souls do not wander up and down when they flit out of our bodies, but . . . Christ receiveth them, that he may keep them faithfully. *Acts I:319.*

Burial is . . . a pledge . . . of immortality . . . a mirror of a future life. *Jer. III:108.*

Whoever destroys the resurrection deprives souls . . . of their immortality. *Syn. Gosp. III:48.*

[On John 19:30] The word breath is manifestly used here to denote the immortal soul. *John II:237.*

IMPUTATION

We cannot be deemed just in any other way than by a gratuitous imputation. *Hab.-Hagg. 85.*

True righteousness is nothing else than the imputation of righteousness, when God, out of free grace, acquits us from guilt . . . It is by imputation that believers are righteous before God to the very end. *Syn. Gosp. I:76, 77.*

The saints are justified freely, even unto death . . . He counts them just, by imputation. . . . Nevertheless, in order that their good works may please God, it is necessary that these works themselves should be justified by gratuitous imputation . . . *Gen. I:407, 409.*

Our filthiness deserves . . . that all the angels should spit upon us; but Christ, in order to present us pure and unspotted in presence of the Father, resolved to be spat upon. *Syn. Gosp. III:290.*

God determined that his own Son should be stripped of his raiment, that we, clothed with his righteousness . . . may appear with boldness in company with the angels. *Syn. Gosp. III:298.*

INCARNATION OF CHRIST

By Christ Man we are conducted to Christ God. *John II:277.*

Christ came down to us in his incarnation that he might lift us up to the Father. *Ps. I:467.*

[On Heb. 9:11] The body of Christ . . . the temple in which the whole majesty of God dwells. *Heb. 202.*

[Christ] voluntarily took upon him everything that is inseparable from human nature. *Syn. Gosp. I:167.*

Even during the time that he *emptied himself (Phil. 2:7)* he continued to retain his divinity entire, though it was concealed under the veil of his flesh. *Syn. Gosp. II:317.*

It is impossible to express in language adequate to the subject the glory with which Christ beautified his Church by his advent. *Ps. III:394, 395.*

As often as God appeared under the form of man, an obscure glimpse was afforded of the mystery which was at length manifested in the person of Christ. *Ezek. I:97.*

Whenever the Scripture mentions the purity of Christ, it relates to a real humanity; because to assert the purity of Deity would be quite unnecessary. *Inst. II:xiii.4.*

We do not represent Christ as perfectly immaculate, merely because he was born of the seed of a woman unconnected with any man, but because he was sanctified by the Spirit, so that his generation was pure and holy, such as it would have been before the fall of Adam. *Inst. II:xiii.4.*

The Son of God miraculously descended from heaven, yet in such a manner that he never left heaven; he chose to be miraculously conceived in the womb of the Virgin; to live on the earth, and to be suspended on the cross; and yet he never ceased to fill the universe, in the same manner as from the beginning. *Inst. II:xiii.4.*

We assert such a connection and union of the Divinity and the humanity, that each nature retains its properties entire, and yet both together constitute one Christ. *Inst. II:xiv.1.*

INGRATITUDE

How basely his glory is obscured by our ingratitude! *Is. III:15.*

Ingratitude is like an abyss which absorbs all the fulness of God's blessings. *Jer. V:313.*

Unless we use God's blessings with purity the charge of ingratitude will always lie against us. *Ezek. I:196, 197.*

Forgetfulness of God's benefits [is] a sort of madness. *Is. III:441.*

Our ingratitude shuts the door against God's blessings. *Is. III:16.*

Contempt of God's benefits is a kind of profanation and sacrilege. *Ezek. I:195.*

INSPIRATION OF THE SCRIPTURES

The apostles were the certain and authentic amanuenses of the Holy Spirit, and therefore their writings are to be received as the oracles of God. *Inst. IV:viii.9.*

[The Scripture] obtains the same complete credit and authority with believers, when they are satisfied of its divine origin, as if they heard the very words pronounced by God himself. *Inst. I:vii.1.*

[On Ps. 26:9, etc.] These forms of prayer are dictated by the Holy Spirit. *Ps. I:447.*

The Holy Spirit has so regulated the writings which he has dictated to the Prophets and the Apostles, that he detracts nothing from the order instituted by himself. *Heb. 358.*

God, in using the instrumentality of men, still claims to be considered our chief and only teacher. Thus its due majesty is assigned to the word from the person of its author. *Ps. V:302.*

[Jeremiah] did not announce what his own mind suggested, but what was dictated by the Spirit of God. *Jer. I:331.*

[Jeremiah] was not the author of what he taught, but only a minister. *Jer. III:307.*

The words which God dictated to his servant were called the words of Jeremiah; yet, properly speaking, they were not the words of man, for they did not proceed from a mortal man, but from the only true God. *Jer. IV:334.*

The Spirit of God . . . appointed the Evangelists to be his clerks . . . They all wrote one and the same history, with the most perfect agreement, but in different ways . . . each of them separately, without paying any attention to another. *Syn. Gosp. I:127.*

[God] dictated to the Four Evangelists what they should write. *John I:22.*

[On Acts 1:16] They themselves were not the authors of their prophecies, but the Spirit which used their tongues as an instrument. *Acts I:61.*

There is such an agreement among them [the prophets] that that which is spoken by one is the common testimony of them all, because they all speak with one mouth . . . The Spirit of God speaketh in them all. *Acts II:65.*

In all that Paul has left us in writing, we must consider that it is God who speaks to us by the mouth of mortal man, and that all his doctrine ought to be received with such authority and reverence as if God visibly appeared from heaven. [Quoted from Calvin's French Sermons] *Past. Epp. 182.*

INTELLECT

In the Christian

A sound mind proceeds from [God's] Spirit. *Zech.-Mal. 337.*

[168]

As the Spirit of understanding is given to anyone from heaven, he will become a proper and faithful interpreter of God. *Gen. II:323.*

Obedience is the source, not only of an absolutely perfect and complete faith, but of all right knowledge of God. *Inst. I:vi.2.*

[This knowledge and assent] which we give to the Divine word, . . . is from the heart rather than the head, and from the affections rather than the understanding. *Inst. III:ii.8.*

Whosoever desires to be God's disciple must necessarily be conscious of his own folly, that is, he must come free from a conceit of his own acumen and wisdom, and be willing to be taught by God. *Zech.-Mal. 109.*

Humility is the beginning of true intelligence. *Ezek. I:81.*

God considers those only intelligent who remain in the pure doctrine of his law, and practise piety with simplicity and sincerity. *Dan. II:328.*

If we excel in understanding, we are not to abuse this singular gift of God. *Joel-Obad. 436.*

In the natural man

The manifold agility of the soul, which enables it to take a survey of heaven and earth; to join the past and the present; to retain the memory of things heard long ago; to conceive of whatever it chooses by the help of imagination; its ingenuity also in the invention of such admirable arts, – are certain proofs of the divinity in man. *Inst. I:v.5.*

So thoroughly infected is the mind of man with a depraved curiosity, that the greater part of men are always gaping after new revelations. *Syn. Gosp. II:192.*

We are by nature slothful and tardy until God as it were plucks our ears. *Zech.-Mal. 602.*

This truth [of the resurrection of the body] is too difficult to command the assent of the human mind. *Inst. III:xxv.3.*

The human mind is unable, through its imbecility, to attain any knowledge of God without the assistance of his sacred word. *Inst. I:vi.4.*

How small is the measure of our intelligence, for God's judgments are a profound abyss. *Ezek. II:60, 61.*

We know nothing vainer than the minds of men. *Dan. I:149.*

The doctrine of the gospel is a heavenly mystery (1 Cor. 2:14) which cannot be comprehended by the most learned and talented among men. *Dan. I:155.*

In heavenly mysteries the whole power of the human mind is utterly unavailing. *John I:273.*

The human mind has a natural inclination towards vanity and errors. *Syn. Gosp. II:280.*

The minds of men are destitute of that sagacity which is necessary for perceiving the mysteries of heavenly wisdom which are hidden in Christ; . . . till God opens our eyes . . . *Syn. Gosp. II:290.*

The gospel is heavenly wisdom but our mind grovels on the earth. *John I:333.*

There is no such moderation in men as to judge rightly and calmly of God's works. *Jer. IV:169.*

All who arrogate to themselves wisdom rise up against God, because they rob God of the honour due to him. *Jer. V:197.*

[Saul of Tarsus] . . . thought very well of his great perspicacity, which was . . . mere blindness. *Acts I:383.*

Man's mind conceiveth nothing of God but that which is gross and earthly. *Acts I:291.*

In seeing without him we see not; it is he . . . which openeth the eyes of the mind. *Acts I:383.*

There is nothing more deadly than to lean on our own wisdom. *Acts II:17.*

[170]

Athens . . . the mansion house of wisdom, the fountain of all arts, the mother of humanity, did exceed all others in blindness and madness. *Acts II:145, 146.*

Man's understanding . . . a shop of all errors. *Acts II:146.*

The mind of man is [God's] true image. *Acts II:154.*

Every truth that is preached of Christ is quite paradoxical to human judgment. *Rom. 121.*

The minds of men are in the hand of God. *Gen. II:73.*

In all the brains of men not one particle of salt is to be found. *Four Last Bks of Moses II:330.*

Satan has so many devices by which he deludes and blinds our minds, that there is not a man who knows the hundredth part of his own sins. *Ps. I:328.*

The human mind is naturally so prone to falsehood, that it will sooner imbibe error from one single expression, than truth from a prolix oration. *Inst. II:ii.7.*

Human sagacity is here [in matters of faith] so completely lost, that the first step to improvement, in the Divine school, is to forsake it. *Inst. III:ii.34.*

The effects of the Fall

The depravity of the human mind is such that it obscures the divine majesty, and places above it those things which ought to have been subject to God. *Is. III:221.*

There is no end of sinning, when men give themselves up to their own inventions. *Jer. I:413.*

The Jews were so corrupted by long habit that they could not repent, for the devil had so enslaved them that they were not in their right mind; they no longer had any discernment, and could not discriminate between good and evil. *Jer. II:191.*

Unbelief . . . is always proud . . . This arises from the depravity of men. *John I:275.*

The madness of the human mind is certainly immense . . .
more disposed to accuse God . . . than to blame itself for its
blindness. *Rom. 203.*

Men, following their own sense, or minds, or feelings, soon
become a prey to the delusions of Satan. *Gen. Epp. 326.*

[On 1 Cor. 2:14, *foolishness to him*] It is not owing simply to the
obstinacy of the human will, but to the impotency, also, of the
understanding. *Cor. I:116.*

The limits of Christian inquiry

One rule of modesty . . . not to speak, or think, or even desire to
know, concerning obscure subjects, anything beyond the
information given us in the Divine word. *Inst. I:xiv.4.*

Nothing is more absurd . . . than to measure the power of God
by our own understanding. *Jer. V:170.*

God's providence . . . ought not to be subjected to human
judgment. *Jer. V:164.*

Those who inquire curiously into everything, and are never at
rest, may be called Questionarians. *Past. Epp. 339.*

Natural perspicacity is a gift of God, and the liberal arts, and all
the sciences by which wisdom is acquired, are gifts of God . . .
They must occupy the place of handmaid, not of mistress. *Cor.
I:145.*

The faithful ought carefully to keep themselves aloof from those
wild opinions, which are afloat in the world. *Ps. I:151.*

It would be a degrading thing for God, before whose tribunal
we all must one day stand, to be subjected to our judgments, or
rather to our foolish temerity. *Gen. I:306.*

We know by our experience how difficult it is to keep within due
bounds those who are puffed up with a silly opinion of their own
wisdom. *Letters 54.*

INTERCESSION OF CHRIST

There is no way of obtaining favour with God but through the intercession of Christ. *Is. III:286.*

The intercession of Christ is a continual application of his death for our salvation . . . Whosoever obtains favour for us, must be furnished with a sacrifice. *Gen. Epp. 171.*

Thirty years ago [i.e. about 1520] this so remarkable an article of our faith, that Christ is our advocate, was nearly buried . . . He cannot be an advocate who is not a priest . . . He sanctifies our prayers by the odour of his sacrifice. *Gen. Epp. 172.*

The two parts of [Christ's] priesthood . . . the sacrifice of the death of Christ, and his continual intercession. *Past. Epp. 60.*

[On John 16:27] The value of his sacrifice . . . is always powerful and efficacious; the blood . . . is a continual intercession for us . . . We have the heart of the Heavenly Father, as soon as we have placed before Him *the name* of his Son. *John II:158.*

[On Matt. 27:12] Christ was at that time silent, that he may now be our advocate. *Syn. Gosp. III:277.*

All our prayers should be founded on the intercession of Christ. [Calvin's Geneva Catechism of 1536, 1541] *Tracts II:75.*

Christ, by his death, purchased for himself the honour of being the eternal advocate and peacemaker, to present our prayers and our persons to the Father; to obtain supplies of grace for us, and enable us to hope we shall obtain what we ask. [The Necessity of Reforming the Church] *Tracts I:191.*

[In the O.T.] no prayers were acceptable . . . but those which were joined with sacrifice, that they might always turn their minds to the Mediator. *Ps. IV:482.*

God can listen to no prayers without the intercession of Christ. *Four Last Bks of Moses II:295.*

INTERMEDIATE STATE

Christ, when commending his soul to his Father, undertook the guardianship of the souls of all his people. *Ps. I:503.*

[On Gen. 47:30] It appears from this passage, that the word 'sleep', whenever it is put for 'die', does not refer to the soul, but to the body. *Gen. II:417.*

[Of Stephen's death] This word *sleep* noteth a meek kind of death . . . It must be referred unto the body, lest any imagine foolishly . . . that the souls do also sleep. *Acts I:321.*

To *sleep in Jesus* [1 Thess. 4:13, 14] means to retain in death the union which we have with Christ. *Thess. 363.*

Although the souls of the dead are now living, and enjoy quiet repose, yet the whole of their felicity and consolation depends exclusively on the resurrection. *Cor. II:21.*

JESTING

Jesting . . . carries in it a portion of conceit not at all in keeping with the character of a godly man. *Eph. 306.*

[On Col. 4:6] As witticisms are insinuating, and for the most part procure favour, he indirectly prohibits believers from the practice of familiar use of them. *Philipp.-Col. 226.*

[Pagans] evaded the grossness of the sin of [immorality] by ribaldry and scurrilous jests. *Four Last Bks of Moses III:70.*

[Wedding jests] have come from Satan's workshop. *Cor. I:224.*

JEWS

I have had much conversation with many Jews: I have never seen either a drop of piety or a grain of truth or ingenuousness – nay, I have never found common sense in any Jew. *Dan. I:185.*

[The Jews] laboured under a hereditary disease of obstinacy (Matt. 12:39) . . . and try to find a subterfuge for not obeying his word. *Syn. Gosp. II:93, 94.*

[On Acts 13:46] The fellowship of the Gentiles did not take from the Jews the right of the first begotten . . . they were always the chief in the Church of God (Acts 1:18; Rom. 1:16). *Acts I:551.*

[On evangelization of the Jews] Christ has assigned to the Jews the first rank. *Syn. Gosp. III:378.*

[On Rom. 11:25] The manner of their conversion will be unique and unprecedented. *Rom. 254.*

[On Zech. 12:9] Jerusalem was to be the mother of all Churches . . . From thence God had determined to send forth the royal sceptre, that the son of David might rule over the whole world. *Zech.-Mal. 358.*

It was . . . the adoption of God alone which prevented the total destruction of the Jews. *Jon.-Nah. 390.*

JOY

Stable joy proceedeth from faith alone. *Acts II:123.*

It is not enough to rejoice, unless our joy look straight towards God, and unless we keep him alone always in our view. *Is. II:381.*

The joy we derive from [God's] paternal favour towards us may surpass all the pleasures of the world. *Ps. II:20.*

By . . . *joy* [Paul] means that spiritual consolation by which believers are sustained under their afflictions. *Cor. II:285.*

The inward joy, which faith brings to us can overcome all fears, terrors, sorrows and anxieties. *Hab.-Hagg. 175.*

There is nothing in afflictions which ought to disturb our joy. *Gen. Epp. 279.*

[On Ps. 47:1, 2] The Holy Spirit has exhorted the faithful to continue clapping their hands for joy, until the advent of the promised Redeemer. *Ps. II:207.*

JUDGMENT

Human Judgment

Let us learn . . . to be prepared, though we do well, to be evil spoken of. *Four Last Bks of Moses IV:102.*

. . . contented to have our piety shining at the judgment-seat of God, although it may be defaced by the calumnies of men. *Ps. IV:452.*

Divine Judgment

What is God without his judgment? *Jer. V:426.*

It is a useful exercise to consider God's judgments, yea, this is the chief prudence of the faithful. *Ezek. II:168.*

[God's] judgments are always founded on his goodness. *Jer. III:383.*

War is one of God's judgments. *Hab.-Hagg. 300.*

For the present God judges the world only in part. *II Thess. 389.*

The wicked are incapable of profiting by the judgments of God. *Ps. II:315.*

[On Pharaoh] Hardness of heart is the sin of man, but the hardening of the heart is the judgment of God. *Four Last Bks of Moses I:141.*

It is the peculiar privilege of the Church, to know what the Divine judgments mean, and what is their tendency. *Gen. I:479.*

The specimens given by the Lord, both of his clemency and of his severity, are only begun. *Inst. I:v.10.*

The body is not affected by a fear of spiritual punishment; that falls only on the soul. *Inst. I:xv.2.*

After the impious have wilfully shut their own eyes, it is the righteous vengeance of God upon them, to darken their understandings, so that, seeing, they may not perceive. *Inst. I:iv.2.*

They, whose minds are alienated from the righteousness of God, earnestly desire the subversion of that tribunal, which they know to be established for the punishment of transgressions against it. *Inst. I:iv.4.*

The conscience cannot sustain the load of iniquity, without an immediate discovery of the Divine judgment. *Inst. II:viii.3.*

Whenever we read of the Divine benevolence or wrath, the former comprehends eternal life, the latter eternal destruction. *Inst. II:viii.4.*

Vengeance is so connected with sin, that it cannot be severed from it. *Four Last Bks of Moses IV:287.*

. . . the judgment of God, which our prodigious dulness makes us excessively slow to comprehend. *Is. II:383.*

It is the work of God, when wicked men are ruined, though he may employ the agency of men in executing his judgments. *Is. I:455.*

The truth of God is not only fruitful in the salvation of men, but also in their perdition (*2 Cor. 2:15, 16*). *Jer. I:407.*

Judgment . . . the rigour which [God] exercises against the transgressors of his Law. *Jer. I:501.*

Nothing is more difficult than to lead men to a serious acknowledgment of God's judgment. *Jer. IV:25.*

When men reject the word of teaching, they cannot escape the other word, which denounces the judgment of God. *Jer. IV:322.*

The peculiar office of the Law is to summon consciences to the judgment-seat of God. *John II:140.*

The gospel cannot be faithfully preached without summoning the whole world, as guilty, to the judgment-seat of God. *John I:285.*

The ungodly are moved by no threats; nay, they laugh to scorn all God's judgments. *Joel-Obad. 127.*

Nothing belongs more peculiarly to God than the office of judging the world; and this he does by his word and his Prophets. *Joel-Obad. 355.*

It is an extreme curse, when God gives us loose reins, and suffers us, with unbridled liberty, to rush as it were headlong into evils, as though he had delivered us up to Satan, to be his slaves. *Jon.-Nah. 196.*

Just in proportion as men grow rampant in sin, may it be anticipated that the Divine judgments are about to descend upon them. *Ps. II:333.*

[On 2 Cor. 5:10] Paul, from a holy desire of acting aright, constantly sisted himself before the bar of God. *Cor. II:225.*

[God] . . . commands his threatenings to be proposed to the elect, and reprobate, in common. *Gen. I:255.*

[God] . . . chastises his own people in the flesh, that their soul may be saved from eternal destruction. *Gen. I:515.*

God's judgment upon Christ for his people

It was proper that the Son of God should be solemnly condemned by an earthly judge, that he might efface our condemnation in heaven. *Syn. Gosp. III:268.*

By the condemnation of Christ, our condemnation before God is blotted out. *John II:207.*

[On Gabbatha, John 20:13] It was proper that Christ should have been condemned from *a lofty place* that he, coming from heaven as the supreme Judge, may acquit us at the last day. *John II:223.*

The Last Judgment

It is not our business to canvass the judgments of God, before whose tribunal we must all hereafter stand. *Four Last Bks of Moses IV:269.*

Our guilt will be double when we come to the judgment-seat of God, if we shut our eyes when he exhibits the light, and shut our ears when he teaches by his word. *Is. III:308.*

The last judgment shall be nothing else than an approbation or ratification of the doctrine of the Gospel. *John II:52.*

[On Ps. 36:12] Those who would hasten prematurely the time of God's vengeance upon the wicked . . . do err; . . . we ought to leave it to the providence of God to fix the period when . . . he shall rise up to judgment. *Ps. II:15.*

The Law was given to cite slumbering consciences to the judgment-seat, that, through fear of eternal death, they might flee for refuge to God's mercy. *Four Last Bks of Moses I:327.*

Strictly speaking, Christ will come, not for the destruction of the world, but for purposes of salvation. This is the reason that the Creed mentions only the life of blessedness. *Inst. III:xxv.9, 261.*

The penal sanctions are annexed [to the Law] to render unrighteousness more execrable, lest the sinner, amidst the fascinations of sin, should forget that the judgment of the Legislator awaits him. *Inst. II:viii.4.*

JUSTICE OF GOD

Definition

[On Jer. 9:24] *Justice* is to be taken for that faithful protection of God, by which he defends and preserves his own people; and *judgment*, for the rigour which he exercises against the transgressors of his Law. *Jer. I:501.*

Whenever you hear the glory of God mentioned, think of his justice. *Inst. III:xxiii.8.*

These things are undivided, his power and his justice, though justice often does not appear. *Jer. V:193.*

Different from human standards

The judgment-seat of heaven is not subject to our laws. *Josh. 163.*

A mercy which impairs the authority of God at the will of man, is detestable. *Josh. 158.*

Those who substitute [God's] permission in place of his act, not only deprive him of his authority as judge, but . . . subject him to a weighty reproach, since they grant him no more of justice than their senses can understand. *Four Last Bks of Moses I:102.*

Because God's judgments are hidden they are not therefore unjust. *Four Last Bks of Moses III:436.*

It is acting a most perverse part, to set up the measure of human justice as the standard by which to measure the justice of God. *Inst. III:xxiv.17.*

We should reflect that we are not treating of the righteousness of a human court, but of that of the heavenly tribunal; in order that we may not apply any diminutive standard of our own, to estimate the integrity of conduct required to satisfy the Divine justice. *Inst. III:xii.1.*

God's principles of justice

Without the sword, laws are dead. *Syn. Gosp. I:195.*

There is no justice where there is no obedience rendered to God. *Zech.-Mal. 613.*

[God] is . . . no less worthy to be praised on account of his rigour, than on account of his mercy. *Ps. III:391.*

No one can be injurious to his brother without wounding God himself . . . He deems himself violated in their person. *Gen. I:295, 296.*

[On the Deluge. God] would have spared his own workmanship, had he seen that any milder remedy could have been effectually applied. *Gen. I:273.*

[God's] will is the most perfect rule of all justice. *Ezek. I:315.*

The Lord, therefore, is the King of kings; who, when he has opened his sacred mouth, is to be heard alone, above all, for all, and before all. *Inst. IV:xx.32.*

Scripture . . . [sets] God before us as our judge, whenever the purpose is to allay our troubles. *Hab.-Hagg. 98.*

JUSTIFICATION BY FAITH

Definition

An acceptance, by which God receives us into his favour, and esteems us as righteous persons; . . . it consists in the remission of sins and the imputation of the righteousness of Christ. *Inst. III:xi.2.*

Our justification [consists] in a voluntary act of God, by which he condescends to forget all our iniquities. *Ps. II:296.*

To be loved by God and to be justified in his sight are synonymous terms. *Syn. Gosp. II:399.*

The efficient cause is the mercy of God, Christ is the substance of our justification, and the Word, with faith, the instrument. *Rom. 73.*

Importance

Justification . . . is the principal hinge by which religion is supported. *Inst. III:xi.1.*

Whenever the knowledge of it is taken away, the glory of Christ is extinguished, religion abolished, the Church destroyed, and the hope of salvation utterly overthrown. [Calvin's Reply to Sadoleto] *Tracts I:41.*

The safety of the Church depends as much on this doctrine as human life does on the soul. If the purity of this doctrine is in any degree impaired, the Church has received a deadly wound. [On the Necessity of Reforming the Church] *Tracts I:137.*

Justifying Faith

Why is our justification ever ascribed to faith? Because our faith directs us to Christ in whom is the complete perfection of justification, and thus our justification may be ascribed equally to the faith taught and the doctrine which teaches it. *Dan. II:377.*

[On Hab. 2:4] The just . . . brings nothing before God except faith. *Hab.-Hagg. 75.*

Faith is not to be taken here for man's integrity, but for that faith which sets man before God emptied of all good things, so that he seeks what he needs from [God's] gratuitous favour. *Hab.-Hagg. 75.*

Faith [is not] the *efficient*, but only the *formal* cause of righteousness. *Gen. I:407.*

Faith does not justify us for any other reason, than that it reconciles us to God . . . not by its own merit, but because we receive the grace offered to us in the promises. *Gen. I:407.*

What of works?

The merit of works ceases when righteousness is sought by faith. *Gen. I:407.*

There is nothing intermediate between being justified by faith and justified by works. *Ps. V:251.*

If justification be the principle from which love originates, what righteousness of works can precede it? *Inst. III:xiv.6.*

Not only our persons, but even our works, are justified by faith alone. *Inst. III:xvii.10.*

The saints are justified freely, even unto death . . . He counts them just, by imputation . . . Nevertheless, in order that their good works may please God, it is necessary that these works themselves should be justified by gratuitous imputation, but some evil is always inherent in them. *Gen. I:407, 409.*

Opposition to this doctrine

Satan has laboured at nothing more assiduously than to extinguish, or to smother the gratuitous justification of faith, which is here . . . asserted [Gen. 15:6] . . . Abram obtained righteousness . . . by imputation. *Gen. I:405.*

The trite dogma of the schools: that men are justified partly by the grace of God and partly by their own works. [Antidote to the Council of Trent] *Tracts III:108.*

The principal cause of obscurity . . . that we are with the greatest difficulty induced to leave the glory of righteousness entire to God alone. *Tracts III:108.*

[182]

The whole dispute is as to the Cause of Justification . . . For however small the portion attributed to our work, to that extent faith will waver, and our whole salvation be endangered. *Tracts III:116, 117.*

Affirmation

[On Jer. 23:6] *Jehova justitia nostra. Jer. III:136.*

We cannot be deemed just in any other way than by a gratuitous imputation. *Hab.-Hagg. 85.*

This eternal justice depends upon the enduring effect of the death of Christ, since the blood of Christ flowed as it were before God, and while we are daily purged and cleansed from our pollution, God is also daily appeased for us. *Dan. II:217.*

The grace of justification is inseparable from regeneration, although they are distinct things. *Inst. III:xi.11.*

[God] justifies them . . . so completely, that they may boldly appear in heaven, as being invested with the purity of Christ. *Inst. III:xi.11.*

KINDNESS

Nothing is more acceptable to God than kindness. *Is. IV:195.*

The faithful, by their clemency and kindness, open up a channel through which the favour of God flows to them. *Ps. IV:325.*

KINGDOM OF GOD AND KINGDOM OF HEAVEN

Christ's kingdom . . . is set forth under the image . . . of an earthly and civil government. *Jer. IV:253.*

God is properly said to rule or reign among the faithful, whom he governs by his Spirit. So God's kingdom begins and has its origin when regeneration takes place. *Jer. V:119.*

Why is the preaching of the gospel so often styled the kingdom of God, but because it is the sceptre by which the heavenly King rules his people? [Calvin's Reply to Sadoleto] *Tracts I:36.*

God in the person of Christ, began to reign on mount Zion, when the doctrine of the gospel from thence went forth to the extremities of the world. *Jon.-Nah. 278.*

The kingdom of God means . . . the spiritual life, which is begun by faith in this world, and gradually increases every day according to the continued progress of faith. *John I:108.*

The kingdom of Christ is only begun, and the perfection thereof is deferred until the last day. *Acts I:xx.42.*

The kingdom of heaven is continually growing and advancing to the end of the world. *Syn. Gosp. I:320.*

This kingdom consists of two parts; the one, God's correcting by the power of his Spirit all our carnal and depraved appetites, which oppose him in great numbers; the other, his forming all our powers to an obedience to his commands. *Inst. III:xx.42.*

The kingdom of God is grounded and contained in the knowledge of the redemption purchased by Christ. *Acts II:431.*

The preaching of the gospel is called the kingdom of heaven, and the sacraments may be called the gate of heaven, because they admit us into the presence of God. *Gen. II:118.*

The kingdom of heaven means the renovation of the Church. *Syn. Gosp. I:279.*

The kingdom of God among men is nothing else than a restoration to a happy life . . . It is true and everlasting happiness . . . 'newness of life' (Rom. 6:4). *Syn. Gosp. I:178.*

The kingdom of Christ is strengthened more by the blood of the martyrs than by the aid of arms. *John II:211.*

In this world we taste but the beginning of Christ's kingdom. *Is. I:392.*

KINGLY RULE OF CHRIST

Christ was sent in order to bring the whole world under the authority of God and obedience to him. *Is. III:287.*

Wherever the doctrine of the gospel is preached in purity, there we are certain that Christ reigns. *Is. I:382.*

The gospel is like a sceptre by which Christ subdues all people and rules them for himself. *Ezek. II:212.*

The kingdom of Christ is spiritual, and so is everything connected with it. *Jer. III:143.*

Christ, both in himself and his members, reigns without any danger of change. *Dan. I:189.*

The perpetuity of Christ's reign is twofold, . . . first, in the whole body of believers, . . . second, in . . . each believer. *Dan. I:188.*

[Christ] did not commence his reign till he was publicly ordained the Master and Redeemer of his people. *Dan. II:214.*

[The Triumphal Entry] He openly declares that he commences his reign by advancing to death. *John II:16.*

[Matt. 28:18–20] extolled in magnificent language the reign of Christ over the whole world. *Syn. Gosp. III:391.*

The kingdom of Christ extends, no doubt, to all men, but it brings salvation to none but the elect. *John II:165, 166.*

Unless Christ were seated at his Father's right hand, and had obtained supreme dominion, causing every knee to bend before him, the Church could never exercise its power. *Dan. II:78.*

Christ's kingdom and his dignity cannot be perceived by carnal eyes, nor even comprehended by the human intellect. *Dan. II:73.*

The Son of God hath always reigned, even from the first beginning of the world, yet after that, being revealed in the flesh, he published his gospel, he began then to erect a more famous tribunal-seat than before, whence he doth now appear most plainly, and to be also most glorious. *Acts I:xviii.*

It is for us that he reigns, for ever and ever. *Ps. I:154.*

Christ can only obtain a tranquil kingdom by fighting. *Ps. I:295.*

These two things – his offspring and his throne, are conjoined. *Ps. III:446.*

In spite of the opposition of the world [the kingdom of Christ] is erected in an astonishing manner by the invincible power of God . . . All that was accomplished in the person of Christ extends to the gradual development of his kingdom, even until the end of the world. *Ps. IV:394.*

The whole world became an enlarged mount Zion upon the advent of Christ. *Ps. V:158.*

God would never allow [the Church] to be altogether destroyed, since upon the event of its destruction he would cease to be a king. *Ps. V:179.*

Christ's kingdom is inseparable from his priesthood. *Ps. V:157.*

KNOWLEDGE OF GOD

Definition

True and substantial wisdom principally consists of two parts, the knowledge of God, and the knowledge of ourselves. [Opening words of the Institutes] *Inst. I:i.1.*

Spiritual wisdom . . . consists chiefly in three things – to know God, his paternal favour towards us, on which depends our salvation, and the method of regulating our lives according to the rule of the law. *Inst. II:ii.18.*

There is one understanding for terrestrial things, and another for celestial ones. *Inst. II:ii.13.*

A knowledge of all the sciences is mere smoke, where the heavenly science of Christ is wanting. *Cor. I:82.*

We cannot attain to a clear and solid knowledge of God, without a mutual acquaintance with ourselves. *Inst. I:xv.1.*

There is a twofold knowledge, – the knowledge of faith, received from his word, – and the knowledge of experience, as we say, derived from actual enjoyment. *Joel-Obad. 136.*

Knowledge of God

The source of this knowledge

What is the beginning of true learning but a prompt alacrity to hear the voice of God? *Inst. I:vii.5.*

Obedience is the source, not only of an absolutely perfect and complete faith, but of all right knowledge of God. *Inst. I:vi.2.*

The true knowledge of God corresponds to what faith discovers in the written Word. *Ps. IV:133.*

True acquaintance with God is made more by the ears than by the eyes. *Four Last Bks of Moses III:378.*

[On Is. 8:20, *To the law and to the testimony*] Everything which is added to the word must be condemned and rejected. It is the will of the Lord that we depend wholly on his word, and that our knowledge shall be confined within its limits . . . Everything that is introduced by men on their own authority will be nothing else than a corruption of the word. *Is. I:290.*

Knowledge is connected with faith, because we are certain and fully convinced of the truth of God, not in the same manner as human sciences are learned, but when the Spirit seals it on our hearts. *John I:279.*

Hindrances to this knowledge

Errors can never be eradicated from the human heart, till the true knowledge of God is implanted in it. *Inst. I:83.*

Whatever deficiency of natural ability prevents us from attaining the pure and clear knowledge of God, yet, since that deficiency arises from our own fault, we are left without any excuse. *Inst. I:v.15.*

The fruit of this knowledge

[On 1 John 2:3] The knowledge of God is efficacious . . . To know him is immediately to love him. *Gen. Epp. 174.*

The more anyone advances in the knowledge of God, every kind of blessing increases also equally with the sense of Divine love. *Gen. Epp. 367.*

A mature knowledge of things makes a man modest. *Past. Epp. 74.*

This is our wisdom, to be learners to the end. *Zech.-Mal. 125.*

The limits of this knowledge

The knowledge of the godly is never so pure, but that some dimness or obscurity hangs over their spiritual vision. *Eph. 212.*

We should be soberly wise in those points, the certain knowledge of which cannot be elicited from Scripture; for our curiosity is not only frivolous, but also perverse and injurious, when we desire to know more than God has revealed. *Four Last Bks of Moses III:423.*

[On Exod. 33:18] This is the rule of sound and legitimate and profitable knowledge, to be content with the measure of revelation, and willingly to be ignorant of what is deeper than this. *Four Last Bks of Moses III:377.*

Warnings

[On 2 Tim. 2:14] How dangerous to the Church is that knowledge which leads to debates . . . disregards piety, and tends to ostentation. *Past. Epp. 220.*

Accursed . . . be that knowledge which makes men proud, and is not regulated by a desire of edifying. *Cor. I:273.*

Our minds, through their sluggishness, easily contract rust, which infects and corrupts all knowledge of God till it be entirely destroyed. *Is. III:382.*

[On Eph. 3:19] . . . the disease of desiring to obtain useless knowledge. *Eph. 264.*

All knowledge of God without Christ is a vast abyss which immediately swallows up all our thoughts. *Gen. Epp. 53.*

LAST DAYS

[On 1 Pet. 1:6] What is elsewhere called the last time, is the whole from the coming of Christ . . . But Peter had a regard to the end of the world. *Gen. Epp. 31.*

Last Days

The Scriptures, in using this phrase [*the end of the days*] always point to the manifestation of Christ, by which the face of the world was renewed. *Dan. II:255.*

Everywhere in Scripture, especially in the New Testament, the manifestation of Christ is placed in the last times. *Hos. 136.*

Whenever . . . the day of the Lord is mentioned in Scripture, let us know that God is bound by no laws, that he should hasten his work according to our hasty wishes; but the specific time is in his own power, and at his own will. *Zech.-Mal. 616.*

LAW OF GOD

True and pure religion was so revealed in the Law, that God's face in a manner shone forth therein. *Four Last Bks of Moses I:419.*

The nearer anyone under the Law approached to God, the more did Christ shine forth in him. *Four Last Bks of Moses I:487.*

Definition

The law included the whole body of Scripture, up to the advent of Christ. *Cor. I:452.*

The Law proceeded from God, and Moses was not its author, but its minister. *Heb. 247.*

. . . the Law, which . . . Christ came to establish, as a rule, for a holy life. *Inst. IV:xvi.15.*

The Law consists chiefly of three parts: first, the doctrine of life; secondly, threatenings and promises; thirdly, the covenant of grace. *Is I:xxvi.*

The 'Law' contains both commandments and promises. *Is. II:169.*

By the word *Law* we understand what peculiarly belonged to Moses; for the Law contains the rule of life, and the gratuitous covenant of life; and in it we . . . are instructed as to faith, and as to the fear of God. *Heb. 167.*

There are two parts in Christianity which correspond with the two tables of the Law . . . He who separates the one from the other, has nothing but what is mutilated and mangled. *Heb. 145.*

The Law is the everlasting rule of a good and holy life. *Gal. 119.*

The Purpose of the Law

The Law is like a mirror, in which we behold, first, our impotence; secondly, our iniquity which proceeds from it; and lastly, the consequence of both, our obnoxiousness to the curse; just as a mirror represents to us the spots on our face. *Inst. II:vii.7.*

Being a spiritual Legislator, [God] addresses himself to the soul as much as to the body. [Commandments 6, 7 and 8]. *Inst. II:viii.6.*

Paul, by the word *law*, frequently intends the rule of a righteous life, in which God requires of us what we owe to him, affording us no hope of life, unless we fulfil every part of it, and, on the contrary, annexing a curse if we are guilty of the smallest transgression. *Inst. II:ix.4.*

The tendency of the doctrine of the law is to connect man with his God . . . to make him cleave to the Lord in sanctity of life. *Inst. II:viii.51.*

The Law avails, not only for the beginning of repentance, but also for our continual progress. *Gen. I:482.*

It is not unusual in Scripture, to seek a description of a pious and holy life, from the Second Table of the Law. *Gen. I:482.*

The Law was given to cite slumbering consciences to the judgment-seat, that, through fear of eternal death, they might flee for refuge to God's mercy. *Four Last Bks of Moses I:327.*

The life of the Law is man's death (*Rom. 7:9*). *Four Last Bks of Moses I:316.*

There is a certain vivifying killing of the soul . . . [God] draws some to salvation, others he drives into ruin. *Heb. 102.*

No mortal will be found who can perform the Law. But in the gospel God receives, with fatherly indulgence, what is not absolutely perfect. *Four Last Bks of Moses I:414.*

Free affection is the foundation and beginning of duly obeying the Law, for what is drawn forth by constraint, or servile fear, cannot please God. *Four Last Bks of Moses I:381.*

The death which [the Law] inflicts is life-giving. *Four Last Bks of Moses III:198.*

As soon as the Law presents itself before us, the curse of God falls upon our heads . . . This is the theological use of the Law. *Four Last Bks of Moses III:197.*

[On Is. 45:19] The principal end and use of the Law, to invite men to God. *Is. III:421.*

The seat of the Law is not in the brain, but in the heart. *Is. IV:73.*

The Law . . . not only contains a rule of life . . . but . . . also rules their hearts before God and angels. *Zech.-Mal. 220.*

The peculiar office of the Law [is] to summon consciences to the judgment-seat of God. *John II:140.*

The Law . . . requires perfect love; we do not yield it. Our duty was to run, and we go on slowly limping. [Antidote to the Council of Trent] *Tracts III:88.*

The Law was as it were the representation of the glory of God . . . a mirror before their eyes. *Jer. V:227.*

The Permanence of the Law

The perpetuity of the Law is grounded in Christ. *Acts II:50.*

The doctrine of the Law remains, therefore, through Christ, inviolable; which by tuition, admonition, reproof, and correction, forms and prepares us for every good work. *Inst. II:vii.14.*

The fathers who lived under the Law had the same hope of eternal life . . . as they had the same grace of adoption in common with us, then faith must have rested on the same promises. *Heb. 185.*

The Law and the Prophets

The prophets often borrowed their chief sentences from Moses, of whom they were the interpreters. *Jer. IV:171.*

The perfection of wisdom was found in the Law, from which the prophets drew whatever we read in their writings. *Jer. III:180.*

Trace the prophets to the Law ... The prophecies are appendages of the Law. [Calvin's Preface to Comm. on Is.] *Is. I:xxvi, xxviii.*

The Law and the Covenant

[The Law at Sinai] It was then registered, as it were, in the public records, when the covenant was ratified by the written Law. *Ps. III:231.*

The Law is called *the testimony of God's mouth. Ps. IV:467.*

The whole doctrine of the Law, the chief part of which is the free covenant of salvation. *Ps. IV:477.*

Law and Gospel

[On Heb. 10:1] Under the Law was shadowed forth only in rude and imperfect lines what is under the Gospel set forth in living colours and graphically distinct ... To both the same Christ is exhibited, the same righteousness, sanctification, and salvation; and the difference only is in the manner of painting or setting them forth. *Heb. 222.*

When Christ or the Apostles are treating of a perfect life, they always refer believers to the Law. *Four Last Bks of Moses III:69.*

He who is the foundation of the covenant of grace, held also the highest rank in the giving of the Law. *Gal. 102.*

The *law* was the grammar of theology, which, after carrying its scholars a short way, handed them over to *faith. Gal. 108.*

If the Law be separated from Christ, it is a dead letter; Christ alone gives it life. *Ezek. II:176, 177.*

In all the ceremonies of the Law [faith] beholds the salvation which has been manifested in Christ. *John II:241.*

Moses had no other intention than to invite all men to go straight to Christ. *John I:217.*

The fathers . . . did not see God in any other way than wrapped up in many folds of figures and ceremonies. *John I:54, 55.*

The abrogation of the Law

The assertions of Paul respecting the abrogation of the law evidently relate, not to the instruction itself, but to the power of binding the conscience. *Inst. II:vii.15.*

Ceremonies . . . have been abrogated, not as to their effect, but only as to their use. *Inst. II:vii.16.*

None of these were abolished by Christ, but only that part which regarded the ancient priesthood. *Heb. 167.*

[On the ceremonies of the Law] It was only the use of them that was abolished, for their meaning was more fully confirmed. *Syn. Gosp. I:278.*

Christ and the Law

By putting on himself the chains, he takes them off from the other. So Christ chose to become liable to keep the Law, that exemption from it might be obtained for us. *Gal. 118, 119.*

Preaching the Law

We ought to imitate the Prophets, who conveyed the doctrine of the Law in such a manner as to draw from it advices, reproofs, threatenings, and consolations, which they applied to the present condition of the people. *Is. I:xxx.*

The law of conscience

All are rendered inexcusable, as they carry in their hearts a law which is sufficient to make them a thousand times guilty. *Hab.-Hagg. 51.*

Opposition to the Law

[Sinners] inveterately hate the law itself, and execrate God the lawgiver. *Inst. II:vii.10.*

LAZINESS

We are by nature slothful and tardy, until God as it were plucks our ears. *Zech.-Mal. 602.*

Slothfulness gradually prevails over the faithful, unless it be corrected. *Inst. II:v.11.*

Indolence almost always springs from excessive confidence. *Syn. Gosp. II:409.*

[On 1 Thess. 5:18] Those also quench the Spirit whose laziness renders void the gift of God. *Thess. 376.*

Three vices which are found to prevail much [among pastors]; sloth, desire of gain, and lust for power. *Gen. Epp. 142.*

[God] remains, as it were, forgetful of us, while he beholds us slothful and dumb. *Inst. III:xx.3.*

LIBERTY

It is a free servitude, and a serving freedom. *Gen. Epp. 84.*

Christian liberty . . . an appendix to justification. *Inst. III:xix.1.*

Christian liberty is, in all its branches, a spiritual thing. *Inst. III:xix.9.*

As our liberty should be subject to charity, so charity itself ought to be subservient to the purity of the faith. *Inst. III:xix.13.*

Man contains, as it were, two worlds, capable of being governed by various rulers and various laws. This distinction will prevent what the gospel inculcates concerning spiritual liberty from being misapplied to political regulations. *Inst. III:xix.15.*

Liberty . . . will be destructive to us, until God undertakes the care of us, and prepares and forms us, that we may bear his yoke . . . When we obey God, we possess true and real happiness. *Jer. IV:15.*

The liberty of believers in external things cannot be reduced to certain rules. *Inst. III:x.4.*

[Ascetics] committed the very dangerous error of imposing on the conscience stricter rules than those which are prescribed to it by the word of God. *Inst. III:x.1.*

God confers his blessings on us for the support of life, not for luxury.*Inst. III:xix.9.*

LIFE

A gift of God

[On Dan. 6:25–27. Darius] calls him *the living God*, not only because he has life in himself, but out of himself, and is also the origin and fountain of life. *Dan. I:392.*

The life of the soul is our union with God. *Heb. 205.*

This life, though transitory, and full of innumerable distresses, is an invaluable gift of God. *Syn. Gosp. III:201.*

. . . one of [God's] daily favours, that our ears hear, and our eyes see; for if he does not every hour quicken our senses, all their power will immediately give way. *Syn. Gosp. III:355.*

The true limit of loving life is . . . when we carry it in our hands, and offer it to God as a sacrifice. *John II:29.*

He who has fixed the limits of our life, has also entrusted us with the care of it. *Inst. I:xvii.4.*

[On Gen. 1:22. God] blesses his creatures when he commands them to increase and grow; that is, he infuses into them fecundity by his word. *Gen. I:90.*

[God] . . . pronounces that marriage will really prove to men the best support of life. *Gen. I:129.*

Its many blessings

God does not prolong the lives of his people that they may pamper themselves . . . but to magnify him for his benefits which he is daily heaping upon them. *Ps. IV:385.*

[On Ps. 91:15] Longevity is never to be compared with eternity . . . A privilege peculiarly belonging to the Lord's people [is] that they are *satisfied with life*. *Ps. III:493.*

Life's limits

[On Ps. 49:10] A definite limit has been assigned to every man's life . . . [hence] the folly of those who dream of spending an eternity in this world. *Ps. II:243.*

He who is most skilful in arithmetic . . . is unable to count fourscore years in his own life. *Ps. III:473.*

This frail and perishing life ought to be little regarded by men who have been created for a heavenly immortality. *Syn. Gosp. I:462.*

Life and Death

We sojourn in this world . . . held wrapped in the shadow of death, until our real life be manifested. *Gen. II:208.*

The simple fact of the shortness of our life should put down all arrogance and pride. *Ps. V:262.*

The life which God has given he may take away as often as he pleases. *Josh. 118.*

[On Ezek. 16:6, *Live!*] Death is converted into life; since he is the sovereign and Lord of both. *Ezek. II:99.*

If he leads us onwards to death, we must be assured it is best for us to die, and injurious to us to enjoy life any longer. *Dan. I:229.*

Let us . . . learn so to love this life as to be prepared to lay it down whenever the Lord pleases; let us also learn to desire death, but so as to live to the Lord. *Jon.-Nah. 129.*

The godly have no other reason for living here than that, being sojourners in the world, they may travel rapidly towards their heavenly country. *John I:241.*

LIGHT

One of the miracles of God, to bring light out of darkness. *Gen. II:449.*

[On Gen. 1:16, *to rule*] The sun is still a servant, and the moon a handmaid . . . He has them as his charioteers to convey light suited to the season. *Gen. I:87, 88.*

[On Is. 60:3] There is no other light of men but when God shines on them by his word. *Is. IV:277.*

Contempt of the light is followed by darkness. *John II:39.*

Out of Christ there is no life-giving light in the world, but everything is covered by the appalling darkness of earth. *Syn. Gosp. I:77.*

LORD'S SUPPER (*see also* Sacraments)

Baptism testifies to us our purgation and ablution; the eucharistic supper testifies our redemption. Water is a figure of ablution, and blood of satisfaction. *Inst. IV:xiv.22.*

The Supper of Jesus Christ is an action so sacred, that it ought not to be soiled by any human inventions whatsoever. *Letters 99.*

The Supper is given us as a mirror in which we may contemplate Jesus Christ crucified . . . and raised. [Short Treatise on the Supper] *Tracts II:169.*

Jesus Christ is there offered to us in order that we may possess him, and in him all the fulness of grace which we desire. [Short Treatise on the Supper] *Tracts II:173.*

All the benefit which we would seek in the Supper is annihilated if Jesus Christ be not given to us as the substance and foundation of all. [Short Treatise on the Supper] *Tracts II:170.*

The sacraments derive their virtue from the word when it is preached intelligibly. [Short Treatise on the Supper] *Tracts II:191.*

The Spirit . . . transfuses life into us from the flesh of Christ. [Calvin's Second Defence of the Sacraments, 1556] *Tracts II:249.*

When celebrating the Supper, we shall indeed worship Him as present, but with minds upraised to heaven. [True Method of Reforming the Church] *Tracts III:281.*

[197]

The whole force of the consecration . . . is directed to us, not to the bread or the wine; and indeed to us, as obeying the command of Christ. [True Method of Reforming the Church] *Tracts III:281.*

We have no express command to constrain all Christians to use a specified day . . . The practice of all well-ordered churches should be to celebrate the Supper frequently, so far as the capacity of the people will admit. [Short Treatise on the Supper] *Tracts II:179.*

The devil has introduced the fashion of celebrating the Supper without any doctrine, and for doctrine has substituted ceremonies . . . pure apishness and buffoonery. [Short Treatise on the Supper] *Tracts II:190.*

[On I Cor. 11:23–26] The institution of Christ is a sure rule, so that if you turn aside from it but a very little, you are out of the right course. *Cor. I:372.*

It is not an empty or unmeaning sign . . . but those who receive this promise by faith are actually made partakers of his flesh and blood. *Syn. Gosp. III:209.*

There are three mistakes against which it is . . . necessary to be on our guard; first, not to confound the spiritual blessing with the sign; secondly, not to seek Christ on earth, or under earthly elements; thirdly, not to imagine any other kind of *eating* than that which draws into us the life of Christ by the secret power of the Spirit, and which we obtain by faith alone. *Syn. Gosp. III:209.*

LOVE TO GOD

The source and cause of obedience is the love wherewith we embrace God as our Father. *Four Last Bks of Moses III:225.*

The principle of worshipping God [is] a diligent love of him. *Dan. II:148.*

We can never separate love and obedience. *Dan. II:149.*

[On 1 John 2:3] The knowledge of God is efficacious . . . To know him is immediately to love him. *Gen. Epp. 174.*

The true *love* of Christ . . . is regulated by the observation of his doctrine as the only rule. *John II:91.*

The commencement of godliness is the *love* of God . . . Under the *love* of God is included the reverence due to him. *Syn. Gosp. III:58.*

No man will actually obey God but he who *loves* him . . . Our life will not be regulated aright till the love of God fill all our senses. *Syn. Gosp. III:58.*

The observance of the commandments consists not in the love of ourselves, but in the love of God and our neighbour . . . His is the best and most holy life, who lives as little as possible to himself. *Inst. II:vii.54.*

[On John 14:21] A more abundant knowledge of Christ is here represented as an extraordinary reward of our love to Christ. *John II:97.*

LOVE TO OTHERS

Piety is the root of charity. *Ezek. II:221.*

Where there is no love the Spirit of God does not rule there. *Zech.-Mal. 227.*

There will never be true charity toward neighbours, unless where the love of God reigns. *Syn. Gosp. III:59.*

The love which the children of the world have for each other is not a true love, but is a mercenary love. *Syn. Gosp. III:59(fn.).*

In God brotherly love seeks its cause, from him it has its root, and to him it is directed. *John II:76.*

Self-love keeps all our senses bound in such a manner that brotherly love is altogether banished. *John II:77.*

[Christ] loved all his people, that they may love each other. *John II:116.*

Faith and love . . . the sum-total of godliness. *Thess. 354.*

[On 1 Cor. 8:1] Whatever is devoid of love is of no account in the sight of God. *Cor. I:273.*

We must not reflect on the wickedness of men, but contemplate the Divine image in them; which, concealing and obliterating their faults, by its beauty and dignity allures us to embrace them in the arms of our love. *Inst. III:vii.6.*

Charity is ingenious in hiding the faults of brethren. *Gen. II:380.*

All contracts which are not formed according to the rule of charity, are vicious in the sight of God. *Gen. II:411.*

Let him who would engage in the duties of love, prepare himself for a life of labour . . . There is nothing to which we are more prone than to weariness in well-doing. *Heb. 143, 144.*

[On Heb. 13:1] Nothing flows away so easily as love. We cannot be Christians without being brethren. *Heb. 339, 340.*

All the acts and duties of love are so many sacrifices. *Heb. 351.*

The duties of love to our neighbour ought never to be injurious to faith. *Gal. 50.*

Love forms the chief part of Christian perfection. *Gal. 159.*

We shall never love our neighbours with sincerity, according to our Lord's intention, till we have corrected the love of ourselves. The two affections are opposite and contradictory. *Gal. 161.*

[On Eph. 5:21] Where love reigns, mutual services will be rendered. *Eph. 317.*

Love and faith – the whole perfection of a Christian man. *Past. Epp. 349.*

In order to preserve love we must bear with many things. *Gen. Epp. 102.*

The chief point in preserving Charity is to maintain Faith sacred and entire. [Psychopannychia] *Tracts III:416.*

Free affection is the foundation and beginning of duly obeying the Law, for what is drawn forth by constraint, or servile fear, cannot please God. *Four Last Bks of Moses I:381.*

[On Mic. 4:3] Though the gospel is at this day purely preached among us, when yet we consider how little progress we make in brotherly love, we ought justly to be ashamed of our indolence. *Jon.-Nah. 264.*

Except . . . we endeavour to relieve the necessities of our brethren, and to offer them assistance, there will not be in us but one part of true conversion. *Jon.-Nah. 264.*

The beginning of love is from the grace of Christ. *Cor. II:404.*

Distrust clings to us, deeply rooted, which keeps us back from all offices of love, until it is subdued by the grace of the same Spirit. *Cor. II:284.*

MAN

Man as Created

[God] appointed man . . . lord of the world . . . Thus man was rich before he was born. *Gen. I:96.*

We must not regard the intrinsic merit of men, but must consider the image of God in them, to which we owe all possible honour and love. *Inst. III:vii.6.*

Three gradations are to be noted in the creation of man; that his dead body was formed out of the dust of the earth; that it was endued with a soul . . . and that on this soul God engraved his own image, to which immortality is annexed. *Gen. I:112.*

The state of man was not perfected in the person of Adam (I Cor. 15:45) . . . Before the fall man's life was only earthly. *Gen. I:112, 113.*

The idea of a Deity impressed upon the mind of man is indelible. *Inst. I:iii.3.*

Some of the philosophers of antiquity have justly called man a microcosm, or world in miniature. *Inst. I:v.3.*

By [man's] being made of earth and clay, a restraint was laid upon pride. *Inst. I:xv.1.*

The proclaiming of [God's] glory on the earth . . . the very end of our existence. *Ps. IV:358.*

Seeing, hearing, walking, and feeling, are God's precious gifts. *Ps. IV:428.*

Nothing can be ascribed to man without taking it from God. *Is. II:393.*

We were created and born on the express condition, that we should devote ourselves to the knowledge of God. *Is. III:168.*

God . . . made man alone erect, and bade him look at what may be regarded as his own habitation. *Is. III:231.*

The whole strength of men depends on the grace of God; and . . . a sound mind proceeds from his Spirit. *Zech.-Mal. 337.*

What aptness and readiness soever is in men, it ought to be reckoned amongst the gifts of God. *Acts I:262.*

Those affections which God hath given to man's nature are, of themselves, no more corrupt than the author himself. *Acts I:327.*

Man as Fallen

[On Heb. 2:15, 16] That [God] preferred us to angels was not owing to our excellency, but to our misery. *Heb. 73.*

[On Ps. 1:1] The general character of men's lives is nothing else but a continual departure from the law of God. *Ps. I:2.*

Every man makes a god of himself, and virtually worships himself. *Ps. IV:84.*

Man, without the knowledge of God, being the most miserable object that can be imagined . . . *Ps. IV:132.*

Whatever men claim for themselves, they take from God. *Is. II:330.*

Such is the perverseness of men, that they always seek opportunities of despising or disallowing the works of God. *Four Last Bks of Moses I:22.*

If men claim even the least thing for themselves, they cannot call God their praise. *Jer. II:367.*

Whatever merit men claim for themselves, they take away from God. *Jer. IV:217.*

Nothing is more displeasing to God than for men to be *authadeis*, 'self-willed' (*2 Pet. 2:10*), that is, devoted to their own inclinations. *Is. IV:379.*

No righteousness will ever be found in mortal man, unless he obtain it from Christ. *Dan. II:216, 217.*

Nothing is more easy than to corrupt the pure worship of God, when men esteem God after their sense and wit. *Acts II:158.*

This wickedness is in men, naturally to deform God's glory with their inventions. *Acts II:159.*

The majority of men, immersed in their errors, are blind amidst the greatest opportunities of seeing. *Inst. I:v.8.*

Notwithstanding all the displays of the glory of God, scarcely one man in a hundred is really a spectator of it. *Inst. I:v.8.*

Herein appears the vile ingratitude of men – that while they ought to be proclaiming the praises of God for the wonderful skill displayed in their formation, and the inestimable bounties he bestows upon them, they are only inflated with the greater pride. *Inst. I:v.4.*

Men attempt to express in the work of their hands such a deity as they have imagined in their minds. *Inst. I:xi.8.*

When the Spirit calls men *darkness* [John 1:4], he at once totally despoils them of the faculty of spiritual understanding. *Inst. II:ii.19.*

God . . . is at perpetual war with the unmeasured audacity of men; anything we undertake without his approval will end miserably. *Gen. I:331.*

God, not man, the measure of all things
The whole humility of man consists in the knowledge of himself. *Ps. I:133.*

In the Church we must always be on our guard lest we pay too great a deference to men. [Calvin, in a letter to Melanchthon] *Letters 74.*

The recesses of the heart are so hidden, that no judgment can be formed of man by any human being. *Jer. II:356.*

All are apostates and deserters from God who turn to men and fix their hope in them. *Jer. II:346.*

All thought of God is excluded, when the industry, or valour, or success, or any other quality of men is extolled. *Dan. I:146.*

Men cannot be humbled otherwise than by placing death before them. *Ezek. II:43.*

[We ought not] to extol the persons of men so as to obscure the glory of God. *John I:150.*

It is the property of God to bring the counsels of men to nought. *Acts I:223.*

Men arrogate too much to themselves when they think that they excel in anything . . . Men cannot bear their own success . . . but madly triumph against God. *Jon.-Nah. 466.*

MARRIAGE

Marriage is a covenant consecrated by God. *Four Last Bks of Moses III:77.*

Solomon, in *Proverbs 2:17*, calls marriage the covenant of God, for it is superior to all human contracts. *Zech.-Mal. 553.*

God is the founder of marriage. *Zech.-Mal. 552.*

Marriage . . . is the fountain of mankind. *Zech.-Mal. 552.*

Marriage is the preservation of the human race. *Jer. II:302.*

[On Jer. 16:2] The law of man's creation, we know, was this, 'increase and multiply' (*Gen. 1:22; 8:17; 9:1, 7*). *Jer. II:301.*

[On Gen. 2:18] God ordains the conjugal life for man, not for his destruction, but to his salvation. *Gen. I:129.*

God pronounces that marriage will prove to men the best support of life. *Gen. I:129.*

The Lord would declare himself to be the maintainer of matrimonial fidelity, so that none who violate another's bed should escape his vengeance. He is surety between the man and his wife and requires mutual chastity from each. [In adultery] God himself is grievously wronged. *Gen. II:297.*

[On Num. 5, 'the spirit of jealousy'] By this rite . . . God proclaims Himself the guardian and avenger of conjugal fidelity. *Four Last Bks of Moses III:87.*

[The jealousy of God] This jealousy has reference to the sacred and spiritual marriage, whereby God has bound His people to Himself. *Four Last Bks of Moses IV:350.*

It is not lawful for the children of a family to contract marriage, except with the consent of the parents . . . But . . . the parties make their contract spontaneously, by mutual consent. *Gen. II:14, 27.*

Disorder in marriage

The artifice of Satan, in attempting the defamation of marriage, was twofold: first, that by means of the odium attached to it he might introduce the pestilential law of celibacy, and, secondly, that married persons might indulge themselves in whatever licence they pleased. *Gen. I:134.*

Unless we think and speak honourably of marriage, reproach is attached to its Author and Patron [God]. *Gen. I:134.*

All the troubles men find in marriage, they ought to impute to sin. *Gen. I:428.*

Mahomet allowed to men the brutal liberty of chastising their wives, and thus he corrupted that conjugal love and fidelity which binds the husband to the wife. *Dan. II:346.*

[Jokes about marriage] have come from Satan's workshop. *Cor. I:224.*

A desire for divorce is at variance with our profession. *Cor. I:244.*

When the bond of marriage is broken, than which none among men is more sacred, the whole of human society sinks into decay. *Gen. II:181.*

Nothing is less accordant with the divine institution than polygamy. *Gen. I:136.*

[On Gen. 6:2] It is not fornication which is here condemned . . . but too great indulgence of licence in choosing themselves wives. *Gen. I:239.*

The single life

Virginity . . . is an excellent gift; but is given only to a few. *Cor. I:232.*

The Scripture declares . . . that the gift of continence is a special grace [Matt. 19; 1 Cor. 7]. Those . . . renouncing marriage for the whole of their life, cannot be acquitted of rashness; . . . by so doing they tempt God. *Letters 136.*

Celibacy – this modern tyranny. *Inst. IV:xii.28.*

. . . the diabolical system of celibacy. *John I:323.*

MARTYRDOM

The martyr is made by his cause, and not by his punishment. *Dan. I:224.*

The kingdom of God is strengthened more by the blood of the martyrs than by the aid of arms. *John II:211.*

[The martyrs] did not set us an example of constancy in asserting the truth that we should now desert it, when handed down to us so signed and sealed; but they taught us the art by which, trusting to the Divine protection, we stand invincible by all the powers of death, hell, the world, and Satan! [On Shunning the Unlawful Rites of the Ungodly] *Tracts III:411.*

God would use your blood to sign his truth . . . It pleases him to employ you to the death in maintaining his quarrel. [Calvin's letter to five young prisoners at Lyons, 15 May 1553] *Letters 149, 150.*

MASS

The opinion that the Supper is a sacrifice derogates from that of Christ, and must therefore be condemned as devilish. [Short Treatise on the Supper] *Tracts II:183.*

To the Mass has been wholly transferred what was proper to the death of Christ, namely, to satisfy God for our sins, and so reconcile us to him. Moreover, the office of Christ has been transferred to those whom they name priests. [Short Treatise on the Supper] *Tracts II:184.*

A theatrical exhibition was got up, and substituted for the Supper . . . [It] ought more properly to be termed excommunion. [On the Necessity of Reforming the Church] *Tracts I:137, 138.*

To return to the ceremonies which are abolished, is to repair the veil of the temple which Jesus rent in his death . . . A multitude of ceremonies in the Mass is a form of Judaism quite contrary to Christianity. [Short Treatise on the Supper] *Tracts II:192.*

We loudly maintain that the sacrifice of the Mass is nothing else than an impious profanation of the Lord's Supper. [Antidote to the Council of Trent] *Tracts III:59.*

The devil has introduced the fashion of celebrating the Supper without any doctrine, and for doctrine has substituted ceremonies . . . pure apishness and buffoonery. [Short Treatise on the Supper] *Tracts II:190.*

Their Mass is diametrically opposed to the sacred Supper of our Lord. *Cor. I:372.*

The Mass, that head of all abominations. [On Shunning the Unlawful Rites of the Ungodly] *Tracts III:360.*

MEDIATOR

[Christ] is the Mediator of reconciliation . . . of intercession . . . of all doctrine. *Gal. 102.*

There was never since the beginning any communication between God and man, save only by Christ; for we have nothing to do with God, unless the Mediator be present to purchase his favour for us. *Acts I:276.*

[On Gal. 3:19] Since the beginning of the world, God has held no intercourse with men, but through the agency of his eternal Wisdom or Son. *Gal. 102.*

Christ is the ladder by which we ascend to God the Father. *Syn. Gosp. I:436.*

God can listen to no prayers without the intercession of Christ. *Four Last Bks of Moses II:295.*

Not even their gratitude was acceptable to [God], except through the sacrifice of the Mediator. *Four Last Bks of Moses 295.*

MEEKNESS

By *the meek* Christ means persons of mild and gentle dispositions. *Syn. Gosp. I:261.*

Where the Spirit of Christ is not, there will be no true meekness. *Is. I:385.*

That gentleness . . . which Christ showed, he requires also from his servants. *Cor. II:318.*

A desire for revenge reigns in all unbelievers, while, on the other hand, God governs his own children by the spirit of meekness and [kindness]. *Ps. I:98.*

It is hope alone . . . which of itself produces meekness. *Ps. II:27.*

MILLENNIUM

[On Dan. 7:27] This vision ought not to be explained of the final advent of Christ, but of the intermediate state of the Church. The saints began to reign under heaven, when Christ ushered in his kingdom by the promulgation of his Gospel. *Dan. II:75.*

MINISTRY

The ministry of men, which God employs in his government of the Church, is the principal bond which holds believers together in one body. *Inst. IV:iii.2.*

[God] leaves ministers possessed of nothing, considered in themselves. *Inst. IV:i.6.*

No one is a fit teacher in the Church, who has not been the disciple of the Son of God, and rightly instructed in his school, since his authority alone ought to prevail. *Gen. Epp. 158.*

No one . . . can faithfully teach the Church, except he is diligent in banishing errors. *Gen. Epp. 199.*

The [people] are more ready to acknowledge us as preachers than as pastors. [Calvin to Henry Bullinger, 1538] *Letters 45.*

The word of the Lord is so precious to himself, that he would be regarded by us as present, whenever he speaks through his ministers. *Gen. I:475.*

The infirmity of the minister does not destroy the faithfulness, power and efficacy of God's word. *Gen. II:94.*

No one is a sincere minister of God's word, but he who, despising reproach, and being ready, as often as it may be necessary, to attack various offences, will frame his method of teaching according to the command of God. *Gen. II:311.*

The man who holds the office of teacher must apply himself to the reception of truth before he attempt to communicate it. *Ps. II:237.*

To pastors and ministers the Lord commits his Church as his beloved wife. *Is. I:163.*

[On Is. 11:4] Christ acts by [ministers] in such a manner that he wishes their *mouth* to be reckoned as his *mouth*, and their *lips* as his *lips*. *Is. I:381.*

[On Is. 50:4] The most important duty of the ministers of the word is, to comfort wretched men . . . to point out what is true rest and serenity of mind. *Is. IV:53.*

Nothing is more ruinous to the Church than for God to take away faithful pastors. *Jer. I:181.*

There are many mercenaries in the Church [who] preach the [truth of God] for gain (2 Cor. 2:17). *Jer. II:286.*

[On the term *clergy*] I could wish . . . that some other more appropriate name had been given them . . . For Peter calls the whole Church *the clergy*, that is, *the inheritance of the Lord. Inst. IV:iv.9.*

The office of teaching is committed to pastors for no other purpose than that God alone may be heard there. *Is. I:95.*

[On Is. 49:2] To all the ministers of the Word must be applied what is here affirmed concerning Christ; for to them is given such efficacy of the Word, that they may not idly beat the air with their voices, but may reach the hearts and touch them to the quick. *Is. IV:10.*

[On Is. 51:16] In order to be covered with that shadow of the Lord [his ministers must be] certain that what they utter is the word of God . . . and that they do so by God's command. *Is. IV:82.*

The priesthood of the New Testament consists in slaying men, as a sacrifice to God, by the spiritual sword of the Word. *Syn. Gosp. III:384.*

[On John 3:11] Christ . . . enjoins on all his ministers a law of modesty, not to put forward their own dreams or conjectures – not to preach human inventions. *John I:117, 118.*

Let the minister attempt nothing trusting to his own wit and industry, but let him commit his labour to the Lord, upon whose grace the whole success dependeth. *Acts I:468.*

Even in our time [c.1550] God so enriches certain churches more than others, that they be seminaries to spread abroad the doctrine of the gospel. *Acts I:498.*

Teachers were not appointed merely to lead men to faith in Christ in one day or in one month, but to perfect the faith which has been begun in them. *Thess. 355.*

We are especially liable to be wearied in healing the diseases of our brethren. *Thess. 373.*

Doctrine, which solidly edifies, is commonly attended by little display. *Past. Epp. 117.*

[Paul] calls himself . . . a minister of the Church, *a minister of God* (1 Cor. 4:1), *a minister of the gospel* (Col. 1:23). *Philipp.-Col. 167.*

[On 1 Tim. 6:13] [This charge] is a proof how rare and hard a virtue it is, to persevere in the ministry, in a proper manner, till the end. *Past. Epp. 163.*

The call to the ministry

This secret call . . . is the honest testimony of our heart, that we accept the office offered to us, not from ambition or avarice, or any other unlawful motive, but from a sincere fear of God, and an ardent zeal for the edification of the Church. *Inst. IV:iii.11.*

As often as God chooses men as His ministers, although they are in themselves good for nothing, He forms and prepares them for their work. *Four Last Bks of Moses I:91.*

Two things are necessary – a Divine call, and faithfulness and integrity . . . A simple and naked call is not sufficient. *Jer. III:178.*

There are no regular teachers, but those on whom God has conferred the office. *Syn. Gosp. I:178.*

The qualifications

[On Num. 4.1, age for levitical service] Not only is strength and vigour of body requisite for spiritual warfare, but seriousness and gravity also. If they had been admitted in their youth, their levity might have detracted from the reverence due to sacred things. *Four Last Bks of Moses III:459.*

All godly teachers [should] ask from the Spirit of God what otherwise they could not at all possess . . . All things necessary for discharging their office are gifts of the Holy Spirit. *Is. IV:52, 53.*

Two things are required in God's servants, even knowledge and undaunted courage. *Jer. I:355.*

None are good teachers but those who have been good scholars . . . they alone are *learned*, who, by continually learning, do not refuse to make constant progress. *Is. IV:54,55.*

He who knows not how to strive knows not how to serve God and the Church, and is not fitted for administering the doctrine of the Word. *Is. IV:58.*

When God searches the minds and hearts of men by his word, ministers of the word are necessary to exercise this jurisdiction, men endued with wisdom, understanding, and prudence. *Jer. I:468.*

No one is a true pastor whom the Lord does not rule by his Spirit. *Zech.-Mal. 333.*

No man is qualified to become a teacher of heavenly doctrine, unless his feelings respecting it be such, that he is distressed and agonized when it is treated with contempt. *Syn. Gosp. I:447.*

Those whom Christ calls to the pastoral office he likewise adorns with the necessary gifts. *John II:268.*

Those that intrude themselves confidently, and in a spirit much elated, or who discharge the ministry of the word with an easy mind, as though they were fully equal to the task, are ignorant at once of themselves and of the task. *Cor. I:99.*

[On 2 Tim. 1:7] God governs his ministers by *the Spirit of power*, which is the opposite of cowardice. *Past. Epp. 191.*

The excellence of gifts produces carelessness, which is also accompanied by sloth. *Past. Epp. 189.*

[Calvin cites the practice of the Early Church] No one might minister in the Church but one who had received sufficient previous instruction, who from his early youth had imbibed sound doctrine, who from a strict discipline had acquired a certain habitual gravity, and more than common sanctity of life, who had been abstracted from secular occupations, and accustomed to spiritual cares and studies. *Inst. IV:341.*

Authority in the ministry

The only way to edify the Church is, for the ministers themselves to study to preserve to Jesus Christ his lawful authority. *Inst. IV:viii.1.*

Whatever authority and dignity is attributed by the Holy Spirit in the Scripture either to the priests and prophets under the law, or to the apostles and their successors, it is all given, not in a strict sense to the persons themselves, but to the ministry over which they were appointed, or, to speak more correctly, to the word, the ministration of which was committed to them. *Inst. IV:viii.2.*

Christ appoints pastors to his Church, not to *rule* but to *serve*. *Syn. Gosp. II:424.*

[Christ] is the only Pastor; . . . yet he admits many pastors under him, provided that he hold the preeminence over them all, and that by them he alone govern the Church. *Syn. Gosp. III:79.*

All the authority that is possessed by pastors, . . . is subject to the word of God . . . We must beware of giving any authority to men, as soon as they depart from the word of God. *John I:315.*

[Christ] continues, and will eternally continue to be, the only Teacher of the Church . . . He alone keeps possession of the whole power, while [the apostles] claim nothing for themselves but the ministry. *John II:266, 267.*

Frantic men require inspirations and revelations from heaven, and . . . contemn the minister of God, by whose hand they ought to be governed. *Acts I:355.*

Ministers of the Gospel are porters . . . of the kingdom of heaven, because they carry its keys . . . The key is placed . . . in the hands of the ministers of the word. *Syn. Gosp. II:292.*

We know by experience what great force principal churches have to keep other lesser churches in order. *Acts II:85.*

Fidelity in the ministry

[On Is. 62:1] None are good and faithful teachers but they who hold the salvation of the Church so dear as to spare no labours. *Is. IV:320.*

A good and faithful pastor ought . . . not only to abstain from impure doctrines . . . but also to detect all corruptions which are injurious to religion, to recover men from the deceptions of Satan, and . . . avowedly to carry on war with all superstitions. *Zech.-Mal. 379.*

All ministers of the word . . . ought to be exceedingly careful that the glory of [Christ's] resurrection should be always exhibited by them in connection with the ignominy of his death. *Syn. Gosp. II:300.*

[On Matt. 24:45] He demands extraordinary care from the principal servants . . . Drowsiness would be peculiarly disgraceful and inexcusable in pastors. *Syn. Gosp. III:165, 166.*

[On Acts 25:10] The ministers of Christ ought to have no less care to make their innocency known than to save their life. *Acts II:362.*

Christ's servants ought to be concerned as to their own reputation only insofar as is for the advantage of the Church. *Cor. II:228.*

There are very few of those who bear the title of ministers, in the present day [c.1550] who have the mark of sincerity impressed upon them. *Past. Epp. 191.*

[On Luke 15:7] A good teacher ought not to labour less to recover those that are *lost*, than to preserve those which are in his possession. *Syn. Gosp. II:340.*

A Bible-based ministry

The government of the church, by the preaching of the word, is . . . declared to be no human contrivance, but a most sacred ordinance of Christ . . . They who despise or reject this ministry offer insult and rebellion to Christ its Author. *Eph. 277, 278.*

[On Phil. 2:16. Paul] makes us resemble the lamps; while he compares the word of God to the wick, from which the light comes. *Phil. 72.*

Assiduous in prayer

These two things are united – teaching and praying. God would have him whom he has set a teacher in his Church, to be assiduous in prayer. *Jer. III:380.*

That the greater part of teachers either languish through indolence, or utterly give way through despair, arises from nothing else than that they are sluggish in the duty of prayer. *John II:122.*

Mutual harmony among ministers

Mutual love among ministers is demanded above all things, that they may be employed, with one accord, in building up the Church of God. *John II:123.*

Pastors . . . are precious pearls from God's treasuries, and the rarer they are, they are so much the more worthy of esteem. *Phil. 84.*

When ministers are lowered, contempt of the word arises. *Cor. I:149.*

The deadly plague of ambition

Teachers . . . have no plague more to be dreaded than ambition. *Syn. Gosp. I:269.*

No man surpasses another through his own industry, but through the undeserved kindness of God. *Syn. Gosp. I:442.*

Nothing has a more powerful tendency to withdraw teachers from a faithful and upright dispensation of the word, than to pay respect to men. *Syn. Gosp. III:42.*

No man can faithfully discharge the office of teacher in the Church, unless he be void of ambition, and resolve to make it his sole object to promote . . . the glory of God. *John I:292.*

It is ambition alone which . . . shuts the door against holy communion [among fellow ministers]. *Acts I:337(fn.).*

[215]

This . . . is the fountain of all evils . . . the deadly poison of all Churches, when ministers seek their own interests rather than those of Christ. *Cor. I:67.*

Opposition in the ministry

[Jeremiah] calls the warfare which awaits all pastors *the day of sorrow* [Jer. 17:16], for if they please men they cannot be the servants of God. *Jer. II:373.*

Whosoever . . . rejects the ministry of the Church . . . can neither have any fellowship with Christ nor be a child of God. *Is. IV:42.*

Satan . . . brings forward as many causes of offence as he can, that he may destroy or weaken the courage of a good pastor. *John II:288.*

Who is there that will be exempt from Satan's bite, when even Christ himself was not spared . . . ? *Cor. II:301.*

It is one of the tricks of Satan to defraud godly ministers of support, that the Church may be deprived of such ministers. *Gal. 177.*

Ministers . . . are engaged in an incessant warfare, for Satan will not allow them to promote the gospel without maintaining a conflict. *Phil. 80.*

Warnings for ministers

[On Exod. 18:13. Jethro's advice to Moses] Let . . . God's servants learn to measure carefully their powers, lest they should wear out, by ambitiously embracing too many occupations. For this . . . is a very common malady. *Four Last Bks of Moses I:303.*

The haughtiest and proudest of all men are they who shelter themselves under the name of God, and glory in the title of the Church. *Is. III:25.*

All prophets and ministers of God ought to watch against being covetous of gifts. *Dan. I:199.*

They will bend every moment to any breeze . . . because they have never taken root in God's truth. *Dan. I:209.*

[216]

Private men indeed sin; but in pastors there is the blame of negligence, and still more, when they deviate even the least from the right way, a greater offence is given. *Joel-Obad. 33.*

The guilt of the old is always the heaviest. *Joel-Obad. 35.*

There ought to be moderation in our respect for God's prophets . . . that he alone may be exalted. *Dan. I:194.*

God allows more power and liberty to Satan over wicked and ungodly ministers than over other ordinary men. *John I:280.*

Many men excel oftentimes in the gifts of the Spirit, who have an unclean heart. *Acts I:344, 345.*

There is no one of us that can take to himself the least jot of glory without sacrilegious robbing of God . . . All those make . . . open war against God which exalt themselves . . . That cannot be done without our overthrow. *Acts I:494, 495.*

Godly teachers must take . . . heed, first, that they favour not the affections of the flesh too much under the colour of zeal; secondly, that they break not out with headlong and unseasonable heat where there is yet place for moderation; thirdly, that they give not themselves over to foolish and uncomely railing. *Acts I:509.*

Oftentimes the immoderate heat of pastors in going about matters does no less hurt than their sluggishness. *Acts II:85.*

[On Acts 15:36] Churches do easily decay . . . unless they are looked to continually. *Acts II:85.*

We [ministers] ought to make so great account of the calling of God, that no unthankfulness of men may be able to hinder us. *Acts II:129.*

We must always speak of the efficacy of the ministry in such a manner that the entire praise of the work may be reserved for God alone. *Cor. I:289.*

This is the artifice of Satan – to seek some misconduct on the part of ministers, that may tend to the dishonour of the gospel. *Cor. II:248.*

Confidence in ourselves produces carelessness and arrogance. *Philipp.-Col. 67.*

[On 2 Tim. 2:5] Let [ministers of the word] see what things are inconsistent with their office [and] what it is that draws them away from Christ. *Past. Epp. 211.*

[On 2 Tim. 3:14] One worthless person will always be more effectual in destroying, than ten teachers in building. *Past. Epp. 246.*

Priorities

[On John 21:15, 16] No service can be more agreeable to Christ than that which is bestowed on *feeding his flock. John II:289.*

I think that there has never been, in ordinary life, a circle of friends so sincerely bound to each other as we have been in our ministry. [Calvin, in his dedication of his commentary on Titus to 'two eminent servants of Christ, William Farel and Peter Viret, his dearly beloved brethren and colleagues'. Geneva, 29 November 1549] *Past. Epp. 276.*

MIRACLES

[On John 11:40] A miracle is called *the glory of God. John I:444.*

[Miracles are] intended to prepare us for faith, or to confirm us in faith. *John I:448.*

Miracles must never be separated from the word. *Acts I:203.*

Miracles added to the word are seals. *Is. I:239.*

We must not contrive new miracles for the purpose of adding to the authority of Christ. *Is. I:42.*

Miracles prepare men to believe, but if miracles only occurred without the knowledge of God being added to his Word, faith will vanish away. *Dan. I:237.*

Faith does not depend on miracles, or any extraordinary sign, but is the peculiar gift of the Spirit, and is produced by means of the word ... There is nothing to which the flesh is more inclined than to listen to vain revelations. *Syn. Gosp. II:193, 194.*

[On Mark 16:17, miraculous signs] Though Christ does not expressly state whether he intends this gift to be temporary, or to remain perpetually in the Church, yet it is more probable that miracles were promised only for a time. *Syn. Gosp. III:389.*

How many do we find . . . demanding miracles, while others murmur against God because he does not indulge their wishes. *Ps. IV:43.*

When [God] permits false prophets to work miracles to deceive, it is to prove men's hearts. *Four Last Bks of Moses I:149.*

Impostors in their working of miracles are the ministers of God's vengeance, in order that the reprobate may be taken in their snares. *Four Last Bks of Moses I:443.*

Since the salvation of the Church has ever been the design of God in working miracles, why should the faithful be cast down? *Hab.-Hagg. 162.*

[On Mic. 4:6, 7] The Church is so preserved in the world, that it sometimes rises again from death; in short, the preservation of the Church, almost every day, is accompanied with many miracles. *Jon.-Nah. 275.*

The resurrection at the last day . . . will surpass all other miracles. *Ps. III:414.*

Any miracles . . . which seek to glorify the creature and not God, and which bolster up untruths and not the Word of God, are manifestly of the devil. *Rom. 312.*

MISSION OF CHRIST

God's purpose

It was not at random that the doctrine of the Gospel was preached to all nations, but by the decree of God, by whom it had been long ago ordained. *Is. III:425.*

[On Mic. 4:2. God] designed that the whole world should be subject to [Christ] *Jon.-Nah. 253.*

[219]

[On Mic. 4:11–13] Here the prophet specifies the end for which God had purposed to subject the heathen nations to his chosen people, – that he might be glorified. *Jon.-Nah. 289.*

[On Gen. 48:16] The faith of the fathers was always fixed on [Christ's] future mission. *Gen. II:429.*

[On Mic. 4:3, *afar off*] God would not be the king of one people only, or of Judea alone, but . . . his kingdom would be propagated to the extremities of the earth. *Jon.-Nah. 262.*

[On Zech. 12:9] Jerusalem was to be the mother of all churches . . . From thence God had determined to send forth the royal sceptre, that the Son of David might rule over the whole world. *Zech.-Mal. 358.*

[On Gen. 48, Jacob blessing Joseph] God, having scattered seed over the whole world, should gather together a Church for himself, out of all nations. *Gen. II:423.*

[On Ps. 150:6] The same songs, which were then only heard in Judea, would resound in every quarter of the globe. *Ps. V:321.*

Christ's Commission

God in the Person of Christ, began to reign on Mount Zion, when the doctrine of the Gospel from thence went forth to the extremities of the world. *Jon.-Nah. 278.*

[On the parable of the sower. Christ] was about to drive his plough through every country of the world. *Syn. Gosp. II:120.*

[On Matt. 21:19] No certain limits are prescribed, but the whole world is assigned to them, to be reduced to obedience to Christ; that by disseminating the gospel wherever they could, they might erect his kingdom in all nations. *Inst. IV:320.*

. . . to reduce the whole world under [Christ's] sway, and to publish a doctrine which subdues all pride, and lays prostrate the whole of the human race. *Syn. Gosp. III:381, 382.*

[The apostolic Church] These few and simple creatures did more prevail against the troublesome tumults of the world, with the base and simple sound of their mouth, than if God should openly have thrown down lightnings from heaven. *Acts I:xxvi, xxvii.*

The voice of a small and dispersed body of men resounded even to the extremities of the world . . . a miracle of heavenly power. *Syn. Gosp. III:394.*

The Church's goal

There is nothing which we ought to desire more earnestly than that the whole world should bow to the authority of God. *Is. IV:286.*

It ought to be the great object of our daily wishes, that God would collect churches for himself from all the countries of the earth, that he would enlarge their numbers, enrich them with gifts, and establish a legitimate order among them. *Inst. III:xx.42.*

[On Mount Zion, Is. 28:17] At the present day [c.1550] *Mount Zion* is everywhere for the Church has spread to the ends of the world. *Is. II:292.*

A prayer of John Calvin

May we daily solicit thee in our prayers, and never doubt, but that under the government of thy Christ, thou canst again gather together the whole world . . . when Christ shall exercise the power given to him for our salvation and for that of the whole world. *Jon.-Nah. 393.*

MODESTY

A mature knowledge of things makes a man modest. *Past. Epp. 74.*

Let us learn to lay upon ourselves the restraint of modesty. *Is. III:185.*

MONOTHEISM

Among all nations a persuasion has existed concerning a supreme God who reigns alone. *Dan. I:133.*

[221]

It was ever a principle held by all nations, that there is some supreme Deity; for though they devised for themselves various gods, yet they all believed that there is one supreme God. *Jer. V:135.*

The philosophers with one mouth teach, that there are not many gods, but some supreme Deity who is the source of divinity; and this is what has been believed by all heathen nations. *Zech.-Mal. 428.*

MORTIFICATION

The only source of our mortification is our participation in the death of Christ. *Rom 125.*

The mortification of the flesh is the effect of the cross of Christ. *Gal. 169.*

The death of the flesh is the life of the Spirit. *Gal. 169.*

Burial expresses a continued process of mortification. *Col. 185.*

MUSIC

[On Ps. 33:2] Musical instruments in celebrating the praises of God would be no more suitable than the burning of incense, the lighting up of lamps, and the restoration of the other shadows of the law. *Ps. I:539.*

Music [was] useful as an elementary aid to the people of God in ancient times (*Ps. 92:3*) . . . Now that Christ has appeared, and the Church has reached full age, it were only to bury the light of the Gospel, should we introduce the shadows of a departed generation. *Ps. III:495.*

[On Ps. 149] The musical instruments he mentions were peculiar to the infancy of the Church, nor should we foolishly imitate a practice which was intended only for God's ancient people. *Ps. V:312.*

[Of Miriam's timbrels] Musical instruments were among the legal ceremonies which Christ at his coming abolished; and, therefore we, under the Gospel, must maintain a greater simplicity. *Four Last Bks of Moses I:263.*

NATURAL MAN

Men think themselves half absolved when no one severely reproves them. *Jer. III:151.*

. . . in all their reasoning faculties they miserably fail. *John I:32.*

The term *flesh* . . . is employed to describe man's whole nature. *Cor. I:124.*

[On 1 Cor. 2:14, *foolishness to him*] It is not owing simply to the obstinacy of the human will, but to the impotency, also, of the understanding. *Cor. I:116.*

[Nicodemus'] magisterial haughtiness . . . We reject with diabolical pride everything that is not explained to our reason. *John I:117, 116.*

[On Peter in Matt. 16:22] There is no beast more furious than this wisdom of the flesh . . . It is only from the word of God that we ought to be wise. *Syn. Gosp. II:301, 302.*

Darkness is the name here given to the whole nature of man before regeneration. *Eph. 309.*

The whole life of man, until he is converted to Christ, is a ruinous labyrinth of wanderings. *Gen. Epp. 50.*

NATURAL THEOLOGY

It will always be evident to persons of correct judgment, that the idea of a Deity impressed on the mind of man is indelible. *Inst. I:iii.3.*

The exact symmetry of the universe is a mirror, in which we may contemplate the otherwise invisible God. *Inst. I:v.1.*

The majority of men, immersed in their errors, are blind amidst the greatest opportunities of seeing. *Inst. I:v.8.*

Notwithstanding all the displays of the glory of God, scarcely one man in a hundred is really a spectator of it. *Inst. I:v.8.*

Such knowledge of God as now remains in men is nothing else than a frightful source of idolatry, and of all superstitions. *John I:113.*

[On Acts 14:17] It made men without excuse, and yet was not sufficient to salvation. *Acts II:19.*

NATURE

We must always start with this principle, that everything in nature depends upon the will of God, and that the whole course of nature is only the prompt carrying into effect of his orders. *Ps. V:301.*

The expression that nature is God, may be used in a pious sense by a pious mind . . . but . . . it is dangerous . . . to confound the Deity with the inferior course of his works. *Inst. I:v.5.*

We must come to this conclusion respecting the existence of fleas, caterpillars and other noxious insects . . . These were created by God, but by God as an Avenger. *Gen. I:104.*

NOVELTY

God's service is corrupted if any strange invention be mingled with it. Let us . . . learn not to intrude our own imaginations or inventions in God's service. *Four Last Bks of Moses II:329, 330.*

[On the altar raised by the two-and-a-half tribes at Jordan] They sinned not lightly in attempting a novelty . . . and in a form which was very liable to be misconstrued . . . Let us learn to attempt nothing rashly . . . Let us . . . beware of disturbing pious minds by the introduction of any kind of novelty. *Josh. 253, 254.*

Let us so adhere to the word of God that no novelty may captivate us and lead us astray. *Hos. 125.*

[On Tit. 2:15] They had such an itch for novelty, that hardly any space was left for edification. *Past. Epp. 323.*

NUMBERS IN SCRIPTURE

[On Dan. 7:7] When plurality is denoted, the number ten is used. *Dan. II:25.*

[On the ten horns, Dan. 7:19, 20] A finite number is put for an indefinite one. *Dan. II:55.*

[On Dan. 12:11, 12] In numerical calculations I am no conjuror. *Dan. II:391.*

NUMBERS IN THE CHURCH

We ought not to judge by the largeness of the number, unless we choose to prefer the chaff to the wheat. *Is. I:53.*

[On Is. 4:3] We are wont always to desire a multitude, and to estimate by it the prosperity of the Church. On the contrary, we should rather desire to be few in number, and that in all of us the glory of God may shine brightly. *Is. I:155.*

In proportion as we see the strength of the Church weakened and brought low, we may be more fully convinced that God has in his power the means of multiplying a small number. *Is. III:140.*

OATHS AND VOWS

An oath . . . is a part of divine worship. *Jer. V:78.*

God makes an oath that he might apply a remedy to the weakness of our faith. *Jer. V:78.*

[On the third commandment] Whenever we swear by God's name, we profess that we are under his power; and that we cannot escape if we swear falsely. *Jer. I:269.*

Unless we abide by our promises God will always be the avenger of fraud and treachery. *Four Last Bks of Moses IV:286, 287.*

OBEDIENCE

God expects our obedience

He must be obeyed not partially, but universally. *Four Last Bks of Moses I:346.*

They only obey God who depend on His authority alone. *Four Last Bks of Moses I:345.*

Slavish and constrained obedience differs little from rebellion. *Ps. IV:485.*

Fear is the true preparation for obedience. *Dan. II:116.*

[Adam in Eden] Abstinence from the fruit of one tree was a kind of first lesson in obedience, that man might know he had a Director and Lord of his life. *Gen. I:126.*

Faith and obedience

Our faith begins with obedience . . . Obedience to God, goes before understanding. *Is. III:270.*

There is no obedience without faith; and there is no faith without the word. *Is. IV:390, 391.*

To *hear* the Lord is to obey his word. *Is. IV:393.*

The basis of true religion is obedience. *Jer. I:395.*

We never really and from the heart obey, except when we rely on his promises and hope for a happy success. *Hab.-Hagg. 343.*

We cannot rely on his promises, without obeying his commandments. *Syn. Gosp. I:219.*

All the commandments of God contain a hidden promise, that so often as we obey him, all that work which we take in hand must needs fall out well. *Acts I:349.*

The Word of God directs our Obedience

Our whole happiness lies in obeying the word of God. There is no hope of salvation if we do not obey God and his word. *Is. IV:159, 160.*

. . . the spiritual sword of the Gospel wherewith Christ killeth us, that he may make us obey him (Rom. 15:16) *Acts I:185*.

The word of the Lord constrains us by its majesty, as if by a violent impulse, to yield obedience to it. *Cor. I:100*.

The Holy Spirit enables our obedience

[On Ps. 119:17] He declares it to be owing to the peculiar grace of the Holy Spirit, that any person keeps the law of God. *Ps. IV:412, 413*.

It is not in our power to obey what God commands us, except this power proceeds from him. *Ezek. I:109*.

Whence cometh aptness to be taught, and a mind to obey, but from his Spirit? *Acts II:97*.

Love for God prompts our obedience

The source and cause of obedience is the love wherewith we embrace God as our Father. *Four Last Bks of Moses III:225*.

We can never separate love and obedience. *Dan. II:149*.

No man will actually obey God but he who loves him. *Syn. Gosp. III:58*.

The obedience which believers render to [Christ] is . . . the effect of his love. *John II:113*.

Our obedience proves our adoption as sons

He who truly desires to worship him, will study to pay him the obedience of a son, and the submission of a servant. *Inst. III:ii.26*.

The end of regeneration is, that the life of believers may exhibit a symmetry and agreement between the righteousness of God and their obedience; and that thus they may confirm the adoption by which they are accepted as his children. *Inst. III:vi.1*.

God has adopted them on the condition of directing themselves and their whole life to obedience to him. *Is. III:284*.

The practice of obedience

Noah obeyed God, not in one particular only, but in all. *Gen. I:261.*

We are taught . . . to follow God through every obstacle. *Gen. II:15.*

[On Gen. 22] . . . as with closed eyes, [Abraham] goes whither he is directed. *Gen. I:563.*

[On Gen. 12:4] In this place the obedience of faith is commended, and not as one act simply, but as a constant and perpetual course of life. *Gen. I:350.*

Obedience is the end of our calling (Rom. 1:5; 16:26). *Is. IV:164.*

As soon as God issues any command, we must obey, even if our senses refuse. *Ezek. I:164.*

When God wishes to stir us up to obedience, he does not always promise a happy result of our labour . . . Let us learn to leave the event in the hand of God. *Ezek. I:111, 112.*

The subterfuges which seem to remove danger, are much more agreeable to our effeminate carnal nature than simple obedience to the word of God. [On Shunning the Unlawful Rites of the Ungodly] *Tracts III:364.*

It is a genuine proof of obedience when we simply obey God, however numerous the obstacles. *Jon.-Nah. 24.*

There is not anything in the whole world which ought not to give way to God's command. *Jon.-Nah. 25.*

Obedience and Christian maturity

Obedience is the source, not only of an absolutely perfect and complete faith, but of all right knowledge of God. *Inst. I:vii.2.*

What is the beginning of true learning but a prompt alacrity to hear the voice of God. *Inst. I:vii.5.*

We preserve a sense of his majesty and the purity of his worship, no longer than we implicitly attend to his voice. *Inst. II:i.4.*

Obedience

God's acceptance of our obedience

Through the interposition of pardon, the will to obey is pleasing to God instead of perfect obedience . . . In the gospel God receives, with Fatherly indulgence, what is not absolutely perfect. *Four Last Bks of Moses I:414.*

The fruits of obedience

Obedience is . . . the mother of piety. *Four Last Bks of Moses I:453.*

Obedience . . . the mistress of humility. *Four Last Bks of Moses IV:78.*

OLD AGE

Old age has this among other evils, that it renders men more indolent and morose. *Gen. I:268.*

The more God has lengthened out their lives the more should they be exercised in singing his praises. *Ps. V:308.*

We may, with tranquil minds, suffer this frail tabernacle to be dissolved . . . The chief part of a good old age consists in a good conscience and in a serene and tranquil mind. *Gen. II:37.*

The shorter the term of life [that] remains to us, the more diligent ought we to be in executing our office. *Gen. Epp. 379.*

[On Eph. 4:13] No mention is made of old age, for in the Christian progress no place for it is found. *Eph. 284.*

The guilt of the old is always the heaviest. *Joel-Obad. 35.*

OLD TESTAMENT

Revelation in the Old Testament

Inscribed on all [the types] was the word of God. *Hab.-Hagg. 131.*

[On the O.T. saints] They had the mirror, we have the substance. *Gal. 107.*

The ancient prophecies were dictated by Christ. *Gen. Epp. 40.*

[229]

[The O.T. prophets] They spread the table, that others might afterwards feed on the provisions laid on it. *Gen. Epp. 41.*

The old dispensation was symbolical . . . the new spiritual. *Heb. xiv.*

The cherubim . . . were peculiar to the old state of tutelage under the legal dispensation. *Inst. I:xi.3.*

It is impossible really to understand and believe the Old Testament and to deny the New. *Heb. xiv.*

Whoever can read and hear what God has revealed once for all to the world, by Moses and the Prophets, is inexcusable. *Jer. I:483.*

Salvation in the Old Testament

The fathers were partakers of the same gospel as ourselves, so far as relates to the faith of a gratuitous salvation. *John I:21.*

The fathers who lived under the Law had the same hope of eternal life . . . as they had the same grace of adoption in common with us, then faith must have rested on the same promises. *Heb. 185.*

The ancients were reconciled to God in a sacramental manner by the victims, [sacrifices], just as we are now cleansed through baptism . . . These symbols were useful only as they were exercises unto faith and repentance. *Four Last Bks of Moses II:324, 325.*

The Fathers, (according to the offer made to them through the word of God), are by faith made partakers of this life . . . sustained by the very same promise of salvation by which Adam was first raised from the fall. *Gen. I:65.*

The new covenant so flowed from the old, that it was almost the same in substance, while distinguished in form. *Ezek. II:178.*

Christ in the Old Testament

God never revealed himself to the Fathers but in his eternal Word and only-begotten Son. *Is. I:201.*

If the Law be separated from Christ it is like a dead letter; Christ alone gives it life. *Ezek. II:176, 177.*

[On Hagg. 1:7, 8] The people were preserved by the visible Temple in the hope of the future Christ . . . that they might worship God spiritually under the external symbols. *Hab. -Hagg. 332.*

[The Old Testament saints] . . . breathed after Christ, like hungry persons, and yet possessed a serene faith. *Syn. Gosp. II:111.*

Christ is as truly heard at the present day in the Law and the Prophets as in the Gospel. *Syn. Gosp. II:315.*

In the whole of the legal priesthood, in the sacrifices, and in the form of the sanctuary, we ought to seek Christ. *Syn. Gosp. III:360, 361.*

All the fathers, from the beginning of the world, drew from Christ all the gifts which they possessed. *John I:51.*

Christ, with His Gospel has been *promised* and always expected from the beginning of the world. *Rom. 15.*

Every doctrine of the law, every command, every promise, always points to Christ. *Rom. 221.*

This is the true perpetuity of the ceremonies, that they should rest in Christ, who is their full truth and substance. *Four Last Bks of Moses II:205.*

The Holy Spirit in the Old Testament

The faithful under the ancient covenant were gifted and endowed with a spirit of regeneration. *Ezek. II:177.*

All godly men, since the beginning of the world were endued with the same spirit of understanding, of righteousness, and sanctification, wherewith the Lord doth at this day illumine and regenerate us. *Acts I:86.*

[231]

The Church in the Old Testament

The infancy of the Church lasted until the end of the Law, but as soon as the Gospel had been preached, it immediately arrived at manhood. *John I:173.*

The priestly order was as it were the nursery of the prophets. *Jer. I:33.*

The grace of regeneration was promised to the ancient people when God consecrated the seventh day. *Ezek. II:302.*

Heaven in the Old Testament

[Abraham] calmly passed from his earthly pilgrimage into heaven. *Gen. I:451.*

The fathers under the Law embraced by faith, while they lived, that inheritance of the heavenly life into which they were admitted at death. *Syn. Gosp. II:188.*

Quotations from the Old Testament in the New

In all their quotations from Scripture the apostles take scrupulous care to arouse us to a more careful perusal of them. *Rom. 96.*

Whenever any proof from Scripture is quoted by the apostles, though they do not translate word for word, and sometimes depart widely from the language, yet it is applied correctly and appropriately to their subject. *Syn. Gosp. I:133.*

OPPOSITION

Nothing that is attempted in opposition to God can ever be successful. *Is. IV:206.*

There is sufficient power in God to subdue all enemies. *Hab.-Hagg. 309.*

The more brightly the light of doctrine shines, so as to press more closely on wicked men, they are driven to a greater pitch of madness. *Syn. Gosp. II:159.*

We imagine that everything that Satan does for the purpose of hindering our salvation blocks up the path of God. *Is. III:220.*

[On Is. 51:15] There are no raging billows which God cannot allay and calm in order to deliver his Church. *Is. IV:81.*

It is customary with Satan to exaggerate in words the power of the enemies, and to represent the dangers as greater than they really are. *Is. III:90.*

The ungodly . . . in molesting the faithful whom God has taken under his protection, openly wage war against him. *Ps. I:244.*

When anyone begins to rely on God, he must lay his account with and arm himself for sustaining many assaults from Satan. *Ps. I:520.*

[On Ps. 64:8] God is ever watching, as it were, his opportunity of converting the stratagems of the wicked into means just as completely effective of their destruction, as if they had intentionally employed them for that end. *Ps. II:449.*

Whenever an injury is inflicted on men, God in their person, is offended. *Four Last Bks of Moses II:359.*

The paternal favour of God towards the elect, is like a fan to excite against them the enmity of the world . . . A blind ferocity impels them to an unintentional resistance against God. *Gen. II:262, 264.*

 . . . the hardship and misery of our condition in the state of warfare under the cross, in which we have to continue as long as we live. *Inst. II:xv.4.*

[On Heb. 1:13] These two things, then, ought to be borne in mind, – that the kingdom of Christ shall never in this world be at rest, but that there will be many enemies by whom it will be disturbed; and secondly, that whatever its enemies may do, they shall never prevail. *Heb. 49.*

Whenever the wicked assault us, the Spirit calls upon us to engage in prayer . . . If any man . . . neglects the exercise of prayer, he defrauds God of the honour which belongs to him, in not referring his cause to him, and in not leaving him to judge . . . it. *Ps. I:236.*

He must resist all fears and all intrigues . . . Oftentimes the enemies of the truth assail them by flatteries . . . These things have often been said to us. *Joel-Obad. 344, 345.*

ORDINATION

[Christ] did not commence his reign until he was publicly ordained the Master and Redeemer of his people. *Dan. II:214.*

Unless we abide by our promises, God will always be the avenger of fraud and treachery. *Four Last Bks of Moses IV:286, 287.*

ORIGINAL SIN

Original sin . . . that hereditary corruption . . . the depravation of a nature previously good and pure. *Inst. II:i.5.*

[Ps. 51:5] intimates that we are cherished in sin from the first moment that we are in the womb . . . born into the world with the seed of every iniquity . . . Sin . . . exists within us as a disease fixed in our nature. *Ps. II:290.*

Original sin . . . an hereditary pravity and corruption of our nature, diffused through all the parts of the soul, rendering us obnoxious to the Divine wrath, and producing in us those works which the Scripture calls 'works of the flesh'. *Inst. II:i.8.*

From a putrefied root, therefore, have sprung putrid branches, which have transmitted their putrescence to remoter ramifications. *Inst. II:i.7.*

This depravity never ceases in us, but is perpetually producing new fruits . . . like the emission of flame and sparks from a heated furnace. *Inst. II:i.8.*

Everything in man, the understanding and will, the soul and body, is polluted and engrossed by this concupiscence . . . Man is himself nothing else but concupiscence. *Inst. II:i.8.*

We have . . . by nature a heart of stone, and there is in all an innate hardness from the womb, which God alone can mollify and amend. *Heb. 84.*

Original sin is sufficient for the condemnation of all men. *Ezek. II:241.*

Although we perish through the fault of another [Adam], yet the fault of each individual is joined with it. *Ezek. II:218.*

In original sin are included blindness of mind and perverseness of heart. [Brief Confession of Faith] *Tracts II:131.*

PATIENCE

Patience is the fruit and proof of faith. *Thess. 388.*

Patience is the inseparable companion of faith. *Rom. 176.*

Faith, love, patience – the sum of Christian perfection. *Past. Epp. 311.*

Patience – the seasoning of faith and love. *Past. Epp. 311.*

Where there is no patience, there is not even a spark of faith. *Jer. V:413.*

Hope is the foundation of patience. *Jer. V:419.*

The patience of the saints differs widely from stupidity. *Syn. Gosp. I:150.*

The patience of Christ – *expectatio Christi. Thess. 416.*

The hope of blessed immortality . . . the mother of patience. *Thess. 363.*

The children of God overcome, not by sullenness, but by patience. *Ps. I:464.*

Patience is a kind of silence by which the godly keep themselves in subjection to his authority. *Ps. III:373.*

God will not only keep our affections under restraint by his commandments, but will also train them to patience by his promises. *Ps. I:240.*

[On Gen. 15:12] The Lord, for the purpose of exercising the patience of his people, suspends his promise more than four centuries. *Gen. I:416.*

It is only in the Lord's school we can ever learn to maintain composure of mind, and a posture of patient expectation and trust under the pressure of distress. *Ps. IV:20.*

It behoves the faithful to be tranquil and quiet, and wait patiently for God, during times of perplexity and confusion. *Hab.-Hagg. 60.*

No man wishes to sow the seed, but all wish to reap the harvest before the season arrives. *Syn. Gosp. III:118.*

We would have God ever act in haste . . . because we do not consider that the fitness of times is determined by his will. *Jer. V:49.*

Believers . . . should lay their account with a long exercise of patience. *Syn. Gosp. III:122.*

PEACE

Peace with God

Peace is a free gift and flows from the pure mercy of God. *Syn. Gosp. I:121.*

Our consciences will never enjoy peace till they rely on the propitiation for sins. *Eph. 230.*

. . . to hope for peace, whilst we wage war with God. *Four Last Bks of Moses III:276.*

[On Is. 32:18] Assured peace . . . is enjoyed by none but believers, who appeal to the heavenly tribunal, not only by their piety, but by their reliance on the mercy of God. *Is. II:424.*

Faith ever brings us to peace with God . . . because the will of God alone is sufficient to appease our minds. *Jer. I:342.*

Peace within

Ungodliness is never at rest; but where faith exists, there the mind is composed. *Is. I:232.*

[On Is. 9:7] It is impossible that Christ should be *King*, without also keeping his people in calm and blessed *peace*. *Is. I:314.*

Strong faith quiets the conscience, and composes the spirit. *Ps. IV:363.*

The repose of a well-regulated mind is a signal mark of God's favour . . . Tranquillity of mind . . . can only arise from having God as our Keeper, and from resting under his protection. *Four Last Bks of Moses III:265, 266.*

[On Heb. 7:1, *king of peace*] This peace . . . is the fruit of that righteousness . . . Yet I prefer to understand it here of that inward peace which tranquillizes the conscience and renders it confident before God. *Heb. 156.*

The help of God comes to our aid in a secret and gentle manner, like the still-flowing streams, yet it imparts to us more tranquillity of mind than if the whole power of the world were gathered together for our help. *Ps. II:199.*

God . . . offers us peace . . . on this condition, that we make war with our own lusts . . . being at peace with God by being enemies to ourselves. *Ezek. II:20.*

Peace with others

[On 1 Cor. 14:33] Accursed is that *peace* of which revolt from God is the bond, and blessed are those contentions by which it is necessary to maintain the kingdom of Christ. *Cor. I:466.*

[On Heb. 12:14] Men are so born that they all seem to shun peace. *Heb. 324.*

The truth of His Gospel is the only bond of peace. [True Method of Reforming the Church] *Tracts III:240.*

The peace of the Church is founded on his eternal and unchangeable purpose . . . the heavenly decree. *Is. II:213.*

We ought to enjoy, in this our pilgrimage on earth, as much peace and satisfaction as if we were put in full possession of our paternal inheritance and home. *Ps. II:33.*

PERFECTION

Our present perfection in Christ

Faith doth not make us clean, as a virtue or quality poured into our souls; but because it receiveth that cleanness which is offered in Christ. *Acts II:50, 51.*

Christ doth offer and present us clean and just in the sight of his Father, by putting away our sins daily, which he hath once purged by his blood. *Acts II:51.*

The highest perfection of the godly in this life, is an earnest desire to make progress. *Eph. 261.*

Faith, love, patience – the sum of Christian perfection. *Past. Epp. 311.*

In the children of God, even after they are regenerated, there always abide the remainders of carnal desires . . . God receives, with fatherly indulgence, what is not absolutely perfect. *Four Last Bks of Moses I:414.*

When Christ or the Apostles are treating of a perfect life, they always refer believers to the Law. *Four Last Bks of Moses III:69.*

No sinless perfection

. . . the saintlings, who lay claim to angelic perfection. *Jer. II:211.*

Beware of the intrigues of Satan . . . for we see that some leave the Church because they require in it the highest perfection . . . and seek to form for themselves a new world, in which there is to be a perfect Church . . . They depart from God himself, and violate the unity of the Church. *Hab.-Hagg. 351.*

[Perfectionism] . . . the delirious dreams of fanatics. [Antidote to the Council of Trent] *Tracts III:157.*

[Sinless perfection] . . . that devilish figment . . . that as soon as we are grafted into the body of Christ, all the corruption that is in us must be destroyed. *Ps. III:439.*

[238]

Perfection

Those fanatics who bewitch both themselves and others with a vain opinion of their having attained to perfect righteousness. *Ps. IV:136.*

. . . those Cyclopses and monsters in heresy . . . who speak so much of perfection in holiness. *Ps. V:250.*

[Perfectionism] . . . this imposture of the devil. *Four Last Bks of Moses II:357.*

PERSECUTION

Definition

I call it persecution for righteousness' sake, not only when we suffer in defence of the gospel, but also when we are molested in the vindication of any just cause. *Inst. III:viii.7.*

We must expect in this world to meet with the secret treachery of friends, as well as with undisguised persecution. *Ps. II:336.*

[On Gen. 15:17] The condition of the Church could not be painted more to the life, than when God causes a burning torch to proceed out of the smoke. *Gen. I:420.*

[On Zeph. 2:8] God intimates here that he does not depart from his elect when the wicked spit, as it were, in their faces. *Hab.-Hagg. 246.*

Satan's aim

No war was ever carried on so continuously and professedly against the Church, as those which occurred after the Caesars arose, and after Christ was made manifest to the world . . . The wrath of Satan was excited against all God's children on account of the manifestation of Christ. *Dan. II:57.*

God's purpose and provision

The salvation of his Church is so precious in the sight of God, that he regards the wrong done to the faithful as done to himself. *Jer. V:146.*

[239]

[On Zeph. 3:12, 13] The Church is subdued by the cross, that she may know her pride, which is so innate and so fixed in the hearts of men. *Hab.-Hagg. 295.*

[On Mark 10:30] The cross . . . is attached to their back, yet so sweet is the seasoning of the grace of God . . . that their condition is more desirable than the luxuries of kings. *Syn. Gosp. II:408.*

Persecution is a touchstone to try faith. *John II:161.*

The more the Church is diminished, it may the more increase through the heavenly blessing.*Acts I:495.*

It goeth well with the godly, because they triumph gloriously before God and his angels in all injuries which they suffer . . . Those persecutions which we must suffer for the testimony of the gospel, are remnants of the sufferings of Christ. *Acts II:115.*

The Son of God doth suffer not only with us, but also in us. *Acts II:297.*

Persecutions are in a manner seals of adoption to the children of God. *Phil. 48.*

It is a true test of our piety, when, being plunged into the lowest depths of disasters, we lift up our eyes, our hopes, and our prayers, to God alone. *Ps. II:167.*

[On Ps. 44:22] Let us always have present to our view this condition of the Church, that as we are adopted in Christ, we are appointed to the slaughter. *Ps. II:171.*

Our greatest comfort under persecution is conscious rectitude. *Ps. II:329.*

The certain outcome

[The oppressed Church] shall stand erect . . . being renewed and multiplied from age to age by various resurrections. *Is. III:134.*

The Church doth always overlive her enemies. *Acts I:495.*

[On Ps. 41:5] The more that God sees his own people cruelly treated, he is so much the more disposed mercifully to succour them. *Ps. II:118.*

Tyrants may burn their flesh and their bones, but the blood remains to cry aloud for vengeance; and intervening ages can never erase what has been written in the register of God's remembrance. *Ps. II:356.*

[On Ps. 68] Those who persecute the Church are here spoken of as God's enemies. *Ps. III:7.*

We shall lose nothing of our right, if we bear injuries with moderation and equanimity . . . God will be so much the more ready to vindicate us, the more modestly we submit ourselves to endure all things. *Gen. I:208.*

Calvin's 'Song of Victory', composed in Latin in honour of Jesus Christ, in 1541, and translated from the French rhyme:

> But the precious blood shed by martyrs,
> That it might be as a testimony rendered to its God,
> Will in the Church of God serve as seed
> From which children will come forth, filled with understanding.
> *Phil. 30, fn.*

PERSEVERANCE

Definition

[The elect differ] in no respect from others, except in being protected by the special mercy of God from rushing down the precipice of eternal death . . . That they go not to the most desperate extremes of impiety, is not owing to any innate goodness of theirs, but because the eye of God watches over them, and his hand is extended for their preservation. *Inst. III:xxiv.10.*

Our perseverance grounded in God

All our progress and perseverance are from God. *Gen. Epp. 373.*

Perseverance [is] God's singular gift. *Ezek. I:380.*

The faithful promise themselves security in God, and nowhere else. *Ps. I:143.*

The permanency of our salvation does not depend on us, but on the secret election of God. *Syn. Gosp. III:141.*

The perseverance of faith . . . flows from election. *Rom. 252.*

We have no perseverance in ourselves unless God daily, nay, momentarily strengthen us, and follow us up with his favour. *Ezek. II:90.*

Both will and effort would immediately fail in us, were he not to add his gift of perseverance. *Hab.-Hagg. 346.*

It is impossible that we could stand one moment in the contest with such enemies as Satan, sin, and the world, did we not receive from God the grace which secures our perseverance. *Ps. III:37.*

[On Ps. 144:1] The constancy and perseverance [David] had shown was signally a gift from God. *Ps. V:260.*

It would be of little advantage to us to have once obtained him as ours, if he did not secure our possession of him against the assaults which Satan daily makes upon us. *Ps. I:225.*

Redemption would be incomplete, if he did not by continual advances carry us forward to the ultimate end of salvation. *Inst. II:xvi.1.*

He vouchsafes to the elect alone, the living root of faith, that they may persevere even to the end. *Inst. III:ii.11.*

Our perseverance is not founded on our own power or industry, but on Christ. *Rom. 105.*

Accomplished by the indwelling Holy Spirit

We persevere in piety only insofar as God is present to sustain us by his hand, and confirm us in perseverance by the agency of his Spirit. *Josh. 261.*

[On Ps. 63:8] David here speaks of the grace of perseverance, which would be bestowed upon him by the Spirit. *Ps. II:440.*

The Holy Spirit not only originates faith, but increases it by degrees, till he conducts us by it all the way to the heavenly kingdom. *Inst. III:ii.33.*

Our part

The highest perfection of the godly in this life is an earnest desire to make progress. *Eph. 261.*

Perseverance . . . the gift of God, but the exhortation to fear is not uncalled for, lest our flesh, through too great indulgence, should root us out. *John II:110.*

Repentance does not consist in one or two works, but in perseverance. *Dan. I:236.*

[On Hab. 2] *I will watch to see* . . . refers to perseverance . . . All our observations become evanescent, except we continue to watch. *Hab.-Hagg. 60.*

Let all who would persevere in a life of holiness give their whole minds to the hope of Christ's coming. *Thess. 339.*

PHILOSOPHY

Philosophy is nothing else than a persuasive speech, which insinuates itself into the minds of men by elegant and plausible arguments . . . a corruption of spiritual doctrine. *Col. 181.*

[On Col. 2:9] He who is not contented with Christ alone, desires something better and more excellent than God. *Col. 182.*

Aristotle, a man of genius and learning . . . employed his naturally acute powers of mind to extinguish all light. *Ps. IV:266.*

[On I Cor. 2:13] . . . blown up with philosophical loftiness. *Cor. I:114.*

Our philosophy is to receive in simplicity what the Scripture shows us. [Confession of Faith in the name of the Reformed Churches of France, 1542] *Tracts II:161.*

Let God be found true [Rom. 3:4] . . . the primary axiom of all Christian philosophy. *Rom. 60.*

PRAISE

Ordained by God for his whole creation

There is not a corner in heaven or on earth where God is not praised. *Ps. IV:143.*

The whole world is a theatre for the display of the Divine goodness, wisdom, justice and power; but the Church is the orchestra, as it were, – the most conspicuous part of it. *Ps. V:178.*

The chief part of Christian worship

The most holy service that we can render to him is, to be employed in praising his name. *Is. I:204, 205.*

The principal object for which holy assemblies are convened, is to afford the worshippers of God an opportunity of presenting to him sacrifices of praise. *Ps. IV:312, 313.*

[On Ps. 66:4] Praise is the best of all sacrifices (Ps. 50:14, 23), and the true evidence of godliness. *Ps. II:468.*

God's aids for fitting praise

Christ leads our songs, and is the chief composer of our hymns. *Heb. 67.*

The proclamation of God's praises is always promoted by the teaching of the gospel. *Heb. 66.*

The praises of God, insofar as they proceed from our mouths, are impure, until they are sanctified by Christ. *Ps. III:76.*

The heart goes before the tongue. *Col. 218.*

We only praise God aright when we are filled and overwhelmed with an ecstatic admiration of the immensity of his power. *Ps. V:273.*

Warnings

. . . not that he needs our praise, but it is profitable for ourselves. *Is. I:397.*

[244]

Praise

We pollute all his benefits, except we return for them . . . the sacrifice of praise. *Hab.-Hagg. 299.*

It will not be lawful to transfer to man even the smallest portion of praise. *Is. IV:351.*

We cannot transfer the smallest portion of the praise due to him without awful sacrilege. *Ps. V:183, 184.*

The Psalmist reminds the Lord's people, that unless they were assiduous in his praises, they were chargeable with defrauding him of what was justly due to him for his benefits. *Ps. V:181.*

PRAYER

Farewell, friendly reader; and if you receive any benefit from my labours, let me have the assistance of your prayers with God our Father. [The closing words of Calvin's Preface to the Institutes] *Inst. I:19.*

On Prayer, the Principal Exercise of Faith, and the Medium of our Daily Reception of the Divine Blessings. [Heading to Inst. III, Chap. xx] *Inst. III:xx.*

Prayer is nothing else than the opening up of our heart before God. *Is. IV:353.*

The Principal Exercise of Faith

Faith . . . lies idle and even dead without prayer. *Ps. V:281.*

That primary exercise of faith, even prayer. *Jer. IV:68.*

Faith . . . goes before all prayer in order and in time. *Syn. Gosp. I:352. 353.*

The test of all *faith* lies in *prayer*. *Syn. Gosp. III:19.*

The modesty of faith consists in permitting God to appoint differently from what we desire. *Syn. Gosp. III:233.*

We cannot rightly pray unless we are persuaded for certain of success. *Rom. 230.*

None can really pray to God but those who with a pure heart fear and rightly worship him. *Gen. Epp. 224.*

The discipline of the cross is necessary, so that earnest prayer may become vigorous in us. *Zech.-Mal. 403.*

Our own scanty desires hinder [God] from pouring out his gifts upon us in greater abundance. *Syn. Gosp. I:414.*

God will have our prayers to be founded first on his gratuitous goodness, and then on the constancy of his faithfulness and truth. *Zech.-Mal. 40.*

Faith is ever the mother of prayer. *Joel-Obad. 106.*

Our faith cannot be supported in a better way than by the exercise of prayer. *Hab.-Hagg. 133.*

Prayer is founded on faith. *Jer. V:301.*

To taste of God's mercy opens to us the door of prayer. *Jer. V:433.*

Prayers flowed from doctrine. *Is. III:111.*

Till we have a persuasion of being saved through the grace of God there can be no sincere prayer. *Ps. V:229.*

Our applications to the throne of grace will be proportional to the degree in which we are conscious of integrity. *Ps. II:381.*

There is no hope of obtaining any favour from God unless he is reconciled to us. *Ps. I:419.*

Prayer is the offspring of faith, and uniformly accompanied with patience and mortification of sin. *Ps. II:270.*

Our desires and prayers . . . proceed from the calm stillness which faith and patience produce in our hearts. *Ps. II:84.*

The ability of praying rightly is a peculiar gift. *Inst. III:xx.5.*

Prayer the medium of our reception of God's blessings

Prayer digs out those treasures, which the gospel of the Lord discovers to our faith. *Inst. III:xx.2.*

We [are] permitted to pour into [God's] bosom the difficulties which torment us, in order that He may loosen the knots which we cannot untie. *Gen. I:489.*

Though men pray for blessings on each other, God declares himself to be the sole Dispenser of perfect happiness. *Gen. II:240.*

[On Ps. 25:7] Our sins are like a wall between us and God, which prevents him from hearing our prayers. *Ps. I:419.*

When overtaken by adversity, we are ever to conclude that it is a rod of correction sent by God to stir us up to pray. *Ps. V:249.*

Christ, by his death, purchased for himself the honour of being the eternal advocate and peacemaker to present our prayers and our persons to the Father; to obtain supplies of grace for us, and enable us to hope we shall obtain what we ask. [The Necessity of Reforming the Church] *Tracts I:191.*

The invocation of God's Name

There is now no sacrifice . . . more pleasing to God than the invocation of His name. *Four Last Bks of Moses II:203.*

The invocation of God's name is his peculiar work; for men do not pray through the suggestion of the flesh, but when God draws them. *Hab.-Hagg. 284.*

The invocation of [God's] name in a despairing condition is a sure port of safety. *Joel-Obad. 105.*

Prayer and the Spirit of Adoption

The pardon which we daily receive flows from our adoption, and on it also are all our prayers founded. *Ps. II:456.*

God gives us the Spirit, to be the director of our prayers, to suggest what is right, and to regulate our affections. *Inst. III:xx.5.*

Whenever the wicked assault us, the . . . Spirit calls upon us to engage in prayer . . . If any man . . . neglects the exercise of prayer, he defrauds God of the honour which belongs to him, in not referring his cause to him, and in not leaving him to judge . . . it. *Ps. I:236.*

Except one is guided by the Spirit of God, he cannot pray from the heart. *Jon.-Nah. 221.*

The beginning of prayer is from that hidden cleansing of the Spirit. *Hab.-Hagg. 284.*

The intercession of Christ on our behalf

Our prayers are acceptable to God only insofar as Christ sprinkles and sanctifies them with the perfume of his own sacrifice. *Ps. I:336.*

[In the Old Testament] no prayers were acceptable to [God] but those which were joined with sacrifice, that they might always turn their minds to the Mediator. *Ps. IV:482.*

There is nothing meritorious in our prayers; . . . whenever God hears them, it is in the exercise of his free goodness. *Ps. IV:483.*

God can listen to no prayers without the intercession of Christ. *Four Last Bks of Moses II:295.*

All our prayers should be founded on the intercession of Christ. [Catechism of the Church of Geneva] *Tracts II:75.*

There is no way of obtaining favour from God but through the intercession of Christ. *Is. III:286.*

[On John 16:27, Christ's intercession] The value of his sacrifice . . . is always powerful and efficacious; the blood . . . is a continual intercession for us . . . We have the heart of the Heavenly Father, as soon as we have placed before him *the name* of his Son. *John II:158.*

Prayer and the Word

It is . . . an axiom, that our prayers are faulty, so far as they are not founded on the word. *Gen. I:509.*

There is nothing more efficacious in our prayers than to set His own word before God, and then to found our supplications upon His promises, as if He dictated to us, out of His own mouth what we were to ask. *Four Last Bks of Moses IV:75.*

We cannot possibly exercise true confidence in prayer, except by resting firmly on God's word. *Dan. II:136.*

It is a usual thing with the saints to plead before God what he has promised to them. *Zech.-Mal. 40.*

Unless the promises of God shine on us and invite us to prayer, no sincere prayer can ever be drawn from us. *Zech.-Mal. 403.*

We cannot pray without the word . . . leading the way. Thus everyone who has no faith in the promises, prays dissemblingly. *Gen. Epp. 283.*

Defective prayer

There ought to be nothing ambiguous in our prayers. *Gen. II:18.*

We must pray for no more than God permits. *Inst. III:xx.5.*

If we address to God a confession which is contrary to our real sentiments, we are guilty of telling him an impudent falsehood. *Inst. III:xii.6.*

How many . . . pray . . . in a clamorous spirit, and . . . by the inordinate anxiety and restlessness which they evince, seem resolved to dictate terms to the Almighty. *Ps. II:344.*

The only means of checking an excessive impatience is an absolute submission to the Divine will. *Ps. II:344.*

God can never be expected to undertake a cause which is unworthy of defence. *Ps. II:374.*

. . . that diseased but deeply-rooted principle in our nature, which leads us to hide our griefs, and ruminate upon them, instead of . . . pouring out our . . . complaints before God. *Ps. II:425.*

Our prayers . . . are worthless when we are agitated with doubts. *Ps. IV:343.*

Doubtful prayer is no prayer at all. *Ps. V:232.*

Howling rather than praying. *Ps. V:234.*

Many boldly plead the name of God in their own behalf, although they are unaffected by any real care or love for it. *Four Last Bks of Moses IV:75.*

To tempt God [is] . . . to prescribe to him the mode in which He is to act, according to our own desires. *Four Last Bks of Moses IV:78.*

Let us learn . . . when we feel . . . sluggish and cold in prayer, to collect all the aids which can arouse our feelings and correct the torpor of which we are conscious. *Dan. I:361.*

God cannot approve of any prayers, unless they spring equally from repentance and faith. *Dan. II:170.*

Nothing is more at variance with faith than the foolish and irregular desires of our flesh. *Syn. Gosp. II:326, 327.*

Many pray in such a way that they still murmur against God. *Thess. 375.*

Method in prayer

Public prayers are to be composed . . . in the vernacular tongue, which may be . . . understood by the whole congregation. *Inst. III:xx.33.*

It is good to have certain hours appointed for prayer, not because we are tied to hours, but lest we be unmindful of prayer. *Acts I:418.*

The legitimate method of praying is, that the faithful should answer to God who calls them; and thus there is such a mutual agreement between his word and their vows, that no sweeter and more harmonious symphony can be imagined. *Gen. II:191.*

When God descends to us he, in a certain sense, abases himself and stammers with us, so he allows us to stammer with him. *Gen. II:238.*

The finest rhetoric and the best grace which we can have before him consists in pure simplicity. *Ps. I:236.*

Unless we fix certain hours in the day for prayer, it easily slips from our memory. *Dan. I:362.*

The scope of our prayers

When we pray, we ought, according to the rule of charity, to include all, for we cannot fix on those whom God has chosen or whom he has rejected. *Jer. II:248.*

We ought to pray for all without exception. *Jer. III:43.*

Prayer

The prayers which we offer for all are still limited to the elect of God . . . We leave to the judgment of God those whom he knows to be reprobate. *John II:172, 173.*

General

The answer of our prayers is secured by the fact, that in rejecting them, [God] would, in a certain sense, deny his own nature. *Ps. II:452.*

In prayer two things are necessary – faith and humility; by faith we rise up to God, and by humility we lie prostrate on the ground. *Jer. IV:332.*

Scripture frequently describes the whole of worship as *calling upon God* (Is. 12:4). *Is. I:402.*

These two things are united – teaching and praying; God would have him whom he has set as a teacher in his Church to be assiduous in prayer. *Jer. III:380.*

[God] regards our prayers as the chief and supreme sacrifice by which we do homage to his Majesty. [Calvin's Confession of Faith in the Name of the Reformed Churches of France, 1542] *Tracts II:146.*

The falls of the brethren . . . stimulants to prayer. *Gen. Epp. 267.*

The true proof of faith is the assurance when we pray that God will really perform what he has promised us. *Dan. II:135.*

A prayer of John Calvin

Grant, Almighty God, that as we are wholly nothing and less than nothing, we may know our nothingness, and having cast away all confidence in the world as well as in ourselves, we may learn to flee to thee as suppliants, . . . and so persevere in humility and in calling on thy name . . . that we may know that thou art always present with those who truly and from the heart call upon thee, until we shall at length be filled with the fulness of all those blessings, which are laid up for us in heaven by Christ our Lord. Amen. [Prayer at the end of Lecture 66 on Jeremiah] *Jer. II:355.*

[251]

PREACHING

Focus

Among so many excellent gifts with which God has adorned mankind, it is a peculiar privilege, that he deigns to consecrate men's lips and tongues to his service, that his voice may be heard in them. *Inst. IV:i.5.*

The first preacher

Through six successive ages . . . the voice of Adam might daily resound, in order to renew the memory of the creation, the fall, and the punishment of man; to testify of the hope of salvation which remained after chastisement, and to recite the judgments of God, by which all might be instructed. *Gen. I:229.*

Definition

The office of teaching is committed to pastors for no other purpose than that God alone may be heard there. *Is. I:95.*

[On Jer. 1:9, 10] A rule is prescribed to all God's servants that they bring not their own inventions, but simply deliver, as from hand to hand, what they have received from God. *Jer. I:43.*

No one ought to be deemed a sound teacher, but he who speaks from God's mouth. *Jer. III:167, 168.*

Sent by God is he only whose doctrine is according to the rule of the Law, and of the Prophets, and of the Gospel. *Jer. III:408, 409.*

To assert the truth is only one half of the office of teaching . . . except all the fallacies of the devil be also dissipated. *Jer. III:423.*

As soon as men depart, even in the smallest degree from God's word, they cannot preach anything but falsehoods, vanities, impostures, errors, and deceits. *Jer. II:226, 227.*

God's servants ought to speak from the inmost affection of their heart. *Ezek. I:130.*

By the preaching of the Gospel, Christ was ever to be raised on high. *John I:121.*

Preaching

We must gently govern those who are apt to be taught and gentle, but we must cite the stubborn unto God's judgment-seat. *Acts II:427.*

[On *prophets* in 1 Cor. 12:28. A gift] not merely for interpreting Scripture, but also for applying it wisely to present use . . . endowed with no common wisdom and dexterity in taking a right view of the present necessity of the Church. *Cor. I:415.*

The pastor ought to have two voices; one, for gathering the sheep, and another, for warding off . . . wolves. *Past. Epp. 296.*

The duty of a good teacher is rather to exhort to a holy life than to occupy the minds of men with useless questions. *Past. Epp. 317.*

Biblical content

God begets and multiplies his Church only by means of his word . . . It is by the preaching of the grace of God alone that the Church is kept from perishing. *Ps. I:388, 389.*

Purity of doctrine is preserved unimpaired in the world, and propagated by the ministry of pastors, whilst piety would soon decay if the living preaching of doctrine should cease. *Four Last Bks of Moses II:230.*

Though the Law was written, yet God would ever have the living voice to resound in His Church, just as now-a-days preaching is inseparably united with Scripture. *Four Last Bks of Moses II:235.*

The uniform characteristics of a well-ordered Church are the preaching of sound doctrine, and pure administration of the sacraments . . . A Church which, from incorruptible seed, begets children for immortality and, when begotten, nourishes them with spiritual food, (the seed and food being the Word of God), and which, by its ministry, preserves entire the truth which God deposited in its bosom. [The Necessity of Reforming the Church] *Tracts I:214.*

We ought to imitate the Prophets, who conveyed the doctrine of the Law in such a manner as to draw from it advices, reproofs, threatenings and consolations, which they applied to the present condition of the people. *Is. I:xxx.*

An assembly in which the preaching of heavenly doctrine is not heard does not deserve to be reckoned a Church. *Is. III:213.*

God sustains us by his word in the deepest afflictions as upon a vast sea, and as long as his teaching remains to us we have as it were a chart of guidance which will bring us safely into harbour. *Ezek. I:273.*

Men have nothing in them but what is tasteless, till they have been seasoned with the salt of heavenly doctrine. *Syn. Gosp. I:270.*

Let those who desire to be wise . . . and to teach others well, appoint themselves these bounds, that they utter nothing but out of the pure fountain of the word. *Acts II:425.*

The Church maintains the truth, because by preaching the Church proclaims it. *Past. Epp. 91.*

The truth of God is maintained by the pure preaching of the gospel. *Past. Epp. 91.*

The Scripture is the fountain of all wisdom, from which pastors must draw all that they place before their flock. *Past. Epp. 115.*

The Church can only be edified by the preaching of this word. *Inst. IV:i.5.*

God's majesty accompanies his word preached

The majesty of God is . . . indissolubly connected with the public preaching of his truth . . . If his word is not allowed to have authority, it is the same as though its despisers attempted to thrust God from heaven. *Jer. I:280.*

[On Luke 4:16] The majesty of Scripture deserves that its expounders should make it apparent, that they proceed to handle it with modesty and reverence. *Syn. Gosp. I:227.*

So often as the Word of God is set before us, we must think . . . that God is present, and doth call us. For, from this respect of God ariseth the majesty of God's word, and reverence in hearing the same. *Acts I:435.*

Preaching

The preaching of the Gospel . . . is inwardly replete with a kind of solid majesty. *Cor. I:176.*

Teachers cannot firmly execute their office except they have the majesty of God before their eyes. *Jer. I:44.*

The ministry of the Holy Spirit with the word

When the minister executes his commission faithfully, by speaking only what God puts into his mouth, the inward power of the Holy Spirit is joined with his outward voice. *Ps. IV:199.*

There is . . . an inward efficacy of the Holy Spirit when he sheds forth his power upon hearers, that they may embrace a discourse by faith. *Ezek. I:61.*

Wherever the gospel is preached, it is as if God himself came into the midst of us. *Syn. Gosp. III:129.*

The power of the Spirit is extinguished as soon as the Doctors blow their flutes . . . to display their eloquence. *Past. Epp. 174.*

Focus on the preacher

The infirmity of the minister does not destroy the faithfulness, power, and efficacy of God's word. *Gen. II:94.*

All the ministers of God should . . . embrace in the first place . . . that divine word which they preach to others. *Ps. II:237.*

We cannot communicate true knowledge unless we deliver it not merely with our lips, but as something which God has revealed to our own hearts. *Ps. III:479.*

God commits both charges to the ministers of His word, to be the proclaimers of His vengeance, as well as the witnesses of His grace. *Four Last Bks of Moses III:347.*

It is the will of our Master that his gospel be preached. Let us obey his command, and follow whithersoever he calls. What the success will be is not ours to inquire. [The Necessity of Reforming the Church] *Tracts I:200.*

The sound of our voices is not ineffectual, when it renders the world without excuse. *Is. I:216.*

[255]

Prophets and priests are two eyes as it were in the Church. *Jer. V:472.*

None are fit to undertake the prophetic office, unless those who are armed with fortitude and perseverance. *Ezek. I:121, 122.*

Why were prophets called forth, unless to collect the people of God? *Ezek. I:154.*

All prophets who have deserted their office are guilty before God. *Ezek. I:161.*

Micah divides this power of the prophets into two kinds . . . wisdom or judgment, and . . . courage . . . Let them excel in doctrine; and . . . let them not bend to please the world. *Jon.- Nah. 233, 234.*

The teachers of the Church ought to be prepared by long study for giving to the people, as out of a storehouse, a variety of instruction concerning the word of God. *Syn. Gosp. II:134.*

All ministers of the Word . . . ought to be exceedingly careful that the glory of his resurrection should be always exhibited by them in connection with the ignominy of his death. *Syn. Gosp. II:300.*

No man is fit to be a teacher in the Church save only he who . . . submits himself . . . [to] be a fellow-disciple with other men. *Acts I:390.*

Nothing is more contrary to the pure and free preaching of the gospel than the straits of a faint heart. *Acts II:187.*

[The teacher should] speak not so much with the mouth, as with the dispositions of the heart. *Cor. I:39.*

Doctrine which solidly edifies is commonly attended by little display. *Past. Epp. 117.*

A bishop will never teach well, who is not also ready to learn. *Past. Epp. 295.*

The aim of a good teacher, [is] to turn away the eyes of men from the world, that they may look up to heaven. *Past. Epp. 283.*

I think that we should speak of God with the same religious caution which should govern our thoughts of him. *Inst. I:xiii.3.*

I am naturally fond of brevity. *Inst. III:vi.1.*

The preaching of the word, the sceptre of Christ's government of his Church

God governs his Church by the external preaching of the word. *Four Last Bks of Moses I:335.*

Why is the preaching of the gospel so often styled the kingdom of God, but because it is the sceptre by which the heavenly King rules his people? [Calvin's Reply to Sadoleto] *Tracts I:36.*

The preaching of the gospel, which is committed to [the Church], is the spiritual sceptre of Christ, by which he displays his power. *Is. III:414.*

The government of the church, by the preaching of the word, is . . . declared to be no human contrivance, but a most sacred ordinance of Christ . . . They who reject or despise this ministry offer insult and rebellion to Christ its Author. *Eph. 277, 278.*

Sound method of preaching

It appears to me that there is very little preaching of a lively kind in the Kingdom; but that the greater part deliver it by way of reading from a written discourse. [Calvin to the Duke of Somerset, England, 1548] *Letters 95.*

In our natural vanity most men are more delighted by foolish allegorics, than by solid erudition. *Four Last Bks of Moses II:130.*

The legitimate use of Scripture is perverted when it is enunciated in an obscure manner such as no one can understand. *Four Last Bks of Moses II:232.*

All exhortations are fleeting and ineffective which are founded on anything else but simple confidence in the grace of God. *Four Last Bks of Moses IV:314.*

[Commentators] who play with the husk, and find no kernel. *Ezek. I:xv.*

Some [ministers] are always fulminating through a pretence of zeal; . . . they show no sign of benevolence. . . . Hence they have no authority, and all their admonitions are hateful. *Dan. I:270.*

God claimed to himself the right of speaking; . . . he orders all men to be silent and not to offer anything of their own . . . God wishes to exclude whatever men fabricate or invent for themselves. *Ezek. I:149.*

[On Mic. 4:1, 2] We . . . see how necessary it is to moderate threatenings and terrors, when prophets and teachers have a regard to the children of God. *Jon.-Nah. 250.*

It is too common a fault that men desire to be taught in an ingenious and witty style. *John I:119.*

We must always take care that the wisdom of God be not polluted with any borrowed and profane lustre. *Cor. I:114.*

[On 1 Cor. 3:13, 'wood, hay and stubble'] God will have his Church trained up by the pure preaching of his own word, not by the contrivances of men. *Cor. I:137.*

Then only are reproofs beneficial, when they are in a manner seasoned with honey. *Cor. II:402.*

The minds of the godly become dim . . . and contract rust, when admonitions cease. *Gen. Epp. 412, 413.*

Whosoever . . . attends to such preachers as amuse us with a mere exhibition of our virtues, will make no progress in the knowledge of himself, but will be absorbed in the most pernicious ignorance. *Inst. II:i.2.*

Deviations

We know how haughtily false teachers elevate themselves. *Jer. III:202.*

There be many mercenary brawlers at this day . . . God has justly blinded them. *Jer. III:387.*

[On Ezek. 13:17, 18] Satan's lies were not spread among the people so much by men as by women . . . Female prophets existed whenever God wished to brand men with a mark of ignominy. *Ezek. II:27.*

It cannot be, that a complete liberty in teaching should exist, except when the pastor is exempt from all desire of gain. *Jon.- Nah. 241.*

The free offer of the gospel to all (see also Free Offer)

The Gospel is preached indiscriminately to the elect and to the reprobate; but the elect alone come to Christ, because they have been 'taught by God'. *Is. IV:146.*

God offers his word indiscriminately to the good and bad; but it works by his Spirit in the elect . . . as to the reprobate . . . it renders them without excuse. *Ezek. I:113.*

[On Jonah's preaching in Nineveh] God does not . . . always keep to the same course; but, when he pleases, he so efficaciously touches the hearts of men, that the success of his word exceeds all expectations. *Jon.-Nah. 103.*

It is the Lord who *pierces the ears* (*Ps. 40:7*), and no man obtains or accomplishes this by his own industry. *Syn. Gosp. II:101.*

God does not always bestow salvation on men when he sends his word to them . . . He sometimes intends to have it proclaimed to the reprobate. *Syn. Gosp. III:101.*

The preaching of Christ among them was nothing else than the announcement of that eternal decree. *Eph. 193.*

Opposition to such preaching

All who are sent to teach the word, are sent to carry on a contest . . . We have a contest with the devil, with the world, and with all the wicked. *Jon.-Nah. 234, 235.*

When anyone is drawn into arduous and difficult struggles he is, at the same time, especially strengthened by the Lord. *Jon.- Nah. 232.*

The more brightly the light of doctrine shines, so as to press more closely on wicked men, they are driven to a greater pitch of madness. *Syn. Gosp. II:159.*

Those who reject the word of God render it, by their unbelief, deadly and destructive. *Syn. Gosp. III:101.*

No man is fit to preach the gospel, seeing the whole world is set against it, save only he which is armed to suffer. *Acts I:381.*

Christ cannot be preached without proving to be resurrection for some, and destruction for others . . . Both . . . have reference to the day of judgment. *Rom. 50.*

Whoever . . . rejects the faithful teachers of the word, shows that he is a despiser of God himself. *Jer. III:445.*

A prayer of Calvin, with which he used to open his lectures on the word: Grant us, Lord, to meditate on the heavenly mysteries of Thy wisdom, with true progress in piety, to Thy glory and our edification. Amen. *Ezek. I:50.*

PREDESTINATION (*see also* Election, Reprobation)

Definition

Eternal Election, or God's Predestination of Some to Salvation and of Others to Destruction. [Heading to Chap. 21, Book III of The Institutes] *Inst. III:xxi.1.*

Predestination we call the eternal decree of God, by which he has determined in himself, what he would have to become of every individual of mankind. For they are not all created with a similar destiny; but eternal life is foreordained for some, and eternal damnation for others. Every man, therefore, being created for one or other of these ends, we say he is predestined either to life or to death. *Inst. III:xxi.5.*

God has a sufficiently just cause for election and reprobation in His own will. *Rom. 201.*

Predestination and salvation

[On Is. 4:3] God has no other book than his eternal counsel, in which he has predestinated us to salvation by adopting us for his children. *Is. I:155.*

[260]

[On Dan. 12:2. God's book] is that eternal counsel which predestinates us to himself, and elects us to the hope of eternal salvation. *Dan. II:373.*

. . . that predestination by which God chooses every single individual according to his own will, and at the same time appoints and sanctifies him. *Jer. I:36.*

God does not deliberate or consult, but has once for all decreed before the creation of the world what he will do. *Jer. V:92.*

Men do not gain the favour of God by their free-will, but are chosen by his goodness alone before they were born. *Hos. 418, 419.*

Predestination and faith

[Christ] connects faith with the eternal predestination of God. *Syn. Gosp. II:40.*

Faith flows from the outward predestination of God, and . . . is not given indiscriminately to all . . . The predestination of God is in itself hidden, but it is manifested to us in Christ alone. *John II:xxi.1, 171.*

Predestination and assurance

. . . the utility of this doctrine . . . productive of the most delightful benefit. *Inst. III:xxi.1.*

Though the discussion of predestination may be compared to a dangerous ocean, yet, in traversing over it, the navigation is safe and serene, and I will also add pleasant, unless any one freely wishes to expose himself to danger. *Inst. III:xxiv.4.*

A certain knowledge of our predestination [is] that testimony of adoption which Scripture makes common to all the godly. [Antidote to the Council of Trent] *Tracts III:155.*

Predestination and the church

What is the Church? The body and society of believers whom God hath predestinated to eternal life. [Calvin's Catechism of the Church of Geneva, 1536, 1541] *Tracts II:50.*

[261]

The peace of the Church is founded on his eternal and unchangeable purpose . . . the heavenly decree. *Is. II:213.*

Criticism

Ignorance of this principle evidently detracts from the Divine glory, and diminishes real humility . . . They who desire to extinguish this principle . . . pluck up humility by the roots. *Inst. III:xxi.1.*

To desire any other knowledge of predestination than what is unfolded in the word of God, indicates as great folly, as to wish to walk through impassable roads, or to see in the dark. *Inst. III:xxi.2.*

Nor let us be ashamed to be ignorant of some things relative to a subject in which there is a kind of learned ignorance. *Inst. III:xxi.2.*

Those lunatics who . . . overturn, as far as they can, that prime article of our faith concerning God's eternal predestination . . . demonstrate their malice no less than their ignorance. *Four Last Bks of Moses III:361.*

Calvin's testimony

In full view of his approaching death, Calvin dictated his Last Will and Testament on 25 April 1564, reciting:
I John Calvin, servant of the Word of God in the Church of Geneva . . . have no other hope or refuge than his predestination upon which my entire salvation is grounded . . . *Letters 29.*

PRIDE

Its root

The whole human race is infected with the disease of pride. *Gen. II:264.*

. . . this most deadly disease of pride. *Four Last Bks of Moses I:398.*

Pride is the mother of all contempt of God. *Ezek. II:156.*

Pride

Pride is the mother of disdain. *Syn. Gosp. II:338.*

Where pride is, there is ignorance of God. *Cor. I:274.*

Nothing is so arrogant as ignorance. *Cor. I:274.*

Herein appears the vile ingratitude of men – that, while they ought to be proclaiming the praises of God for the wonderful skill displayed in their formation, and the inestimable bounties he bestows on them, they are only inflated with the greater pride. *Inst. I:v.4.*

There is no man who does not cherish within him some idea of his own excellence . . . this most noxious pest of ambition and self-love. *Inst. III:vii.4.*

The talents with which God has favoured us, are not excellences originating from ourselves, but free gifts of God; of which, if any are proud, they betray their ingratitude. *Inst. III:vii.4.*

As far as any man is satisfied with himself, so far he raises an impediment to the exercise of the grace of God. *Inst. III:xii.8.*

[Merit] – the consummate haughtiness of its import can only obscure the Divine grace, and taint the minds of men with presumptuous arrogance. *Inst. III:xv.2.*

We know by our own experience how difficult it is to keep within due bounds those who are puffed up with a silly opinion of their own wisdom. *Letters 54.*

The disease of pride . . . Pride is the mother of all wrongs. *Ps. I:136.*

We have no worse fault than that devilish arrogance which robs God of his due praise, and which yet is so deeply rooted in us. *Ps. IV:133.*

It is an evil as it were innate in us, that we become elated and proud whenever God deals bountifully with us. *Jer. I:382.*

We know nothing vainer than the minds of men. *Dan. I:149.*

Men arrogate too much to themselves when they think that they excel in anything. *Jon.-Nah. 466.*

Its evil character

In proportion as we arrogate to ourselves do we derogate from [God]. *Ps. II:316.*

We are not at liberty to share the honour of success with God. *Ps. II:409.*

Nothing is more difficult than for men to strip themselves of their blind arrogance whereby they detract some portion of the praise from God's mercies. *Four Last Bks of Moses I:379.*

All who exalt themselves wage war with God. *Four Last Bks of Moses IV:48.*

The haughtiest and proudest of all men are they who shelter themselves under the name of God, and glory in the title of the Church. *Is. III:25.*

. . . such diabolical pride as to rob God and adorn themselves with the spoils. *Is. III:100.*

Men sin more through insolence and pride than through ignorance. *Is. III:226.*

Nothing is more contrary to faith than pride. *Jer. III:374.*

[On Ezek. 13:1–3. False prophets] are just like upstarts puffed up with wonderful self-conceit; for the devil, who reigns in them, is the father of pride. *Ezek. II:8.*

He is a sacrilegious person who takes even an inch of Christ's praise that he may deck man therewith. *Acts I:461.*

There is nothing less tolerable in the servants of Christ than ambition and vanity. *Acts II:240.*

That man can never be rightly framed to obey Christ whose looks are lofty, and whose heart is proud. *Acts II:242.*

The Corinthians were giants in pride, children in faith. *Cor. I:169.*

Accursed be that knowledge which makes men proud, and is not regulated by a desire of edifying. *Cor. I:273.*

Many are proud of the gifts of God. *Past. Epp. 325.*

Pride

Its evil fruit

[On the *giants* of Gen. 6:4] Their first fault was pride . . . Pride produced contempt of God. *Gen. I:246.*

Pride is always the companion of unbelief. *Gen. II:173.*

Proud men do not regard themselves as free, so long as anyone has the pre-eminence over them. *Gen. II:187.*

Whoever proudly arrogates to himself more than is his due, will almost necessarily treat others with contempt. *Ps. I:513.*

[On Is. 3:16, 17] From whence comes luxury in men and women but from pride? *Is. I:144.*

We ought not to be . . . proud of God's favours . . . for security breeds contempt. *Jer. III:119.*

We always attribute something to pride, which renders our senses obtuse, so as to be incapable of the glory of God. *Ezek. I:81.*

Pride takes away every fear. *Hos. 191.*

Divine restraint

By [man's] being made of earth and clay, a restraint was laid upon pride. *Inst. I:xv.1.*

The elect . . . never become docile until the pride of the flesh is laid low. *Gen. II:321.*

The best fruit of afflictions is, when thereby we are brought to purge our minds from all arrogance, and to bend them to meekness and modesty. *Ps. III:201.*

[God] denominates all unbelievers *proud* [Ps. 119:21], because it is true faith alone which humbles us, and all rebellion is the offspring of pride. *Ps. IV:415.*

The simple fact of the shortness of our life should put down all arrogance and pride. *Ps. V:262.*

When God wishes to become familiarly known to us, he strips us of all pride and all security; . . . humility is the beginning of true intelligence. *Ezek. I:81.*

[265]

As we are extremely prone to arrogance and pride, we ought carefully to seek to conduct ourselves in a meek and humble manner, when favoured with God's singular benefits. *Hab.-Hagg. 293.*

The higher that every one of us shall be extolled, let him submit himself unto God with modesty and fear. *Acts I:238.*

Divine cure

Men ever swell with inward pride until God thoroughly cleanse them . . . This Satanic pride . . . is innate, and . . . cannot be shaken off by us, until the Lord regenerates us by his Spirit. *Hab.-Hagg. 52.*

Divine judgment

God cannot endure the presumption of men, when inflated by their own greatness and power. *Hab.-Hagg. 257.*

It is . . . necessary that they who ascribe to themselves even the smallest thing, should be reduced to nothing. *Hab.-Hagg. 295.*

The pride of Herod . . . shut the door on the grace of God. *Syn. Gosp. III:279.*

The Lord, who is the Teacher of the humble, blinds the proud. *John II:212.*

[On 1 Cor. 8:3. God] erases all proud persons from the book of life (*Phil. 4:3*) and from the roll of the pious. *Cor. I:275.*

. . . a most righteous punishment of human arrogance, that they who swerve from the purity of Scripture become profane. *Past. Epp. 175.*

Every person who, by his over-weening pride, breaks up the unity of the Church, is pronounced by Paul to be a 'heretic'. *Past. Epp. 341.*

All who seek to elevate themselves, shall have God as their enemy, who will lay them low. *Gen. Epp. 148.*

The great end which God has in view, when he prostrates the pride of the ungodly, is the comfort of his own people. *Ps. II:315.*

Those who arrogate the least fraction of strength to themselves
apart from God, only ruin themselves through their own pride.
Ps. II:409.

PROMISES OF GOD

[On 2 Cor. 1:20] Christ . . . is the groundwork of *all the promises
of God* . . . When promises are given . . . there is a special
reason – that in them [God] declares himself to be a Father . . .
We are not qualified for enjoying the promises of God, unless
we have received the remission of our sins . . . The promise, by
which God adopts us to himself as his sons, holds the first place
among them all. *Cor. II:136, 137.*

God's design in the promises

The promises of God should be believed by us, to give to his
power the praise which it deserves. *Is. III:217.*

Whatever God promises, belongs to his elect . . . not . . . to all.
Jer. III:128.

The design of all God's promises . . . to keep us from being
disturbed, to give us quietness of mind, and to cause us to look
for the help promised to us. *Jer. IV:437.*

Through the promises alone it is that we can have a taste of
God's paternal goodness. *Jer. V:322.*

When any promise of God is set before us it is like a small light
kindled in darkness. *Jer. V:361.*

Our salvation is rendered safe and certain through God's
promise alone. *Hab.-Hagg. 70.*

Men ought not to expect more than God promises. *Syn. Gosp.
I:373.*

God stimulates us the more powerfully to the performance of
duty by promising than by ordering. *Josh. 150.*

God's glory paramount

[On Is. 42:8] The glory of God is chiefly visible in his fulfilment
of what he has promised. *Is. III:296.*

In all the promises this condition is implied, that there must be incitements to us to promote the glory of God. *Cor. II:263.*

God's covenant the guarantee

On the general covenant depended all particular promises. *Jer. IV:249.*

All the promises have been founded on a covenant . . . because God had adopted the people. *Joel-Obad. 137.*

The promises, which now and then occurred, [in the Old Testament prophets] were like streams which flowed from the first spring, even their gratuitous covenant. *Hab.-Hagg. 355.*

Promises are related to the covenant as their only source. *Rom. 195.*

Christ the foundation

All the promises that were given to believers from the beginning of the world were founded upon Christ. *Cor. II:138.*

The efficacy of God's promises depends on Christ alone. *Jer. IV:249.*

Our sacraments . . . contain that *Yea and Amen* of all *the promises of God* (2 Cor. 1:20). *Philipp.-Col. 193.*

The promises of God are . . . only profitable to us when they are confirmed by the blood of Christ . . . His blood like a seal is engraven on our hearts. *Heb. 212.*

[On Is. 17:1] The prophets, when they promise anything hard to be believed, are wont immediately afterwards to mention Christ; for in him are ratified all the promises (*2 Cor. 1:20*). *Is. III:283.*

The role of the Holy Spirit

It is the part of the Holy Spirit to confirm within us what God promises in his word. *Cor. II:141.*

When we have received the Spirit of God his promises are confirmed to us, and no dread is felt that they will be revoked. *Eph. 209.*

Promises of God

The promise to Abraham

[On Gen. 25:7] . . . contented, both in life and death, with the bare promise of God. *Gen. II:36.*

Destitute of food for the body, [Abram] feeds himself upon the sole promise of God. *Gen. I:358.*

[Abraham] was unwilling to measure, by his own understanding, the method of fulfilling the promise, which he knew depended on the incomprehensible power of God. *Gen. I:564.*

Our prayers and God's promises

There is nothing more efficacious in our prayers than to set His own word before God, and then to found our supplications upon His promises, as if He dictated to us out of his own mouth what we were to ask. *Four Last Bks of Moses IV:75.*

What [faith] properly looks to in the Word of God is the free promises, and especially Christ, their pledge and foundation. [Antidote to the Council of Trent] *Tracts III:250.*

What benefit do God's promises confer on us, unless we embrace them by faith? *Dan. II:134, 135.*

[On Hab. 2:2, 3] We ought . . . [to] be so satisfied with his promises as though what is promised were really possessed by us. *Hab.-Hagg. 64.*

We never really and from the heart obey, except when we rely on his promises and hope for a happy success. *Hab.-Hagg. 343.*

It is a usual thing with the saints to plead before God what he has promised to them. *Zech.-Mal. 40.*

God freely invites us to himself for this end, that our prayers may harmonize with his promises. *Zech.-Mal. 292.*

Unless the promises of God shine on us, and invite us to prayer, no sincere prayer can ever be drawn from us. *Zech.-Mal. 403.*

In the act of believing, we give our assent to God who speaks to us, and hold for certain what he has promised to us that he will do. *Syn. Gosp. I:51.*

Our faith answers to his promises. *Syn. Gosp. I:126.*

[269]

This is the true proof of faith, when we never suffer ourselves to be torn away from Christ, and from the promises. *John II:81.*

The end and use of promises is to excite us to prayer. *John II:165.*

Faith . . . ought to rest exclusively on the promises and word of God. *John II:281.*

Faith dependeth upon the promises. *Acts I:450.*

Our faith should be borne up on wings by the promises of God. *Rom. 187.*

As soon as we cease to be aware of the promises of God we completely fail. *Thess. 388.*

Faith leans on the sole promise of gratuitous adoption. *Gen. Epp. 36.*

There is a mutual relation between God's promises and our faith. *Ps. I:494.*

There are three stages in our progress. First, we believe the promises of God; next, by relying on them, we obtain that *confidence*, which is accompanied by holiness and peace of mind; and, last of all, comes *boldness*, which enables us to banish fear, and to come with firmness and steadiness into the presence of God. *Eph. 257.*

It is the true wisdom of faith to consider all his benefits as the result or fruit of his promises. *Ps. IV:492.*

Faith cannot stand, unless it be founded on the promises of God. *Gen. I:346.*

God's promises and our need

As often as [God] reiterates his promises men are reminded of their forgetfulness, or their sloth, or their fickleness. *Josh. 167.*

We are more terrified frequently by the empty mask of a single man than we are strengthened by all the promises of God. *Is. III:231.*

We ought not to judge of the promises of God from our condition, but from his truth. *Is. IV:21.*

[270]

Promises of God

In the promises of God, as in a mirror, we ought to behold those things which are not yet visible to our eyes, even though they appear to us to be contrary to reason. *Is. IV:102.*

Whenever God repeats the promises of his favour, he does not utter words heedlessly and without reason; but since he sees . . . in us so much dulness, that one promise is not sufficient, he confirms it by repetitions. *Jer. II:174.*

Faith, sustained by promises, elevates us above all the world. *Jer. IV:333.*

We are to cherish the hope of the promises until God completes his work. *Jer. V:276.*

When [the prophets] add promises, it is then as though they called the faithful to a private conference, and spake in their ear. *Hab.-Hagg. 35.*

We cannot rely on his promises, without obeying his commandments. *Syn. Gosp. I:219.*

Promises are necessary to us, to excite and encourage us to holiness of life. *Syn. Gosp. III:182.*

The main thing in the worship of God is to embrace His promises with obedience. *Rom. 99.*

The only cure for covetousness is to embrace the promises of God. *Syn. Gosp. I:340.*

As often as we are weighed down by adversity, or involved in very great distress, we ought to meditate upon the promises of God . . . so that . . . we may break through all the temptations which assail us. *Ps. I:36.*

[God] never feeds men with empty promises. *Gen. I:538.*

Our doubt and distrust

We weigh God's promises in our own scale. *Four Last Bks of Moses IV:211.*

Of what advantage to us will the promises of God be, if we distrust him? *Is. IV:57.*

[271]

Nothing does more hinder or prevent us from embracing the promises of God than to think of what may be done naturally, or of what is probable. When . . . we thus consult our own thoughts, we exclude the power of God. *Jer. V:277.*

We cannot depart from the promises which have been sanctioned by an oath in God's name, without seeming to slight the Almighty himself. *Ezek. II:203.*

Fear, proceeding from unbelief, cannot be otherwise dissipated but by God's promises made to us, which chase away all doubts. *Zech.-Mal. 213.*

God punishes the unbelief of those who doubt his promises. *Gen. Epp. 284.*

Distrust is cured by meditating upon the promises of God. *Acts I:46.*

God's delays

God has his own seasons to fulfil what he has promised . . . not what we desire. *Hab.-Hagg. 307.*

His people must wait as long as God pleases to exercise them under the cross. *Hab.-Hagg. 309.*

There is no place for faith, if we expect God to fulfil immediately what he promises. *Hab.-Hagg. 68.*

Whenever God promises anything, we ought to receive it as a present thing, though yet hidden and even remote. There is no distance which ought to impede our faith. *Jer. V:22.*

The liberality of God

The hand of God is joined with his mouth. *Jer. V:31.*

The promises of God and the fulfilment of them are linked together by an indissoluble bond. *Is. IV:98.*

God, in all his promises, is set before us as if he were our willing debtor. *Ps. IV:444.*

[On Ps. 48:8] It is not his way to be more liberal in promising than faithful in performing what he has promised. *Ps. II:223.*

To those only who are guided by his promises does he stretch out his hand. *Is. III:305.*

We ought to be armed with God's promises, so that we may with courageous hearts follow wherever he may call us. *Zech.- Mal. 217.*

PROPHECY

The prophets were sent for the express purpose, that God might keep his people under the guidance of his word. *Syn. Gosp. II:192.*

Nothing more is permitted to prophets than that they should be the witnesses, or ambassadors, or heralds of the grace which God freely deigns to bestow at his own pleasure upon whom he will. *Four Last Bks of Moses IV:187.*

The priestly order was as it were the nursery of the prophets. *Jer. I:33.*

The perfection of wisdom was found in the Law, from which the prophets drew whatever we read in their writings. *Jer. III:180.*

Prophecies were as so many embassies. *Jer. V:80.*

God has often so distributed the gifts of his Spirit, that he has honoured with the prophetic office even the ungodly and unbelieving; for it was a special gift, distinct from the grace of regeneration. *Jon.-Nah. 334.*

God always distinguished his own prophets from false prognosticators [by enduing] them with the power of teaching and exhorting. *Gen. II:326.*

[On Heb. 3:7, '*as the Holy Ghost saith*'] The words adduced from the books of the prophets are those of God and not of men. *Heb. 83.*

[On Rom. 12:6] Prophecy at the present day is simply the right understanding of Scripture and the particular gift of expounding it. *Rom. 269.*

[On Acts 13:1] Prophets signify excellent interpreters of Scripture. *Acts I:497.*

God does not at this day predict hidden events; but he would have us to be satisfied with his Gospel. *Jer. III:372, 373.*

PROSPERITY

The cause of all prosperity is the favour of God. *Jer. IV:496.*

Prosperity inebriates men, so that they take delight in their own vanities. *Jer. V:479.*

During [Israel's] prosperity they were drowned in negligence and contempt . . . When [God] indulges us we abuse his kindness. *Ezek. I:228.*

When men grow wanton, it arises from becoming intoxicated with prosperity. *Ezek. II:304.*

A prayer of Calvin

Grant, Almighty God, that since the depravity of our nature is so great that we cannot bear prosperity without some wantonness of the flesh . . . and without becoming even arrogant against Thee, O grant that we may profit under the trials of the cross, and when Thou hast blest us, may we with lowly hearts . . . submit ourselves to Thee . . . through Christ our Lord. Amen. [Prayer at close of Lecture 126 on the Minor Prophets] *Hab.-Hagg. 298.*

PROTECTION

[On Jer. 1:8] The defence of God alone is sufficient to protect us. *Jer. I:42.*

Nothing can be safer than to make God the guardian and protector of our life. *Dan. I:229.*

Our life can never be in the hand of men, for God is its faithful keeper. *Jer. III:328.*

Our safety is concealed under the faithful protection of God, which is only made known to us by the word and promises. *Zech.-Mal. 434.*

The invocation of [God's] name in a despairing condition is a sure port of safety. *Joel-Obad. 105.*

We have not the slightest cause to fear that our integrity will make us a prey to the ungodly, when God promises us safety under his hand. *Ps. I:441, 442.*

It is God's peculiar prerogative to vindicate his people from all unjust reproaches. *Ps. I:516, 517.*

[On Ps. 46:10] In doing injury to the saints, they are making war against God. *Ps. II:204.*

God has more than enough, both of weapons and of strength, to preserve and defend his Church which he has adopted. *Ps. II:205.*

[On Ps. 48:6] A nod alone on the part of God is sufficient to deliver us. *Ps. II:223.*

The defence of God is greater than all dangers, so faith triumphs over fear. *Gen. I:400.*

PROVIDENCE

The whole world is governed by God for our salvation . . . that those whom he has elected may be saved. *Is. I:434.*

The most important truth of all, that God governs the world by his providence. *Ps. II:249.*

Nothing is more useful than a knowledge of this doctrine. *Inst. I:xvii.3.*

Nothing can happen but what is subject to his knowledge, and decreed by his will. *Inst. I:xvi.3.*

The winding course of Divine providence. *Gen. II:318.*

Not chance, fortune or luck

If God is the judge of the world, fortune has no place in its government. *Dan. II:173.*

We are not afflicted by chance, but through the infallible providence of God. *Gen. Epp. 40.*

The providence of God, as it is taught in Scripture, is opposed to fortune and fortuitous accidents. *Inst. I:xvi.2.*

Objections

Because I affirm and maintain that the world is managed and governed by the secret providence of God, a multitude of presumptuous men rise up against me, and allege that I represent God as the Author of sin. *Ps. I:xlvi.*

There is nothing of which it is more difficult to convince men than that the providence of God governs this world. *Is. I:406, 407.*

God's providence . . . ought not to be subjected to human judgment. *Jer. V:164.*

[On Hab. 1:7] God thus intimates that he can use the vices of men in executing his judgments, and yet contract hence no spot nor blemish. *Hab.-Hagg. 28.*

Let us . . . learn to see . . . by the eyes of faith, both in accidental circumstances (as they are called) and in the evil designs of men, that secret providence of God, which directs all events to a result pre-determined by himself. *Gen. II:253.*

Explanations

The providence of God ought not always to be contemplated abstractedly by itself, but in connection with the means which he employs. *Inst. I:xvii.4.*

Those profit most who acquiesce in God's judgments, although they do not perceive the reason of them, yet modestly adore them. *Ezek. II:83.*

Those things which seem contingent are yet ruled by the certain providence of God. *Jer. V:428.*

We are taught to recognize God's providence in both prosperity and adversity. *Dan. II:172.*

We can form no judgment of God's providence, except by the light of celestial truth. *Hab.-Hagg. 62.*

Ignorance of the providence of God is the cause of all impatience. *Philipp.-Col. 118.*

The providence of God . . . shines forth principally for the sake of the faithful, because they only have eyes to behold it. *Ps. I:97.*

God's providence of the world is not presently apparent. *Ps. II:235.*

Second causes should not prevent us from recognizing the providence of God. *Ps. V:297.*

The providence of God watches for our salvation, even when it most seems to sleep. *Gen. II:232.*

God foreknows things that are future, because he had determined to do them; but they ignorantly and perversely separate the providence of God from his eternal counsel and his continual operation. *Gen. II:325.*

Although God converts to good in the end whatever Satan and the reprobate plot and practise against him or his people; yet the Church, in which God rules with undisturbed sway, has in this respect a special privilege. By his providence, which to us is incomprehensible, he directs his work in regard to the reprobate externally; but he governs his believing people internally by his Holy Spirit. *Ps. III:476.*

Benefits

Sacred is the security which reclines on his providence. *Josh. 93.*

[On Hab. 1:12] Except . . . we be fully persuaded, that God by his secret providence regulates all these confusions, Satan will . . . every moment shake that confidence which ought to repose in God. *Hab.-Hagg. 42.*

God embraces us so lovingly in Christ that he turns to our advantage and welfare everything that befalls us. *Thess. 375.*

Our only remedy is to fix our eyes upon the providence of God. *Ps. II:22.*

[On Ps. 44:10] When the faithful represent God as the author of their calamities, it is not in the way of murmuring against him, but that they may, with greater confidence, seek relief, as it were, from the same hand which smote and wounded them. *Ps. II:159.*

There is nothing better . . . for us, in our adversity, than to give ourselves to meditation upon the providence and judgment of God. *Ps. II:160.*

Nothing will more effectually preserve us in a straight and undeviating course, than a firm persuasion that all events are in the hand of God, and that he is as merciful as he is mighty. *Ps. II:430.*

The promotion of our best interests [is] the great end for which God dwells amongst us. *Ps. V:151.*

The [promised] land was not so much fertile by nature, as because God daily watered it by His secret blessing to make it so. *Four Last Bks of Moses II:285.*

The necessary consequences of this knowledge are, gratitude in prosperity, patience in adversity, and a wonderful security respecting the future. *Inst. I:xvii.7.*

PUNISHMENT

The atrocity of punishment shows the atrocity of sin. *Jer. IV:552.*

Whenever mention is made of Sodom and Gomorrah all pardon and alleviation of punishment are excluded (Is. 1:9). *Jer. V:86.*

God would not be God, except he were to punish sins . . . Whenever God pardons, he leads sinners to repentance; so that he never suffers sins to be unpunished. *Jer. I:273.*

God has an endless variety of scourges for punishing the wicked. *Is. II:182.*

We are to judge the grievousness of our sins by the greatness of our punishment. *Jer. V:461.*

God has innumerable hidden methods of punishing transgressors. *Ezek. I:235.*

The contempt of [God's threatenings] doubles both the crime and the punishment. *Four Last Bks of Moses I:153.*

God . . . has surrounded the human race with rottenness, in order that everywhere our eyes should light on the punishment of sin. *Four Last Bks of Moses II:18.*

The punishment of God's people

God purifies us now by temporal punishments, that we may be then free from final vengeance. *Jer. V:76.*

The punishments inflicted by God on his servants are only temporary and limited, and intended as medicine, inasmuch as all we suffer are helps to our salvation (Rom. 8:28). *Jer. V:75.*

God extends without any difference temporal punishments to his own children and to the unbelieving, and that in order that it may be made evident that our hope ought not to be fixed on this world. *Jer. III:297.*

Properly speaking, God is not angry with his elect, whose diseases he cures by afflictions as it were by medicines. *Ps. III:161.*

RACE

Mankind is knit together with a holy knot. *Acts I:539.*

The whole human race is united by a sacred bond of fellowship. *Syn. Gosp. III:61.*

By the sole bidding of God both nations and kingdoms are propagated, and are also abolished and destroyed. *Jon.-Nah. 446.*

REASON

The light of human reason differs little from darkness. *Eph. 290.*

We are not even competent to think aright. *Four Last Bks of Moses I:413.*

In all their reasoning faculties they miserably fail. *John I:32.*

This is impious and intolerable audacity, to set forth the offspring of man's earthly brain as if it were a divine revelation. *Four Last Bks of Moses I:449.*

Unless we have divine teaching to enlighten us, our own reason will beget nothing but mere vanity. *Four Last Bks of Moses II:162.*

Human reason, as well as human passions, is widely at variance with the Divine law. *Ps. IV:447.*

What madness it is to embrace nothing but what commends itself to human reason! What authority will God's word have, if it is not admitted any farther than we are inclined to receive it? *Ps. IV:193.*

The gospel can be understood by faith alone – not by reason, nor by the perspicacity of the human understanding. *Philipp.-Col. 174.*

As carnal sense wickedly limits the power of God to human means, so it improperly subjects his inscrutable counsel to human reasonings. *Is. III:218.*

Our faith begins with obedience . . . Obedience to God goes before understanding. *Is. III:270.*

When God's works have the appearance of being unreasonable, we ought humbly to admire them, and never to judge them according to our computation. *Jer. V:192.*

In the promises of God, as in a mirror, we ought to behold those things which are not yet visible to our eyes, even though they appear to us to be contrary to reason. *Is. IV:102.*

[On John 20:29] Christ commends faith on this ground, that it acquiesces in the bare word, and does not depend on carnal views or human reason. *John II:278.*

As often as we measure the promises and the works of God, by our own reason, and by the laws of nature, we act reproachfully towards him. *Gen. I:474.*

Men . . . choose to seek their safety in hell itself, rather than in heaven, whenever they follow their own reason. *Gen. I:510.*

RECONCILIATION

The righteousness of faith is a reconciliation with God . . . The Divine wrath remains on all men, as long as they continue to be sinners. *Inst. III:xi.21.*

[Christ] propitiated God by his own blood, and reconciled him to men. *Heb. 236.*

Whence do we receive reconciliation, but because Christ has appeased the Father by his obedience? *Syn. Gosp. III:200.*

[Of David] . . . this great blessing that God is reconciled to him. *Ps. I:253.*

The principal blessing of the everlasting covenant – gratuitous reconciliation. *Ps. V:250.*

There was but one way of reconciliation, i.e. when God should be propitiated by sacrifice. *Four Last Bks of Moses II:303.*

Reconciliation . . . does not depend on repentance, but on the gratuitous favour of God. *Jer. IV:332.*

[God's] mere goodwill reconciles him to us. *Dan. I:139.*

God is irreconcilable to the impenitent. *Jon.-Nah. 422.*

As soon as a sinner willingly condemns himself . . . he is already reconciled to God. *Hab.-Hagg. 136.*

The beginning of acceptable service is reconciliation. *Heb. 205.*

It is the highest honour conferred on the Gospel, that it is declared to be the *embassy* of mutual *reconciliation* between God and men (2 Cor. 5:20). *Syn. Gosp. II:294.*

[On Eph. 2:17] All that Christ had done towards effecting a reconciliation would have been of no service, if it had not been proclaimed by the gospel. *Eph. 239, 240.*

We are reconciled to God upon condition that every man endeavour to make his brethren partakers of the same benefit. *Ps. I:535.*

[281]

God continually reconciles Himself to the Church when He sets before it the sacrifice of Christ in the Gospel. *Four Last Bks of Moses II:297.*

REDEMPTION

The entire blessing of redemption consists mainly in these two things, remission of sins, and spiritual regeneration. *Philipp.-Col. 159.*

Christ is no Redeemer except to those who turn from iniquity, and lead a new life. *Gen. Epp. 165.*

Redemption is the first gift of Christ that is begun in us, and the last that is completed (Rom. 8:23). *Cor. I:94.*

It is the ordinary practice of Scripture, whenever redemption is mentioned, to exhort to repentance. *Is. III:383.*

Noah . . . had received his own life, and that of the animals, as the gift of God's mercy alone. *Gen. I:283.*

The common deliverance of God's chosen people from Egypt . . . God designed . . . to be a perpetual memorial . . . the archetype or original copy of the grace of God. *Ps. I:269.*

Redemption would be incomplete if it did not by continued advances carry us forward to the ultimate end of salvation. *Inst. II:xvi.1.*

[On Hagg. 2:6–9. God] will rather change the appearance of the whole world, than that redemption should not be fully accomplished. *Hab.-Hagg. 358.*

[The resurrection] – the closing scene of our redemption. For the lively assurance of our reconciliation with God arises from Christ having come from hell as the conqueror of death. *Syn. Gosp. III:338.*

I expect, with Paul, a reparation of all the evils caused by sin. *Inst. III:xxv.11.*

REFORMERS AND THE REFORMATION

Doctrine

Ours the Church, whose supreme care it is humbly and religiously to venerate the word of God, and submit to its authority. [Calvin's Reply to Sadoleto] *Tracts I:50.*

By purity of doctrine [we] preserve the unity of the Church. [Necessity of Reforming the Church] *Tracts I:174.*

The chief ground of gladness and joy is when God restores to us pure and sound doctrine; for no scarcity of wheat ought to terrify and alarm us so much as a scarcity of the word. *Is. II:371.*

[On Justification by Faith alone] The safety of the Church depends as much on this doctrine as human life does on the soul. If the purity of this doctrine is in any degree impaired, the Church has received a deadly wound. [Necessity of Reforming the Church] *Tracts I:137.*

[Of the Church of Geneva, 1553] God has graciously restored to us uncontaminated purity of doctrine, religion in its primitve state, the unadulterated worship of God, and a faithful administration of the Sacraments. *John I:17.*

Worship

Every addition to His word, especially in this matter, is a lie. [Necessity of Reforming the Church] *Tracts I:129.*

God rejects, condemns, abominates, all fictitious worship, and employs his Word as a bridle to keep us in unqualified obedience. [Necessity of Reforming the Church] *Tracts I:133.*

In the whole body of worship which had been established there was scarcely a single observance which had an authoritative sanction from the Word of God. [Necessity of Reforming the Church] *Tracts I:189.*

A theatrical exhibition was got up, and substituted for the Supper. [Necessity of Reforming the Church] *Tracts I:137.*

Reformation is God's work

The restoration of the Church is the work of God, and no more depends on the hopes and opinions of men than the resurrection of the dead . . . It is the will of our Master that His gospel be preached. Let us obey His command and follow whithersoever He calls. What the success will be it is not ours to inquire. [Necessity of Reforming the Church] *Tracts I:200.*

When we repair the ruins of the Church we give our labours to the Lord . . . Yet the restoration of the Church is His own work. *Is. I:xxiii.*

The restoration of the Church proceeds solely from the grace of God. *Is. II:420.*

The restoration of the Church is at God's disposal. *Is. III:360.*

[On Is. 44:26] Let us not doubt that there will always be a Church; and when it appears to be in a lamentably ruinous condition, let us entertain good hope of its restoration. *Is. III:389.*

[On Acts 14:16, revival] There can no reason . . . be brought why the Lord had mercy rather on one age than on another, save only because it seemed good to him that it should be so. *Acts II:18.*

[On Is. 49:11] When the Church is about to be completely restored, no obstruction, however great and formidable, can hinder God from being finally victorious. *Is. IV:27.*

[On Jer. 29:14] Who could have thought that what we now see with our eyes, would ever take place? [c.1550] *Jer. III:439.*

Opposition

When Christ goes forth with His Gospel serious commotions arise . . . Those who pretend that the Gospel is the source of disturbances, accuse us falsely and unjustly. *Dan. I:lxviii.*

When Dr Martin Luther, and other persons . . . were beginning to reprove the grosser abuses of the Pope, they scarcely had the slightest relish for pure Christianity; but after that the Pope had thundered against them, and cast them out of the

Roman synagogue by terrific bulls, Christ stretched out His hand, and made Himself fully known to them. [Comment on John 9:35] *John I:388.*

Would to God that there were no Corinth in our times! [Geneva, 1546] *Cor. I:470.*

Thirty years have passed away since my voluntary exile from France, because thence were exiled the truth of the Gospel, pure Religion, and the true Worship of God. [Calvin's Dedication of Commentaries on Jeremiah to Frederick III of the Palatinate] *Jer. I:xxiii.*

They can find nothing more atrocious . . . than the word Calvinism . . . They endeavour, by bringing forward Calvinism, to affix to your Highness some mark of infamy. [The same, dated Geneva, 23 July 1563] *Jer. I:xvii, xxii.*

All those who undertake to promote the doctrine of salvation and the well-being of the Church must be armed with invincible firmness . . . We have such an invincible Leader, that the more he is assailed the greater will be the victories and triumphs gained by his power. *Heb. xxv.*

There are many among them [the Churches of the Reformation] who insidiously corrupt the simple and genuine doctrine of the Gospel . . . who disturb all things by their own inventions. *Jer. III:194.*

Yearning for peace and unity

[On Mic. 4:3] Though the Gospel is at this day purely preached among us, when we yet consider how little progress we make in brotherly love, we ought justly to be ashamed of our indolence. *Jon.-Nah. 264.*

Calvin's reply to Archbishop Cranmer, who had proposed a General Synod for the closer union of the Reformed Churches: The Lord, as he has done from the beginning of the world, will preserve in a miraculous manner, and in a way unknown to us, the unity of a pure faith from being destroyed by the dissensions of men. [Letter of April 1552] *Letters 131.*

[285]

I would not grudge to cross even ten seas, if need were, on account of it . . . A serious and properly adjusted agreement between men of learning upon the rule of Scripture is still a desideratum . . . I think it right for me, at whatever cost of toil and trouble, to seek to attain this object. But I hope my own insignificance will cause me to be passed by. [The same] *Letters 133.*

On the state of the medieval Church at the time of Calvin

Impiety so stalked abroad, that almost no doctrine of religion was pure from admixture, no ceremony free from error, no part . . . of Divine worship untarnished by superstition. [Calvin's Reply to Sadoleto] *Tracts I:49.*

The light of divine truth had been extinguished, the word of God buried, the virtue of Christ left in profound oblivion, and the pastoral office subverted. [Calvin's Reply to Sadoleto] *Tracts I:49.*

Calvin's modesty

Some inconsiderable persons, taken from the common people, have been selected by [God] as his architects, to promote this work [of reformation] by pure doctrine. *Is. I:xxiii.*

REGENERATION

The necessity for regeneration

Man must be born again, because he is flesh. *Inst. II:iii.1.*

We have nothing of the Spirit, except by regeneration. *Inst. II:iii.1.*

The grace of God has no charms for men till the Holy Spirit gives them a taste for it. *Inst. III:xxiv.14.*

[Men] . . . are born of Adam, they are depraved creatures, and therefore can conceive only sinful thoughts, until they become the new workmanship of Christ, and are formed by his Spirit to a new life. *Gen. I:284.*

[286]

Regeneration

Origin of regeneration

The commencement of regeneration is an abolition of what is from ourselves. *Inst. II:v.15.*

The cause [is] in the Father, the matter in the Son, and the efficacy in the Spirit. *Inst. IV:xv.6.*

[God] . . . enrols [the elect] in the catalogue of his saints only when, having regenerated them by the Spirit of adoption, he impresses his own mark upon them. *Ps. III:403.*

Regeneration is like another creation; and if we compare it with the first creation, it far surpasses it. *Ezek. II:262.*

It is God's peculiar work to raise the dead. *Zech.-Mal. 262.*

In the Old Testament

The faithful under the ancient covenant were gifted and endowed with a spirit of regeneration. *Ezek. II:177.*

The grace of regeneration was promised to the ancient people when God consecrated the seventh day. *Ezek. II:302.*

Circumcision . . . a sacrament of regeneration. *Four Last Bks of Moses III:241.*

[*Born again*] – the . . . expression which Christ employed was not contained in the Law and the Prophets. *John I:109.*

Regeneration and adoption

The Spirit of regeneration is the seal of adoption. *Philipp.-Col. 147.*

The Lord admits none into his school but little children. *Cor. I:76.*

[God] declares his election when he regenerates his elect by his Holy Spirit, and thus inscribes them with a certain mark, while they prove the reality of this sonship by the whole course of their lives, and confirm their own adoption. *Dan. II:372.*

Regeneration of children of the covenant

If any of those who are the objects of divine election, after having received the sign of regeneration, depart out of this life

[287]

before they have attained years of discretion, the Lord renovates them by the power of his Spirit, incomprehensible to us, in such a manner as he alone foresees will be necessary. *Inst. IV:xvi.21.*

Regeneration and justification

The grace of justification is inseparable from regeneration, although they are distinct things. *Inst. III:xi.11.*

The fruits of regeneration

God's kingdom begins and has its origin when regeneration takes place. *Jer. V:119.*

The fear of God is not otherwise produced than by the regeneration of the Spirit. *Jer. IV:212.*

Spiritual regeneration by which he creates anew his image in his elect. *Ps. IV:84.*

The end of regeneration is that the life of believers may exhibit a symmetry and agreement between the righteousness of God and their obedience; and that thus they may confirm the adoption by which they are accepted as his children. *Inst. III:vi.1.*

God does not form new souls in us, when he draws us to his service; but changes what is wrong in us: for we should never be attentive to his word, were he not to open our ears; and there would be no inclination to obey, were he not to turn our hearts. . . . Both will and effort would immediately fail in us were he not to add his gift of perseverance. *Hab.-Hagg. 346.*

There still remains in a regenerate man a fountain of evil, continually producing irregular desires . . . This warfare will be terminated only by death. *Inst. III:iii.10.*

RELIGION

Its foundation

It is the foundation of all true religion to depend on the mouth or word of God; and it is also the foundation of our salvation. *Jer. III:460.*

Religion

No religion is pleasing to God unless founded on truth. *Dan. II:103.*

Apart from Christ, all religion is deceitful and transitory. *Is. II:201.*

The beginning of religion . . . humbly and soberly to submit to God's word. *Zech.-Mal. 229.*

There is . . . no religion approved by God except what is based on His word. *Zech.-Mal. 501.*

True religion differeth from feigned religions, because the word of God alone is the rule thereof. *Acts II:425.*

Its perversion

Religion . . . the beginning of all superstitions, not in its own nature, but through the darkness which has settled down upon the minds of men. *Ps. IV:62.*

All human inventions and admixtures in religion are profane, and tend to corrupt the service of God. *Ps. IV:240.*

All religious services which are not perfumed with the odour of faith, are of an ill-savour before God. *Gen. I:282.*

Religion, separated from knowledge, is nothing but the sport and delusion of Satan. *Jer. IV:526.*

Whoever adulterates the pure religion, (which must necessarily be the case of all who are influenced by their own imagination), he is guilty of a departure from the one God. *Inst. I:v.13.*

Ridiculed by the pagan

The Romans dared to insult all religions with freedom and petulance, and to promote atheism as far as they possibly could. *Dan. II:349.*

[The emperors] made a laughing stock of all divinities, and ridiculed the very name and appearance of piety, and used it only for the purpose of retaining their subjects in obedience. *Dan. II:342.*

REMNANT (*see also* Church)

[On Jer. 31:8] We are by no means to expect that God will so restore his Church in the world, that all shall be renewed by his Spirit, and unite in true religion; but he gathers his Church on all sides, and yet in such a way, that his gratuitous mercy ever appears, because there shall be remnants only. *Jer. IV:69.*

The covenant remains valid in the remnant. *Jer. III:132.*

God always preserves a hidden seed, that the Church should not be extinguished; for there must always be a Church in the world, but sometimes it is preserved miserably, as . . . in a sepulchre. *Ezek. II:165.*

[On Rom. 11:25] The salvation of the remnant (whom the Lord will finally gather to Himself) is hidden beneath the seal of God's ring. *Rom. 254.*

REPENTANCE

Definition

The Hebrew word for repentance denotes conversion or return. The Greek word signifies change of mind and intention. *Inst. III:iii.5.*

[Repentance is] a true conversion of our life to God, proceeding from a sincere and serious fear of God, and consisting in the mortification of our flesh and of the old man, and in the vivification of the Spirit. *Inst. III:iii.5.*

The two branches of true penitence – the mortification of the flesh, and the vivification of the spirit. *Inst. III:iii.8.*

Repentance is nothing else but a reformation of the whole life according to the Law of God. *Hos. 432.*

Repentance . . . an inward turning of man unto God, which showeth itself afterwards by external works. *Acts I:218.*

The need for repentance

If we . . . wish our sins to be buried before God, we must remember them ourselves. *Ezek. II:174.*

If we desire . . . our sins to be blotted out before God (Mic. 7:19) . . . we must recall them often and constantly to our remembrance. *Ezek. II:181.*

God buries our sins and we recall them to memory. *Ezek. II:184.*

The roots of repentance

The very beginning of repentance is grief felt on account of sin, together with self-condemnation. *Gen. II:96.*

We do nothing effectually until we tear up our sins by the roots, and thoroughly devote ourselves to God. *Gen. II:110.*

Men are seldom if ever drawn to repentance, except by the fear of punishment. *Gen. II:229.*

The only way of obtaining the favour of God is by prostrating ourselves with a wounded heart at the feet of his Divine mercy. *Ps. II:306.*

Penitence should precede our reconciliation to God. *Four Last Bks of Moses II:460.*

Every chastisement is a call to repentance. *Is. II:123.*

Repentance . . . has its place in the heart. *Is. II:123.*

Adversity does not fall out to us by chance, but is the method by which God arouses us to repentance. *Is. III:107.*

The beginning of repentance is the confession of guilt. *Jer. I:177.*

The beginning of true repentance is to renounce all deceptions and fallacies, and to seek the light, which can alone discover to us our evils. *Jer. I:426.*

It is penitence that leads us to God. *Jon.-Nah. 243.*

What is repentance but condemnation, which yet turns out to be the means of salvation? *Jon.-Nah. 423.*

Except a sinner sets himself in a manner before God's tribunal, he is never touched by a true feeling of repentance. *Zech.-Mal. 364.*

All the miseries which we endure are a profitable invitation to repentance. *Syn. Gosp. II:346.*

Repentance is a sacred thing, and therefore needs careful examination. *Syn. Gosp. II:366.*

True repentance is displeasure at sin, arising out of fear and reverence for God, and producing . . . a love and desire of righteousness. *Syn. Gosp. III:269.*

A man cannot truly devote himself to repentance, unless he knows himself to be of God. *Inst. III:iii.2.*

Repentance – a work of God

[On Heb. 6:6] The apostle warns us that repentance is not at the will of man, but that it is given by God. *Heb. 139.*

[On Is. 1:25] Repentance is a true and peculiar work of the Holy Spirit. *Is. I:80.*

No one repents of his own accord. *Is. II:25.*

Repentance is the peculiar gift of God. *Jer. III:228.*

God is not called the helper in repentance, but the author of it. *Jer. III:229.*

Repentance is the gift of God. *Jer. III:435.*

The Papists . . . speaking of repentance, hold that man, through his own freewill, returns to God; and on this point is our greatest contest with them at this day. *Jer. IV:102.*

Men never entertain a real hatred towards sin, unless God illuminates their minds, and changes their hearts. *Jer. IV:102.*

None repented but those to whom it was given . . . Repentance is a singular gift of God. *Ezek. I:229.*

There is no hope of repentance for the reprobate. *Ezek. I:404.*

[On Mal. 3:7, 8] The Papists very foolishly conclude, that repentance is in the power of man's freewill. *Zech.-Mal. 583.*

The foundation of repentance is the mercy of God, by which he restores the lost. *Syn. Gosp. I:179.*

[Jesus], in looking at Peter, added . . . the secret efficacy of the Spirit, and thus, . . . penetrated into his heart. *Syn. Gosp. III:265.*

Repentance is the gift and work of God. *Past. Epp. 234.*

Faith and repentance

True penitence is always the consequence of true faith. *Inst. II:587.*

Repentance not only immediately follows faith, but is produced by it. *Inst. III:iii.1.*

The first step of healing is repentance. *Is. I:219.*

No man will have recourse to the mercy of God, or obtain reconciliation, till he be moved by a true feeling of repentance . . . accompanied by faith. *Is. II:80.*

We cannot be reconciled to God through the blood of Christ, unless we first repent of our sins . . . Repentance is joined to [salvation] in such a manner that it cannot be separated. *Is. IV:268, 269.*

Repentance as well as faith proceeds from the truth taught . . . It is the fruit of truth . . . It is . . . an impious sacrilege to separate them. *Jer. III:310, 311.*

The gospel contains nothing else but repentance and faith. *Ezek. II:174.*

Repentance is voluntary . . . [a] return by a change of mind to the God from whom they had revolted; and this cannot be done without faith and the love of God. *Dan. I:255.*

Repentance throws men downwards, and faith raises them up again. *Dan. II:184.*

We cannot enjoy the favour of God . . . except we from the heart repent. *Zech.-Mal. 19.*

God does not despise even weak repentance, provided that it be sincere. *Syn. Gosp. III:266.*

We never obtain forgiveness of sins without repentance. *Cor. II:275.*

The evidences of repentance

Circumcision was a sign of repentance. *Gen. I:454.*

This is the true fruit of penitence when we do not defend ourselves, but silently confess ourselves convicted. *Ezek. II:184.*

Repentance begin[s] in the mind and the heart, and then pass[es] on to outward works . . . the only testimonies to real repentance. *Dan. I:279.*

Repentance . . . the commencement of true docility. *John I:154.*

Lifelong repentance

True repentance is firm and constant, and makes us war with the evil that is in us, not for a day or a week, but without end and without intermission. [Short Treatise on the Supper of our Lord] *Tracts II:178.*

Repentance does not consist in one or two works, but in perseverance. *Dan. I:236.*

The faithful ought throughout their whole life to repent . . . for we must ever contend with the flesh. *Jon.-Nah. 104.*

The exercise of repentance ought to be uninterrupted throughout our whole life. *Syn. Gosp. II:341.*

False repentance

[Of Cain, King Saul and Judas] Their repentance . . . was only . . . the ante-chamber of hell. *Inst. III:iii.4.*

They who are given up to a reprobate mind are never touched with genuine penitence. *Gen. II:96.*

Preaching repentance

It is the ordinary practice of Scripture, whenever redemption is mentioned, to exhort to repentance. *Is. III:383.*

Men cannot be led to repentance in any other way than by holding out assurance of pardon. *Is. IV:167.*

There can be no room for consolations till they have been preceded by the doctrine of repentance. *Is. IV:85.*

[294]

The doctrine of repentance ought always to accompany the promise of salvation. *Is. IV:166.*

There can be no exhortation to repentance without a hope of favour. *Jer. II:402.*

Men never understand the favour of God until they are subdued by many and severe reproofs . . . They ought . . . to be urged to the practice and duty of repentance. *Jer. IV:27.*

Those [preachers] who falsely use God's name bury the doctrine of repentance . . . As they hunt for favour, they omit the doctrine that may offend. *Jer. IV:32.*

Two prayers of Calvin

Grant, Almighty God, that as the devil ceases not to soothe us by his allurements . . . O grant that thy word may shine in our minds and hearts . . . and may we so assiduously exercise repentance through the whole course of our life, that we may ever be displeased with ourselves on account of our sins; and may we judge ourselves daily . . . until having at length finished our warfare, which we have to carry on continually with our sins, we shall come to that blessed rest which has been procured for us in heaven, by Jesus Christ our Lord. Amen. [Prayer concluding Lecture 18 on Jeremiah] *Jer. I:261, 262.*

Grant, Almighty God, since we are so dull and heavy, that we may awake in time at thy threats, and submit ourselves to thy power . . . that through the whole course of our life we may proceed in the continual pursuit and meditation of true repentance; and having put off the vices and filth of the flesh, we may be reformed into true purity, until at length we arrive at the enjoyment of celestial glory, which is laid up for us in Christ Jesus our Lord. Amen. [Prayer concluding Lecture 15 on Ezekiel] *Ezek. I:217.*

REPROBATION

Definition

Eternal Election, or God's Predestination of Some to Salvation, and of Others to Destruction. [Heading to Chap. 21, Book III, The Institutes] *Inst. III:xxi.*

Predestination, by which God adopts some to the hope of life, and adjudges others to eternal death, no one, desirous of the credit of piety, dares absolutely to deny. *Inst. III:xxi.5.*

The word *world*, throughout [John 17] denotes the reprobate. *John II:184.*

God sovereign

There is no absurdity in the act of avenging the sins of the fathers upon their reprobate children; since, of necessity, all those whom God has deprived of his Spirit, are subject to his wrath. *Gen. I:305.*

Whatever poison Satan produces, God turns it into medicine for his elect . . . He turns the food of reprobates into poison, their light into darkness . . . their life into death. *Gen. II:488.*

The weight of God's wrath lies on the reprobate. *Is. II:385.*

There is no hope of repentance to the reprobate. *Ezek. I:404.*

Man responsible

Experience shows, that the reprobate are sometimes affected with emotions very similar to those of the elect, so that, in their own opinion, they are in no respect different from the elect. *Inst. III:ii.11.*

The reprobate will be delivered over into eternal fire with their bodies . . . the instruments of perpetrating evil. *Gen. I:166.*

Death makes the great distinction between the reprobate and the sons of God, whose condition in the present life is commonly one and the same, except that the sons of God have by far the worst of it. *Gen. I:417.*

[On Gen. 50:20. The reprobate] are not induced to sin, as the faithful are to act aright, by the impulse of the Spirit, but they are the authors of their own evil, and follow Satan as their leader. *Gen. II:488.*

All who depart from [God] are reprobate. *Ps. IV:415.*

Security arms the reprobate against God. *Four Last Bks of Moses I:192.*

[On Pharaoh] I am certainly not ashamed of speaking as the Holy Spirit speaks, nor do I hesitate to believe what so often is spoken of in Scripture, that God gives the wicked over to a reprobate mind, gives them up to vile affections, blinds their minds and hardens their hearts.*Four Last Bks of Moses I:102.*

Impostors in their working of miracles are the ministers of God's vengeance, in order that the reprobate may be taken in their snares. *Four Last Bks of Moses I:443.*

Whilst God earnestly invites the reprobate to repentance and the hope of salvation, He has no other object than that they may be rendered inexcusable by the detection of their impiety. *Four Last Bks of Moses IV:170.*

This is the distinction between the elect and the reprobate . . . that the elect simply rely on the word, but do not disregard works, while ungodly men scorn and disdain the word, though God speak a hundred times. *Is. I:185.*

Such blinding and hardening . . . must be ascribed exclusively to the depravity of man. *Is. I:217.*

Satan caresses the reprobate. *Is. IV:249.*

The first . . . and natural use of God's word is to bring salvation to men . . . but it turns into poison to the reprobate. *Jer. III:199.*

The devil, by his artifice fascinates the reprobate, when he renders God's word either hateful or contemptible. *Jer. III:205.*

. . . the reprobate and abandoned, who do not acknowledge God, except in death. *Ezek. I:403.*

. . . this temporary and vanishing conversion of the reprobate. *Dan. I:233.*

[On Matt. 26:14. Satan] is said to *enter* into the reprobate, when he takes possession of all their senses, overthrows the fear of God, extinguishes the light of reason, and destroys every feeling of shame. *Syn. Gosp. III:193.*

[On John 6:60] Out of the word of God the reprobate are . . . accustomed to form stones to dash themselves upon. *John I:270.*

[297]

The reprobate . . . suck venom from the most wholesome food, and gall from honey. *John I:277*.

. . . sign of a reprobate mind, when one cannot endure the doctrine of Christ. *John I:354*.

Explanations

To those whom [God] devotes to condemnation, the gate of life is closed by a just and irreprehensible, but incomprehensible, judgment. *Inst. III:xxi.7*.

By excluding the reprobate from the knowledge of his name and the sanctification of his Spirit, he affords an indication of the judgment that awaits them. *Inst. III:xxi.7*.

They who are given up to a reprobate mind are never touched with genuine penitence. *Gen. II:96*.

God chastises [His erring people] and often punishes them more severely than the reprobate, whom he spares to utter destruction. *Ps. I:570*.

God acts as a Father towards his elect and as a judge towards the reprobate. *Jer. II:66*.

The one thing which distinguishes his Elect from the Reprobate is, that . . . he presents the former with new eyes . . . and inclines their hearts to obey His word. [Antidote to the Council of Trent] *Tracts III:253*.

God offers his word indiscriminately to the good and the bad, but it works by his Spirit in the elect . . . as to the reprobate . . . it renders them without excuse. *Ezek. I:113*.

God . . . claims to himself alone the difference between the elect and the reprobate. *Ezek. II:250*.

The reprobate are sometimes endued by God with the gifts of the Spirit, to execute the office with which he invests them. *John II:64*.

Objections

Many . . . as if they wished to avert odium from God, admit election in such a way as to deny that anyone is reprobated. But

[298]

this is puerile and absurd, because election itself could not exist without being opposed to reprobation. *Inst. III:xxiii.1.*

Others endeavour to overthrow God's eternal purpose of predestination by which he distinguishes between the reprobate and the elect. *Ps. I:xlvi.*

[Reprobation] This doctrine, which filthy dogs endlessly assail with their barking, everywhere appears in the Scriptures. *Four Last Bks of Moses III:380.*

Practical Duty

As we cannot distinguish between the elect and reprobate, it is our duty to pray for all who trouble us, to desire the salvation of all men. *Ps. IV:283.*

It does not belong to us to determine before the time who the reprobate and the irreclaimable are . . . We ought to pray for all without exception. *Jer. III:43.*

The prayers which we offer for all are still limited to the elect of God . . . We leave to the judgment of God those whom he knows to be reprobate. *John II:173.*

We ought not rashly to conclude that anyone has brought on himself the judgment of eternal death. *Gen. Epp. 270.*

REPUTATION

Christ's servants ought to be concerned as to their own reputation, only in so far as is for the advantage of the Church. *Cor. II:228.*

We must beware of relying on the good opinion of men. *John II:130.*

[On 2 Cor. 12:1] It is humility alone, that can give stability to our greatness in the sight of God. *Cor. II:366.*

It is well for us that God not only wipes away the reproaches with which the wicked load us, but also so ennobles them, that they surpass all the honours and triumphs of the world. *Ps. III:54.*

RESPONSIBILITY

God deals with men according to their disposition. *Jer. IV:327.*

Whatever deficiency of natural ability prevents us from attaining the pure and clear knowledge of God, yet, since that deficiency arises from our own fault, we are left without any excuse. *Inst. I:v.15.*

The blame lies solely with ourselves, if we do not become partakers of this salvation; for he calls all men to himself, without a single exception, and gives Christ to all, that we may be illuminated by him. *Is. III:295.*

The greater honour which anyone receives from the Lord, the more severely is he to be blamed, if he afterwards makes himself the slave of Satan, and deserts his post. *Gen. II:247.*

They are worthier of a heavier punishment, who have been religiously brought up from their childhood. *Jer. II:257.*

After the impious have wilfully shut their own eyes, it is the righteous vengeance of God upon them, to darken their understandings, so that, seeing they may not perceive. *Inst. I:iv.2.*

RESURRECTION

Importance

The resurrection of Christ is the most important article of our faith. *John II:247.*

[On Acts 1:21] The resurrection . . . the chief point of the gospel. *Acts I:67.*

The main article of religion – the resurrection of the dead. *Cor. I:38.*

If the resurrection is overthrown, the dominion of sin is set up anew. *Cor. II:20.*

The resurrection at the last day, which will surpass all other miracles. *Ps. III:414.*

We ascribe our salvation partly to the death of Christ, and partly to his resurrection; we believe that sin was abolished, and death destroyed, by the former; that righteousness was restored, and life established, by the latter. *Inst. II:xvi.13.*

[The resurrection] – the closing scene of our redemption. For the lively assurance of our reconciliation with God arises from Christ having come from hell as the conqueror of death. *Syn. Gosp. III:338.*

The resurrection of Christ

In order to know [Christ's] glory, we must proceed from his death to his resurrection. *Is. IV:114.*

The glory of His resurrection . . . caused his death itself to be a splendid triumph. *John II:213.*

The gift of the Spirit was a fruit of the resurrection of Christ. *Acts I:100.*

The holy apostles were chosen by the holy decree of God, that by their testimony the truth of Christ's resurrection might stand. *Acts I:446.*

Our salvation was begun by the sacrifice by which our sins were expiated, and finally completed by His resurrection. *Rom. 102.*

The resurrection of Christ is the commencement of his reign. *Gal. 24.*

In the resurrection of Christ we all have a sure pledge of our own resurrection . . . Christ did not rise for himself, but for us. *Past. Epp. 214.*

In order that a good conscience may lead us peacefully and quietly to the grave, it is necessary to rely upon the resurrection of Christ . . . for we then go willingly to God. *Gen. II:473.*

Preaching Christ's resurrection

All ministers of the Word . . . ought to be exceedingly careful that the glory of his resurrection should be always exhibited by them in connection with the ignominy of his death. *Syn. Gosp. II:300.*

When the death of Christ is mentioned, we ought always to take into view at once the whole of the three days, that his death and burial may lead us to a blessed triumph and to a new life. *Syn. Gosp. II:330.*

[On John 12:1] The odour of his resurrection has now sufficient efficacy, without spikenard and costly ointments, to quicken the whole world. *John II:14.*

The resurrection of the Christian

He alone has made a solid proficiency in the gospel who has been accustomed to continual meditation on the blessed resurrection. *Inst. III:xxv.1.*

[On Ps. 49:14, 15] *In the morning* . . . a beautiful and striking metaphor . . . the morning which will introduce eternity . . . [which] points us to a long day of an extraordinary kind, when God himself shall rise upon us as the sun, and surprise us with the discovery of his glory. *Ps. II:249, 251.*

Christ so frequently connects *the resurrection* with eternal life, because our salvation will be hidden till that day. *John I:266.*

If the hope of a resurrection is taken away . . . the whole structure of piety falls to the ground. *Cor. II:66.*

The 'resurrection' of the soul

Faith is the resurrection of the soul. [True Method of Reforming the Church] *Tracts III:250.*

We never know aright our Lord's resurrection, until . . . we venture to rejoice that we have been made partakers of the same life . . . For . . . it is chiefly by the faith of the resurrection that we are now quickened. *Syn. Gosp. III:348.*

Faith is a spiritual resurrection of the soul. *John I:436.*

The 'resurrection' of the church

The life of the Church is not without a resurrection; nay, it is not without many resurrections. *Jon.-Nah. 275.*

Resurrection

The resurrection of the body

God watches over the scattered dust of his own children, gathers it again, and will suffer nothing of them to perish. *Ps. II:442.*

God does not collect fresh materials . . . for the fabrication of men, but calls the dead out of their sepulchres. *Inst. III:xxv.7.*

The resurrection of Christ, by its quickening vigour, penetrated every sepulchre. *Syn. Gosp. III:341.*

Although the souls of the dead are now living, and enjoy quiet repose, yet the whole of their felicity and consolation depends exclusively on the resurrection. *Cor. II:21.*

Burial and resurrection

The sacred rite of burial descended from the holy fathers, to be a kind of mirror of the future resurrection. *Gen. II:477.*

To embalm corpses . . . was done as a public symbol of future incorruption. *Gen. II:477.*

The rites of burial arouse us to the hope of the resurrection and everlasting life. *Four Last Bks of Moses III:248.*

Burial . . . the symbol of the last resurrection, which we still look for . . . As *the earth* supports the living, so it covers the dead and keeps them till the coming of Christ. *Is. I:449, 450.*

Burying has been held as a sacred custom in all ages; for it was a symbol of the last resurrection. *Jer. I:416.*

Immoderate [funeral] expense quenches the sweet savour of Christ's resurrection. *John II:246.*

Old Testament figures

The translation of Enoch was . . . to be as a visible representation of a blessed resurrection . . . an instruction for all the godly . . . He was taken to a better abode . . . he was received into a heavenly country (Heb. 11:5). *Gen. I:231, 232.*

His people's passage through the Red Sea and victory over warlike giants, was a species of resurrection. *Ps. III:30.*

[303]

[On Deut. 21:23] The rights of sepulture are ordained for man, both as a pledge and symbol of the resurrection, and also to spare the eyes of the living. *Four Last Bks of Moses III:47.*

Unbelief concerning the resurrection

This truth is too difficult to command the assent of the human mind. *Inst. III:xxv.3.*

To refuse credit to testimonies so numerous and authentic, is not diffidence, but perverse and unreasonable obstinacy. *Inst. III:xxv.3.*

Whoever destroys the *resurrection* deprives souls of their immortality. *Syn. Gosp. III:48.*

It was the finishing stroke of the vengeance of God to blind the Jews, that the resurrection of Christ was buried by the perjury of the soldiers . . . The world voluntarily gives itself up to be blinded by the snares of Satan. *Syn. Gosp. III:351.*

[On Acts 26:7] The state of the Church is come to that pass, that the priests set themselves against the common hope of all the faithful. *Acts II:374.*

Those . . . who entertain doubts concerning the resurrection do great injury to Christ, and . . . as Paul says in Rom. 10:6, take Christ down from heaven. *Thess. 363.*

REVELATION ·

Definition

The Word of God . . . is . . . to be understood of the eternal wisdom residing in God, whence the oracles, and all the prophecies, proceeded. *Inst. I:xiii.7. 145.*

As all Divine revelations are justly entitled *the word of God*, so we ought chiefly to esteem that substantial Word the source of all revelations, who is liable to no variation, who remains with God . . . and who is God. *Inst. I:xiii.7.*

God will not and cannot have himself separated from his word. *Jer. IV:542.*

These two things are opposite to each other and do not mutually agree, general and perpetual science, and special revelation. *Dan. I:124.*

The majesty of God is . . . incomprehensible to us; but he makes himself known by his works and by his word. *Hab.-Hagg. 130.*

As men submit themselves to God, the gift of revelation is prepared for them. *Zech.-Mal. 146.*

No doctrine is to be allowed, except what he has himself revealed. *Zech.-Mal. 532.*

The doctrine of Scripture is so full and complete in every respect, that whatever is defective in our faith ought justly to be attributed to ignorance *of the Scriptures. John II:253.*

The Lord does not shine upon us, except when we take his word as our light . . . Without the word nothing is left for men but darkness. *Gen. Epp. 388.*

Necessity for revelation

There was never since the beginning any communication between God and man, save only by Christ; for we have nothing to do with God, unless the Mediator be present to purchase his favour for us. *Acts I:276.*

The proper discrimination between truth and falsehood . . . does not arise from the sagacity of our own mind, but comes to us from the Spirit of wisdom. *Syn. Gosp. III:356.*

[On Is. 60:3] There is no other light of men but when God shines on them by His word. *Is. IV:277.*

They who seek for the least spark of light or drop of purity out of Christ, plunge themselves into a labyrinth, where they wander in mortal darkness, and inhale the deadly fumes of false virtues unto their own destruction. *Four Last Bks of Moses II:198.*

All those things which are invisible to our eyes, or far above the comprehension of our minds, must either be believed on the authority of the oracles of God, or entirely rejected. *Inst. III:xxv.5.*

We perceive it to have been the design of the Lord, to deliver nothing in his sacred oracles, which we might not learn to our edification. *Inst. I:xiv.16.*

General revelation in God's creation

The glory of God is written and imprinted in the heavens . . . They give forth a loud and distinct voice, which reaches the ears of all men . . . a visible language. *Ps. I:313.*

Special revelation

God never revealed Himself to the fathers [in the Old Testament] but in His eternal Word and only-begotten Son. *Is. I:201.*

Christ, the only light of truth, the soul of the law, the end of all the prophets. *Is. II:322.*

Whenever God has *appeared* to his servants, he has also *spoken* to them . . . *Gen. II:388.*

We . . . are truly wise, when we depend on God's words, and submit our feeling to His revelations. *Four Last Bks of Moses I:348.*

[Moses] faithfully handed [the Commandments] down from the dictation of God's own mouth. *Four Last Bks of Moses I:385.*

[Moses] wrote his five books not only under the guidance of the Spirit of God but as God Himself had suggested them, speaking to him out of His own mouth. *Four Last Bks of Moses III:328.*

Moses . . . uttered nothing of himself, but only what God had dictated by his mouth. *Josh. 37.*

There is nothing contained in this book which was not made known to Isaiah by God Himself . . . no human reasonings, but the oracles of God . . . nothing but what was revealed by His Spirit. *Is. I:36.*

Revelation was progressive

[The Old Testament saints] had the mirror, we have the substance. *Gal. 107.*

Revelation

The Lord reveals his secrets to the elect when he sees a fit season. *Is. III:367.*

This is the order and economy which God observed, in dispensing the covenant of his mercy, that as the course of time accelerated the period of its full exhibition, he illustrated it from day to day with additional revelations. *Inst. II:x.20.*

God's accommodation to us in His revelation

[On Gen. 1:16] Since the Spirit of God here opens a common school for all, it is not surprising that he should chiefly choose those subjects which would be intelligible to all. *Gen. I:87.*

When God descends to us he, in a certain sense, abases himself, and stammers with us, so he allows us to stammer with him. *Gen. II:238.*

God lisps, as it were, with us, just as nurses are accustomed to speak to infants. *Inst. I:xiii.1.*

The truths of revelation are so high as to exceed our comprehension; but, at the same time, the Holy Spirit has accommodated them so far to our capacity, as to render all Scripture profitable for instruction. *Ps. II:239.*

God prattles to us in Scripture in a rough and popular style. *John I:119.*

Our reverent submission necessary

That the revealed will of God ought to be reverently acquiesced in, we will receive, without disputation, those mysteries which offend either the proud, or such as would be over-careful to remove the difficulties. *Ps. IV:194.*

[On Exod. 33:18] This is the rule of sound and legitimate and profitable knowledge, to be content with the measure of revelation, and willingly to be ignorant of what is deeper than this. *Four Last Bks of Moses III:377.*

Deviations

[Heading to Chap. 9, Bk I, The Institutes] The Fanaticism which Discards the Scripture, Under the Pretence of Resorting

[307]

to Immediate Revelations, Subversive of Every Principle of Piety. *Inst. I:ix.1.*

The Psalmist . . . did not hunt after secret revelations, and set the word at nought, as many fanatics do, but connected the external doctrine with the inward grace of the Holy Spirit. *Ps. V:14.*

Well . . . does Chrysostom admonish us to reject all who, under the pretence of the Spirit, lead us away from the simple doctrine of the gospel – the Spirit having been promised not to reveal new doctrine, but to impress the truth of the gospel on our minds . . . For when they boast extravagantly of the Spirit, the tendency certainly is to sink and bury the Word of God, that they may make room for their own falsehoods. [Reply to Sadoleto] *Tracts I:36.*

In sacred things every human mixture is absolute profanation. *Is. I:210.*

[On Is. 30:1] Two things are here connected, the word and the Spirit of God, in opposition to fanatics, who aim at oracles and hidden revelations without the Word. *Is. II:347.*

As soon as we yield the least to our own imaginations, we necessarily turn aside from the right way, which God has made known to us in his Word. *Jer. I:483.*

God so shines forth in his word, that he does not appear as God, except his word remains safe and uncorrupted. *Jer. III:27.*

Everything is a deceit which has not God himself as its Author. *Jer. III:193.*

So thoroughly infected is the mind of man with a depraved curiosity, that the greater part of men are always gaping after new revelations. *Syn. Gosp. II:192.*

[On Luke 16:30] God has included in his word all that is necessary to be known . . . Faith does not depend on miracles, or any extraordinary sign, but is the peculiar gift of the Spirit, and is produced by means of the word . . . There is nothing to which the flesh is more inclined than to listen to vain revelations. *Syn. Gosp. II:193, 194.*

Many are too presumptuous in boasting of the authority of God; fanatics . . . give out their own inventions as the oracles of God. *John I:300.*

We should be soberly wise in those points, the certain knowledge of which cannot be elicited from Scripture, for our curiosity is not only frivolous, but also perverse and injurious, when we desire to know more than God has revealed. *Four Last Bks of Moses III:423.*

This is impious and intolerable audacity, to set forth the offspring of man's earthly brain as if it were a divine revelation. *Four Last Bks of Moses I:449.*

REVENGE

[On Herod's attitude to the infant Messiah] . . . the ulcer of revenge. *Syn. Gosp. I:160.*

He which revengeth himself doth take God's office from him. *Acts I:258.*

Revenge is a passion unbecoming the children of God. *Jer. II:278.*

A desire of revenge reigns in all unbelievers, while, on the other hand, God governs his own children by the spirit of meekness and benignity. *Ps. I:98.*

REVERENCE

Reverence always begets modesty. *John II:27.*

To be silent at the presence of God . . . is to submit to God's authority. *Hab.-Nah. 204.*

So often as the Word of God is set before us, we must . . . think . . . that God is present, and doth call us. From this respect of God, ariseth the majesty of God's word, and reverence in hearing the same. *Acts I:435.*

Faith is always connected with a seemly and spontaneous reverence for God. *Thess. 407.*

It is . . . a reverence due to God, immediately to receive, as beyond controversy, whatever he declares to us. *Gen. Epp. 262.*

God wishes that reverence which he exacts from us be given to his own Word. *Ezek. I:359.*

[On Luke 4:16] The majesty of Scripture deserves that its expounders should make it apparent, that they proceed to handle it with modesty and reverence. *Syn. Gosp. I:227.*

REVIVAL

[The oppressed Church] shall stand erect . . . being renewed and multiplied from age to age by various resurrections. *Is. III:134.*

[On Is. 51:3] As the Lord suddenly produced from one man [Abraham] so numerous an offspring, so he will also people his Church by wonderful and unknown methods, and not once only, but whenever she shall be thought to be childless and solitary. *Is. IV:68.*

It is God's peculiar office to raise up and renew what had formerly been destroyed. *Is. IV:309.*

We ought always to entertain favourable hopes of the restoration of the Church, though she be plunged under thick darkness and in the grave. *Is. IV:321.*

Although the Church does not make professions of towering greatness . . . yet the Lord imparts a secret vigour which causes it to spring up and grow beyond human expectation. *Is. III:140.*

No difficulties can prevent the Lord from delivering and restoring His Church whenever he shall think fit. *Is. III:205.*

[On Is. 62:7] It is [God] alone who promotes, by [the pastors'] agency, the restoration of the Church. *Is. IV:328, 329.*

The Prophets, when speaking of the restoration of the Church, included the whole kingdom of Christ from the beginning to the end. *Jer. IV:117.*

God has his settled seasons of visitations. *Jer. V:69.*

There is a fixed time of visitation, and that is dependent on God's will. *Jer. V:167.*

God would overcome all those impediments, which Satan and the whole world may throw in the way, when it is his purpose to restore his Church. *Hab.-Hagg. 386.*

[On Mal. 3:17] God has His season and opportunity, in order that there may be no presumption in us to prescribe to him the time when he is to do this or that. *Zech.-Mal. 606.*

Though the melancholy desolation which surrounds us, seems to proclaim that there is nothing left of the Church, let us remember that the death of Christ is fruitful, and that God wonderfully preserves his Church as it were in hiding places. *Inst. IV:i.2.*

REWARDS

Reward depends on the free mercy of God only. *Jer. IV:176.*

The Lord does not always recompense our piety by earthly rewards. *Is. III:85.*

The Lord almost always places the reward of labours and the crown of victory in heaven. *Inst. III:xv.4.*

For none but him who has fought lawfully is the crown prepared. *Syn. Gosp. II:420.*

I expect, with Paul, a reparation of all the evils caused by sin. *Inst. III:xxv. 11.*

[On Heb. 6:10] Reward . . . is reserved for works, not through merit, but through the free bounty of God alone, [and only if] we be first received into favour through the kind mediation of Christ . . . He recognises himself, and the work of his Spirit, in them. *Heb. 142.*

RIGHTEOUSNESS

God's righteousness
This righteousness . . . flows from God and through Christ. *Gen. Epp. 367.*

God's righteousness means his faithfulness . . . God displays his righteousness in performing his promises to his servants. *Ps. I:499.*

The righteousness of God is to be understood of his faithfulness which he observes in maintaining and defending his own people. *Ps. II:229.*

The righteousness of God [is] the faithfulness which he observes towards his own people, when he cherishes, defends and delivers them. *Ps. III:90.*

[On Ps. 36:10] With the mercy of God he connects his righteousness, combining them as cause and effect. *Ps. II:13.*

True righteousness is nothing else than the imputation of righteousness, when God, out of free grace, acquits us from guilt . . . It is by imputation that believers are righteous before God to the very end. *Syn. Gosp. I:76, 77.*

Christ's righteousness

[On Heb. 7:1] As the King of righteousness [he] communicates to us the righteousness of God, partly when he makes us to be counted righteous by a gratuitous reconciliation, and partly when he renews us by his Spirit, that we may lead a godly and holy life. *Heb. 156.*

[Christ's righteousness] . . . is ours, because Christ is righteous not for himself, but possesses a righteousness which he communicates to us. *Jer. III:146.*

God determined that his own Son should be stripped of his raiment, that we, clothed with his righteousness . . . may appear with boldness in company with his angels. *Syn. Gosp. III:298.*

Christ was stripped of his garments that he might clothe us with righteousness; . . . his naked body was exposed to the insults of men, that we may appear in glory before the judgment-seat of God. *John II:230.*

Christ himself permitted his garments to be torn in pieces like a prey, that he might enrich us with the riches of his victory. *Syn. Gosp. III:298, 299.*

Righteousness

Our righteousness

No righteousness will ever be found in mortal man, unless he obtain it from Christ. *Dan. II:216, 217.*

Not only do we receive righteousness by grace through faith but, as the moon borrows her light from the sun, so does the same faith render our works righteous. *Ps. IV:233.*

We are righteous only in so far as Christ reconciles the Father to us. *Rom. 75.*

We are with the greatest difficulty induced to leave the glory of righteousness entire to God alone. [Antidote to the Council of Trent] *Tracts III:108.*

The fear of God is the root or origin of all righteousness. *Ps. IV:448.*

Righteousness flows from only one principle – the fear of God. *Ezek. II:234.*

ROMAN CATHOLICISM AT THE TIME OF THE REFORMATION

Context

Our acknowledgment of societies to be churches of Christ must be accompanied by an explicit condemnation of everything in them that is improper or defective. *Gal. 25.*

We are ever now and then enforced to show and testify how much Papistry differeth from Christianity, and what a hurtful plague it is to be yoked with the unfaithful enemies of Christ. *Acts I:125.*

We differ from Papists, that while we are both of us called Christians, and profess to believe in Christ, they picture to themselves one that is torn, disfigured, divested of his excellence, denuded of his office, in fine, such as to be a spectre rather than Christ himself; we, on the other hand, embrace him such as he is here described by Paul – loving and efficacious. [Colossians] distinguishes the true Christ from a fictitious one. [Intro. to Colossians] *Col. 134.*

[313]

The very fountain of all the contentions, by which the Church for these thirty years has been so sorely disturbed, will be found to be, that they who seek to be deemed first among Christ's disciples, cannot bear to submit to His truth. Ambition as well as audacity has so far prevailed, that the truth of God lies buried under innumerable lies, that all his institutions are polluted by the basest corruptions; his worship is in every part vitiated, the doctrine of faith is wholly subverted, the sacraments are adulterated, the government of the Church is turned into barbarous tyranny . . . and in the place of Christianity is substituted a dreadful profanation. *Heb. Preface xxi.*

The light of divine truth had been extinguished, the word of God buried, the virtue of Christ left in profound oblivion, and the pastoral office subverted. [Reply to Sadoleto] *Tracts I:49.*

Impiety so stalked abroad, that almost no doctrine of religion was pure from admixture, no ceremony free from error, no part . . . of divine worship untarnished by superstition. [Reply to Sadoleto] *Tracts I:49.*

Popery . . . patches sewed together, taken out of every kind of superstitions, not only heathen and Jewish, but likewise such as have been recently contrived by Satan. *Is. IV:416.*

If Peter were now alive, they would tear him in pieces; they would stone Paul; and if Christ himself were still in the world, they would burn him with a slow fire. *Syn. Gosp. III:97.*

Theology

Their whole doctrine contains nothing else than big words and bombast, because it is inconsistent with the majesty of Scripture, the efficacy of the Spirit, the gravity of the prophets, and the sincerity of the apostles . . . It is . . . an absolute profanation of real theology. *Past. Epp. 174.*

We may safely denounce an anathema on the whole theology of the Pope, for it wholly obscures the true light. *Gen. Epp. 179.*

[314]

Scripture

Abandoned ... by the Word of God, they flee for aid to antiquity. [Necessity of Reforming the Church] *Tracts I:218*.

The Papists ... accustomed to set aside the true meaning of the Scriptures, and to spoil all the mysteries of God by their own fooleries ... *Is. I:41*.

The word of God ... is ridiculed in the present day by Papists, as if it were a fable, and fiercely persecuted by fire and sword. *John I:346*.

I will most truly declare that we have thrown more light upon the Scriptures than all the doctors who have appeared under the Papacy since its commencement. [Antidote to the Council of Trent] *Tracts III:76*.

The Church

Although the devil has long reigned in the Papacy, yet he could not altogether extinguish God's grace: nay, a Church is among them. *Ezek. II:120*.

We ... deny not that those over which you preside are Churches of Christ. [Reply to Sadoleto] *Tracts I:50*.

It is better a hundred times to separate from [the Papists] than to be united together, and thus to form an ungodly and wicked union against God. *Jer. IV:211*.

They are to cling with a death-grasp to all their impieties, while we who desire nothing but the reign of Christ, and maintain the pure doctrine of the Gospel, are to be judged heretics. [Antidote to the Council of Trent] *Tracts III:39*.

The Papacy ... has nothing in common with the ancient form of the Church. [Antidote to Council of Trent] *Tracts III:264*.

[315]

The Person and Work of Christ

There are especially two parties who find the Epistle to the Hebrews in no way favourable – the Papists and the Socinians. The Sole Priesthood of Christ, and His Sole and Sufficient Sacrifice are here so distinctly stated. *Heb. v.*

[The Papacy] brought feigned washings from the lake of hell, to make dry the blood of the Son of God . . . Instead of the Holy Ghost; he . . . erected man's freewill . . . the true Christ is banished far from Papistry. *Acts I:xxii.*

The whole of Popery . . . is built on ignorance of Christ. *Col. 177.*

Under Popery . . . every person had a different method of washing away his sins. *Is. II:328.*

Worship

What is the worship of God in the papacy in these days but a confused jumble, which they have thrown together from numberless fictions? . . . fabricated by the will of man. *Ezek. II:310.*

In the whole body of worship which had been established, there was scarcely a single observance which had an authoritative sanction from the Word of God. [Antidote to the Articles of the Faculty of Sacred Theology of Paris] *Tracts I:189.*

Ceremonies

What horrible confusion doth reign in Popery . . . a huge heap of ceremonies . . . Instead of one veil of the old temple, an hundred. *Acts II:92.*

[On auricular confession] That tyrannical decree of the Pope, by which he turns us away from God, and sends us to his priests to obtain pardon. *Ps. I:532.*

Antichrist

Antichrist . . . has now for ages exercised dominion in God's sanctuary. *Joel-Obad. 138.*

... the wretched bondage of that detestable monster, Antichrist, whose tyranny is exercised over the whole world. *Is. III:133.*

Roman antichrist invites us to himself, under the pretence of unity, and pronounces all to be schismatics who do not spontaneously submit to ... the yoke of his tyranny. [Calvin on Letter of Pope Paul III] *Tracts I:259.*

The Papacy

The Popish hierarchy I execrate as diabolical confusion, established for the very purpose of making God Himself to be despised, and of exposing the Christian religion to mockery and scorn. [Brief Confession of Faith] *Tracts II:134.*

[The Papacy] never acts without dissimulation. [Calvin on Letter of Pope Paul III] *Tracts I:279.*

The Papacy ... whose Baalim are angels and dead men. *Jer. I:371.*

... the Pope and his clergy, the very filth of the world ... Those savages who boast that they are bishops, and prelates and governors. *Jer. II:173.*

The Papacy ... an immense chaos of errors. *Ezek. I:150.*

The Papacy ... inclose pardon of sins in lead and parchment. *Cor. II:239.*

Papists ... have a diabolical synagogue. *Eph. 285.*

The Papists ... peddle the stinking conglomeration of their own superstitions. *Thess. 412.*

The Papists ... are given up to a reprobate mind. *Hab.-Hagg. 84.*

The Court of Rome, that forge of all craft and trickery. [Reply to Sadoleto] *Tracts I:28.*

[Popery] ... an immense chaos and horrible labyrinth. *Acts II:122.*

[317]

We know well that under the Pope there is a bastard sort of Christianity, and that God will disavow it at the last day, seeing that He now condemns it in His Word. [Letter to the Duke of Somerset, 1548] *Letters 98.*

SABBATH

[On Is. 66:2] The Sabbath includes all the exercises of religion. *Is. IV:177.*

The Sabbath was the symbol of sanctification (Exod. 31:13, 14). *Ezek. II:301.*

The Sabbath was a sacrament . . . a visible word. *Ezek. II:302.*

The grace of regeneration was promised to the ancient people when God consecrated the seventh day. *Ezek. II:302.*

[On Gen. 2:3, God blessing the seventh day] That benediction is nothing else than a solemn consecration by which God claims for himself the meditations and employments of men on the seventh day. *Gen. I:105.*

The Sabbath was not prescribed as a day of idleness, but a season when we should collect our whole energies for meditation upon the works of God. *Ps. III:496.*

God inculcates no other commandment more frequently, nor more strictly requires obedience to any. *Four Last Bks of Moses II:435.*

The whole worship of God is sometimes included by synecdoche in the word Sabbath (Jer. 17:21; Ezek. 20:12). *Four Last Bks of Moses III:238.*

[On Lev. 26:34, Sabbath-breakers] God in a manner associated the land . . . together with man . . . The land was disturbed by ceaseless inquietude . . . since it bore on its shoulders, as it were, and not without great distress, such impious despisers of God. *Four Last Bks of Moses III:238.*

[On Acts 13:14] Even at this day we must use holy days; for we must omit all other things that we may the more freely serve God. *Acts I:513.*

SACRAMENTS (*see also* Baptism, the Lord's Supper)

Purpose

Their only aim . . . to make us look to Christ for everything requisite to our salvation. [Calvin's Brief Confession of Faith] *Tracts II:134.*

The first object of [the sacraments] is to assist our faith towards God; the second, to testify our confession before men. *Inst. IV:xiv.13.*

. . . aids of our faith and appendices of doctrine. *Inst. IV:xiv.13.*

Scope

The sacraments of both Testaments have the same Author, the same promises, the same truth, and the same fulfilment in Christ. [Antidote to the Council of Trent] *Tracts III:172.*

Word and sacrament

There is never any sacrament without an antecedent promise of God. *Inst. IV.xiv.3.*

There is no true administration of the sacrament without the word. *Inst. IV:xvii.39.*

[Christ] communicates his riches and blessings to us by his word, so he distributes them to us by His sacraments. [Form of Administering the Sacraments] *Tracts II:115.*

A sacrament consists of the word and the outward sign. *Inst. IV:xiv.4.*

. . . *mirrors,* in which we may contemplate the riches of grace which God imparts to us. *Inst. IV:xiv.6.*

The sacraments derive their virtue from the word when it is preached intelligibly. [Calvin's Short Treatise on the Supper] *Tracts II:191.*

All signs are as it were dead, except life is given them by the word. *Jer. III:353.*

The word of God . . . throws life into the sacraments. *Ezek. I:110.*

Sacraments cannot be distinguished from empty shows, unless by the word of God. *Ezek. I:170.*

Sacraments . . . their efficacy consists in the command and promise of God. *Ezek. I:171.*

In Sacraments God alone properly acts; men bring nothing of their own. [Antidote to the Council of Trent] *Tracts III:176.*

This is the chiefest thing in all sacraments, that the Word of God may appear engraven there, and that the clear voice may sound. *Acts I:443.*

Our sacraments . . . contain that *Yea and Amen* of all the *promises of God* (2 Cor. 1:20). *Col. 193.*

Christ-centred

The office of the sacraments is precisely the same as of the word of God; which is to offer and present Christ to us, and in Him the treasures of his heavenly grace. *Inst. IV:xiv.17.*

The Lord, in the sacraments, brings himself under obligation to us, as if he had given it in his own hand-writing. *Syn. Gosp. I:184.*

Necessity of faith

Whatever grace is conferred upon us by the sacraments is . . . to be ascribed to faith. He who separates faith from the Sacraments, does just as if he were to take the soul away from the body. [Antidote to the Council of Trent] *Tracts III:174.*

We cannot obtain the grace offered in the Sacraments, unless we are capacitated by faith. [Antidote to the Council of Trent] *Tracts III:175.*

Abuse of the sacraments

What is a sacrament, taken without faith, but the most certain ruin of the Church? *Inst. IV:xiv.14.*

If the *word* is taken away, the whole power of the sacraments is gone. *Eph. 320.*

The chief part of the sacraments consists in the word . . . Without it they are absolute corruptions. *Is. I:212.*

. . . the extravagant encomiums on the sacraments which are found in the writings of the fathers. *Inst. IV:xiv.26.*

SALVATION

Definition

The efficient cause of eternal life being procured for us, was the mercy of our heavenly Father, and his gratuitous love towards us; . . . the material cause is Christ and his obedience, by which he obtained a righteousness for us . . . the formal and instrumental cause . . . faith . . . The final cause . . . both the demonstration of the Divine righteousness and the praise of the Divine goodness. *Inst. III:xiv.17.*

The source

The cause of salvation . . . is the undeserved love of God. *Is. III:323.*

Salvation ought to be ascribed exclusively to his election, which is of free grace. *Is. IV:21.*

[On Is. 43:8] His glory . . . is intimately connected with the salvation of his people. *Is. III:326.*

God never forgets His Church, whose salvation . . . he promotes by hidden methods. *Is. III:399.*

The beginning of our salvation . . . is God's election by free grace; and the end of it is the obedience which we ought to render to him. *Is. III:399.*

On our calling is our salvation founded. *Jer. V:64.*

God has nothing else in view in addressing men, but to call them to salvation. *Jer. III:211.*

That general commencement of our salvation . . . is founded on the word of God. *Syn. Gosp. II:266.*

God seeketh us and not ours. *Acts I:304.*

The salvation of men is traced to its true and native source, the free act of adoption. [Introduction to Commentary on Ephesians] *Eph. 191.*

The only cause of our salvation is adoption . . . This flows from the mere love of God alone. *Gen. Epp. 203.*

Every part and particle of our salvation depends on God's mercy only. *Four Last Bks of Moses II:319.*

The substance

There is no part of our salvation which may not be found in Christ. *Acts II:247.*

Christ . . . the chief governor, in accomplishing the salvation of the Church. *Acts I:284.*

Our salvation consists in the doctrine of the cross (*1 Cor. 1:23*). *Syn. Gosp. III:274, 275.*

The whole accomplishment of our salvation, and all the parts of it, are contained in His death. *John II:235.*

Our salvation was begun by the sacrifice by which our sins were expiated, and finally completed by His resurrection. *Rom. 102.*

In Scripture the word salvation is throughout set in opposition to death. *Rom. 27.*

We must seek all the parts of our salvation in Jesus Christ; for we shall not find a single drop of it anywhere else. [From a French sermon of Calvin's] *Past. Epp. 335 (fn.).*

There is nothing necessary for salvation which faith finds not in Christ. *Gen. Epp. 244.*

[On Heb. 11:6] A man, prostrate in himself, and smitten with the conviction that he deserves eternal death, and in self-despair, is to flee to Christ as the only asylum for salvation. *Heb. 272.*

We ascribe our salvation partly to the death of Christ, and partly to his resurrection; we believe that sin was abolished, and death destroyed, by the former; that righteousness was restored, and life established, by the latter. *Inst. II:xvi.13.*

Salvation

All our salvation depends upon these two points: first, that Christ has been given to us to be our priest; and, secondly, that he has been established king to govern us. *Ps. V:74.*

It was usual with all the prophets, whenever they gave the people the hope of salvation, to bring forward the coming of the Messiah, for in him have God's promises always been yea and amen (*2 Cor. 1:20*). *Jer. III:136.*

Christ is called Saviour because he bestows a complete salvation. *Syn. Gosp. I:117.*

Christ . . . willingly submitted to wear fetters on his flesh, that our souls might be freed from fetters of a far worse description. *Syn. Gosp. III:252.*

The scope

The doctrine of repentance ought always to accompany the promise of salvation. *Is. IV:166.*

[On John 10:9] . . . a double door thrown open for the admission both of Jews and Gentiles. *Eph. 241.*

The word

Our salvation . . . being shut up in God's word, is not subject to change . . . but is anchored in a safe and peaceful haven. *Ps. IV:468.*

We . . . only yield to God the praise of salvation, when we continue to keep our hope firmly fixed on his word . . . We ought to repose on his bare promises. *Ps. V:4.*

The preparation

No one longs after Christ, unless he first abandons all confidence in his works, and rests all his hope of salvation in gratuitous pardon. *Four Last Bks of Moses III:262.*

[323]

SANCTIFICATION

Definition

A true conversion of our life to God . . . consisting in the mortification of our flesh and of the old man, and in the vivification of the Spirit. *Inst. III:iii.5.*

Every one's advancement in piety is the secret work of the Spirit. *Inst. III:xxiv.13.*

Election and sanctification

In election we perceive the beginning of sanctification. *Is. IV:21.*

[On Jer. 1:4, 5] Sanctification is the same as the knowledge of God . . . that knowledge is not mere prescience, but that predestination, by which God chooses every single individual according to his own will; for no one, Paul declares (*2 Cor. 2:16*), is according to his own nature fitted for the work. *Jer. I:36.*

Justification and sanctification

The manner of their justification must of necessity be very different from that of their renovation to newness of life. For the latter God commences in his elect, and as long as they live carries on gradually, and sometimes slowly . . . He justifies them, however, not in a partial manner, but so completely, that they may boldly appear in heaven, as being invested with the purity of Christ. *Inst. III:xi.11.*

Sanctification and righteousness are separate blessings of Christ. *Inst. III:xi.14.*

Christ . . . justifies no man whom he does not also sanctify. *Inst. III:xvi.1.*

The efficacy of his Sacrifice is eternal – and . . . the benefit of it is received by us every day. [The True Method of Reforming the Church] *Tracts III:309.*

Mortification

By a communication of himself, he 'mortifies' our 'members which are upon the earth' . . . and slays our old man, that it may not flourish and bear fruit any more . . . In the death and burial of Christ, therefore, we have a twofold benefit proposed for our enjoyment – deliverance from the thraldom of death, and the mortification of our flesh. *Inst. II:xvi.7.*

If we truly partake of his death, our old man is crucified by its power, and the body of sin expires, so that the corruption of our former nature loses all its vigour. *Inst. III:iii.9.*

The very word *mortification* reminds us how difficult it is to forget our former nature; for it implies that we cannot be formed to the fear of God, and learn the rudiments of piety, without being violently slain and annihilated by the sword of the Spirit. *Inst. III:iii.8.*

There still remains in a regenerate man a fountain of evil, continually producing irregular desires . . . This warfare will be terminated only by death. *Inst. III:iii.10.*

The death of the flesh is the life of the Spirit. *Gal. 169.*

The mortification of the flesh is the effect of the cross of Christ. *Gal. 169.*

Sanctification is through Christ, by His Spirit

The pious, in their warfare against Satan, obtain the victory by no other arms than those which are furnished by God. *Inst. II:v.11.*

Christ cannot be known without the sanctification of his Spirit. Consequently, faith is absolutely inseparable from a pious affection. *Inst. III:ii.8.*

That we may appear before the face of God to salvation, it is necessary for us to be perfumed with his fragrance, and to have all our deformities concealed and absorbed in his perfection. *Inst. III:xi.23.*

Christ was sanctified from his earliest infancy, that he might sanctify in himself all his elect, of every age [year], without any difference. *Inst. IV:xvi.18.*

[Christ] not only as God sanctifies us, but there is also the power of sanctifying in his human nature. *Heb. 64.*

When anything grows in us, and our endowments manifest themselves more conspicuously, our progress is only derived from the continued operation of the Spirit. *Four Last Bks of Moses III:292.*

God bestows upon us, by the hand of the Son, all that is necessary for spiritual life. *John I:243.*

In . . . sanctification . . . our hearts are formed to keep the law. *Rom. 81.*

[On 1 Cor. 15:10. God] confers upon us not merely the power of doing well, but also the inclination and the accomplishment. *Cor. II:15.*

Sanctification a gradual work

Being at a great distance from perfection, it behoves us to make continual advances; and being entangled in vices, we have need to strive against them every day. *Inst. III:iii.4.*

We Christians are miserable indeed if we grow old in making no improvement. *Inst. IV:xiv.8.*

Believers need incessant culture. *John II:108.*

His Spirit will ever form them anew to be better and better, that they may walk to the end in newness of life. *John II:114.*

The true attainments of Christians are when they make progress in *knowledge* and *understanding*, and afterwards in *love*. *Philipp.-Col. 31.*

Christ by his Spirit does not perfectly renew us at once, or in an instant, but he continues our renovation throughout life. *Gen. Epp. 209.*

The more anyone advances in the knowledge of God, every kind of blessing increases also equally with the sense of Divine love. *Gen. Epp. 367.*

Aids to sanctification

[On John 14:21] A more abundant knowledge of Christ is here represented as an extraordinary reward of our love to Christ. *John II:97.*

It is always profitable that the sense of sin should remain. *Gen. II:377.*

We enjoy most of the light of his countenance when we are favoured with the radiance of his truth. *Inst. III:v.9.*

We should sooner be confounded than corrected with the scourges of adversity, unless he rendered us docile by his Spirit. *Inst. II:v.13.*

Let us . . . walk through the world, as persons debarred from all repose, who have no other resource than the mirror of the word. *Gen. I:376.*

Sanctification does not mean sinless perfection.

God does indeed destroy the kingdom of sin in them . . . but though it ceases to reign, it continues to dwell in them. *Inst. III:iii.11.*

Sin always exists in the saints, till they are divested of the mortal body; because their flesh is the residence of that depravity of concupiscence, which is repugnant to all rectitude. *Inst. III:iii.10.*

Evidence of sanctification

No one ought to be reckoned among the disciples of Christ, unless we perceive *the glory of God* impressed on him, as with a seal, by the likeness of Christ. *John II:185.*

Opposition

There is nothing in which Satan takes less delight than the *purification* of believers. *Syn. Gosp. III:217.*

The more sincerely a man surrenders himself to God, the more will he be assailed by the tongues of the vile and the venomous. *Ps. IV:423.*

SATAN

His origin

Since the devil was created by God . . . this wickedness which we attribute to his nature is not from creation, but from corruption . . . acquired by his defection and fall. *Inst. I:xiv.16.*

The principle of evil with which Satan was endued was not from nature, but from defection. *Gen. I:142.*

. . . the heresy of the Manichees, who imagined that the devil is wicked by nature, and derives origin and beginning from himself. [Calvin's Catechism of the Church of Geneva, 1536, 1541] *Tracts II:130.*

Character

Satan is an ingenious contriver of falsehoods. *Gen. I:246.*

Satan . . . the ape of God. *Gen. II:69.*

The devils are called the princes of the air, not because they govern it according to their will, but only so far as the permission to wander in it is accorded to them. *Four Last Bks of Moses I:180.*

The devil has many mercenaries. *Jer. III:47.*

The devil has ever falsely assumed God's name. *Jer. III:372.*

To Satan no sight is beautiful but deformity itself, and no smell is sweet but filth and nastiness . . . His highest delight is that *emptiness* by which the neglect of Divine grace is followed. *Syn. Gosp. II:85.*

Satan endeavours, by every possible method, to take anything from Christ. *John I:31.*

The devil is called *the prince of this world,* not because he has a kingdom separated from God (as the Manicheans imagined), but because, by God's permission, he exercises his tyranny over the world. *John II:104.*

Satan . . . the father of all cruelty. *Acts I:322.*

Sometimes [God] maketh the devils as hangmen. *Acts I:492.*

[God] useth Satan as the minister of His wrath, and, as it were, an hangman. *Acts I:444.*

What is Satan but God's executioner to punish man's in-gratitude? *Eph. 221*.

God intended . . . to exhibit in the person of his Son, as in a very bright mirror, how obstinately and perseveringly Satan opposes the salvation of men. *Syn. Gosp. I:210*.

It is customary with Satan to exaggerate in words the power of the enemies, and to represent the dangers as greater than they really are. *Is. III:90*.

Satan, although ten times conquered, is still perpetually hurried forward with indefatigable obstinacy. *Four Last Bks of Moses I:180*.

Satan is a wonderful adept at deceiving, and deludes men with so many wiles in the name of God. *Gen. I:401*.

. . . the artifice of Satan in attempting the defamation of marriage. *Gen. I:134*.

The design of almost everything that the Scripture teaches concerning devils, is that we may be careful to guard against their insidious machinations, and may provide ourselves with such weapons as are sufficiently firm and strong to repel the most powerful enemies. *Inst. I:xiv.13*.

. . . this warfare is terminated only by death . . . Great armies wage war against us. *Inst. I:xiv.13*.

It is the native property of the Divine word, never to make its appearance without disturbing Satan, and rousing his opposi-tion. *From the Dedication to the Institutes*.

Satan assails Adam and Eve

Adam and Eve knew that all animals were given, by the hand of God, into subjection to them, they yet suffered themselves to be led away by one of their own slaves into rebellion against God. *Gen. I:141*.

Because [Satan] could not drag God from his throne, he assailed man, in whom his image shone . . . He endeavoured, in the person of man, to obscure the glory of God. *Gen. I:146*.

Satan . . . wished to inject into the woman a doubt [concerning] the word of God . . . She begins to give way, by inserting the adverb 'perhaps'. *Gen. I:148, 149.*

Satan accuses God of falsehood, of envy, and of malignity, and our first parents subscribe to a calumny thus vile and execrable. *Gen. I:153.*

Satan . . . is never wont to engage in open war until we voluntarily expose ourselves to him, naked and unarmed. *Gen. I:149.*

Satan's strategies

[Calvin's Introduction to Ps. 51] Nothing but satanic influence can account for the stupor of conscience which could lead [David] to despise or slight the Divine judgment which he had incurred . . . [He] laboured under a fatal insensibility as to his present exposure to Divine wrath. *Ps. II:282.*

Satan has so many devices by which he deludes and blinds men's minds, that there is not a man who knows the hundredth part of his own sins. *Ps. I:328.*

[On Ps. 42:6] The soul of man serves the purpose . . . of a workshop to Satan, in which to forge a thousand methods of despair. *Ps. II:137.*

The devil . . . is constantly seeking to pervert and corrupt the truth of God . . . He can put a specious gloss upon things . . . and is a sufficiently acute theologian. *Ps. III:485, 486.*

Light emerges more clearly . . . when Satan endeavours to shut it out. *Dan. I:227.*

Satan could not himself move a finger [against Job] except by the permission of God; nay, except it was commanded him. *Hos. 284.*

The wicked . . . and the devil who is their head, fulfil God's biddings . . . They are constrained, willing or unwilling, to obey God . . . The Lord turns all their efforts to answer the end which he has decreed. *Joel-Obad. 54.*

Satan . . . can do nothing without the command of God, to whose dominion he is subject. *Is. IV:356.*

God himself is said to harden and to blind, when he gives up men to be blinded by Satan, who is the minister and executioner of his wrath. *Is. IV:356.*

Except the world willingly sought falsehoods, the power of the devil to deceive would not be so great . . . A liberty was justly given to Satan to deluge the whole land with falsehood. *Jer. II:228.*

It has been God's will in all ages to try the faith of his servants by permitting to Satan and his ministers the liberty of pretending falsely his holy name. *Jer. III:191.*

Even the devil himself contributes in some way to the *glory* of God, though contrary to his wish. *Is. I:117.*

As [Satan] does nothing but by the command of God, it is therefore said that God does what Satan does. The statement commonly made that it is done by God's permission, is an excessively frivolous evasion. *Is. II:65.*

We imagine that everything that Satan does for the purpose of hindering our salvation blocks up the path of God. *Is. III:220.*

Satan, whenever God loosens the chain by which he is bound, is able to bewitch unhappy men. *Four Last Bks of Moses I:429.*

As to the devils and reprobate men . . . [God] holds them bound by a secret control, and prevents them from executing intended destruction. *Ps. III:26.*

Christ's victory over Satan

The world has been brought into a state of good order by the victory of Christ, by which he overturned the authority of Satan. *John II:141.*

The devil is justly said to *go out of* those men to whom Christ exhibits himself as a Redeemer. *Syn. Gosp. II:83.*

[On Heb. 2:14] It is a great consolation to know that we have to do with an enemy who cannot prevail against us . . . The tyranny of Satan was abolished by Christ's death . . . No more account is to be made of him than as though he were not. *Heb. 72.*

Christ has once defeated Satan, but Satan is ever ready to renew the battle. *Rom. 325.*

No man is rescued from the tyranny of the devil . . . till the grace of God go before; for no man will redeem himself. *Is. III:73.*

Our victory assured

Satan has no power to keep any whom God has chosen from being saved. *Thess. 409.*

God proclaims war against Satan on our behalf. *Zech.-Mal. 84.*

[On Zech. 3:1, 2] Christ never performs the work of the priesthood, but . . . Satan stands at his side, that is, devises all means by which he may remove and withdraw Christ from his office. *Zech.-Mal. 82.*

The whole of Satan's kingdom is subject to the authority of Christ. *Syn. Gosp. I:430.*

It is impossible that we could stand one moment in the contest with such enemies as Satan, sin, and the world, did we not receive from God the grace which secures our perseverance. *Ps. III:37.*

Satan alienates the minds of those, whom by God's permission he holds in devotion, and bondage, to himself. *Four Last Bks of Moses I:182.*

[God] . . . arms Satan with the efficiency of error, so that they who have refused to obey the truth do not guard against his snares, and are liable to be deceived by his impostures. *Is. III:377.*

[On Jer. 16:19] Satan hunts for nothing more than to involve us in various and intricate disputes, and he is an acute disputant. *Jer. II:329.*

Satan, by various arts and means, tempts the servants of God, and has wonderful turnings and windings, and sometimes transforms himself into an angel of light. *Joel-Obad. 347.*

Satan always comes forth when we resolve to obey God. *Jon.-Nah. 30.*

If we contend with Satan, according to our own view of things, he will a hundred times overwhelm us, and we can never be able to resist. *Hab.-Hagg. 58.*

Satan can easily find out a thousand impediments, by which he may turn us aside from the right course. *Hab.-Hagg. 350.*

What a subtle contriver Satan is . . . to turn us aside, under the cover of zeal, from the course of our vocation . . . Beware of the intrigues of Satan . . . for we see that some leave the Church because they require in it the highest perfection . . . and seek to form for themselves a new world, in which there is to be a perfect Church . . . They depart from God himself, and violate the unity of the Church. *Hab.-Hagg. 350, 351.*

Satan will never cease to make weary those whom he knoweth to serve Christ faithfully, either with open war, or secret lying in wait, or domestical combats. *Acts II:145.*

Satan knoweth that nothing is more fit to lay waste the kingdom of Christ, than discord and disagreement among the faithful. *Acts II:276.*

God allows more power and liberty to Satan over wicked and ungodly ministers, than over ordinary men. *John I:280.*

Satan profanes the Word of God, and endeavours to torture it for our destruction. *Syn. Gosp. I:218.*

Satanic miracles

Satan as we know deludes men's senses with his prodigies and his wonderful arts of fascination; for it happens that the children of God are sometimes deluded. *Ezek. I:280.*

Miracles . . . the door opened for the impostures of Satan. *Syn. Gosp. III:389.*

Whatever miracles [Satan] appears to work are mere delusions; he has no power except upon unbelievers. *Four Last Bks of Moses I:430, 431.*

Satan's dupes

[Of Pharaoh at the Red Sea] God for the sake of magnifying His glory, set a bait to catch the tyrant, just as fish are hooked. *Four Last Bks of Moses I:240.*

No one is deceived by the devil unless he offers himself of his own accord. *Ezek. II:31.*

It is an extreme curse, when God gives us loose reins, and suffers us, with unbridled liberty, to rush as it were headlong into evils, as though He had delivered us up to Satan, to be his slaves. *Jon.-Nah. 196.*

No other reason can be assigned, why the fury of Satan meets with so little resistance, and why so many are everywhere carried away by him, but that God punishes their carelessness, and their contempt of His Word. *Syn. Gosp. I:214.*

God's control over Satan

Satan . . . can do nothing without God's will and consent. *Inst. I:xiv.17.*

Neither the devil nor the wicked regard God's bidding, but are led, without knowing and against their will, wherever God drives them . . . Neither Satan nor the wicked can advance one inch, except as God permits them. *Zech.-Mal. 149.*

Satan . . . can never utter the slightest word unless commanded by God. *Ezek. II:59.*

Satan is the minister of the wrath of God, and His 'executioner', he is armed against us not merely in appearance, but by the orders of the Judge. *Rom. 35.*

The worst of men are in God's hand, as Satan is, who is their head. *Hab.-Hagg. 29.*

SCHISM

Among Christians there ought to be so great a dislike of schism, as that they may always avoid it so far as lies in their power . . . Nor need it be any hindrance that some points of doctrine are not quite so pure. [Calvin to William Farel, letter dated 24 Oct. 1538] *Letters 53.*

We hold as schismatics all who stir up trouble and confusion, tending to rend the Church. [Calvin's Confession of Faith in the Name of the Reformed Churches of France, 1542] *Tracts II:151.*

When schisms arise, we ought to ask who they are who revolt from God and from his pure doctrine. *John I:411.*

[On John 9:16] A schism is a highly pernicious and destructive evil in the Church of God . . . All who do not yield obedience to the truth of God . . . rend the Church by schism. *John I:377, 378.*

Those who are united to [Christ] by pure faith are beyond the risk of schism. *Syn. Gosp. III:143.*

Whosoever tears asunder the Church of God, disunites himself from Christ, who is the head, and who would have all his members to be united together. *Zech.-Mal. 231.*

Whilst schismatics are influenced by nothing but pride to disturb the peace of the Church, they always invent plausible motives [to] conciliate . . . the favour of the ignorant, or even of the unstable and worthless. *Four Last Bks of Moses IV:100.*

[On Heb. 10:26] Those who *sin* . . . are . . . such as forsake the Church, and wholly alienate themselves from Christ . . . those who wilfully renounced fellowship with the Church . . . The apostle here refers only to apostates . . . to those who wickedly forsake Christ, and thus deprive themselves of the benefit of His death. *Heb. 243, 244.*

Roman antichrist invites us to himself, under the pretence of unity, and pronounces all to be schismatics who do not spontaneously submit to . . . the yoke of his tyranny. [Calvin's Remarks on Letter of Pope Paul III] *Tracts I:259.*

SCIENCES

Natural perspicacity is a gift of God, and the liberal arts and all the sciences, by which wisdom is acquired, are gifts of God . . .

They must occupy the place of handmaid, not of mistress. *Cor. I:145.*

If . . . we would avoid a senseless natural philosophy, we must always start with this principle, that everything in nature depends upon the will of God, and that the whole course of nature is only the prompt carrying into effect of his orders. *Ps. V:301.*

A knowledge of all the sciences is mere smoke, where the heavenly science of Christ is wanting. *Cor. I:82.*

To be so occupied in the investigation of the secrets of nature, as never to turn the eyes to its Author, is a most perverted study. *Gen. I:60.*

It is a diabolical science . . . which fixes our contemplations on the works of nature, and turns them away from God. *Ps. I:479.*

[On Ps. 136:7] The Holy Spirit had no intention to teach astronomy . . . The Holy Spirit would rather speak childishly than unintelligibly to the humble and unlearned. *Ps. V:184, 185.*

SECOND ADVENT

Purpose

Strictly speaking, Christ will come, not for the destruction of the world, but for purposes of salvation. This is the reason that the Creed mentions only the life of blessedness. *Inst. III:xxv.9.*

[On Ps. 47:1, 2] The Holy Spirit has exhorted the faithful to continue clapping their hands for joy, until the advent of the promised Redeemer. *Ps. II:207.*

The 'last days' and the 'day of the Lord'

[On Is. 2:2. The last days] He is speaking of the kingdom of Christ . . . Since Christ came . . . we have arrived at *the end of the ages. Is. I:91.*

While the fulness of days began at the coming of Christ, it flows on in uninterrupted progress until he appear the second time for our salvation. *Is. I:92.*

Whenever the day of the Lord is mentioned in Scripture, let us know that God is bound by no laws, that he should hasten his work according to our hasty wishes; but the specific time is in his own power, and at his own will. *Zech.-Mal. 616.*

The *great day of the Lord* . . . the whole kingdom of Christ . . . to the last resurrection. *Acts I:88, 89.*

Times and seasons

[On 1 Thess. 5:1. Paul] now calls them back from a curious and unprofitable inquiry concerning *times* . . . Those who insist that divisions of time should be marked out for them . . . move from one uncertain position to another. *Thess. 367.*

It would . . . be foolish to want to determine the time from presages and portents. *Thess. 367.*

'Soon'

[On Heb. 10:25] From the beginning of the kingdom of Christ, the Church was so constituted that the faithful ought to have considered the Judge as coming soon. *Heb. 242.*

Christ keeps the minds of believers in a state of suspense till the last day. *Syn. Gosp. III:146.*

[Jesus] wished [the disciples] to be uncertain as to his coming, but yet to be prepared to expect him . . . every moment. *Syn. Gosp. III:156.*

It behoves us . . . to see by faith the near advent of Christ. *Gen. Epp. 189.*

Hope, while it is silently expecting the Lord, restrains faith, that it may not be too precipitate. *Inst. III:ii.42.*

Moral power

Our faith cannot stand otherwise than by looking to the coming of Christ. *Gen. Epp. 205.*

When we direct our eyes to this event, this world becomes crucified to us, and we to the world. *Gen. Epp. 45.*

It is the expectation of final redemption alone that keeps us from growing weary. Let all who would persevere in a life of holiness give their whole minds to the hope of Christ's coming. *Thess. 339.*

The single word *watch* . . . denotes that uninterrupted attention which keeps our minds in full activity, and makes us pass through the world like pilgrims. *Syn. Gosp. III:160.*

The . . . looking for Christ's coming must both restrain the importunate desires of our flesh, and support our patience in all adversities; and . . . refresh our weariness. *Acts I:53.*

Satan aims directly at the throat of the Church when he destroys faith in the coming of Christ. *Gen. Epp. 415.*

SECTS

This our age has brought forth some horrible and monstrous sects. *Gen. Epp. 228.*

Faith is the soul of the Church; nothing is more proper to faith than agreement, nothing more contrary than sects. *Acts II:321.*

God punishes men justly, when true religion is so rent asunder by divisions, and truth is obscured by falsehood. *Ezek. II:58.*

. . . certain ferocious men exceed the barbarism of the Papacy. [Calvin's Second Defence of the Sacraments in Answer to the Calumnies of Westphal] *Tracts II:246.*

SECURITY OF BELIEVERS

It cannot be that God will ever forsake those whom he has chosen, as Paul also shows in [Romans chap. 11] *Jer. V:518.*

He who knows God to be on his side, will be superior to the whole world. *Dan. I:239.*

All who are united to Christ, . . . will remain to the end safe from all danger; for what is said of the body of the Church belongs to each of its members, since they are one in Christ. *Syn. Gosp. II:292.*

There should yet be greater security in integrity than in all the resources of fraud and injustice. *Ps. I:564, 565.*

SELF-DENIAL

Summary of the Christian Life. Self-Denial. [Heading to Chap. 7, Book III of The Institutes] *Inst. III:vii.1.*

Self-denial relates partly to men . . . principally, to God. *Inst. III:vii.4.*

Few follow God, because scarcely one in a hundred will bear to be losers. *Gen. II:194.*

To deny ourselves is the beginning of that sacred union which ought to exist between us and Christ. *Ps. II:189.*

The chief praise of Christians is self-renunciation. *Cor. II:233.*

God . . . offers us peace . . . but on this condition, that we make war with our own lusts . . . being at peace with God by becoming enemies to ourselves. *Ezek. II:20.*

SELF-EXAMINATION

The godly should hold to the principle of examining themselves each day and seeing the extent of their progress. *Thess. 387.*

SELF-LOVE

The true limit of *loving life* is . . . when we carry it . . . in our hands, and offer it to God as a sacrifice. *John II:29.*

Self-love so blinds us, that we seek to absolve ourselves from that fault which we freely condemn in others. *Hab.-Hagg. 94.*

. . . that intoxicated self-love, in which irreligious men indulge. *Is. I:121.*

Self-love keeps all our senses bound in such a manner that brotherly love is altogether banished. *John II:77.*

[339]

If men claim even the least thing for themselves, they cannot call God their praise . . . If we are inflated with the conceit of our own power, or of our own righteousness, the door is closed against us. *Jer. II:367.*

There is no venom more deadly than that slothfulness which is produced in us, either by earthly happiness, or by a false and deceitful opinion of our own righteousness and virtue. *Syn. Gosp. II:43.*

Philautia [Gk.], self-love, blinds us so much as to be the parent of all iniquities. *Four Last Bks of Moses III:195.*

Philautia . . . the source from which flow all the vices. *Past. Epp. 238.*

No man is qualified to be a disciple of Christ, until he has been divested of self. *John I:392.*

We ought always to beware of making the smallest claim for ourselves. *Is. III:100.*

The observance of the commandments consists not in the love of ourselves, but in the love of God and our neighbour; that his is the best and most holy life, who lives as little as possible to himself; and that no man leads a worse or more iniquitous life, than he who lives exclusively to himself, and makes his own interest the sole subject of his thoughts and pursuits. *Inst. II:viii.54.*

If anyone deviate from the path of love, who can deny that his soul is in an unhealthy state? *Inst. II:viii.50.*

SELF-PRAISE

A man that extols himself is a fool and an idiot. *Cor. I:160.*

Those that will be truly wise will never glory but in God. *Cor. II:228.*

It is a disgusting and odious thing in itself for one to be the trumpeter of his own praises. *Cor. II:165.*

SEPARATION

It is always fatally dangerous to be separated from the Church. *Inst. IV:i.4.*

Very many, under the pretext of zeal, are excessively displeased, when everything is not conducted to their wish, and, because absolute purity is nowhere to be found, withdraw from the Church in a disorderly manner, or subvert and destroy it by unreasonable severity. *Syn. Gosp. II:119.*

[On Matt. 9:14] We ought especially to beware lest the unity of faith be destroyed, or the bond of charity broken, on account of outward ceremonies. *Syn. Gosp. I:405.*

Strangers who separate themselves from the Church have nothing left for them but to rot amidst their curse . . . A departure from the Church is an open renouncement of eternal salvation. *Is. III:43.*

[On Heb. 10:25] There is so much morosity almost in all, that individuals would gladly make churches for themselves if they could . . . It behoves us the more earnestly to cultivate unity, as the more eagerly watchful Satan is, either to tear us by any means from the Church, or stealthily to seduce us from it. *Heb. 240, 241.*

Provided religion continue pure as to doctrine and worship, we must not be so much stumbled at the faults and sins which men commit, as on that account to rend the unity of the Church . . . God's sacred barn-floor will not be perfectly cleansed before the last day. *Ps. I:204, 205.*

Although it may not be in our power to cleanse the Church of God, it is our duty to desire her purity. *Ps. I:382.*

The severity becoming the Church must be tempered with a spirit of gentleness [lest] a remedy . . . become a poison. *Inst. IV:510.*

SERVICE OF GOD

Importance

The highest honour in the Church is not government, but service. *Syn. Gosp. III:81.*

Whatever we do for God's servants, he acknowledges as done to himself. *Jer. IV:436.*

Except . . . we endeavour to relieve the necessities of our brethren, and to offer them assistance, there will not be in us but one part of true conversion. *Jon.-Nah. 264.*

Qualifications

Forget yourself, if you would serve God. *Philipp.-Col. 78.*

God considers us as serving him in none of our works, but such as are truly done by us to his honour. *Inst. III:xix.5.*

[On Heb. 12:28] No service is approved by him except it be united with humility and due reverence. *Heb. 338.*

To serve God is the purpose for which we have been born, and for which we are preserved in life. *Ps. IV:318.*

No person can serve God aright, but he who has been taught in His school. *Ps. IV:460.*

The chief part of the service of God . . . to have a pure and upright heart. *Is. IV:346.*

It is not in man to form his heart for God's service. *Jer. IV:211.*

The beginning of acceptable service is reconciliation. *Heb. 205.*

Our service cannot be approved of God, except it be founded on his Word. *Hab.-Hagg. 350.*

[On Hagg. 1:14] No one is fit to offer sacrifices to God, or to do any other service, but he who has been moulded by the hidden operation of the Spirit. *Hab.-Hagg. 347.*

The first step towards serving Christ is to lose sight of ourselves, and think only of the Lord's glory and the salvation of men. *Cor. I:39.*

He who knows not how to strive knows not how to serve God and the Church, and is not fitted for administering the doctrine of the Word. *Is. IV:58.*

[342]

Disposition

God requires from us no slavish service; he will have us to come to him cheerfully. *Ps. IV:477.*

Men are ordinarily mercenary in serving God . . . True godliness is disinterested. *Ps. V:21.*

Fear . . . the whole service of God. *Four Last Bks of Moses IV:351.*

The most holy service that we can render to him is, to be employed in praising his name. *Is. I:204, 205.*

[On Ps. 37:5] We render to [God] the honour to which he is entitled only when we intrust to him the government and direction of our lives. *Ps. II:21.*

Warnings

. . . to offer to God the shell of an empty nut. *Is. IV:415.*

We are all good soldiers so long as things go well with us. *Ps. II:330.*

God is served amiss when He is served by halves, since He abominates a double heart (*Prov. 11:20*). *Four Last Bks of Moses II:378, 379.*

We know in how great liberties the world indulges itself in the service of God; for whilst it lightly and contemptuously obtrudes mere trifling upon Him as if He were a child, it still fancies that its duty is properly discharged. *Four Last Bks of Moses II:379.*

God's service is corrupted if any strange invention be mingled with it . . . Let us . . . learn not to intrude our own imaginations or inventions in God's service. *Four Last Bks of Moses II:329, 330.*

We hold that it is not for us to invent what to us seems good, or to follow what may have been devised in the brain of other men, but to confine ourselves simply to the purity of Scripture. [Calvin's Confession of Faith in the Name of the Reformed Churches of France, 1542] *Tracts II:147.*

A prayer of Calvin: Grant, Almighty God, . . . that we may not continue torn asunder, everyone pursuing his own perverse inclinations, at a time when Christ is gathering us to thee; nor let us only profess with the mouth and in words that we are under thy government, but prove that we thus feel in real sincerity: and may we then add to the true and lawful worship of thy name brotherly love towards one another, that with united efforts we may promote each other's good . . . that we may ever be able . . . to call on thee as our Father, through Christ our Lord. Amen. [Concluding prayer after Lecture 88 on the Minor Prophets] *Jon.-Nah. 268.*

SILENCE

The silence of long-suffering . . . is more effectual before God than any cries, however loud. *Four Last Bks of Moses IV:45.*

. . . the holy silence of faith. *Acts I:433.*

. . . advancement in this grace of silence. *Ps. II:423.*

SIMPLICITY

God has commanded us to cultivate simplicity. *Gen. II:366.*

There is nothing which God more earnestly recommends to us than simplicity. *Is. II:129.*

The simplicity of faith is our spiritual chastity. *Jer. III:112.*

SIN

Sin and a Sovereign God

God Uses the Agency of the Impious, and Inclines Their Minds to Execute His Judgments, Yet Without the Least Stain of His Perfect Purity. [Heading to chap. 18, Bk I, The Institutes] *Inst. I:xviii.*

The spirit of confusion and mental blindness seizes on those who have been obstinate in their wickedness. *Four Last Bks of Moses I:149.*

God is the author of the 'evil' of punishment, but not of the 'evil' of guilt. *Is. III:403.*

[344]

The hatred of sin proceeds from the fear of God. *Hab.-Hagg. 172.*

Definitions

The term 'ungodliness' . . . comprehends . . . everything that is repugnant to the serious fear of God. *Inst. III:viii.3.*

The contempt of [God's] word ever led [Israel] to sin. *Heb. 92.*

[On Ps. 19:12] If God should discover our secret faults, there would be found in us an abyss of sins so great as to have neither bottom nor shore. *Ps. I:329.*

[On Ps. 19:13] *Presumptuous sins* . . . known and evident transgressions, accompanied with proud contempt and obstinacy. *Ps. I:330.*

Sinners . . . those who are all asleep and content in their sins, without any desire of righteousness. *Inst. III:xx.10.*

The expression [in Ps. 51:5] intimates that we are cherished in sin from the first moment that we are in the womb . . . born in the world with the seed of every iniquity . . . sin . . . exists within us as a disease fixed in our nature. *Ps. II:290.*

All wickedness flows from a disregard of God. *Rom. 67.*

The dreadful desert of sin. *Ps. II:296.*

Adam's sin and ours

Although we perish through the fault of another [Adam], yet the fault of each individual is joined with it. *Ezek. II:218.*

The first principle of theology . . . namely, that God can see nothing in the corrupt nature of man . . . to induce Him to show His favour. *Rom. 200.*

Our old self crucified in our conversion

If we truly partake of his death, our old man is crucified by its power, and the body of sin expires, so that the corruption of our former nature loses all its vigour. *Inst. III:iii.9.*

Indwelling sin in the believer

There still remains in a regenerate man a fountain of evil, continually producing irregular desires . . . This warfare will be terminated only by death. *Inst. III:iii.10.*

Sin always exists in the saints, till they are divested of the mortal body; because their flesh is the residence of that depravity of concupiscence which is repugnant to all rectitude. *Inst. III:iii.10.*

God does indeed destroy the kingdom of sin in them . . . but though it ceases to reign, it continues to dwell in them. *Inst. III:iii.11.*

Every sin should convince us of the general truth of the corruption of our nature. *Ps. II:290.*

There is no action so perfect as to be absolutely free from stain. *Four Last Bks of Moses I:35.*

The Law . . . requires perfect love; we do not yield it. Our duty was to run, and we go on slowly limping. [Antidote to the Council of Trent] *Tracts III:88.*

In us there is no affection unaccompanied by sin. *Syn. Gosp. III:227.*

Our remembrance of past sin

It is always profitable that the sense of sin should remain. *Gen. II:377.*

If . . . we wish our sins to be buried before God, we must remember them ourselves. *Ezek. II:174.*

If we desire . . . our sins to be blotted out before God (*Mic. 7:19*) . . . we must recall them often and constantly to our remembrance. *Ezek. II:181.*

Sin and the wrath of God

Wherever sin is . . . it is accompanied with the wrath and vengeance of God. *Inst. III:xi.2.*

Vengeance is so connected with sin, that it cannot be severed from it. *Four Last Bks of Moses IV:287.*

Hardening in sin

The effect of the habit of sinning is, that men grow hardened in their sins, and discern nothing, as if they were enveloped in thick darkness. *Ps. I:192.*

[On Ps. 38:5] David acknowledges that he has been out of his right mind when he obeyed the lusts of the flesh in opposition to God . . . Sin is always conjoined with folly or madness. *Ps. II:58.*

Indulgence in sin increases by concealment and connivance. *Four Last Bks of Moses III:275.*

The sinner stupefies himself into forgetfulness of the distinction between good and evil. *Four Last Bks of Moses III:277.*

When men add sin to sin, God loosens his reins, and allows them to destroy themselves. *Dan. I:244.*

[On John 3:19] *Hatred of the light* arises only from a mind that is wicked and conscious of its guilt. *John I:128.*

Sin's consequences

We must reckon our sins to be the cause of all the evils which we endure. *Is. III:31.*

To our sins . . . it ought to be imputed, that we are liable to diseases, pains, old age, and other inconveniences. *Is. IV:401.*

We throw heaven and earth into confusion by our sins. For were we in right order as to our obedience to God, doubtless all the elements would be conformable, and we should thus observe in the world an angelic harmony. *Jer. I:301.*

We are to judge of the grievousness of our sins by the greatness of our punishment. *Jer. V:461.*

God would not be God, except he were to punish sins . . . Whenever God pardons, he leads sinners to repentance; so that he never suffers sins to be unpunished. *Jer. I:273.*

Sin not due to ignorance

That Platonic dogma is false, that ignorance alone is the cause of sin. *Gen. Epp. 46.*

Men sin more through insolence and pride than through ignorance. *Is. III:226.*

Miscellaneous thoughts

[On Nadab and Abihu, Lev. 10] How greatly God abominates all the sins whereby the purity of religion is corrupted. *Four Last Bks of Moses III:431.*

All who are sent to teach the word are sent to carry on a contest . . . We have a contest with the devil, with the world, and with all the wicked. *Jon.-Nah. 234, 235.*

. . . that we may be alienated from the vices rather than from the persons of men. *Gen. II:361.*

It very often happens that those who are not wicked foster the sins of their brethren by conniving at them. *Josh. 103.*

SORROW

The best remedy for the mitigation and the cure of sadness, is placed in the word of God. *Gen. I:374.*

The principal mitigation of sorrow is the consolation of the future life. *Gen. II:274.*

Patiently to bear the cross does not consist in absolute stupefaction and privation of all sense of sorrow [as, for example, among the Stoics] . . . We have nothing to do with that iron-hearted philosophy . . . For if all tears be reprobated, what judgment shall we form concerning the Lord himself, from whose body distilled tears of blood? *Inst. III:772, 773.*

Excessive grief always precipitates us into rebellion . . . The mitigation of sorrow is chiefly to be sought for, in the hope of a future life. *Gen. II:477.*

Since our flesh has no self-government, men commonly exceed bounds both in sorrowing and in rejoicing. *Gen. II:480.*

The ceremony of mourning over the dead arose from a good principle; namely, that the living should meditate on the curse entailed by sin upon the human race. *Gen. II:476.*

[348]

Sadness and anxiety lock up the soul, and restrain the tongue from celebrating the goodness of God. *Syn. Gosp. I:52, 53.*

That diseased but deeply-rooted principle in our nature, which leads us to hide our griefs, and ruminate upon them, instead of . . . pouring out our . . . complaints before God. *Ps. II:425.*

[On Ps. 37:13, God laughing] We learn to weep patiently while God laughs so that our tears may be a sacrifice of obedience . . . We, by beholding with the eye of faith, his laughter, become partakers thereof, even in the midst of sorrow. *Ps. II:29.*

SOUL

By the 'soul' I understand an immortal, yet created essence, which is the nobler part of [man]. *Inst. I:xv.2.*

Psychopannychia, A Refutation of the Errors entertained by some Unskilful Persons who Ignorantly Imagine that in the Interval between Death and the Judgment, the Soul Sleeps; together with an Explanation of the Condition and Life of the Soul after this Present Life. *Tracts III:413.*

It is a brutish error . . . to despoil that part of us in which Divinity is eminently displayed. *Inst. III:xxv.6.*

Christ, when commending his soul to his Father, undertook the guardianship of the souls of all his people. *Ps. I:503.*

Those *psychoktonoi* [Gk., soul-slayers], who murder souls, though without inflicting a wound . . . [Psychopannychia]. *Tracts III:414.*

SOVEREIGNTY OF GOD (*see also* Predestination, Providence)

Over the world

[God] holds events by His secret bridle and allows nothing to happen without His heavenly decree. *Dan. II:314.*

We recognise all the tumults of the world as springing from the fixed counsel of God. *Dan. II:293.*

The life and death of every kingdom and nation are in the hand and at the will of God. *Jer. III:356.*

Whoever raises his eyes to heaven will see the greatest harmony between those things which have the appearance of opposition below. *Ezek. I:76.*

It is the property of God to bring the counsels of men to nought. *Acts I:223.*

That time is most fit for God to work in when there is no hope or counsel to be looked for at man's hands. *Acts I:268.*

As we ought to presume nothing of ourselves, so we should presume everything of God. *From the Dedication to the Institutes. .*

The majesty of God is otherwise far above the reach of mortals, who are like worms crawling upon the earth. *Inst. II:vi.6.*

Whatever we think, and whatever we say of him, should savour of his excellence, correspond to the sacred sublimity of his name, and tend to the exaltation of his sublimity. *Inst. II:viii.22.*

The hearts of men are so under Divine government, that they can be inclined to equity, or hardened in inflexible rigour. *Gen. II:345.*

. . . one of the miracles of God, to bring light out of darkness. *Gen. II:449.*

. . . that everyone may behold, by faith, God from on high holding the helm of the government of the world. *Gen. II:488.*

The hearts of all men are entirely under God's control, to harden or to soften them according to His sovereign pleasure. *Ps. IV:243.*

God by His secret inspiration moves, forms, governs and draws men's hearts, so that even by the wicked he executes whatever He has decreed. *Four Last Bks of Moses IV:172.*

Good men, who fear to expose the justice of God to the calumnies of the impious, resort to this distinction, that God *wills* some things, but *permits* others to be done . . . Away, then, with that vain figment, that, by the *permission* of God only, and

[350]

not by His *counsel* or *will*, those evils are committed which he afterwards turns to a good account . . . This method of acting is secret, and far above our understanding. *Gen II:378.*

Over the wicked and Satan

Satan . . . can do nothing without God's will and consent. *Inst. I:xiv.17.*

While God directs the courses of unclean spirits hither and thither at his pleasure, he regulates this government in such a manner, that they exercise the faithful with fighting, attack them in ambuscades, harass them with incursions, push them in battles, and frequently fatigue them, and throw them into confusion, terrify them, and sometimes wound them, yet never conquer or overwhelm them; but subdue and lead captive the impious, tyrannize over their souls and bodies, and abuse them like slaves by employing them in the perpetration of every enormity. *Inst. I:xiv.18.*

In the same crime he [the Christian] will distinctly contemplate the righteousness of God and the iniquity of man, as they respectively discover themselves. *Inst. I:xvii.9.*

After the impious have wilfully shut their own eyes, it is the righteous vengeance of God upon them, to darken their understandings, so that, seeing, they may not perceive. *Inst. I:iv.1.*

God . . . by a secret influence so rules them and their tongues, their minds and hearts, their hands and their feet, that they are constrained, willing or unwilling, to do his will and pleasure. *Jer. III:251.*

God holds the impious under his guidance, as it were, for executing his judgments; but God has a method, wonderful and incomprehensible to us, which impels them hither and thither, so that he does not involve himself in any alliance with their fault. *Ezek. I:269.*

[On Ps. 64:8] God is ever watching, as it were, his opportunity of converting the stratagems of the wicked into means just as completely effective of their destruction, as if they had intentionally employed them for that end. *Ps. II:449.*

[351]

Over the people of God

God on high governs all things in such a manner as to promote the benefit of his elect. *Is. III:395.*

Except . . . God governs the world there is no salvation for the faithful. *Hab.-Hagg. 86.*

Whenever . . . we are disturbed at the paucity of believers, let us . . . remember that none, but those to whom it was given, have any apprehension of the mysteries of God. *Inst. I:vii.5.*

It is well for us that God not only wipes away the reproaches with which the wicked load us, but also so ennobles them, that they surpass all the honours and triumphs of the world. *Ps. III:54.*

SPEECH

The tongue, the *portrait* of the mind. *Syn. Gosp. I:366.*

. . . so rare a gift of the Spirit is moderation in language. *Ps. V:237.*

. . . too common a fault that men desire to be taught in an ingenious and witty style. *John I:119.*

As witticisms are insinuating, and for the most part procure favour, [Paul] indirectly prohibits believers from the practice and familiar use of them. *Philipp.-Col. 226.*

STATE (*see also* Government)

The Lord, therefore, is the King of kings; who, when he has opened his sacred mouth, is to be heard alone, above all, for all, and before all . . . We are subject to those men who preside over us; but no otherwise than in him. *Inst. IV:xx.32.*

Laws . . . the strong nerves of civil polity. *Inst. IV:xx.14.*

Executions on the gallows, when the wicked suffer, may be said to be sacrifices to God: for the Lord arms the magistrate with the sword. *Hab.-Hagg. 205.*

When the sense of shame is overcome, and the reins are given to lust, a vile and outrageous barbarism necessarily succeeds . . . and a most confused chaos is the result. *Gen. I:497.*

Nothing is more dangerous than to live where the public licence of crime prevails; yea, there is no pestilence so destructive, as that corruption of morals, which is opposed neither by laws nor judgments, nor any other remedies. *Gen. I:491.*

Man contains, as it were, two worlds, capable of being governed by various rulers and various laws. This distinction will prevent what the gospel inculcates concerning spiritual liberty from being misapplied to political regulations. *Inst. III:xix.15.*

STUDY

[On 2 Tim. 4:13, books and parchments] This passage gives to all believers a recommendation of constant reading, that they may profit by it. *Past. Epp. 266.*

The Lord . . . is a most faithful master, so that he hath scholars which are apt to be taught and studious. *Acts I:116.*

None are good teachers but those who have been good scholars . . . They alone are 'learned' who, by continually learning, do not refuse to make constant progress. *Is. IV:54, 55.*

SUCCESS

Success in our ministry is a singular blessing from God. *Philipp.-Col. 73.*

So often as God showeth to his servants any fruit of their labour, he doth . . . prick them forward with a goad, that they may proceed more courageously in their work. *Acts II:420.*

All thought of God is excluded, when the industry, or valour, or success, or any other quality of man is extolled. *Dan. I:146.*

This is man's ingratitude; whenever they find anything worthy of praise in themselves or others, they claim it directly as their own, and thus God's glory is diminished by the depravity of those who obtain their blessings from him. *Dan. I:143.*

[Calvin speaks of God's servants] bargaining with [God] . . . For unless God shows us the present fruit of our labour, we languish, and so . . . withdraw ourselves from his authority. *Ezek. I:117, 118.*

Signal success commonly draws its companion envy along with it. *Gen. I:398.*

We know how liable men are to be snared by the blandishments of prosperous and smiling fortune. *Gen. I:398.*

How much soever God may use the labours of men in building his Church, yet he himself performs everything. *Heb. 80, 81.*

We are not at liberty to share the honour of success with God. *Ps. II:409.*

[On Is. 39:2] Nothing is more dangerous than to be blinded by prosperity. *Is. III:184.*

It is an evil as it were innate in us, that we become elated and proud whenever God deals bountifully with us. *Jer. I:382.*

SUFFERING (*see also* Afflictions)

The silence of longsuffering . . . is more effectual before God than any cries, however loud. *Four Last Bks of Moses IV:45.*

It goeth well with the godly, because they triumph gloriously before God and his angels in all injuries which they suffer . . . Those persecutions, which we must suffer for the testimony of the gospel, are remnants of the sufferings of Christ. *Acts II:115.*

The Son of God doth suffer not only with us, but also in us. *Acts II:297.*

God . . . does not call His people to triumph before He has exercised them in the warfare of suffering. *Rom. 176.*

The endurance of the cross is the gift of God . . . Even the sufferings themselves are the evidences of the grace of God. *Philipp.-Col. 48.*

Suffering

The miseries of the godly are more happy than . . . all the . . . delights of the world. *Acts II:25.*

It is far better for the sons of God to be blessed, though mutilated and half-destroyed, than to desire that peace in which they shall fall asleep. *Gen. II:199.*

. . . aroused from slumber by suffering. *Gen. II:236.*

We should sooner be confounded than corrected with the scourges of adversity, unless he rendered us docile by his Spirit. *Inst. II:v.13.*

We murmur against God, if he does not grant us a quiet nest. *Gen. I:356.*

Whatever felicity is promised us in Christ, consists not in . . . a life of joy and tranquillity . . . security from every injury . . . but that it is peculiar to the heavenly state. *Inst. II:xv.4.*

SUPERSTITION

Religion . . . the beginning of all superstitions, not in its own nature, but through the darkness which has settled down upon the minds of men. *Ps. IV:62.*

The insane zeal of superstition. *Four Last Bks of Moses II:116.*

Such knowledge of God as now remains in men is nothing else than a frightful source of idolatry and of all superstitions. *John I:113.*

The Church cannot be rightly formed, until all superstitions be rejected and banished. *Zech.-Mal. 379.*

Superstition is always cruel. *John I:313.*

Superstition is always fearful. *Acts II:155.*

Superstition, when it has once gone beyond the proper limits, proceeds in sinning without end. *Inst. IV:xvii.37.*

[355]

TEACHER

[On Ps. 143:10] There are three ways in which [God] acts the part of our Teacher, instructing us by his word, enlightening our minds by the Spirit, and engraving instruction upon our hearts, so as to bring us to observe it with a true and cordial consent. *Ps. V:256, 257.*

No one will ever be a good teacher, who does not show himself to be teachable. *Cor. I:462.*

No one . . . ought to be deemed a sound teacher, but he who speaks from God's mouth. *Jer. III:167, 168.*

TEMPTATION (*see also* Satan)

As a trial from God

God fights with us with his left hand, and defends us with his right hand . . . that we may become victorious in the struggle. *Hos. 425.*

It is not said that Satan, or any mortal man, wrestled with Jacob, but God himself; to teach us that our faith is tried by him; and whenever we are tempted, our business is truly with him. *Gen. II:195.*

Having challenged us to this contest . . . he both fights *against* us and *for* us . . . While he assails us with one hand he defends us with the other. *Gen. II:196.*

It is a wonderful marshalling of the contest, when God on one side makes himself an antagonist, and, on the other, fights in us against his own temptations, or against all those wrestlings by which he tries our faith. *Hos. 423.*

[On Heb. 5:7] In this contest the Son of God had to engage . . . because he sustained as a man in our flesh the judgment of God. *Heb. 122.*

As the assault of Satan

All temptations, from whatever quarter . . . were forged in the workshop of that enemy. *Syn. Gosp. III:217.*

[356]

Temptation

Who is there that will be exempt from Satan's bite, when even Christ himself was not spared by them. *Cor. II:301.*

Satan never ceases diligently to suggest those things which may incite us to sin. *Gen. II:295.*

Satan's snares

Satan has numberless artifices by which he dazzles our eyes and bewilders the mind. *Ps. III:121.*

As often . . . as we open our eyes two gates are opened for the devil to enter our hearts, unless God guard us by his Holy Spirit. *Ps. IV:428.*

We are tempted both by adversity and by prosperity. *Syn. Gosp. I:328.*

Temptations are either from prosperous, or from adverse events. *Inst. III:xx.46.*

Elegance of form was the occasion of great calamity to holy Joseph . . . Satan . . . is accustomed to turn the gifts of God into snares whereby to catch souls. *Gen. II:295.*

[Of Potiphar's wife] The eyes were as torches to inflame the heart to lust. *Gen. II:295.*

The more bountifully God deals with any one, the more carefully ought he to watch against such snares. *Ps. I:492.*

Our susceptibility

No one is deceived by the devil unless he offers himself of his own accord. *Ezek. II:31.*

[On Ps. 119:101] With a nature so corrupted as ours is, amidst so many allurements, and with minds so fickle, we are in the greatest danger of being led astray. *Ps. IV:476.*

If any temptation thrusts itself upon us we immediately magnify a fly into an elephant. *Ps. III:96.*

Everyone is a tempter to himself; for the devil never ceases to agitate our minds. *Hab.-Hagg. 62.*

[357]

[On Matt. 26:70] Peter's fall . . . is a bright mirror of our own weakness. *Syn. Gosp. III:260.*

Fatal temptation! when, while God is threatening us with death, we not only securely sleep, but hold God Himself in derision. *Gen. I:150.*

All temptations are, as it were, so many fans; if they hurry us on into consent, the fire is lighted. *Four Last Bks of Moses III:189.*

Use of temptations

Unless we are daily sharpened by various temptations, we immediately gather rust and other evils. *Hos. 427.*

What are temptations, or what is their object, but to afford us an occasion to exhibit, as on a field of battle, an example and proof of our strength and firmness. *Hos. 423.*

Our armour

The Lord seasonably sets limits to our temptations. *Ps. V:93.*

By His word He has armed His elect for certain victory . . . Whoever has profited, as he ought, by heavenly doctrine, will easily repel all the tricks of Satan by steadfast and victorious faith. *Is. III:270.*

It would be of little advantage to us to have once obtained him as ours, if he did not secure our possession of him against the assaults which Satan daily makes upon us. *Ps. I:225.*

It is meditation upon the Divine Law which furnishes us with armour to resist. *Ps. I:283.*

At every apprehension of temptation it becomes us to arouse ourselves with promptitude for repelling Satan's assaults. *Cor. II:374.*

[On Ps. 62:1, 2] . . . the many titles which [David] applies to God, each of which is to be considered as a foil by which he would ward off the attacks of the tempter. *Ps. II:419.*

[God's] power and His clemency . . . are the two wings wherewith we fly upwards to heaven; the two pillars on which we rest, and may defy the surges of temptation. *Ps. II:431.*

Temptation

Our victory

To flee unto God . . . the only armour which renders us invincible. *Gen. II:302.*

Nothing is more powerful to overcome temptation than the fear of God. *Gen. II:297.*

The faithful . . . can come forth conquerors in their temptations, only by being injured and wounded in the conflict [Jacob's thigh]. *Gen. II:198.*

The conquerors of all temptations are those who love God. *Gen. Epp. 288.*

God's speaking is opposed to all the obstreperous clamours of Satan . . . The only unfailing security for the faithful is to acquiesce in God's word. *Hab.-Hagg. 62.*

TESTIMONY

It means more to testify than to teach. *Acts II:384.*

We shall give 'testimony' to [God] for maintaining His glory. *Past. Epp. 192.*

[On Ps. 116:10] Faith cannot remain inoperative in the heart, but it must, of necessity, manifest itself. Hence the Holy Spirit unites, with a sacred bond, the faith of the heart with outward confession. *Ps. IV:366.*

Testimonies from Calvin:

I have observed . . . a simple style of teaching . . . I have felt nothing to be of more importance than to have a regard to the edification of the Church. [Intro. to the Psalms] *Ps. I:xlix.*

We shall die, but in death even be conquerors, not only because through it we shall have a sure passage to a better life, but because we know that our blood will be as seed to propagate the Divine truth which men now despise. [The closing words of The Necessity of Reforming the Church] *Tracts I:234.*

The things which I set before you are not those which I have meditated with myself in my shady nook, but those which the invincible martyrs of God realised amid gibbets, and flames, and ravenous beasts . . . They did not set us an example of constancy in asserting the truth, that we should now desert it, when handed down to us so signed and sealed; but they taught us the art by which, trusting to the Divine protection, we stand invincible by all the powers of death, hell, the world, and Satan! Farewell. [Closing words of On Shunning the Unlawful Rites of the Ungodly] *Tracts III:411*.

The testimony of Theodore Beza to Calvin

Having been a spectator of his conduct for sixteen years, I have given a faithful account both of his life and of his death, and I can now declare, that in him all men may see a most beautiful example of the Christian character, an example which it is as easy to slander as it is difficult to imitate. [Closing words of Beza's Life of Calvin] *Tracts I:c.*

THANKSGIVING

It is the highest worship of God . . . when we acknowledge God's goodness by thanksgiving. *Heb. 350.*

[Intro. to Ps. 136] The Psalmist reminds the Lord's people, that unless they were assiduous in His praise, they were chargeable with defrauding Him of what was justly due to Him for His benefits. *Ps. V:181.*

The Holy Spirit, speaking of the true worship of God . . . connects, by an indissoluble bond, these two parts of worship, 'Call upon Me in the day of trouble' and 'after thy deliverance glorify Me' (Ps. 50:15). *Ps. IV:371.*

As every blessing should be sought from God, so, when it has been received, thanksgiving should be rendered for it to God alone. *Is. IV:403.*

Sadness and anxiety lock up the soul, and restrain the tongue from celebrating the goodness of God. *Syn. Gosp. I:53.*

[On 2 Cor. 4:16] Every blessing that God confers upon us perishes through our carelessness, if we are not prompt and active in rendering thanks. *Cor. II:210.*

Thanksgiving

Every instance in which the mercy of God occurs to our remembrance ought to be embraced by us as an occasion of ascribing glory to God. *Gal. 28.*

THEOLOGY AND THEOLOGIANS

All theology, when separated from Christ, is not only vain and confused, but is also mad, deceitful and spurious. *John II:85.*

The first principle of theology, namely, that God can see nothing in the corrupt nature of man . . . to induce him to show him favour. *Rom. 200.*

He ought to be reckoned a true theologian who edifies conscience in the fear of God. *Past. Epp. 283.*

What else was the scholastic theology than a huge chaos of empty and useless speculations? *Past. Epp. 14.*

The duty of a theologian is, not to please the ear with empty sounds, but to confirm the conscience by teaching things which are true, certain and profitable. *Inst. I:xiv.4.*

I gladly abstain from all controversies about mere words; but I could wish that this sobriety had always been observed by Christian writers, that they had avoided the unnecessary adoption of terms not used in the Scriptures, and calculated to produce great offence, but very little advantage. *Inst. III:xv.2.*

All who mingle their own inventions with the word of God, or who advance anything that does not belong to it, must be rejected, how honourable soever may be their rank. *Syn. Gosp. II:176.*

No enemies are more destructive than those who speak the same language as ourselves. *Is. III:90.*

How dangerous to the Church is that knowledge which leads to debates . . . disregards piety, and tends to ostentation! *Past. Epp. 220.*

Doctrine without zeal is either like a sword in the hand of a madman, or . . . else it serves for vain and wicked boasting. *Acts II:20.*

There is a weariness as to simple doctrine which produces innumerable prodigies of errors, when everyone gapes continually for new mysteries. *Gen. Epp. 178.*

Whoever adulterates the pure religion, (which must necessarily be the case of all who are influenced by their own imagination), he is guilty of a departure from the one God. *Inst. I:v.13.*

How will the impious ridicule our faith, and all men call it in question, if it be understood to possess only a precarious authority depending on the favour of men! *Inst. I:vii.1.*

TRADITION

In the Church all human traditions ought to be treated as worthless, since all men's wisdom is vanity and lies. *Dan. II:10.*

To make the commandments of men, and not the word of God, the rule of worshipping Him, is a subversion of all order . . . They provoke God's anger. *Is. II:325.*

The world affects to believe that whatever is customary is lawful. *Gen. II:478.*

[On the Church Fathers] While we make use of their writings, we always remember that 'all things are ours' to serve us, not to have dominion over us, and that 'we are Christ's' alone, and owe him universal obedience. *From the Dedication to the Institutes.*

[On the Papacy] Abandoned by the Word of God, they flee for aid to antiquity. [On the Necessity of Reforming the Church] *Tracts I:218.*

TRINITY

What I denominate a Person, is a subsistence in the Divine essence, which is related to the others, and yet distinguished from them by an incommunicable property. *Inst. I:xiii.6.*

I doubt the propriety of borrowing similitudes from human things, to express the force of this distinction [of Persons in the trinity]. *Inst. I:xiii.18.*

[362]

The ordinance of baptism proves the existence of Three Persons in one Divine essence. *Eph. 269.*

Those who readily and implicitly attend to the Divine word, may have stable ground on which they may confidently rest. *Inst. I:xiii.21.*

[On Zech. 2:10] Christ is the temple of the Godhead. *Zech.-Mal. 75.*

To compose a catalogue of the errors, by which the purity of the faith has been attacked on this point of doctrine, would be too prolix and tedious. *Inst. I:xiii.22.*

TRUTH

The truth of God is immortal. *Gen. II:491.*

Whosoever applies his mind to the study of truth, can never be deceived. *Jer. III:167.*

There cannot be found the least particle of wisdom, light, righteousness, power, rectitude, or sincere truth which does not proceed from [God] and claim him for its author. *Inst. I:ii.1.*

No religion is pleasing to God unless founded on truth. *Dan. II:103.*

Nothing is deemed more precious by God than truth . . . there is nothing more adverse to his nature than falsehood. *Jer. IV:290.*

As his truth is precious to God, so it is a sacrilege that he cannot bear, when his truth is turned into falsehood. *Jer. III:450.*

Truth . . . is to be extended to that sincerity which the faithful ought to possess as to the pure and sincere worship of God. *Zech.-Mal. 194.*

The proper discrimination between truth and falsehood . . . does not arise from the sagacity of our own mind, but comes to us from the Spirit of wisdom. *Syn. Gosp. III:356.*

The truth of God always rises superior to all the obstacles raised by human unbelief. *Syn. Gosp. III:289.*

The truth of God will ever avail to dissipate all the mists in which Satan never ceases to envelop the pure truth. *Jer. III:427.*

There cannot be truth when faith is wanting. *Dan. I:140.*

God never leaves his faithful people destitute of the spirit of discernment, provided they offer themselves cordially and sincerely to be taught by his true and legitimate servants. *Jer. III:426.*

God always bestows on his elect, knowledge and judgment, that they may distinguish truth from falsehood. *Is. III:331.*

We shall be doubly punished, if it shall be found that we have quenched, by neglect or indifference, the light by which the Lord hath enlightened us. *Is. III:381.*

Our hearts through unbelief will hardly receive a simple truth, unless God removes the impediments. *Jer. III:83.*

When Divine Truth is avowedly attacked, we must not tolerate the adulteration of one single iota of it. [Preface to Psychopannychia] *Tracts III:418.*

Light emerges more clearly . . . when Satan endeavours to shut it out. *Dan. I:227.*

Amidst bitter strife and confused noise the truth will not be heard. *Is. III:101.*

The truth of God is not only fruitful in the salvation of men, but also in their perdition (2 Cor. 2:15, 16). *Jer. I:407.*

There should yet be greater security in integrity than in all the resources of fraud and injustice. *Ps. I:564, 565.*

Silence in the Church is the banishment and crushing of the truth. *Past. Epp. 91.*

The Church maintains the truth, because by preaching the Church proclaims it. *Past. Epp. 91.*

[364]

UNBELIEF

Its roots

How prone are we by nature to distrust! *Is. III:323.*

The beginning of infidelity is to be withheld by fear from obedience to God. *Four Last Bks of Moses IV:64.*

Boldness in disputing . . . is the mother of unbelief. *Syn. Gosp. I:46.*

Unbelief . . . is always proud . . . will never understand anything in the words of Christ, which it despises and disdains . . . This arises from the depravity of men. *John I:275.*

Ignorance is closely followed by obstinacy. *John II:57.*

[On Acts 26:7] The state of the Church is come to that pass, that the priests set themselves against the common hope of all the faithful. *Acts II:374.*

[On Ps. 119:21. God] denominates all unbelievers *proud*, because it is true faith alone which humbles us, and all rebellion is the offspring of pride. *Ps. IV:415.*

Our hearts are, by a kind of natural instinct, inclined to unbelief. *Inst. III:iii.20.*

Its character

It is a sure sign of unbelief not to be contented with the things which God gives to us. [Calvin's Catechism for the Church of Geneva] *Tracts II:71.*

When it ought to be quiet, unbelief is always active, prompt, and bold; but when God would have it advance, it is timid, slow and dead. *Four Last Bks of Moses IV:90.*

Unbelieving and irreligious men have no ears. *Is. III:479.*

The majority of men at this day set up their own fictions against God's word. *Jer. I:398.*

Unbelief is always timid. *Jer. IV:440.*

Unbelief is proud. *Ezek. II:184.*

[365]

Unbelief pollutes and contaminates whatever is otherwise in its nature sacred. *Zech.-Mal. 167.*

Impiety is ingenious in obscuring the works of God. *John I:372.*

Infidelity is always blind. *Cor. I:106.*

There is . . . no thicker darkness than that of unbelief. *Heb. 104.*

Pride is always the companion of unbelief. *Gen. II:173.*

Some portion of unbelief is always mixed with faith in every Christian. *Inst. III:ii.4.*

Its gravity

Nothing is more abominable in the sight of God than the contempt of divine truth. *Jer. I:345.*

The highest dishonour that can be done to [God] is unbelief and contempt of his word. *Syn. Gosp. I:319.*

[The Word of God] cannot be more grievously blasphemed than when men refuse to believe it. *Acts I:555.*

No greater injury can be done to God, than when credit is denied to his word. *Gen. I:514.*

We . . . attempt to rob God of his power whenever we distrust his word. *Gen. I:475.*

Its fruits

Nothing tends more than distrust to make us sluggish and useless. *Josh. 27.*

Fear . . . a sign of hopeless unbelief. *Jer. IV:410.*

Unbelief makes us rebels and deserters. *Syn. Gosp. I:46.*

Of all cares, which go beyond bounds, unbelief is the mother. *Syn. Gosp. I:340.*

All the mysteries of God are paradoxes to the mortals who have such audacity that they do not hesitate to rise against them. *Rom. 62.*

Unbelief

[Of Adam's sin] Unbelief was the root of defection . . . Hence flowed ambition, pride . . . also monstrous ingratitude. *Gen. I:153.*

Its cost

Our unbelief hinders God from displaying his power amongst us. *Is. III:335.*

The more audacious a man becomes, the farther God withdraws from him. *Jer. V:429.*

Those who reject the word of God render it, by their unbelief, deadly and destructive. *Syn. Gosp. III:101.*

The gate of salvation is set open unto all men; neither is there any other thing which keepeth us back from entering in, save only our own unbelief. *Acts I:92.*

Our own unbelief is no small hindrance to God's liberality. *Ps. II:34.*

Its impotence

The truth of God always rises superior to all the obstacles raised by human unbelief. *Syn. Gosp. III:289.*

UNION WITH CHRIST

Described

. . . that sacred marriage, by which we are made flesh of his flesh and bone of his bone, and therefore one with him. *Inst. III:i.3.*

The life of the soul is our union with God. *Heb. 205.*

We are partakers of the Holy Spirit, in proportion to the intercourse which we maintain with Christ; the Spirit will be found nowhere but in Christ. *Eph. 262.*

To *sleep in Jesus* (*1 Thess. 4:13, 14*) means to retain in death the union which we have with Christ. *Thess. 363.*

[367]

There is so great a unity between Christ and his members, that the name of Christ sometimes includes the whole body, as in 1 Cor. 12:12. *Col. 164.*

Explained

[On 1 Cor. 6:11] Christ . . . is the source of all blessings to us . . . but Christ himself, with all his blessings, is communicated to us by the Spirit. *Cor. I:212.*

[On 1 Cor. 6:15] The spiritual connection which we have with Christ belongs not merely to the soul, but also to the body (*Eph. 5:30*). *Cor. I:217.*

The Holy Spirit is the bond by which Christ efficaciously unites us to Himself. *Inst. III:i.1.*

All who are united to Christ . . . will remain to the end safe from all danger; for what is said of the body of the Church belongs to each of its members, since they are one in Christ. *Syn. Gosp. II:292.*

We are . . . *in Christ* because we are out of ourselves. *Rom. 72.*

The only source of our mortification is our participation in the death of Christ. *Rom. 125.*

Enjoyed

The mystical union subsisting between Christ and his members, should be matter of reflection not only when we sit at the Lord's Table, but at all other times. *Ps. II:435.*

He who has Christ dwelling in him can want nothing. *Eph. 262.*

Attested

When we hear any mention of our union with God, we should remember that holiness must be the bond of it. *Inst. III:vi.2.*

The more we are afflicted by adversities, our fellowship with Christ is so much the more certainly confirmed! *Inst. III:viii.1.*

UNITY (*see also* Church)

A reality

A holy unity exists amongst us, when, consenting in pure doctrine, we are united in Christ alone. [Necessity of Reforming the Church] *Tracts I:215.*

In ourselves we are scattered; in Christ we are gathered together. *Is. IV:118.*

[On John 10:16] Though this *flock* appears to be divided into different *folds*, yet they are kept within enclosures which are common to all believers, who are scattered throughout the whole world; because the same word is preached to all, they use the same sacraments, they have the same order of prayer, and everything that belongs to the profession of faith. *John I:408.*

We ought . . . to beware lest the unity of the faith be destroyed, or the bond of charity broken, on account of outward ceremonies. *Syn. Gosp. I:405.*

[On Acts 15:37] Unless the servants of Christ take great heed, there be many chinks through which Satan will creep in, to disturb that concord which is among them. *Acts II:86.*

[On Rom. 15:6] God sets so high a store on the unity of His servants that He will not allow His glory to be sounded amid discord and controversy. *Rom. 306.*

Satan . . . leaves no stone unturned with the view of breaking up the unity of the Church. *Cor. I:367.*

How great a blessing unity in the Church is, and with what eagerness pastors should endeavour to secure it. *Philipp.-Col. 50, 51.*

The chief indication of a prosperous condition of the Church is – when mutual agreement prevails in it, and brotherly harmony. *Philipp.-Col. 51.*

Basis of unity

I burned for the unity of thy Church, provided thy truth were made the bond of concord. [Reply to Sadoleto] *Tracts I:60.*

We, who desire nothing else than unity, and whose only bond of union is the eternal truth of God . . . [Necessity of Reforming the Church] *Tracts I:199.*

If we would unite in holding a unity of the Church, let it be by a common consent only to the truth of Christ. [True Method of Reforming the Church] *Tracts III:266.*

With regard to concord or union . . . the principle of a right and lawful agreement is, to have regard to God, to depend on his word, and, with one consent, to obey what he commands. *Jer. IV:212.*

Faith is the soul of the Church; nothing is more proper to faith than agreement, nothing more contrary than sects. *Acts II:321.*

There is no other holy bond of unity than the natural and plain truth of God. *Acts II:321.*

On [Christ] alone the unity of the Church depends. *Eph. 218.*

Unity . . . to which humility is the first step. *Eph. 267.*

The bond . . . of holy unity is the truth of God. *Philipp.-Col. 173.*

Twofold unity – of *spirit* and *soul*. The *first* is, that we have like views; the *second*, that we be united in heart . . . Agreement of views comes first . . . From it springs union of inclination. *Philipp.-Col. 46.*

The bond of holy unity is the simple truth. As soon as we depart from that, nothing remains but dreadful discord. *Gen. Epp. 393.*

The headship of Christ
Beware of separating the Church from Christ its Head. [Necessity of Reforming the Church] *Tracts I:213.*

[Quoting Hilary] 'The name of peace is, indeed, specious, and the idea of unity beautiful, but who knows not that the only united peace of the Church and the Gospel is that which is of Christ?' [Remarks on the Letter of Pope Paul III to the Emperor Charles V] *Tracts I:259.*

The unity of men is of no account before God, except it originates from one head. *Hos. 70.*

[370]

Whosoever tears asunder the Church of God, disunites himself from Christ, who is the head, and who would have all his members to be united together. *Zech.-Mal. 231.*

Those only rest on Christ, who keep the unity of the Church, for he is not set as a foundation stone except in Sion. *Gen. Epp. 68.*

Subject to Scripture

We must by all means seek harmony, but we must see on what conditions we obtain it . . . Let the truth itself be preserved, which cannot be contained but in the word . . . Away with every one who shall corrupt it, choose what language he may. *Is. II:70.*

No unity pleases God, unless men obey his word from the least to the greatest. *Jer. IV:65.*

In order that men may happily unite together, obedience to God's word must be the beginning. *Jer. IV:211.*

Accursed is every union where there is no regard to God and to his word. *Jer. IV:211.*

No union formed by men can possibly lessen the authority of God. *Hab.-Hagg. 267.*

. . . as if the unity of the Church were itself founded on anything else than the authority of Scripture. *John II:230.*

The name of peace is . . . plausible and sweet, but cursed is that peace which is purchased with so great a loss, that we suffer the doctrine of Christ to perish, by which alone we grow together into godly and holy unity. *Acts II:38.*

When the unity of the Church is spoken of, it is to be considered as consisting in nothing else but an unafraid agreement to yield obedience to the Word of God. *Ps. II:215.*

Without compromise of the truth

What greater violation of unity, than when purity of doctrine is adulterated. [Remarks on the Letter of Pope Paul III to the Emperor Charles V] *Tracts I:273.*

[371]

We are all agreed that peace is not to be purchased by the sacrifice of truth. [Mutual Consent in Regard to the Sacraments] *Tracts II:222.*

It is a shameless piece of trickery to defend a conspiracy of lying and godless doctrines under the pretext of peace and unity. *Rom. 324.*

The duties of love to our neighbour ought never to be injurious to faith. *Gal. 50.*

[On Ps. 133:1] We cannot extend this intercourse to those who obstinately persist in error . . . Any concord, which may prevail among men, is insipid, if not pervaded by a sweet savour of God's worship. *Ps. V:164, 165.*

No union with the papacy

It is better a hundred times to separate from [the Papists] than to be united together, and thus to form an ungodly and wicked union against God. *Jer. IV:211.*

[On Gal. 2:5] Where are the men who, by pretended moderation, endeavour to bring about a reconciliation between us and the Papists? As if the doctrine of religion, like a matter affecting money or property, could be compromised. *Gal. 52.*

Violation of this unity

[On Tit. 3:10] Every person who, by his overweening pride, breaks up the unity of the Church, is pronounced by Paul a 'heretic'. *Past. Epp. 341.*

A heresy or sect and the unity of the Church . . . are things totally opposite to each other. *Past. Epp. 342.*

Calvin's prayer, concluding his Reply to Cardinal Sadoleto's Letter: The Lord grant, Sadolet, that you and all your party may at length perceive, that the only true bond of Ecclesiastical unity would exist if Christ the Lord, who hath reconciled us to God the Father, were to gather us out of our present dispersion into the fellowship of his body, that so, through his one Word and Spirit, we might join together with one heart and one soul. *Tracts I:68.*

[372]

UNIVERSALISTIC LANGUAGE

[On Is. 64:10] By employing the word *all* he does not speak of each individual . . . but includes the whole body of Christ. *Is. IV:372.*

When the Holy Spirit names 'all' he means some out of all nations, and not every one universally. *Dan. II:78.*

[On Zeph. 3:9] As to the word *all* it is to be referred to all nations, not to each individual. *Hab.-Hagg. 285.*

[On John 3:16, 17] The word *world* is . . . repeated that no man may think himself wholly excluded, if he only keep the road of faith. *John I:126.*

[On John 12:32] The word *all* . . . must be understood to refer to the children of God, who belong to His flock. *John II:37.*

[On 1 Tim. 2:5] The universal term *all* must always be referred to classes of men, and not to persons . . . he wishes the benefit of his death to be common to all. *Past. Epp. 57.*

[On Heb. 5:9] He seems . . . to have adopted a universal term, *all* . . . that he might show that no one is precluded from salvation who is but teachable and becomes obedient to the Gospel of Christ. *Heb. 125.*

[On 1 John 2:2] Under the word *all*, he . . . designates those who should believe, as well as those who were then scattered through various parts of the world. *Gen. Epp. 173.*

VICTORY

By his word he has . . . armed his elect for certain victory . . . Whoever has profited, as he ought, by heavenly doctrine, will easily repel all the tricks of Satan by steadfast and victorious faith. *Is. III:270.*

When any person has his eyes fixed on God, his heart will be invincible. *John II:47.*

The cross of Christ always contains in itself the victory. *John II:150.*

[373]

The faithful do so get the victory, that they are always humbled under the cross. *Acts I:180.*

It goeth well with the godly, because they triumph gloriously before God and His angels in all injuries which they suffer. *Acts II:115.*

The world has been brought into a state of good order by the victory of Christ, by which he overturned the authority of Satan. *John II:141.*

God . . . does not call His people to triumph before He has exercised them in the warfare of suffering. *Rom. 176.*

[On Ps. 91:15. God] puts much honour upon [his people] in the world, and glorifies himself in them conspicuously, but it is not till the completion of their course that he affords them ground for triumph. *Ps. III:491.*

VIRGIN MARY

The highest happiness and glory of the holy Virgin consisted in her being a member of his Son, so that the heavenly Father reckoned her in the number of new creatures. *Syn. Gosp. II:88.*

The Blessed Virgin . . . 'the associate of Christ'. What is meant by dividing Christ, if this is not? [Antidote to the Council of Trent] *Tracts III:48.*

VOCATION

Every individual's line of life, therefore, is, as it were, a post assigned him by the Lord . . . There will be no employment so mean and sordid . . . as not to appear truly respectable, and be deemed highly important in the sight of God. *Inst. III:x.6.*

Let everyone go whither he shall be called, even if he should not have a single follower. [Letter to the Admiral Coligny, dated 16 January 1561] *Letters 234.*

[On Exod. 18:13, Jethro's advice to Moses] Let . . . God's servants learn to measure carefully their powers, lest they should wear out, by ambitiously embracing too many occupations. For this propensity to engage in too many things . . . is a very common malady . . . God has so arranged our condition, that individuals are only endued with a certain measure of gifts. *Four Last Bks of Moses I:303.*

[On the call to the ministry] This secret call . . . is the honest testimony of our heart, that we accept the office offered to us, not from ambition or avarice, or any other unlawful motive, but from a sincere fear of God, and an ardent zeal for the edification of the Church. *Inst. IV:iii.11.*

[Calvin's comment when he, Farel and Corald were ordered to leave Geneva] Had I been the servant of men I had obtained a poor reward, but it is well that I have served him who never fails to perform to his servants whatever he has promised. [Beza's Life of Calvin] *Tracts I:xxxiii.*

[On the ministry] We ought to make so great account of the calling of God that no unthankfulness of men may be able to hinder us. *Acts II:129.*

WAR

War ought to be nothing else than an attempt to obtain peace. *Is. I:131.*

War is one of God's judgments. *Hab.-Hagg. 300.*

In war all humanity and equity is buried. *Ezek. I:235.*

Wars are not kindled accidentally, or by an arrangement of men, but by the command of God. *Is. I:194.*

The events of all wars depend on God. *Zech.-Mal. 267.*

[Quoting Cicero] 'Wars must not be undertaken except that we may live in unmolested peace.' *Four Last Bks of Moses III:52.*

All wars are stirred by [God's] command, and . . . the soldiers are armed at His will. *Four Last Bks of Moses III:235.*

All who strive to produce anarchy, fight against God. *Gen. I:382.*

[375]

[Abraham, Gen. 14] He went to war endued with the power of the Spirit . . . the heroical virtues of the man. *Gen. I:383, 384.*

WEALTH

[Quoting Chrysostom] All that we have is on the same tenure as the possessions of slaves, which the law pronounces to be the property of their masters. *Inst. III:xiv.15.*

God confers his blessings on us for the support of life, not for luxury. *Inst. III:xix.9.*

If we believe heaven to be our country, it is better for us to transmit our wealth thither, than to retain it here, where we may lose it by a sudden removal. *Inst. III:xviii.6.*

Where riches hold the dominion of the heart, God has lost his authority . . . Covetousness makes us the slaves of the devil. *Syn. Gosp. I:337.*

All the wealth of this world is nothing else but a heap of clay. *Hab.-Hagg. 95.*

Hardly . . . an avaricious man can be found who is not a burden to himself, and to whom his wealth is not a source of trouble. *Hab.-Hagg. 94.*

[On the eighth commandment] Let us remember that all artifices by which the possessions and wealth of our neighbours are transferred to us, whenever they deviate from sincere love into a desire of deceiving, or doing any kind of injury, are to be esteemed acts of theft. *Inst. II:viii.45.*

WILL

As our understanding has need of light, so has our will of uprightness. *Ps. III:388.*

[On 1 Cor. 2:14] It is not owing simply to the obstinacy of the human will, but to the impotency, also, of the understanding. *Cor. I:116.*

Simply to will belongs to man; to will what is evil, to corrupt nature; to will what is good, to grace. *Inst. II:iii.5.*

[The bondage of the will] offends those who know not how to distinguish between necessity and compulsion. *Inst. II:iii.5.*

Whatever we resolve to do that is not approved by God, cannot possibly succeed; for God will subvert all our hopes. *Jer. I:151.*

[Following Augustine] The Lord precedes the unwilling that he may will, and follows the willing that he may not will in vain. *Inst. II:iii.7.*

The will is not destroyed by grace, but rather repaired . . . when, by the correction of its depravity and perverseness, it is directed according to the true standard of righteousness; and also that a new will may be said to be created in man, because the natural will is so vitiated and corrupted, that it needs to be formed entirely anew. *Inst. II:v.15.*

WISDOM

True wisdom

True and substantial wisdom principally consists in two parts, the knowledge of God, and the knowledge of ourselves. [Opening words of The Institutes] *Inst. I:i.1.*

Spiritual wisdom . . . consists chiefly in three things – to know God, his paternal favour towards us, on which depends our salvation, and the method of regulating our lives according to the rule of the law. *Inst. II:ii.18.*

. . . the first step of wisdom, to ascribe nothing to ourselves. *Gen. II:323.*

No small part of our wisdom is a teachable spirit. *Heb. 192, 193.*

[On Eph. 5:17] Paul defines *wisdom* to be *understanding what the will of the Lord is. Eph. 315.*

Comes from God

Wisdom is not the growth of human genius. It must be sought from above. *Ps. II:237.*

All the gifts and power which men seem to possess are in the hand of God, so that he can, at any instant . . . deprive them of the wisdom which he has given them. *Ps. III:198.*

All sound knowledge and wisdom must commence with yielding to God the honour which is his due, and submitting to be restrained and governed by his word. *Ps. III:333.*

It is the peculiar virtue of faith, that we should willingly be fools, in order that we may learn to be wise only from the mouth of God. *Four Last Bks of Moses IV:155, 156.*

There is no wisdom but that which is founded on the fear of God. *Is. II:58.*

All who arrogate to themselves wisdom rise up against God, because they rob God of the honour due to him. *Jer. V:197.*

By Divine illumination, through the Holy Spirit

We are not wise, except when we are illumined by God from above through his Spirit. *Gen. Epp. 325.*

[On 1 John 2:22, an unction from the Holy One] Men are not rightly made wise by the acumen of their own minds, but by the illumination of the Spirit . . . and . . . we are not otherwise made partakers of the Spirit than through Christ. *Gen. Epp. 194.*

It were not enough to have . . . the outward sound, did not God illuminate our minds by the Spirit of understanding, and correct our obduracy by the Spirit of docility. *Ps. V:47.*

Through His Word

The way by which we become truly wise is, first by submitting ourselves to the Word of God, and not following our own imaginations; and, secondly, by God's opening our understanding and subduing it to the obedience of his will. *Ps. V:47.*

It is only from the word of God that we must learn wisdom. *John I:106.*

[We] have no wisdom but through his word. *Cor. I:144.*

This is all our wisdom, to stay ourselves upon the authority, government, and commandment of God. *Acts II:45.*

[378]

All our wisdom is contained in the Scriptures. *Past. Epp. 252.*

Faith ought to be accompanied by prudence, that it may distinguish between the word of God and the word of men. *Past. Epp. 247.*

[On Peter, at Matt. 16:22] There is no beast more furious than the wisdom of the flesh . . . It is only from the word of God that we ought to be wise. *Syn. Gosp. II:301, 302.*

Through the cross of Christ

[On 1 Cor. 1:17] All the wisdom of believers is comprehended in the cross of Christ. *Cor. I:74.*

The minds of men are destitute of that sagacity which is necessary for perceiving the mysteries of heavenly wisdom which are hidden in Christ . . . till God opens our eyes to perceive his glory in Christ. *Syn. Gosp. II:290.*

The blindness of human conceit

Athens . . . the mansion house of wisdom, the fountain of all arts, the mother of humanity, did exceed all others in blindness and madness. *Acts II:145, 146.*

To search for wisdom apart from Christ means not simply foolhardiness, but utter insanity. *Rom. 15.*

The worst blindness is, when men become inebriated with the false conceit of wisdom. *Joel-Obad. 435.*

There is a heavenly and secret wisdom that is contained in the gospel, which cannot be apprehended by any acuteness or perspicacity of intellect . . . but . . . by the revelation of the Spirit. *Cor. I:41.*

The *wisdom of the world*, in Paul's acceptation, is that which assumes to itself authority, and does not allow itself to be regulated by the word of God. *Cor. I:145.*

[On 2 Cor. 1:12] Paul gives the name of *fleshly wisdom* to everything apart from Christ, that procures for us the reputation of *wisdom. Cor. II:127.*

[379]

The teachable spirit of the Christian

Then only are we truly wise unto righteousness when we obey the word of God. *Syn. Gosp. I:22.*

This is our wisdom, to be learners to the end. *Zech.-Mal. 125.*

When the Lord has furnished us with the spirit of invincible fortitude, we must also pray that he may govern us by the spirit of prudence. *Gen. I:500.*

True wisdom manifests itself in the observance of the law. *Ps. IV:319.*

True wisdom consists in being wise according to the law of God. *Ps. IV:425.*

Micah divides this power of the prophets into two kinds, even into wisdom or judgment, and into courage . . . Let them excel in doctrine . . . let them not bend to please the world. *Jon.-Nah. 233, 234.*

WORKS OF THE BELIEVER (*see also* Good Works)

The contrite heart abjures the idea of merit, and has no dealings with God upon the principle of exchange. *Ps. II:306.*

According to the judgment which God forms of the works of the believer, their worth and valuation depend first, upon the free pardon extended to him as a sinner, and by which he becomes reconciled to God; and, next, upon the divine condescension and indulgence which accepts his services, notwithstanding all their imperfections. *Ps. II:432.*

Not only do we receive righteousness by grace through faith, but as the moon bestows her light from the sun, so does the same faith render our works righteous. *Ps. IV:233.*

No works are imputed unto righteousness, except because God deigns to bestow His gratuitous favour on believers. *Four Last Bks of Moses III:124.*

However defective the works of believers may be, they are nevertheless pleasing to God through the intervention of pardon . . . Reward is given to their efforts, although imperfect, exactly as if they had fully discharged their duty. *Four Last Bks of Moses III:214.*

[God] not only loves the *faithful*, but also their *works* . . . The grace . . . of Christ, and not their own dignity or merit, is that which gives worth to their works. *Gen. I:266.*

Let the faithful observe this moderation, that when they have tried all means, they still ascribe nothing to their own industry. *Gen. II:355.*

WORLD

As created

That beautiful theatre of the world. *Is. III:225 (fn.).*

This most ample and beautiful machine. *Inst. I:v.i.*

The faithful, to whom he has given eyes, see sparks of his glory, as it were, glittering in every created thing. The world was no doubt made, that it might be the theatre of divine glory. *Heb. 266.*

The intention of Moses, in beginning his Book with the creation of the world, is, to render God . . . visible to us in his works. *Gen. I:58.*

God – by other means invisible – clothes himself . . . with the image of the world . . . Let the world become our school if we desire rightly to know God. *Gen. I:60.*

After the world had been created man was placed in it as in a theatre . . . that he, beholding the wonderful works of God, might reverently adore their Author. *Gen. I:64.*

The creation – the book of the unlearned. *Gen. I:80.*

The exact symmetry of the universe is a mirror, in which we may contemplate the otherwise invisible God. *Inst. I:v.I.*

[The Holy Spirit] . . . being universally diffused, sustains and animates all things in heaven and in earth. *Inst. I:xiii.14.*

Since [God] is the Creator of the whole world, it seems to be his proper office to protect its various parts, especially those which excel in beauty. *Jon.-Nah. 483.*

All the changes of the world depend on celestial motion. *Ezek. I:87.*

The world stands through no other power than that of God's word. *Gen. Epp. 416.*

As vitiated by sin

It is evident to all who can see, that the world is inundated with more than an ocean of evils, that it is overrun with numerous destructive pests, that everything is fast verging to ruin, so that we must altogether despair of human affairs, or vigorously and even violently oppose such immense evils. *From the Dedication to the Institutes.*

The world . . . now advancing to its last end, has not yet reached six thousand years. *Inst. I:xiv.1.*

The world always degenerates. *Dan. I:164.*

The worse the world is, and the greater the licentiousness of sin, the more necessity there is for praying God to keep us by his wonderful power, as it were in the very regions of hell. *Jer. II:366.*

Nearly the whole world languished between a weariness of the present life and an inexplicable desire for its continuance. *Gen. II:37,38.*

As soon as we come down to the world, we gather fading flowers . . . We wish to be happy without God, that is, without happiness itself. *Is. II:275.*

As the platform for demonstrating God's salvation

[On Mic. 4:2] God designed . . . that the whole world should be subject to him. *Jon.-Nah. 253.*

The world has been brought into a state of good order by the victory of Christ, by which he overturned the authority of Satan. *John II:141.*

[382]

The whole world became an enlarged mount Zion upon the advent of Christ. *Ps. V:158.*

The world itself was enclosed in the ark. *Gen. I:281.*

The whole world is governed by God for our salvation . . . that those whom he has elected may be saved. *Is. I:434.*

Christ was sent in order to bring the whole world under the authority of God and obedience to him. *Is. III:287.*

Christ has restored to believers the inheritance of the world. *Is. II:426.*

There is power in God to lay prostrate the whole world, and to tread it under his feet, whenever it may please him. *Hab.-Hagg. 132.*

When we have God as our security, we ought . . . boldly to tread the whole world under our feet . . . rather than allow the unbelief of any persons . . . to fill us with alarm. *John I:118.*

This present evil world

The word *world*, throughout [John 17] denotes the reprobate. *John II:184.*

[On Gal. 1:4] The world is . . . contrasted with regeneration, as nature with grace, or the flesh with the spirit. *Gal. 27.*

Whatever is opposed to the spiritual kingdom of Christ is the world. *Gal. 184.*

The Gospel cannot be published without instantly driving the world to rage. *John II:123.*

The faithful, while in this world, are always living among wolves. *Ps. IV:131.*

To know the error and the madness of the world certainly contributes in no small degree to the confirmation of true godliness. *Ps. IV:347.*

For the present God judges the world only in part. *Thess. 389.*

WORLDLINESS

There is no place for us among God's children, except we renounce the world. *Heb. 285.*

The Lord, by calling us to heaven, withdraws us from the earth. *Past. Epp. 320.*

As much as anyone inclines to the world, so much he alienates himself from God. *Gen. Epp. 331.*

We look at nothing but the world, till the Lord has drawn us to Himself. *Past. Epp. 319.*

If meditation on the heavenly life were the prevailing sentiment in our hearts, the world would have no influence in detaining us. *John II:30.*

If we would perceive the worthlessness of this fading life, we must be deeply affected by the view of the heavenly life. *Syn. Gosp. II:305.*

No man can meditate on the heavenly life, unless he be dead to the world, and to himself. *Is. IV:242.*

[On Ps. 31:6, Vanities] . . . Whatever vain hopes . . . we form to ourselves, which may draw us off from our confidence in God. They feed us for a time with magnificent promises, in the end they beguile and disappoint us. *Ps. I:505.*

[On Ps. 37:9] The flesh is always seeking to build its nest for ever here . . . and were we not tossed hither and thither . . . we would . . . forget heaven. *Ps. II:26.*

The joy we derive from his paternal favour towards us may surpass all the pleasures of the world. *Ps. II:20.*

The only way to walk through life happily is to walk holily and harmlessly in the world, in the service and fear of God. *Ps. I:555.*

Christ is little esteemed by us, when the admiration of worldly glory lays hold on us. *Gen. Epp. 301.*

[Demas] enjoyed a propitious gale from the world. *Past. Epp. 264.*

They who desire to be happy in the world, renounce heaven. *Syn. Gosp. I:333.*

We ought to apply our minds to meditation upon a future life, so that this world may become cheap to us. *Dan. I:226.*

All worldly men . . . are justly punished . . . Each is his own executioner. *Ps. V:42.*

Prosperity so intoxicates [men] that, forgetful of their condition, and sunk in insensibility, they dream of an immortal state on earth. *Ps. II:78.*

The world [is] full of Epicureans, who regard religion as a fable. *Jer. IV:402.*

This is the perpetual infatuation of the world; to neglect heaven, and to seek immortality on earth. *Gen. I:327.*

As soon as the least ray of hope beams upon us, from the world, we are torn away from the Lord, and alienated from the pursuit of the heavenly life. *Gen. II:422.*

There is no medium between these two extremes; either the earth must become vile in our estimation, or it must retain our immoderate love. *Inst. III:ix.2.*

The Lord calls all his people, as by the sound of the trumpet, to be wanderers, lest they should become fixed in their nests on earth. *Gen. II:404.*

WORSHIP

Principles

God wishes first of all for inward worship, and afterwards for outward profession. The principal altar . . . ought to be . . . in our minds, for God is worshipped spiritually by faith, prayer and other acts of piety. *Dan. I:211.*

[On 1 Cor. 11:2] What contempt . . . will be incurred if we do not preserve dignity in the Church, by conducting ourselves honourably and becomingly? *Cor. I:351.*

The main thing in the worship of God is to embrace His promises with obedience. *Rom. 99.*

He who truly desires to worship [God] will study to pay him the obedience of a son, and the submission of a servant. *Inst. III:ii.26.*

Public prayers are to be composed . . . in the vernacular tongue, which may be generally understood by the whole congregation. *Inst. III:xx.33.*

The outward service of the sanctuary, which is the sacred bond of intercourse with God . . . a ladder by which [we may] ascend to God . . . *Ps. II:129, 130.*

[On Ps. 42:2] When we see the marks of the divine presence engraven on the word, or on external symbols, we can say with David that there is *the face of God*, provided we come with pure hearts to seek him in a spiritual manner. *Ps. II:130.*

The worship of God is spiritual and consists of two parts, prayer and thanksgiving. *Ps. II:257.*

[On Ps. 138:1] The solemn assembly is, so to speak, a heavenly theatre, graced by the presence of attending angels. *Ps. V:199.*

God cannot be rightly worshipped unless when He has His peculiar attributes acknowledged. *Four Last Bks of Moses I:422.*

No worship pleases God except what He sanctifies. *Four Last Bks of Moses II:328.*

All modes of worship fabricated by men are rejected as unsavoury. *Four Last Bks of Moses II:330.*

Two things are required for legitimate worship: First, that he who approaches God shall be purged from every stain; and secondly, that he should offer nothing except what is pure and free from all imperfection. *Four Last Bks of Moses II:380.*

The chief object of life is to acknowledge and worship God. *Is. III:368.*

Scripture frequently describes the whole of worship [as] *calling upon God* [Is. 12:4]. *Is. I:402.*

The beginning and perfection of lawful worship is a readiness to obey. *Is. IV:381.*

God is not rightly worshipped, except when the heart is free from all guile and deceit . . . There is no worship of God without sincerity of heart. *Jer. I:201.*

If . . . we . . . only follow what God demands, our worship will be pure, but if we add anything of our own, it is an abomination. *Ezek. I:226.*

The principle of worshipping God [is] a diligent love of him. *Dan. II:148.*

Jehovah is not in any place, except where he is rightly worshipped according to the rule of his word. *Hos. 60.*

The worship of God especially consists in praises, as it is said in Ps. 50. *Jon.-Nah. 89.*

[On Matt. 10:32] Confession of Christ is here represented to be a main part of divine worship, and a distinguished exercise of godliness. *Syn. Gosp. I:466.*

We should consider it the great end of our existence to be found numbered amongst the worshippers of God; . . . we should avail ourselves of the inestimable privilege of the stated assemblies of the Church. *Ps. II:318.*

Governed by Scripture

All such rites, . . . as have no foundation in the word of God are unauthorised, and that worship which has not a distinct reference to the word is but a corruption of things sacred. *Ps. II:264.*

No other service of God is lawful, except that of which He has testified His approval in His Word. *Four Last Bks of Moses I:453.*

God rejects, condemns, abominates all fictitious worship, and employs His Word as a bridle to keep us in unqualified obedience. [The Necessity of Reforming the Church] *Tracts I:133.*

True fear of God cannot exist, where the worship is not pure and agreeable to his Word. *Is. IV:207.*

All modes of worship devised contrary to his command, he not only repudiates as void, but distinctly condemns. [True Method of Reforming the Church] *Tracts III:261.*

The right rule then as to the worship of God is, to adopt nothing but what he prescribes. *Jer. IV:543.*

The principal part of worship is obedience, which he prefers to all sacrifices . . . Things we might tolerate ought to be detested by us, because God condemns them so severely. *Ezek. II:135.*

It is not in the power of men to form any modes of worship they please. *Hos. 366.*

There is nothing omitted in the law that is needful for the perfect worship of God. *Hab.-Hagg. 202.*

No one rightly worships God, but he who is taught by his Word. *Zech.-Mal. 448.*

Nothing is more wicked than to contrive various modes of worship without the authority of the word of God. *John I:154.*

God is not properly worshipped but by the certainty of faith, which cannot be produced in any other way than by the word of God. *John I:160.*

The rule for the worship of God, . . . ought to be taken from nothing else than from his own appointment. *John II:214.*

The first difference between true worship and idolatry is this: when the godly take in hand nothing but that which is agreeable to the Word of God. *Acts I:299.*

Old Testament worship distinguished

There was no exercise of imagination in the whole service of the tabernacle, because there is nothing more opposite to the purity of religion than to do anything which is not enjoined. *Four Last Bks of Moses III:305.*

In the imposing services of the Mosaic ritual everything that was presented to the eye bore an impress of Christ. *Gal. 109.*

[On Ps. 149] The musical instruments he mentions were peculiar to this infancy of the Church, nor should we foolishly imitate a practice which was intended only for God's ancient people. *Ps. V:312.*

Corruption of Divine worship

[On Col. 2:33] Consider . . . how forward the mind of man is to artificial modes of worship. *Col. 203.*

Nothing is more easy than to corrupt the pure worship of God, when men esteem God after their sense and wit. *Acts II:158.*

All those modes of worship are false and spurious, which men allow themselves by their own wit to invent, and beyond God's command. *Heb. 184.*

We know in how great liberties the world indulges itself in the service of God; for whilst it lightly and contemptuously obtrudes mere trifling upon him, as if he were a child, it still fancies that its duty is properly discharged. *Four Last Bks of Moses II:379.*

As soon as the purity of the worship of God is impaired, there no longer remains anything perfect or sound, and faith itself is utterly ruined. *Past. Epp. 98.*

As men decline from God in the least degree, his worship is corrupted. *Four Last Bks of Moses I:421.*

Let us . . . beware of disturbing pious minds by the introduction of any kind of novelty. *Josh. 254.*

There is nothing to which men are more prone than to mix up their inventions with God's commands, as if they would be wiser than he is. *Four Last Bks of Moses III:406.*

We perceive in the human mind an intemperate longing for perverse worship. *Josh. 268.*

There is no end, when men once depart ever so little from the pure worship of the only true God; for when anything is blended with it one error immediately produces another. *Jer. II:94.*

As soon as we allow ourselves the liberty to worship God in this or in that way . . . we create gods for ourselves. *Jer. II:336.*

All . . . who seek instruction from statues or pictures gain nothing, but become entangled in the snares of Satan, and find nothing but impostures. *Jer. V:225.*

Whatever men devise of themselves is a pollution of divine worship. *Hos. 452.*

There is . . . naturally in us a perverse lust for mixing with [true religion] some false and ungodly forms of worship. *Hos. 170.*

They trifle with [God] like children with their puppets. *Hab.- Hagg. 369.*

[On Matt. 15:1ff.] We see the extraordinary insolence that is displayed by men as to the form and manner of worshipping God; for they are perpetually contriving new modes of worship. *Syn. Gosp. II:245.*

There is nothing to which men are more prone than to fall away from the pure worship of God. *Syn. Gosp. III:88.*

Modes of worship regulated according to our own fancy . . . rob God of his true honour, and pour upon him nothing but reproach . . . Whenever we mix up our own opinions with the word of God, faith degenerates into frivolous conjectures. *John I:234.*

The Papists do place the spiritual worship of God in man's inventions. *Acts II:94.*

Whatever . . . men bring in [to worship] of themselves is wholly impious, for it adulterates the pure worship of God . . . a tyrannical bondage. *Jer. IV:323.*

The gravity of such departure from Scriptural worship

God . . . cannot endure new modes of worship to be devised . . . All kinds of worship invented by men . . . are accursed and detestable. *Syn. Gosp. II:253, 254.*

To make the commandments of men, and not the word of God, the rule of worshipping him, is a subversion of all order . . . They . . . provoke God's anger. *Is. II:325.*

God cannot long endure his worship to be scoffed at. *Jer. V:214.*

As nothing is more dear to God than his own glory, so there is nothing which he more strongly detests than to have it infringed by any kind of corruptions; and this is done, when any sort of unmeaning service is put in the room of true worship. *Is. I:58.*

[God] pronounces all fictitious modes of worship, however much adorned by a specious guise, to be adulteries and whoredoms. *Hos. 165.*

Although men think that they obey God when they thrust in their own fictions, yet they produce no other effect than to provoke the wrath of God against them. *Ezek. I:222.*

When men introduce their inventions it immediately causes God to depart. *Ezek. I:284.*

Some . . . inculcate acts of worship which are wicked and diametrically opposed to the word of God. Others . . . mingle profane trifles with the worship of God, and corrupt its purity . . . [adding] to the word of God some patches of their own invention. *Syn. Gosp. II:247, 248 and fn.*

Epilogue

John Calvin died on 27 May 1564 at the age of fifty-four.

His last commentary was on the prophecies of Ezekiel. He reached chapter 20, verse 44.

Calvin's co-pastor, Theodore Beza, prepared these commentaries for the press and dedicated them to Gaspar de Coligny, Grand Admiral of France, 'mirror and example of piety', who was struck down in the massacre of St Bartholomew in Paris in 1572.

Here is Calvin's prayer, which closes Lecture 65 on Ezekiel, and may fittingly conclude this anthology:

Grant, Almighty God, since we have already entered in hope upon the threshold of our eternal inheritance, and know that there is a certain mansion for us in heaven, after Christ has been received there, who is our Head, and the first-fruits of our salvation: Grant . . . that we may proceed more and more in the course of thy holy calling until at length we reach the goal, and so enter that eternal glory of which thou affordest us a taste in this world, by the same Christ our Lord. Amen. *Ezek. II:345.*

SOME OTHER
BANNER OF TRUTH
TITLES

A COMMENTARY ON THE MINOR PROPHETS

John Calvin

'I confess that at the outset I was put off by the fear of being thought rash and arrogant if I should attempt such an undertaking after so many other excellent works.'

So wrote John Calvin (1509–1564) in the dedicatory letter of his commentary on Romans, his first printed exposition. That initial hesitation overcome, Calvin went on to produce a commentary series covering much of Scripture, one which is, in the words of William Cunningham, 'not only superior to any that preceded it, but it has continued ever since, and continues to this day, to be regarded by all competent judges, as a work of the highest value'. C. H. Spurgeon concurred: 'Everything that Calvin wrote by way of expositions are more equal in excellence than those of other men; other men rise and fall, but he is almost uniformly good.'

These estimations still hold true, and even in this age of multiplying commentaries those of John Calvin stand out as models of honesty, good sense, and evangelical warmth.

His great gifts as an interpreter are clearly evident here in his treatment of the oft-neglected Minor Prophets. In these volumes he opens up their rich contents to our hearts and minds: here is God's Word concerning false religion, spiritual adultery, injustice, judgement, the remnant, the restoration and sovereign love.

ISBN 0 85151 552 5
5 Volumes.

Also available:

JEREMIAH AND LAMENTATIONS
ISBN 0 85151 552 5
5 Volumes. Cloth-bound.

GENESIS
ISBN 0 85151 093 0
1088pp. Cloth-bound.

DANIEL
ISBN 0 85151 154 6
808pp. Cloth-bound.

SERMONS ON 2 SAMUEL

John Calvin
(Translated by Douglas Kelly)

While John Calvin is chiefly remembered today as a great theologian, it should not be forgotten that he was essentially a pastor. Indeed, it has been said of him that he became a theologian in order to be a better pastor. His preaching gives some of the clearest evidence for this. Still in his early twenties when he began to preach, he continued to do so for the rest of his life – on average five times a week during his long years of ministry in Geneva. From 1549, thanks to the *Company of Strangers*, who employed Denis Raguenier as a scribe, Calvin's sermons were preserved and their riches remain available to us. Now, thanks to the devoted labours of Professor Douglas Kelly of Reformed Seminary, Jackson, Mississippi, the sermons on 2 Samuel 1–13 are made available in English for the first time.

Important as these sermons are for students of Calvin, they are of inestimable value for those who, like him, are pastors or preachers; and equally, for ordinary Christian believers like those to whom they were first preached. Calvin's masterly handling of the historical narrative of this wonderful book of Scripture combines with his deep insight into human character to produce a volume which will be treasured.

ISBN 0 85151 578 9
696pp. Cloth-bound.

Also available:

SERMONS ON EPHESIANS
Translated by Arthur Golding
ISBN 0 85151 170 8
724pp. Cloth-bound.

THE TREASURY OF HIS PROMISES

366 Daily Bible Readings by Graham Miller

The best books of Daily Readings are those which cause the Scriptures themselves to be studied and prized. This is what *The Treasury of His Promises* sets out to do for each day of the year. There is help for prayer and devotion but with the aim of leading the reader beyond a few momentary thoughts to the blessings of Christian meditation. Here is guidance to the reading of the Bible itself, and avenues of thought on doctrine and practice are opened for further reflection.

A leader among evangelical students in New Zealand in the 1930s, after legal and theological training, J. Graham Miller, with his wife, Flora, went to the New Hebrides (Vanuatu) in missionary service. Thereafter working for the advancement of the cause of Christ in those islands, and in churches in New Zealand and Australia, Dr Miller has been widely known and loved. His commitment to the Westminster Confession has rallied a younger generation of Presbyterian ministers in Australia, while his expository preaching has been used of God to the help of many churches, colleges and missionary societies.

Graham Miller's book encourages the prayerful reading and exposition of the Word of God. Younger Christians, especially, will be helped.

ISBN 0 85151 472 3
384pp. Large paperback.

For free illustrated catalogue please write to
THE BANNER OF TRUTH TRUST
3 Murrayfield Road, Edinburgh EH12 6EL
PO Box 621, Carlisle, Pennsylvania 17013, USA